Toward a General Theory of Social Control

Volume 2

SELECTED PROBLEMS

STUDIES ON LAW AND SOCIAL CONTROL

DONALD BLACK *Series Editor*

Center for Criminal Justice
Harvard Law School
Cambridge, Massachusetts 02138

P. H. Gulliver. Disputes and Negotiations:
A Cross-Cultural Perspective

Sandra B. Burman and Barbara E. Harrell-Bond
(Editors). The Imposition of Law

Cathie J. Witty. Mediation and Society:
Conflict Management in Lebanon

Francis G. Snyder. Capitalism and Legal Change:
An African Transformation

Allan V. Horwitz. The Social Control of Mental Illness

Richard L. Abel (Editor). The Politics of Informal Justice, Vol. 1:
The American Experience; Vol. 2: Comparative Studies

William M. O'Barr, Linguistic Evidence: Language, Power, and Strategy
in the Courtroom

Donald Black (Editor). Toward A General Theory of Social
Control, Vol. 1: Fundamentals; Vol. 2: Selected Problems

Toward a General Theory of Social Control

Volume 2

SELECTED PROBLEMS

Edited by

Donald Black

Center for Criminal Justice
Harvard Law School
Cambridge, Massachusetts

 1984

ACADEMIC PRESS, INC.
(Harcourt Brace Jovanovich, Publishers)
Orlando   San Diego   San Francisco   New York   London
Toronto   Montreal   Sydney   Tokyo   São Paulo

ACADEMIC PRESS, INC.
Orlando, Florida 32887

United Kingdom Edition published by
ACADEMIC PRESS, INC. (LONDON) LTD.
24/28 Oval Road, London NW1 7DX

Library of Congress Cataloging in Publication Data
Main entry under title:

Toward a general theory of social control.

(Studies on law and social control)
Includes bibliographies and indexes.
Contents: v. 1. Fundamentals -- v. 2. Selected problems.
1. Sociological jurisprudence--Addresses, essays, lectures. 2. Social control--Addresses, essays, lectures.
3. Deviant behavior--Addresses, essays, lectures.
I. Black, Donald J. II. Series.
K376.T68 1984 340'.115   83-11886
ISBN 0−12−102802−X (v. 2)

PRINTED IN THE UNITED STATES OF AMERICA

84 85 86 87   9 8 7 6 5 4 3 2 1

Contents

Contributors   ix

Preface   xi

Contents of Volume 1   xiii

1

Crime as Social Control   1

DONALD BLACK

Traditional Self-Help   2

Modern Self-Help   5

Theoretical Considerations   12

Conclusion   20

References   21

2

Social Control in Illegal Markets   29

PETER REUTER

Conceptual Issues   30

The Mafia as a Dispute-Settlement System   40

The Mafia, Arbitration, and Extortion   49
Concluding Comments   54
Appendix: Data Sources   56
References   57

3

Social Control under Totalitarianism   59

JAN T. GROSS

The Polish Case   60
The Privatization of the State   66
A Note on Totalitarian Language   72
Conclusions   76
References   76

4

Social Control in Suburbia   79

M. P. BAUMGARTNER

The Setting   80
Method   81
Social Control without Confrontation   82
Social Control and Weak Ties   94
Concluding Remarks   100
References   101

5

Two Models of Social Control in Simple Societies   105

JANE F. COLLIER

The Question of Meaning   107
The Analytical Framework   111
Two Types of Simple Societies   114
Conclusion   134
References   137

6

Social Control and Corporate Organization: A Durkheimian Perspective   141

ALBERT BERGESEN

Some Explanations of Political Witch-Hunts   144
McCarthyism and Status Politics   145
Toward a New Theory of Political Crime   146
The Boundary Crisis Hypothesis   147
Immanence   155
Immanence and Boundary Crises   164
Summary and Conclusion   167
References   168

7

Social Control and Social Formation: A Marxian Analysis   171

DREW HUMPHRIES AND DAVID F. GREENBERG

Class and Social Control   171
The Ideology of Social Control   174
Nonclass Actors   175
Social Control outside the State   176
Mercantile Capitalism   177
Industrial Capitalism   183
Methods of Social Control under Industrial Capitalism   190
Discussion   199
References   202

8

Social Control and Relational Disturbance: A Microstructural Paradigm   209

SHELDON EKLAND-OLSON

Assumptions, Definitions, and Propositions   209
Relational Resilience and Social Control   214
Seriousness and the Mobilization of Outsiders   218
Structural Changes in Social Control   222
Summary   227
References   228

9

What Is a Dispute About? The Political Interpretation of Social Control   235

BARBARA YNGVESSON

Description: The Problem of Perspective   239
Prediction, Explanation, and the Role of the Maverick   251
Concluding Comment   257
References   258

10

Experiments in Social Control   261

PAT LAUDERDALE

Factors in the Reaction to Deviant Behavior   265
Social Control and the Controllers   267
A Theoretical Focus   273
References   276

11

History and Social Control   283

WILLIAM E. NELSON

History as Data   283
Contributions of History to a Theory of Social Control   291
Conclusion   293
References   294

Author Index   297
Subject Index   305

Contributors

Numbers in parentheses indicate the pages on which the authors' contributions begin.

M. P. Baumgartner (79), Center for Criminal Justice, Harvard Law School, Cambridge, Massachusetts 02138

Albert Bergesen (141), Department of Sociology, University of Arizona, Tucson, Arizona 85721

Donald Black (1), Center for Criminal Justice, Harvard Law School, Cambridge, Massachusetts 02138

Jane F. Collier (105), Department of Anthropology, Stanford University, Stanford, California 94305

Sheldon Ekland-Olson (209), Department of Sociology, University of Texas at Austin, Austin, Texas 78712

David F. Greenberg (171), Department of Sociology, New York University, New York, New York 10003

Jan T. Gross (59), Department of Sociology, Yale University, New Haven, Connecticut 06520

Drew Humphries (171), Department of Sociology, Rutgers–The State University of New Jersey, Camden, New Jersey 08102

Pat Lauderdale (261), Center for the Study of Justice, Arizona State University, Tempe, Arizona 85281

William E. Nelson (283), School of Law, New York University, New York, New York 10003

Peter Reuter (29), The Rand Corporation, 2100 M Street, N.W., Washington, D.C. 20037

Barbara Yngvesson (235), School of Social Science, Hampshire College, Amherst, Massachusetts 01002

Preface

Social control includes all of the practices by which people define and respond to deviant behavior. Even so, the scientific study of this subject matter has long been preoccupied with the phenomenon of law. Perhaps this is understandable, for in recent centuries the legal form of social control—that which is an appendage of the state—seems to have enjoyed especially favorable conditions for its growth and prominence, while many other forms have tended to fade into the background. We might easily forget that for most of human history (until the past 100 centuries or so) people managed without law and that, all along, other species of social control have continued to inhabit every society in great variety and profusion. Today as in the past, people with grievances might beat, banish, or kill one another; they might demand restitution, seize or destroy one another's property, or take hostages; they might protest, nag, ridicule, or gossip; they might resort to third parties such as mediators, arbitrators, or judges; they might avoid one another, negotiate, run away, fast, or commit suicide; they might weep, frown, or merely stare. All of these practices are worthy of scientific attention.

The following collection of essays—divided into two volumes—is designed to extend the study of social control beyond law. Moreover, it seeks to establish a conception of social control as a dependent variable, that is, as a thing to be predicted and explained. It also seeks to further a theoretical strategy suitable to this end, the fundamental assumption of which is that social control varies with its location and direction in social space. This strategy—which first appeared in my earlier work, *The Behavior of Law* (New York: Academic Press, 1976)—takes natural science as an appropriate model for social science, disregards the psychological aspects of social life, and incorporates a number of sociological traditions and theories into a single framework. While not all of the authors included in the collection explicitly follow this strategy, their writings are largely consistent with it.

Each of the essays is published here for the first time, though earlier versions of two (Chapters 1 and 3 in Volume 2) appeared elsewhere. Most were written in response to my invitation to the authors to venture beyond their usual realm of study to a more general problem. A few were recruited after I happened upon them in preliminary form, such as in a doctoral dissertation or conference presentation, and several more were proposed by the authors themselves after I invited them to join the project. Volume 1 (*Fundamentals*) opens with programmatic statements about the subject matter and then offers a number of inquiries into the conditions under which particular modes of social control occur. Volume 2 (*Selected Problems*) contains a set of investigations of social control in situations that may be especially interesting from a theoretical standpoint, as well as several essays on explanation and methodology. It should be obvious to the reader that these volumes are only a beginning, primitive in many respects, and that they will inevitably become obsolete as our knowledge expands.

Acknowledgments

I am grateful to the authors for their contributions. Because invitations to participate in the project were extended as early as 1978, and the first chapters were received within the year, most of the authors deserve additional credit for tolerating a long wait before publication. During the planning and preparation of the collection, I benefited immensely from the assistance of M. P. Baumgartner. Mark Cooney also made valuable suggestions, and Michael Oshima prepared a comprehensive Subject Index for each volume. I thank the administrative staff of Harvard Law School's Center for Criminal Justice, notably Kathleen Keeffe and Patricia Keating, for their services as well. And for providing a supportive environment for my work in general, I thank the Center's directors during the past several years: James Vorenberg, Lloyd E. Ohlin, and Philip Heymann.

Contents of Volume 1

1
Social Control as a Dependent Variable
DONALD BLACK

2
The Division of Labor in Social Control
JOHN GRIFFITHS

3
From Disputing to Complaining
LAURA NADER

4
Liability and Social Structure
KLAUS-FRIEDRICH KOCH

5
The Social Organization of Vengeance
JONATHAN RIEDER

6

The Variability of Punishment

PETER N. GRABOSKY

7

Compensation in Cross-Cultural Perspective

VIVIAN J. ROHRL

8

Therapy and Social Solidarity

ALLAN V. HORWITZ

9

The Logic of Mediation

WILLIAM L. F. FELSTINER

10

Rethinking Gossip and Scandal

SALLY ENGLE MERRY

11

Social Control from Below

M. P. BAUMGARTNER

Author Index
Subject Index

1

Crime as Social Control*

DONALD BLACK

There is a sense in which conduct regarded as criminal is often quite the opposite. Far from being an intentional violation of a prohibition, much crime is moralistic and involves the pursuit of justice. It is a mode of conflict management, possibly a form of punishment, even capital punishment. Viewed in relation to law, it is self-help. To the degree that it defines or responds to the conduct of someone else—the victim—as deviant, crime is social control.[1] And to this degree it is possible to predict and explain crime with aspects of the sociological

*A shorter version of this chapter appeared in the *American Sociological Review* 48 (1983): 34–45. Support was provided by the Program in Law and Social Science of the National Science Foundation.

[1]The concept of social control employed here refers specifically—and exclusively—to any process by which people define or respond to deviant behavior (Black, 1976: 105). It is a broad category that includes such diverse phenomena as a frown or scowl, a scolding or reprimand, an expulsion from an organization, an arrest or lawsuit, a prison sentence, commitment to a mental hospital, a riot, or a military reprisal. But this concept entails no assumptions or implications concerning the impact of social control on conformity, social order, or anything else, nor does it address the subjective meanings of social control for those who exercise or experience it (see generally Black, Chapter 1, Volume 1 of the present work). In some cases, for example, an arrest might harden a criminal's commitment to crime, disrupt the order of a community, or violate the moral preferences of the officer who makes it, but every arrest must nevertheless be construed as social control.

1

TOWARD A GENERAL THEORY OF SOCIAL CONTROL
Volume 2: Selected Problems

theory of social control, in particular, the theory of self-help.[2] After an overview of self-help in traditional and modern settings, the following pages briefly examine in turn the so-called struggle between law and self-help, the deterrence of crime, the processing of self-help by legal officials, and, finally, the problem of predicting and explaining self-help itself.

Traditional Self-Help

Much of the conduct described by anthropologists as conflict management, social control, or even law in tribal and other traditional societies is regarded as crime in modern societies. This is especially clear in the case of violent modes of redress such as assassination, feuding, fighting, maiming, and beating, but it also applies to the confiscation and destruction of property and to other forms of deprivation and humiliation. Such actions typically express a grievance by one person or group against another (see Moore, 1972: 67–72). Thus, one anthropologist notes that among the Bena Bena of highland New Guinea, as among most tribes of that region, "rather than being proscribed, violent self-help is prescribed as a method of social control [Langness, 1972: 182]."[3] The same might be said of numerous societies throughout the world. On the other hand, violence is quite rare in many traditional societies, and at least some of it is condemned in all. What follows is not intended as a representative overview, then, since only the more violent societies and modes of self-help are illustrated. First consider homicide.

In one community of Maya Indians in southern Mexico, for example, any individual killed from ambush is automatically labeled "the one who had the guilt." Everyone assumes that the deceased individual provoked his own death through an act of wrongdoing: "Homicide is considered a *reaction* to crime, not a crime in itself [Nash, 1967: 456]." Similarly, it has been observed that in a number of equatorial African societies homicide is rarely predatory—committed for gain—but is nearly always related to a grievance or quarrel of some kind (Bohannan, 1960: 256; see, e.g., Fallers and Fallers, 1960: 78; La Fontaine, 1960: 103). The Eskimo of the American Arctic also kill people in response to vari-

[2]For these purposes, self-help refers to the expression of a grievance by unilateral aggression. It is thus distinguishable from social control through third parties such as police officers or judges and from avoidance behavior such as desertion or divorce. (This conception of self-help derives from work in progress with M. P. Baumgartner.)

[3]Illustrations of traditional self-help are given here in the present tense (known in anthropology as the "ethnographic present"), though many of the practices to be surveyed have changed considerably—if not disappeared altogether—since they were originally observed.

ous offenses, including adultery, insult, and simply being a nuisance (Hoebel, 1954: 83–88; van den Steenhoven, 1956: 32, 63; 1962: chap. 4). The Ifugao of the Philippines hold that any "self-respecting man" must kill an adulterer discovered *in flagrante delicto* (Barton, 1919: 66–70). Under the same conditions, the Sarakatsan shepherds of Greece prefer that the wife be killed first, and then her lover (Campbell, 1964: 152, 199). Societies such as these have, in effect, capital punishment administered on a private basis.

Unlike penalties imposed by the state, however, private executions of this kind often result in revenge or even a feud, a reciprocal exchange of violence that might last months or years (for cross-cultural studies of feuding, see Thoden van Velzen and van Wetering, 1960; Otterbein and Otterbein, 1965; see also Rieder, Chapter 5, Volume 1 of the present work). Moreover, the person killed in retaliation may not be himself or herself a killer, for in these societies violent conflicts between nonkin are virtually always handled in a framework of collective responsibility—or, more precisely, collective liability—whereby all members of a family or other group are accountable for the conduct of their fellows (see, e.g., Moore, 1972; Koch, Chapter 4, Volume 1 of the present work). Among the Cherokee Indians of southeastern North America, for example, "The relatives of the dead man had the duty and the right to kill the manslayer or one of his relatives [Reid, 1970: 74; see also 75]." Blood vengeance is also common among the Eskimo, though in some cases retaliation does not occur until years after the original killing (see Hoebel, 1954: 87–88).

Within a given society, vengeance against a killer may be allowed under some conditions but prohibited under others. For example, the Gisu of Uganda permit a man to kill anyone he finds stealing his property or having sexual relations with his wife or whom he suspects of witchcraft, and in these cases the relatives of the person killed are prohibited from reciprocating in kind (La Fontaine, 1960: 99). The Sarakatsan shepherds distinguish between a killing that should be avenged and counteravenged by the families involved—in theory, until all of the men on one side are dead—and a killing that should be allowed to stand as a private execution: The former normally arises in response to an insult or during a quarrel, whereas the latter is essentially the punishment of someone who has offended the sexual honor of a woman, such as by seducing or raping her (Campbell, 1964: 201–202). In some societies the killer's family or other group may be expected to compensate the victim's survivors for their loss, even when it is recognized that the killing was intended as social control (see, e.g., Howell, 1954: 39–58; Diamond, 1957; Lewis, 1959; Koch, 1974: 82, 86–89; Jones, 1974: 68–69, 99–100).

Violence of other kinds also expresses a grievance in most instances.

Among the Yanomamö of Venezuela and Brazil, for instance, women are routinely subjected to corporal punishment by their husbands:

> Most reprimands meted out by irate husbands take the form of blows with the hand or with a piece of firewood, but a good many husbands are even more brutal. Some of them chop their wives with the sharp edge of a machete or ax, or shoot them with a barbed arrow in some nonvital area, such as the buttocks or leg. Many men are given over to punishing their wives by holding the hot end of a glowing stick against them, resulting in serious burns [Chagnon, 1977: 82–83].

In parts of East Africa, "husbands often assault their wives, sometimes with a slap, sometimes with a fist, a foot, or a stick [Edgerton, 1972: 164]." Among the Qolla of Peru, a husband may beat his wife "when her behavior warrants it," such as when she is "lazy" or "runs around with other men" (Bolton and Bolton, 1973: 64). Women among the Aborigines of Australia are subject to beatings, spearings, and other violence, and these, it might be added, are "less likely to be avenged or compensated than injuries to men [Hiatt, 1965: 126]."[4] Another punishment for women in some societies is rape by a group of men, or "gang rape" (see, e.g., Llewellyn and Hoebel, 1941: 202–210; Murphy, 1960: 109). The punishment of children may also reach a degree of violence that would be viewed as criminal in a modern setting. For instance, the Jalé of highland New Guinea will "severely beat or even burn" a young boy who does not perform his chores satisfactorily (Koch, 1974: 51). The Kirghiz of western Siberia traditionally allow parents to kill their children if they see fit, so it seems likely that they practice a good deal of other corporal punishment as well (Riasanovsky, 1938: 10). Beating, maiming, and related forms of social control of women and children occur in only a limited range of societies, however, and are viewed primarily as offenses in many others (see, e.g., Fried, 1953: 292; van den Steenhoven, 1962: 44–45; Maybury-Lewis, 1967: 67–71).

Property destruction may also be a mode of social control. An extreme form is house burning, a practice quite frequent, for example, in parts of East Africa (Edgerton, 1972: 164) and India (Fürer-Haimendorf, 1943: 318). Animals, gardens, or other property might be destroyed as

[4]In cross-cultural perspective, Aborigine women are notable for their vulnerability to violence. If two men should quarrel over a woman, for example, it would not be uncommon for a third man to attack and even kill the woman, or threaten to do so, justifying this by saying, "She is really the cause of all the trouble [Hiatt, 1965: 119, n. 3; 139–140]." And a man will attack his own sister with a spear if he hears someone swear at her, possibly in this case too because he holds her responsible for the disturbance and for his own distress in the situation. In the process, he might also attack his other sisters, since he strives to treat all of his sisters "in exactly the same manner" (Warner, 1958: 110–113; Hiatt, 1965: 112–119).

well. Among the Cheyenne of the American Plains, a man's horse might be killed (Llewellyn and Hoebel, 1941: 117), and in northern Albania, a dog might be killed, though under some conditions this is regarded as equivalent to the murder of a man (Hasluck, 1954: 76–78). In one case in Lebanon (later punished as a crime), an aggrieved man cut the branches off his adversary's walnut tree (Rothenberger, 1978: 169). Among the Qolla, crops are sometimes damaged as a punishment, such as "when a man methodically uproots his enemy's potato plants before they have produced any tubers [Bolton, 1973: 234]." Netsilik Eskimo parents may subtly encourage their children to destroy an offender's cache of food, so that what appears to be mischief or vandalism may actually be a carefully orchestrated act of revenge (van den Steenhoven, 1962: 74). Young people are similarly mobilized to deal with offending adults in rural Wales (Rees, 1950: 80–84, 126–130; Peters, 1972: 109–124).

Property may also be confiscated as a form of social control, so that what might at first appear to a modern observer as unprovoked theft or burglary proves in many cases to be a response to the misconduct of the victim. Among the Mbuti Pygmies of Zaire, for instance, a seeming theft may be recognized by all as an "unofficial sanction" against a person who has incurred "public disapproval for some reason or another [Turnbull, 1965: 199]." Among the Qolla, the moralistic character of a theft is especially clear "when the object stolen has no value to the thief [Bolton, 1973: 233]." It is also a standard Qolla practice for the relatives of a murder victim to seize the presumed killer's livestock (Bolton, 1970: 233). Lastly, where women are regarded as the property of their fathers or husbands, rape may provide a means of retaliation against a man. This seems to have been involved in some of the gang rapes recorded as crimes in fourteenth-century England, for example, where even a widow might be attacked by a group of men as an act of revenge against her deceased husband (Hanawalt, 1979: 109, 153).[5] In some cases, then, rape may be another kind of confiscation.

Modern Self-Help

A great deal of the conduct labeled and processed as crime in modern societies resembles the modes of conflict management—described above—that are found in traditional societies which have little or no law (in the sense of governmental social control; Black, 1972: 1096). Much of

[5]For an overview of self-help in fourteenth-century England, see Pike (1873: 246–255), who notes—remarkably in the spirit of the present discussion—that "the criminal tendencies of modern times seem in many cases to have been handed down from a period when that which is now considered crime was thought very nearly akin to virtue [p. 247]."

this conduct is intended as a punishment or other expression of disapproval, whether applied reflectively or impulsively, with coolness or in the heat of passion. Some is an effort to achieve compensation, or restitution, for a harm that has been done. The response may occur long after the offense, perhaps weeks, months, or even years later; after a series of offenses, each viewed singly as only a minor aggravation but together viewed as intolerable; or as an immediate response to the offense, perhaps during a fight or other conflict, or after an assault, theft, insult, or injury.

As in tribal and other traditional societies, for example, most intentional homicide in modern life is a response to conduct that the killer regards as deviant. In Houston during 1969, for instance, over one-half of the homicides occurred in the course of a "quarrel," and another one-fourth occurred in alleged "self-defense" or were "provoked," whereas only a little over one-tenth occurred in the course of predatory behavior such as burglary or robbery (calculated from Lundsgaarde, 1977: 237). Only one-fifth of the offenders were strangers to their victims (Lundsgaarde, 1977: 230). Similar patterns were found in Philadelphia during a 5-year period (Wolfgang, 1958: 191). Homicide is often a response to adultery or other matters relating to sex, love, or loyalty, to disputes about domestic matters (financial affairs, drinking, housekeeping) or affronts to honor, to conflicts relating to debts, property, and child custody, and to other questions of right and wrong. Cases mentioned in the Houston study include one in which a young man killed his brother during a heated discussion about the latter's sexual advances toward his younger sisters, another in which a man killed his wife after she "dared" him to do so during an argument about which of several bills they should pay, one where a woman killed her husband during a quarrel in which the man struck her daughter (his stepdaughter), one in which a woman killed her 21-year-old son because he had been "fooling around with homosexuals and drugs," and two others in which people died from wounds inflicted during altercations over the parking of an automobile (Lundsgaarde, 1977).[6] Like the killings in traditional societies described by anthropologists, most intentional homicide in modern society may thus be construed as social control, specifically as self-help, even if it is handled by legal officials as crime.[7] From this standpoint, it is apparent

[6]A similar range of conditions apparently accompanies most homicide everywhere. In modern India, for example, typically the killer "correctly or incorrectly perceives of the victim as a violater of important social norms" such as those pertaining to sexual infidelity, property, or the treatment of women and children (Driver, 1961: 157).

[7]Crimes of self-help may be distinguished from other categories of conduct regarded as criminal, such as certain kinds of economic behavior (e.g., predatory robbery and the selling of illicit goods and services) and recreation (e.g., gambling and underage drinking

that capital punishment is quite common in modern America—in Texas, homicide is one of the 10 leading causes of death—though it is nearly always a private rather than a public affair.[8]

Most conduct that a lawyer would label as assault may also be understood as self-help. In the vast majority of cases the people involved know one another, usually quite intimately, and the physical attack arises in the context of a grievance or quarrel. For example, most arrests for assault in the United States involve offenders and victims with a prior relationship (see, e.g., Vera Institute, 1977: 23–42), even though the police are far less likely to invoke the law when this is the case (Black, 1971: 1097–1098; see also Black, 1980: 155–164). Commonly the assault is a punishment, such as when a husband beats or otherwise injures his wife because she has not lived up to his expectations. In one case that came to the attention of the Boston police, a woman complained that her husband had beaten her because supper was not ready when he came home from work (Black, 1980: 161), a state of affairs, incidentally, which might have been the woman's own way of expressing disapproval of her husband (see Baumgartner, Chapter 11, Volume 1 of this work). In a case handled by the police in Washington, D.C., a woman hit her father-in-law with a baby bottle because he had become intoxicated and "called her vile names [Black, 1980: 161]." Other standards are enforced violently as well. In one instance that occurred in a major northeastern city and that apparently was not reported to the police, a young woman's brothers attacked and beat her boyfriend "for making her a drug addict," and in another a young man was stabbed for cooperating with the police in a burglary investigation (Merry, 1981: 158, 180–181). In a case in Washington, D.C., that resulted in an arrest, a boy shot his gang leader for taking more than his proper share of the proceeds from a burglary (Allen, 1977: 40–43). Years later, the same individual shot someone who had been terrorizing young women—including the avenger's girlfriend—in his neighborhood. Although he pleaded guilty to "assault with a deadly weapon" and was committed to a refor-

---

of alcoholic beverages). This is not to deny that some crime is multidimensional; for instance, an incident might be both moralistic and predatory at the same time, as when someone is killed in a quarrel but then robbed as well.

It is presently impossible to specify with precision what proportion of all crime involves self-help, and in any case this varies across societies and other settings. It can at least be surmised from available evidence, however, that in modern societies such as the United States, at least three-fourths of the nonnegligent criminal homicides are committed as social control (see Wolfgang, 1958: chap. 10; Lundsgaarde, 1977: 237).

[8]Compare Wolfgang and Ferracuti's (1966) argument that homicide and related conduct reflect a "subculture of violence." For a criticism of their view in the light of cross-cultural evidence, see Haft-Picker (1980).

matory, not surprisingly he described himself as "completely right" and his victim as "completely wrong" (Allen, 1977: 62–66, 69–70).

Indigenous people arrested for violence in colonial societies are likely to have a similar point of view: They may be proud of what they have done and admit it quite openly, even while they are being prosecuted as criminals by the foreign authorities.[9] Those apprehended in Europe for the crime of dueling—also a method of conflict resolution—have typically lacked remorse for the same reasons (see Pitt-Rivers, 1966: 29–31). Thus, when asked by a priest to pray for forgiveness before being hanged for killing a man with a sword, one such offender in France exclaimed, "Do you call one of the cleverest thrusts in Gascony a crime? [Baldick, 1965: 62]." As in dueling, moreover, violence in modern societies is often prescribed by a code of honor. He who shrinks from it is disgraced as a coward (see generally Peristiany, 1966; Werthman, 1969; Horowitz and Schwartz, 1974).

Many crimes involving the confiscation or destruction of property also prove to have a normative character when the facts come fully to light. There are, for example, moralistic burglaries, thefts, and robberies. Over one-third of the burglaries in New York City resulting in arrest involve people with a prior relationship (Vera Institute, 1977: 82),

---

[9]This reportedly applied, for example, to the Nuer of the Sudan when they lived under British rule:

> A Nuer dispute is usually a balance of wrongs, for a man does not, except in sexual matters, wantonly commit an act of aggression. He does not steal a man's cow, club him, or withhold his bride-cattle in divorce, unless he has some score to settle. Consequently it is very rare for a man to deny the damage he has caused. He seeks to justify it, so that a settlement is an adjustment between rival claims. I have been told by [a British] officer with wide experience of Africans that Nuer defendants are remarkable in that they very seldom lie in cases brought before Government tribunals. They have no need to, since they are only anxious to justify the damage they have caused by showing that it is retaliation for damage the plaintiff has inflicted earlier [Evans-Pritchard, 1940: 171–172].

Another observer of the Nuer noted that "it is rare that a killer attempts to conceal his guilt, even if in the heat of battle there are no witnesses [Howell, 1954: 66]." This honesty seemed remarkable to the British, for they were accustomed to their own system of justice in which only one side could be recognized as right or wrong, and in which the moral claims of the accused criminal were not generally regarded as relevant.

In Australia, the Aborigines have long been vulnerable to what they call "whitefella law" for certain practices relating to the enforcement of "blackfella law," particularly in regard to religious taboos. In one such case, in which six Aborigines admitted to having followed their tradition of killing a fellow tribesman who had violated a major taboo (by stealing a number of sacred relics and selling them to a white tourist), a white lawyer successfully argued for reduced sentences on the ground that "according to tribal law they were doing only what they had to do" and that "if Your Honour took too severe a view of their breach of our law, Your Honour would in effect be punishing them for adherence to their own code [Eggleston, 1976: 289–293; see also Maddock, 1977; Australian Law Reform Commission, 1980: 37–40]."

and these not infrequently express a grievance the burglar has against the victim. In one such case handled by the Boston police, a woman who had been informed by a neighbor complained that while she was away "her estranged husband had entered her apartment, wrecked it, loaded all of her clothes into his car, and driven away, presumably headed for his new home several hundred miles away [Black, 1980: 115]." Although the specific nature of this man's grievance was not mentioned, it seems apparent that his actions were punitive to some degree, and surely his estranged wife understood this as well. In a case in New York City, one resulting in two arrests for burglary, two black women barged into the home of an elderly white woman at midnight to confront her because earlier in the day she had remonstrated with their children for throwing rocks at her window (Vera Institute, 1977: 88). A crime may also be committed against a particular individual to express the disapproval of a larger number of people, such as a neighborhood or community, as is illustrated by the report of a former burglar who notes in his autobiography that early in his career he selected his victims partly on moralistic grounds:

> We always tried to get the dude that the neighbors didn't like too much or the guy that was hard on the people who lived in the neighborhood. Like, some store-keepers wouldn't let people have credit till the end of the week. We used to call them just plain cheezy. Say you go in there for a loaf of bread and a loaf of bread cost seventeen cents and you didn't have but fifteen cents—he wouldn't let you out there! People like that—just plain scrooges. . . . I like to think that all the places we robbed, that we broke into, was kind of like the bad guys [Allen, 1977: 39–40].

It should be clear, however, that the victims of moralistic crime may be entirely unaware of why they have been selected, especially when the offender is unknown. Such crimes may therefore be understood as secret social control (compare Becker, 1963: 20).[10]

Another possible mode of self-help is robbery, or theft involving violence. In New York City, where over one-third of the people arrested for robbery are acquainted with their victims, the crime often arises from a

---

[10]It might seem to some readers that "secret social control" is a contradiction in terms. Perhaps such a contradiction would exist if the concept of social control were taken to imply an effort to influence the future conduct of a population or, at least, the future conduct of the deviant who is subjected to social control. But recall that in the present analysis social control refers simply to any process by which people define or respond to deviant behavior (see Note 1). This does not imply that social control influences conduct (though it obviously does in many cases) or that it is intended to do so (though often it is).

People of lower social status seem especially prone to use secret forms of social control against their superiors (see Baumgartner, Chapter 11, Volume 1 of the present work). A secret mode used more widely—apparently in all societies—is gossip (see Merry, Chapter 10, Volume 1 of the present work).

quarrel over money (Vera Institute, 1977: 65–71). In one case, a woman reported that her sister and her sister's boyfriend had taken her purse and $40 after assaulting her and threatening to kill her baby, but she later explained that this had arisen from a misunderstanding: The boy-friend wanted reimbursement for a baby carriage that he had bought for her, whereas she thought it had been a gift (Vera Institute, 1977: 69–70). It seems, in fact, that in many instances robbery is a form of debt collec-tion and an alternative to law. The same applies to embezzlement, though it may also simply express disapproval of the employer who is victimized (see Cressey, 1953: 57–59, 63–66).

Conduct known as vandalism, or malicious destruction of property, proves to be a form of social control in many cases as well. Far from being merely "malicious," "non-utilitarian," or "negativistic," with "no purpose, no rhyme, or reason [Cohen, 1955: 25–30, including quoted material in Note 4]," much vandalism in modern society is similar to the moralistic destruction of crops, animals, and other valuables in tradi-tional societies. But whereas, say, a Plains Indian might kill a horse, a modern agent of justice might damage the offender's automobile. Thus, in one American neighborhood where parking spaces on the street are scarce, the residents have evolved their own distribution system, with its own customary rules and enforcement procedures. In the winter, one such rule is that whoever shovels the snow from a parking space is its "owner," and persistent violators may find that their automobile has been pushed into a snow bank, spray painted, or otherwise abused (Thomas-Buckle and Buckle, 1982: 84, 86–87). Vandalism may also be reciprocated in a feudlike pattern of mutual destruction: In one such case in a northeastern city, a young man found that someone had bro-ken the radio antenna on his automobile, learned from some children who had done it, and thereupon proceeded to slash the tires of the offender's automobile (Merry, 1981: 179).

Business places and dwellings are often damaged to punish their owners or inhabitants. Arson, or burning, has a long history of this kind.[11] Less severe sanctions, however, are far more frequent. In one case handled by the police in Washington, D.C., the proprietor of a bar advised his customers to ignore a deaf-mute man trying to solicit money from them, so the man, enraged, broke one of the windows (Black, 1980: 179). In a case occurring in a suburb of New York City, a young man drove his car across someone's lawn during a quarrel, and in another incident in the same town several young men spray painted parts of an

---

[11]On "revenge arson" in fourteenth-century England, for example, see Hanawalt (1979: 90–91); on anonymous letters threatening arson in eighteenth- and nineteenth-century England, see Thompson (1975).

older man's house in the middle of the night because he had called the police to disperse them when they were sitting in their cars drinking beer and listening to music (Baumgartner, pages 92–93 of this volume). If all of the facts were known, then, it seems likely that much seemingly senseless and random vandalism would prove to be retaliation by young people against adults (see Greenberg, 1977: 202–204). Some may even be done by children on behalf of their parents, in a pattern analogous to that found among the Eskimo, mentioned earlier (for a possible example, see Black, 1980: 167–168). If the parents themselves are the offenders, however, other strategies might be followed. Among the Tarahumara Indians of northern Mexico, children with a grievance against their parents often "run away" from home, staying with an uncle or grandparent for a few days before returning (Fried, 1953: 291). Qolla children have a similar custom, locally known as "losing themselves" (Bolton and Bolton, 1973: 15–16). Modern children do this as well, though like vandalism it is commonly regarded as a form of juvenile delinquency.

Finally, it might be noted that the practice of collective liability— whereby all of the people in a social category are held accountable for the conduct of each of their fellows—occurs in modern as well as traditional societies. This is most apparent during a war, revolution, or riot, when anyone might suffer for the deeds of someone else, but during peaceful times too, seemingly random violence may often be understood in the same way. Today a police officer might become the victim of a surprise attack by a stranger, for example, because of the conduct of one or more fellow officers in the past. Seemingly random crime of other kinds may involve collective liability as well. Thus, for instance, a black rapist described his selection of white victims as a process of vengeance against white people in general:

> It delighted me that I was defying and trampling upon the white man's law, upon his system of values, and that I was defiling his women—and this point, I believe, was the most satisfying to me because I was very resentful over the historical fact of how the white man has used the black woman. I felt I was getting revenge [Cleaver, 1968: 14].

Similarly, a former burglar and robber remarked that he once selected his victims primarily from a relatively affluent neighborhood, but not simply because this provided a chance of greater material gain: "I really disliked them people, 'cause it seemed like they thought they was better 'cause they had more [Allen, 1977: 32–33]." People might be held collectively liable because of their neighborhood, social class, race, or ethnicity. Crime by young people against adult strangers may also have this logic in some cases: All adults might be held liable for the conduct of those known personally, such as police, teachers, and parents.[12] Among young people themselves, particularly in large American cities, rival "gangs" may engage in episodic violence resembling the feud in traditional settings, where each member of a feuding group is liable—to injury or even death—for the conduct of the other members (see, e.g., Yablonsky, 1962). A significant amount of crime in modern society may even resemble what anthropologists describe as "raiding," a kind of predatory behavior often directed at people collectively defined as deserving of revenge (see, e.g., Sweet, 1965; Tanner, 1966: 41; Ekvall, 1968: 52–53; Schneider, 1971: 4). And some might properly be construed as "banditry," since it seems to be a kind of primitive rebellion by those at the bottom of society against their social superiors (see Hobsbawm, 1959: chap. 2; 1969). In short, although much crime in modern society directly and unambiguously expresses a grievance by one person against another, this may be only the most visible portion of a much broader phenomenon.

Theoretical Considerations

When a moralistic crime is handled by the police or prosecuted in court, the official definition of the event is drastically different from that of the people involved, particularly from that of the alleged offender. In the case of a husband who shoots his wife's lover, for example, the definition of who is the offender and who is the victim is reversed: The wife's lover is defined as the victim, even though he was shot because of an offense he committed against the woman's husband. Moreover, the lover's offense is precisely the kind for which violent social control—by the husband—is viewed as acceptable and appropriate, if not obligatory, in numerous tribal and other traditional societies. Even in modern society, it might be said that the husband is charged with violating the criminal law because he enforced his rights in what many regard as the customary law of marriage. The victim thus becomes the offender, and vice versa. The state prosecutes the case in its own name, while the

---

[12]Subpopulations such as women, old people, and the poor may be particularly vulnerable to vengeance of this kind. Seen in cross-cultural perspective, this is not inconsistent with systems of collective liability. In some tribal societies, for example, retaliation may be taken against those who are physically less dangerous, such as women and children, and against those who are less likely to be revenged, such as social isolates and visitors (e.g., Koch, 1974). Anyone who happens to be available may also be considered a satisfactory victim (e.g., Harner, 1972: 172). On the other hand, a "code of honor" may govern revenge and limit it, for instance, to adult males able to defend themselves (e.g., Hasluck, 1954: chap. 24; see also Stauder, 1972: 166).

original offender against morality (if alive) serves as a witness against the man he has victimized—surely a perverse proceeding from the standpoint of the defendant (compare Christie, 1977). It is also enlightening in this regard to consider criminal cases arising from quarrels and fights, where each party has a grievance against the other. Here the state often imposes the categories of offender and victim on people who were contesting the proper application of these labels during the altercation in question. Whether there was originally a cross-complaint or not, however, in all of these cases the state defines someone with a grievance as a criminal. The offense lies in how the grievance was pursued. The crime is self-help.

It should be apparent from much of the foregoing that in modern society the state has only theoretically achieved a monopoly over the legitimate use of violence (compare, e.g., Weber, 1919: 78; 1922: 156; Elias, 1939: 201–202). In reality, violence flourishes (particularly in modern America), and most of it involves ordinary citizens who seemingly view their conduct as a perfectly legitimate exercise of social control. It might therefore be observed that the struggle between law and self-help in the West did not end in the Middle Ages, as legal historians claim (e.g., Pike, 1876: chap. 13; Pollock and Maitland, 1898: vol. 2, 574; Pound, 1921: 139–140; see also Hobhouse, 1906: chap. 3). It continues.[13] Many people still "take the law into their own hands." They seem to view their grievances as their own business, not that of the police or other officials, and resent the intrusion of law (see Matza, 1964: chap. 5). They seem determined to have justice done, even if it means that they will be defined as criminals.[14] Those who commit murder, for example, often appear to be resigned to their fate at the hands of the authorities; many wait patiently for the police to arrive; some even call to report their own crimes (see generally Lundsgaarde, 1977). In cases of this kind, indeed, the individuals involved might arguably be regarded as martyrs.

---

[13]The struggle, however, was once vastly more rancorous and spectacular, in many cases involving open confrontations between those engaging in self-help—along with their supporters—and the authorities who regarded their conduct as criminal. In medieval England, for example, a prisoner's friends might forcibly seize him from the sheriff, and in some instances armed bands violently challenged the authorities in the courtroom itself (see, e.g., Pike, 1873: 257–258).

Like so much else, the struggle between law and self-help has become more individualized and for the most part invisible to the general public. Only an occasional riot harkens back to the earlier pattern.

[14]It has been suggested that offenders often condemn their victims merely in order to "neutralize" their own feelings of guilt (Sykes and Matza, 1957: 668; see also Fattah, 1976). In contrast, the argument here is that in many cases condemnations of this kind may be authentic. Some criminals may be telling the truth.

Not unlike workers who violate a prohibition to strike—knowing they will go to jail—or others who defy the law on grounds of principle, they do what they think is right and willingly suffer the consequences.[15]

DETERRENCE AND SELF-HELP

To the degree that people feel morally obligated to commit crimes, it would seem that the capacity of the criminal law to discourage them—its so-called deterrent effect—must be weakened. For example, homicides committed as a form of capital punishment would seem to be more difficult to deter than those committed entirely in pursuit of personal gain (on the deterrability of the latter, see Chambliss, 1967). This is not to deny that moralistic homicide can be discouraged to some extent. In fact, one former resident of Harlem has noted that the inhabitants of that unusually violent area seem to debate in their own minds whether moralistic homicide is ultimately worth its legal consequences: "I think everybody was curious about whether or not it was worth it to kill somebody and save your name or your masculinity, defend whatever it was that had been offended—whether it was you or your woman or somebody in your family [C. Brown, 1965: 220]." He adds that during his years in Harlem this question loomed especially large whenever anyone was executed in prison (C. Brown, 1965: 220). That the desirability of killing another person is entertained at all is remarkable, however, particularly when the death penalty is believed to be a possible result (a belief that appears to be largely unfounded; see next section). Furthermore, because other crimes of self-help carry fewer risks of a legal nature, they should be even harder to discourage than homicide. In any event, a theory of deterrence surely should recognize that the power of punishment to deter crime partly depends on whether a given crime is itself a form of social control (for other relevant variables see, e.g., Andenaes, 1966; Chambliss, 1967; Zimring, 1971).

A related question is the extent to which victimizations are deterred

[15]Others may become fugitives from the law, which may in turn drive them further into a life of crime. On the basis of evidence from southern Italy, for example, it has been suggested that young men typically become bandits after first committing an act of violence in defense of their honor: Despite popular approval of their behavior, they are sought by the police (who define their violence as crime) and thereafter lead a life of banditry merely in order to survive in the absence of a legitimate livelihood (Brögger, 1968: 233–234). According to this interpretation, banditry would seem a classic example of "secondary deviation"—deviant behavior that results from social control (Lemert, 1967). It seems probable that at least a few robbers and thieves in modern societies such as the United States have a similar history.

by self-help rather than by—or in addition to—law. Although many citizens are entirely dependent on legal officials such as the police to handle criminal offenders, others are prepared to protect themselves and their associates by any means at their disposal, including violence. It is well known among potential predators in one American neighborhood, for example, that a number of the residents would be dangerous to victimize, in some cases because they enjoy the protection of family members who act as their champions (see Merry, 1981: 178–179). Such people are left alone. Entire segments of a community may also be avoided from fear of retaliation. For example, for this reason some thieves and robbers may avoid the poor: "One of the most dangerous things in the world is to steal from poor people. . . . When you steal from the poor, you gamble with your life [C. Brown, 1965: 214; see also Allen, 1977: 50–52]." Moreover, since the deterrent effect of social control generally increases with its severity (see Zimring, 1971: 83–90, for qualifications), it should be noted that self-help is often more severe than law. Thus, a burglar or robber might be executed by the intended victim, though burglary and robbery are generally not capital crimes in modern codes of law. Accordingly, to the degree that self-help is effectively repressed by the state, crime of other kinds might correspondingly increase. Among the Gusii of Kenya, for instance, rape dramatically increased after the British prohibited traditional violence against strangers—potential rapists—and, when a rape occurred, violence against the offender and possibly his relatives (Le Vine, 1959: 476–477).[16] Perhaps some of the predatory crime in modern society is similarly a result of a decline in self-help.

THE PROCESSING OF SELF-HELP

Even while the ancient struggle between law and self-help continues, the response of legal officials to those handling their own grievances by violence and other aggression is not nearly so severe as might be supposed. In fact, crimes of self-help are often handled with comparative leniency. An extreme of this pattern was seen historically, for example, in the generous application of the concept of "self-defense" to justify

[16]It appears that predatory behavior within tribal and peasant villages is often effectively deterred by the threat of self-help. This was the impression, for example, of an anthropologist who studied the Nuer of the Sudan: "It is the knowledge that a Nuer is brave and will stand up against aggression and enforce his rights by club and spear that ensures respect for person and property [Evans-Pritchard, 1940: 171; see also Howell, 1954: 231–232]." Why people in any society refrain from victimizing their fellows raises difficult questions of motivation, however, and lies beyond the scope of the present discussion.

homicide—otherwise by law a capital offense—in medieval England: In cases in which a killing involved social control, it appears that juries routinely avoided a conviction by fabricating a version of the incident in which the victim had first attacked the defendant, forcing him to resist with violence in order to save his own life (Green, 1972; 1976: 428–436). Likewise, in more recent centuries European authorities and juries have generally been reluctant to enforce laws against dueling (see Baldick, 1965: chaps. 4–7; Andrew, 1980). Earlier in the present century, the same applied to the handling of so-called lynchings in the American South—executions carried out by a group of private citizens, usually against a black man believed to have victimized a white. Typically no one was arrested, much less prosecuted or punished, though the killers frequently were well known and readily available (see, e.g., Raper, 1933). Today, much violent self-help is still tolerated by American officials and juries. Incidents that a lawyer would normally classify as felonious assault, for example—involving severe bodily injury or the threat thereof—are unlikely to result in arrest if the offender and victim are intimately related (see, e.g., Black, 1980: 180–185; see also Black, 1971: 1097–1098). Where an arrest is made, prosecution and conviction are far less likely when the offense entails an element of self-help. Thus, in Houston, people whom the police arrest for homicide are often released without prosecution, and in many cases this seems to be related to the moralistic nature of the killing.[17] In 1969, 40% of those arrested for killing a relative (such as a spouse or sibling) were released without prosecution, and the same applied to 37% of those arrested for killing a friend or other associate and to 24% of those arrested for killing a stranger (Lundsgaarde, 1977: 232). And when self-help is involved, such as when a burglary or robbery is committed in order to collect an unpaid debt, offenses that do initially result in prosecution are likely to be abandoned or dismissed at a later point in the process (see, e.g, Vera Institute, 1977: 69–70, 87–88). At every stage, then, crimes of self-help often receive a degree of immunity from law.

[17]Until 1973, Texas expressly permitted a husband to kill a man he discovered in an act of adultery with his wife. As of 1972, three American states (Texas, New Mexico, and Utah) defined this by statute as "justifiable homicide," while another (Georgia) did so by judicial decision. The rest of the states have traditionally treated adultery as a "provocation" that automatically reduces the seriousness of a homicide from murder to voluntary manslaughter (LaFave and Scott, 1972: 576). Even so, American juries in these latter states have long been reputed to ignore the written law in such cases and to treat them as justifiable homicide anyway. This is known as an "unwritten law" (see, e.g., W. Roberts, 1922).

In modern American law, homicide committed as self-help is everywhere permitted as "justifiable" if it qualifies as "self-defense," "defense of another," or "prevention of felony" (see, e.g., Torcia, 1979: secs. 125, 127–128).

If the capacity of law to deter crimes of self-help is weak in the first place, surely this leniency, insofar as it is known among the population, makes it weaker still. But it might be wondered why so much self-help occurs in a society such as modern America. Why do so many people criminally pursue their own grievances in a society where law is developed to such a high degree? Why, in particular, are they so violent?

THE THEORY OF SELF-HELP

Several centuries ago, Thomas Hobbes argued that without a sovereign state— without law—a "war of every one against every one" would prevail, and life would be "solitary, poor, nasty, brutish, and short [1651: 100]." Many stateless societies have since been observed by anthropologists, however, and Hobbes's theory has proven to be somewhat overstated: Life without law does not appear to be nearly as precarious as he believed (see, e.g., Middleton and Tait, 1958; Gluckman, 1965; MacCormack, 1976; S. Roberts, 1979). Even so, the idea that violence is associated with statelessness still enjoys considerable support. With various refinements and qualifications, an absence of state authority has been used to explain high levels of violence in settings as diverse as the highlands of New Guinea (P. Brown, 1964; Koch, 1974: chap. 7), Lake Titicaca in the Andes (Bolton, 1970: 12–16), and western Sicily (Blok, 1974: 210–212.[18] It has also been used to explain war and other violent self-help in international relations (e.g., Hoffmann, 1968; Arendt, 1969: 5; Koch, 1974: 173–175). A version of the same approach may be relevant to an understanding of self-help in modern society.

Hobbesian theory would lead us to expect more violence and other crimes of self-help in those contemporary settings where law—governmental social control—is least developed, and, indeed, this appears to fit the facts: Crimes of self-help are more likely where law is less available. This is most apparent where legal protection is withheld as a matter of public policy, such as where a contract violates the law. A gambling debt is not legally enforceable, for example, and the same applies to transactions in illicit narcotics, prostitution, stolen goods, and the like. Perhaps for this reason many underworld businesses find it necessary to maintain, in effect, their own police, such as the "strong-arms" of illegal loan operations and the "pimps" who oversee the work of prostitutes (see, e.g., Allen, 1977: 100). Furthermore, it appears that social control within

---

[18]A cross-cultural survey of 50 societies shows that those with the least "political integration"—which means, *inter alia*, those without a state—are the most likely to have "coercive self-help" as their dominant mode of conflict management (Koch and Sodergren, 1976: 454–455).

settings of this kind is relatively violent (but see Reuter, Chapter 2 of the present volume).

Law is unavailable, or relatively so, in many other modern settings as well, though not necessarily as a matter of public policy. A teenager with a grievance against an adult, for example, will generally be ignored or even reprimanded by the police (Black, 1980: 152–155). Lower-status people of all kinds—blacks and other minorities, the poor, the homeless—enjoy less legal protection, especially when they have complaints against their social superiors, but also when conflict erupts among themselves (see Black, 1976: chaps. 2–6). To the police and other authorities, the problems of these people seem less serious, their injuries less severe, their honor less important.[19] A fight or quarrel among them may even be viewed as itself a "disturbance of the peace," an offense in its own right, regardless of the issues dividing the parties (see Black and Baumgartner, 1983: 106–107). People in intimate relationships, too, such as members of the same family or household, find that legal officials are relatively unconcerned about their conflicts, particularly if they occur in private and do not disturb anyone else (see Black, 1976: 40–44; 1980: chap. 5).[20] In all of these settings neglected by law, crimes of self-help are comparatively common. There are, so to speak, stateless locations in a society such as modern America, and in them the Hobbesian theory appears to have some validity.[21]

[19]It should also be recognized that people in these settings are relatively unlikely to bring their grievances to legal officials in the first place. For instance, most teenagers would not consider calling the police about an adult, and the same generally applies when someone has a grievance against an intimate such as a spouse or friend (but see Black, 1980: chap. 5, especially pp. 124–128). It might even be said that many people choose statelessness as a way of life. This pattern presumably undermines still further the capacity of law to deter crimes of self-help.

[20]To a degree, self-help may function—whether by design or not—as a mechanism through which law is mobilized among those who might otherwise be ignored. In at least one tribal society, the Meta' of the Cameroon, it appears that violence was consciously employed as a technique of this kind: Village elders were empowered to arbitrate disputes only if the parties became violent, and so it was not uncommon for people to initiate a fight in order to obtain a hearing of their case (Dillon, 1980: 664; see also Gluckman, 1967: 79). Children in many societies seem to use the same technique to mobilize adults. In some instances, violence in modern society may similarly serve as a cry for help from people who are less capable of attracting legal attention without it. Reports of violence occasionally may even be fabricated in order to ensure that the police will handle cases that the callers fear—possibly with justification—would otherwise be dismissed as trivial (for a likely example, see Black, 1980: 151). But then, as noted earlier, the police are likely to respond with indifference anyway.

[21]The opposite of statelessness can occur as well, with opposite results: The availability of law can be extended to such a degree that it almost entirely displaces self-help. People can become so dependent on law that they are unwilling to handle their own grievances. It

Before this chapter concludes, it is possible to specify the relationship between law and self-help more precisely. The likelihood of self-help is not merely a function of the availability of law, and, moreover, crimes of self-help are not always handled leniently by legal officials. Different locations and directions in social space have different patterns. In other words, the relationship between law and self-help depends on who has a grievance against whom.

Four patterns can be identified: First, law may be relatively unavailable both to those with grievances and to those who are the objects of self-help, as when people of low status and people who are intimate have conflicts with one another (on the distribution of law, see generally Black, 1976). This pattern has been emphasized earlier in the chapter. Second, law may be relatively unavailable to those with grievances in comparison to those who have offended them. Should the former employ self-help, they may therefore be vulnerable to harsh treatment by legal officials. This is the situation of people with a grievance against a social superior, such as a teenager with a grievance against an adult, and may help to explain why they tend to develop their own techniques of social control, including, for instance, covert retaliation, self-destruction, and flight (see Baumgartner, Chapter 11, Volume 1 of the present work). Those with grievances against a social inferior illustrate a third pattern: Law is readily available to them, but not to those against whom they might employ self-help. In this situation, the aggrieved party seemingly has a choice of law or self-help. A man might easily obtain legal help against his teenaged son, for example, but if he instead simply beats the boy—a kind of self-help—he is unlikely to be handled with severity by the police or other officials (see Black, 1980: 152–155). The fourth possibility, where law is readily available both to those with grievances and to those who have offended them, is seen where people of high status, and also people who are strangers, have conflicts with one another. Here self-help seems to be relatively infrequent. In sum, law and self-help are unevenly distributed across social space, and each is relevant to the behavior of the other.[22]

---

appears, in fact, that this extreme is almost reached by so-called totalitarian societies, such as the Soviet Union under Stalin or Germany under Hitler, where the state insinuates itself throughout the population by actively encouraging citizens to make use of its coercive apparatus however they see fit. Since apparently nearly anyone can have nearly anyone else sent to prison, each person is dangerous to others, and yet vulnerable to them at the same time (see Gross, Chapter 3 of the present volume). The result seems almost what Hobbes called a "war of every one against every one," but within the framework of a state. Under these conditions, self-help tends to wither away.

[22]It should also be understood that other conditions besides the availability of law are relevant to the incidence of self-help in each of its various manifestations. After all, no

Conclusion

The approach taken in this chapter departs radically from traditional criminology (as seen, e.g., in Cohen, 1955; Miller, 1958; Cloward and Ohlin, 1960; Sutherland and Cressey, 1960). Indeed, the approach taken here is, strictly speaking, not criminological at all, since it ignores whatever might be distinctive to crime as such (including, for example, how criminals differ from other people or how their behavior differs from that which is not prohibited). Instead it draws attention to a dimension of many crimes that is usually viewed as a totally different—even opposite—phenomenon, namely, social control. Crime often expresses a grievance.[23] This implies that many crimes belong to the same family as gossip, ridicule, vengeance, punishment, and law itself. It also implies that to a significant degree we may predict and explain crime with a sociological theory of social control, specifically a theory of self-help. Beyond this, it might be worthwhile to contemplate what else crime has in common with conduct of other kinds. As remarked earlier (in Note 7), for instance, some crime may be understood as economic behavior, and some as recreation. In other words, for certain theoretical purposes we might usefully ignore the fact that crime is criminal at all.[24] The crimi-

---

effort has been made here to develop a comprehensive theory of self-help. The analysis has been intended merely to indicate the relevance of such a theory and to offer a single formulation that it might include. Furthermore, it should be clear that despite the emphasis on contemporary society in the present discussion, a sociological theory of self-help would ideally apply to all instances of this phenomenon, traditional as well as modern.

Self-help in traditional societies may provide insights into modern self-help, and vice versa. For example, whereas the anthropological literature on violent self-help in tribal societies might suggest that people resort to this mode of social control in direct relation to the social distance between the aggrieved and the offending party (see, e.g., Evans-Pritchard, 1940: 150–172; Middleton, 1965: 46–52; Koch, 1974: chaps. 4–6), the evidence from modern societies suggests that this pattern is not universal. As noted earlier, for instance, violent self-help is quite frequent in families and other settings where the parties involved are extremely close. But not all modern intimates are violent when they have a grievance: Middle-class people, for example, seem to be far more inclined simply to avoid one another, and, for the matter, they are highly unlikely to use violence against strangers as well (Baumgartner, Chapter 4 of the present volume). In any event, it seems apparent that a theory of self-help should be constructed upon an empirical foundation broader than that characteristically employed by either anthropologists or sociologists.

[23]This analysis could be extended to other kinds of illegal behavior as well. What is legally regarded as a breach of contract or as grounds for divorce, for example, might also be a form of self-help when it occurs.

[24]This is not to deny that the definition of conduct as criminal may be relevant to its form and frequency. Even so, a given category of crime may share more with particular kinds of noncriminal conduct than with other crime. The use of illicit drugs is seemingly more similar to the legal consumption of alcoholic beverages than to robbery or rape, for example, and extortion is seemingly closer to the practices of many landlords, physicians, and corporations than to vandalism, trespassing, or treason.

nality of crime is defined by law, and therefore falls within the jurisdiction of a completely different theory (see especially Black, 1976).

ACKNOWLEDGMENTS

A number of people made helpful comments on an earlier draft: M. P. Baumgartner, John L. Comaroff, Mark Cooney, Jack P. Gibbs, Richard O. Lempert, Craig B. Little, Sally Engle Merry, Alden D. Miller, Calvin K. Morrill, Trevor W. Nagel, Lloyd E. Ohlin, Alan Stone, and Sheldon Stryker.

References

Allen, John
    1977   *Assault with a Deadly Weapon: The Autobiography of a Street Criminal,* edited by Dianne Hall Kelly and Philip Heymann. New York: McGraw-Hill.
Andenaes, Johannes
    1966   "The general preventive effects of punishment." *University of Pennsylvania Law Review* 114: 949–983.
Andrew, Donna T.
    1980   "The code of honour and its critics: The opposition to duelling in England, 1700–1850." *Social History* 5: 409–434.
Arendt, Hannah
    1969   *On Violence.* New York: Harcourt, Brace and World.
Australian Law Reform Commission
    1980   *Aboriginal Customary Law—Recognition?* Discussion Paper No. 17. Sydney: Law Reform Commission.
Baldick, Robert
    1965   *The Duel: A History of Duelling.* London: Chapman and Hall.
Barton, Roy Franklin
    1919   *Ifugao Law.* Berkeley, Calif.: University of California Press, 1969.
Becker, Howard S.
    1963   *Outsiders: Studies in the Sociology of Deviance.* New York: Free Press.
Black, Donald
    1971   "The social organization of arrest." *Stanford Law Review* 23: 1087–1111.
    1972   "The boundaries of legal sociology." *Yale Law Journal* 81: 1086–1100.
    1976   *The Behavior of Law.* New York: Academic Press.
    1980   *The Manners and Customs of the Police.* New York: Academic Press.
Black, Donald, and M. P. Baumgartner
    1980   "On self-help in modern society." Pages 193–208 in *The Manners and Customs of the Police,* by Donald Black. New York: Academic Press.
    1983   "Toward a theory of the third party." Pages 84–114 in *Empirical Theories about Courts,* edited by Keith O. Boyum and Lynn Mather. New York: Longman.
Blok, Anton
    1974   *The Mafia of a Sicilian Village, 1860–1960: A Study of Violent Peasant Entrepreneurs.* New York: Harper & Row.
Bohannan, Paul
    1960   "Patterns of murder and suicide." Pages 230–266 in *African Homicide and Suicide,* edited by Paul Bohannan. Princeton, N.J.: Princeton University Press.

Bolton, Ralph
    1970   "Rates and ramifications of violence: Notes on Qolla homicide." Paper present-
           ed at the International Congress of Americanists, Lima, Peru, August 1970.
    1973   Aggression and hypoglycemia among the Qolla: A study in psychobiological
           anthropology." *Ethnology* 12: 227–257.
Bolton, Ralph, and Charlene Bolton
    1973   "Domestic quarrels among the Qolla." Paper presented at the annual meeting
           of the American Anthropological Association, New Orleans, Louisiana, Octo-
           ber 1973. Published in Spanish as *Conflictos en la Familia Andina*. Cuzco: Centro
           de Estudios Andinos, 1975.
Brögger, Jan
    1968   "Conflict resolution and the role of the bandit in peasant society." *Anthropologi-*
           cal Quarterly 41: 228–240.
Brown, Claude
    1965   *Manchild in the Promised Land.* New York: New American Library, 1966.
Brown, Paula
    1964   "Enemies and affines." *Ethnology* 3: 335–356.
Campbell, J. K.
    1964   *Honour, Family and Patronage: A Study of Institutions and Moral Values in a Greek*
           Mountain Community. Oxford: Clarendon Press.
Chagnon, Napoleon A.
    1977   *Yanomamö: The Fierce People.* 2d edition. New York: Holt, Rinehart and Winston
           (1st edition, 1968).
Chambliss, William J.
    1967   "Types of deviance and the effectiveness of legal sanctions." *Wisconsin Law*
           Review 1967: 703–719.
Christie, Nils
    1977   "Conflicts as property." *British Journal of Criminology* 17: 1–15.
Cleaver, Eldridge
    1968   *Soul on Ice.* New York: Dell.
Cloward, Richard A., and Lloyd E. Ohlin
    1960   *Delinquency and Opportunity: A Theory of Delinquent Gangs.* New York: Free
           Press.
Cohen, Albert K.
    1955   *Delinquent Boys: The Culture of the Gang.* New York: Free Press.
Cressey, Donald R.
    1953   *Other People's Money: A Study in the Social Psychology of Embezzlement.* Glencoe,
           Ill.: Free Press.
Diamond, A. S.
    1957   "An eye for an eye." *Iraq* 19: 151–155.
Dillon, Richard G.
    1980   "Violent conflict in Meta' society." *American Ethnologist* 7: 658–673.
Driver, Edwin D.
    1961   "Interaction and criminal homicide in India." *Social Forces* 40: 153–158.
Edgerton, Robert B.
    1972   "Violence in East African tribal societies." Pages 159–170 in *Collective Violence*,
           edited by James F. Short, Jr., and Marvin E. Wolfgang. Chicago: Aldine Press.
Eggleston, Elizabeth
    1976   *Fear, Favour or Affection: Aborigines and the Criminal Law in Victoria, South Aus-*
           tralia and Western Australia. Canberra: Australian National University Press.

Ekvall, Robert B.
　1968　*Fields on the Hoof: Nexus of Tibetan Nomadic Pastoralism.* New York: Holt, Rinehart and Winston.
Elias, Norbert
　1939　*The Civilizing Process: The Development of Manners,* vol. 1. New York: Urizen Books, 1978.
Evans-Pritchard, E. E.
　1940　*The Neur: A Description of the Modes of Livelihood and Political Institutions of a Nilotic People.* London: Oxford University Press.
Fallers, L. A., and M. C. Fallers
　1960　"Homicide and suicide in Busoga." Pages 65–93 in *African Homicide and Suicide,* edited by Paul Bohannan. Princeton, N.J.: Princeton University Press.
Fattah, Ezzat A.
　1976　"The use of the victim as an agent of self-legitimization: Toward a dynamic explanation of criminal behavior." *Victimology: An International Journal* 1: 29–53.
Fried, Jacob
　1953　"The relation of ideal norms to actual behavior in Tarahumara society." *Southwestern Journal of Anthropology* 9: 286–295.
Fürer-Haimendorf, Christoph von
　1943　*The Chenchus: Jungle Folk of the Deccan.* London: Macmillan.
Gluckman, Max
　1965　*Politics, Law and Ritual in Tribal Society.* New York: Mentor Books, 1968.
　1967　*The Judicial Process among the Barotse of Northern Rhodesia.* 2d edition. Manchester: Manchester University Press (1st edition, 1955).
Green, Thomas A.
　1972　"Societal concepts of criminal liability for homicide in mediaeval England." *Speculum* 47: 669–694.
　1976　"The jury and the English law of homicide, 1200–1600." *Michigan Law Review* 74: 413–499.
Greenberg, David F.
　1977　"Delinquency and the age structure of society." *Contemporary Crises: Crime, Law, Social Policy* 1: 189–223.
Haft-Picker, Cheryl
　1980　"Beyond the subculture of violence: An evolutionary and historical approach to social control." Pages 181–210 in *Crime and Deviance: A Comparative Perspective,* edited by Graeme R. Newman. Sage Annual Reviews of Studies in Deviance, vol. 4. Beverly Hills, Calif.: Sage.
Hanawalt, Barbara A.
　1979　*Crime and Conflict in English Communities, 1300–1348.* Cambridge, Mass.: Harvard University Press.
Harner, Michael J.
　1972　*The Jívaro: People of the Sacred Waterfalls.* Garden City, N.Y.: Anchor Books, 1973.
Hasluck, Margaret
　1954　*The Unwritten Law in Albania.* Cambridge: Cambridge University Press.
Hiatt, L. R.
　1965　*Kinship and Conflict: A Study of an Aboriginal Community in Northern Arnhem Land.* Canberra: Australian National University.
Hobbes, Thomas
　1651　*Leviathan: Or the Matter, Forme and Power of a Commonwealth Ecclesiasticall and Civil.* New York: Macmillan, 1962.

Hobhouse, L. T.
    1906 *Morals in Evolution: A Study in Comparative Ethics.* New York: Henry Holt.
Hobsbawm, Eric
    1959 *Primitive Rebels: Studies in Archaic Forms of Social Movement in the 19th and 20th
          Centuries.* New York: W. W. Norton (originally published as *Social Bandits and
          Primitive Rebels*).
    1969 *Bandits.* New York: Dell, 1971.
Hoebel, E. Adamson
    1954 *The Law of Primitive Man: A Study in Comparative Legal Dynamics.* Cambridge,
          Mass.: Harvard University Press.
Hoffman, Stanley
    1968 "International law and the control of force." Pages 34–66 in *The Relevance of
          International Law,* edited by Karl Deutsch and Stanley Hoffmann. Garden City,
          N.Y.: Anchor Books, 1971.
Horowitz, Ruth, and Gary Schwartz
    1974 "Honor, normative ambiguity and gang violence." *American Sociological Review*
          39: 238–251.
Howell, P. P.
    1954 *A Manual of Nuer Law: Being an Account of Customary Law, Its Evolution and
          Development in the Courts Established by the Sudan Government.* London: Oxford
          University Press.
Jones, Schuyler
    1974 *Men of Influence in Nuristan: A Study of Social Control and Dispute Settlement in
          Waigal Valley, Afghanistan.* New York: Seminar Press.
Koch, Klaus-Friedrich
    1974 *War and Peace in Jalémó: The Management of Conflict in Highland New Guinea.*
          Cambridge, Mass.: Harvard University Press.
Koch, Klaus-Friedrich, and John A. Sodergren (with the collaboration of Susan
Campbell)
    1976 "Political and psychological correlates of conflict management: A cross-cultural
          study." *Law and Society Review* 10: 443–466.
LaFave, Wayne R., and Austin W. Scott, Jr.
    1972 *Handbook on Criminal Law.* St. Paul: West.
La Fontaine, Jean
    1960 "Homicide and suicide among the Gisu." Pages 94–129 in *African Homicide and
          Suicide,* edited by Paul Bohannan. Princeton, N.J.: Princeton University Press.
Langness, L. L.
    1972 "Violence in the New Guinea highlands." Pages 171–185 in *Collective Violence,*
          edited by James F. Short, Jr., and Marvin E. Wolfgang. Chicago: Aldine Press.
Lemert, Edwin M.
    1967 "The concept of secondary deviation." Pages 40–64 in *Human Deviance, Social
          Problems, and Social Control.* Englewood Cliffs, N.J.: Prentice-Hall.
Le Vine, Robert A.
    1959 "Gusii sex offenses: A study in social control." *American Anthropologist* 61:
          965–990.
Lewis, I. M.
    1959 "Clanship and contract in northern Somaliland." *Africa* 29: 274–293.
Llewellyn, Karl N., and E. Adamson Hoebel
    1941 *The Cheyenne Way: Conflict and Case Law in Primitive Jurisprudence.* Norman,
          Okla.: University of Oklahoma Press.

Lundsgaarde, Henry P.
    1977   *Murder in Space City: A Cultural Analysis of Houston Homicide Patterns.* New York:
           Oxford University Press.
MacCormack, Geoffrey
    1976   "Procedures for the settlement of disputes in 'simple societies.'" *The Irish Jurist*
           11 (N.S.): 175–188.
Maddock, Kenneth
    1977   "Two laws in one community." Pages 13–32 in *Aborigines and Change: Australia
           in the '70s,* edited by R. M. Berndt. Canberra: Australian Institute of Aboriginal
           Studies.
Matza, David
    1964   *Delinquency and Drift.* New York: Wiley.
Maybury-Lewis, David
    1967   *Akwē-Shavante Society.* Oxford: Clarendon Press.
Merry, Sally Engle
    1981   *Urban Danger: Life in a Neighborhood of Strangers.* Philadelphia: Temple Univer-
           sity Press.
Middleton, John
    1965   *The Lugbara of Uganda.* New York: Holt, Rinehart and Winston.
Middleton, John, and David Tait (editors)
    1958   *Tribes without Rulers: Studies in African Segmentary Systems.* New York: Human-
           ities Press, 1970.
Miller, Walter B.
    1958   "Lower class culture as a generating milieu of gang delinquency." *Journal of
           Social Issues* 14: 5–19.
Moore, Sally Falk
    1972   "Legal liability and evolutionary interpretation: Some aspects of strict liability,
           self-help and collective responsibility." Pages 51–107 in *The Allocation of Respon-
           sibility,* edited by Max Gluckman. Manchester: Manchester University Press.
Murphy, Robert F.
    1960   *Headhunter's Heritage: Social and Economic Change among the Mundurucú Indians.*
           Berkeley, Calif.: University of California Press.
Nash, June
    1967   "Death as a way of life: The increasing resort to homicide in a Maya Indian
           community." *American Anthropologist* 69: 445–470.
Otterbein, Keith F., and Charlotte Swanson Otterbein
    1965   "An eye for an eye, a tooth for a tooth: A cross-cultural study of feuding."
           American Anthropologist 67: 1470–1482.
Peristiany, J. G. (editor)
    1966   *Honour and Shame: The Values of Mediterranean Society.* Chicago: University of
           Chicago Press.
Peters, E. Lloyd
    1972   "Aspects of the control of moral ambiguities: A comparative analysis of two
           culturally disparate modes of social control." Pages 109–162 in *The Allocation of
           Responsibility,* edited by Max Gluckman. Manchester: Manchester University
           Press.
Pike, Luke Owen
    1873   *A History of Crime in England: Illustrating the Changes of the Laws in the Progress of
           Civilisation,* Vol. 1: *From the Roman Invasion to the Accession of Henry VII.* London:
           Smith, Elder.

1876   *A History of Crime in England: Illustrating the Changes of the Laws in the Progress of Civilisation*, vol. 2: *From the Accession of Henry VII to the Present Time*. London: Smith, Elder.

Pitt-Rivers, Julian
1966   "Honour and social status." Pages 19–77 in *Honour and Shame: The Values of Mediterranean Society*, edited by J. G. Peristiany. Chicago: University of Chicago Press.

Pollock, Frederick, and Frederic William Maitland
1898   *The History of English Law: Before the Time of Edward I*. 2d edition. Cambridge: Cambridge University Press, 1968 (1st edition, 1895).

Pound, Roscoe
1921   *The Spirit of the Common Law*. Boston: Marshall Jones.

Raper, Arthur F.
1933   *The Tragedy of Lynching*. Chapel Hill, N.C.: University of North Carolina Press.

Rees, Alwyn D.
1950   *Life in a Welsh Countryside: A Social Study of Llanfihangel yng Ngwynfa*. Cardiff: University of Wales Press.

Reid, John Phillip
1970   *A Law of Blood: The Primitive Law of the Cherokee Nation*. New York: New York University Press.

Riasanovsky, Valentin A.
1938   *Customary Law of the Nomadic Tribes of Siberia*. Bloomington, Ind.: Indiana University Press, 1965.

Roberts, Simon
1979   *Order and Dispute: An Introduction to Legal Anthropology*. New York: Penguin Books.

Roberts, W. Lewis
1922   "The unwritten law." *Kentucky Law Journal* 10: 45–52.

Rothenberger, John E.
1978   "The social dynamics of dispute settlement in a Sunni Muslim village in Lebanon." Pages 152–180 in *The Disputing Process—Law in Ten Societies*, edited by Laura Nader and Harry F. Todd, Jr. New York: Columbia University Press.

Schneider, Jane
1971   "Of vigilance and virgins: Honor, shame and access to resources in Mediterranean societies." *Ethnology* 10: 1–24.

Stauder, Jack
1972   "Anarchy and ecology: Political society among the Majangir." *Southwestern Journal of Anthropology* 28: 153–168.

Sutherland, Edwin H., and Donald R. Cressey
1960   *Principles of Criminology*. 6th edition. Philadelphia: J. P. Lippincott (1st edition, 1924).

Sweet, Louise E.
1965   "Camel raiding of North Arabian Bedouin: A mechanism of ecological adaptation." *American Anthropologist* 67: 1132–1150.

Sykes, Gresham M., and David Matza
1957   "Techniques of neutralization: A theory of delinquency." *American Sociological Review* 22: 664–670.

Tanner, R. E. S.
1966   "Cattle theft in Musoma, 1958–9." *Tanzania Notes and Records* 65: 31–42.

Thoden van Velzen, H. U. E., and W. van Wetering
    1960   "Residence, power groups and intra-societal aggression: An enquiry into the conditions leading to peacefulness within non-stratified societies." *International Archives of Ethnography* 49 (pt. 2): 169–200.
Thomas-Buckle, Suzann R., and Leonard G. Buckle
    1982   "Doing unto others: Disputes and dispute processing in an urban American neighborhood." Pages 78–90 in *Neighborhood Justice: Assessment of an Emerging Idea*, edited by Roman Tomasic and Malcolm M. Feeley. New York: Longman.
Thompson, E. P.
    1975   "The crime of anonymity." Pages 255–344 in *Albion's Fatal Tree: Crime and Society in Eighteenth-Century England*, by Douglas Hay, Peter Linebaugh, John G. Rule, E. P. Thompson, and Cal Winslow. New York: Pantheon.
Torcia, Charles E.
    1979   *Wharton's Criminal Law*, vol. 2. 14th edition. Rochester, N.Y.: Lawyers Cooperative (1st edition, 1846).
Turnbull, Colin M.
    1965   *Wayward Servants: The Two Worlds of the African Pygmies*. Garden City, N.Y.: Natural History Press.
van den Steenhoven, Geert
    1956   Research Report on "Caribou Eskimo Law." Ottawa: Canadian Department of Northern Affairs and National Resources.
    1962   Leadership and Law among the Eskimos of the Keewatin District, Northwest Territories. Doctoral dissertation, Faculty of Law, University of Leiden.
Vera Institute of Justice
    1977   *Felony Arrests: Their Prosecution and Disposition in New York City's Courts*. New York: Vera Institute of Justice.
Warner, W. Lloyd
    1958   *A Black Civilization: A Social Study of an Australian Tribe*. Revised edition. New York: Harper and Brothers (1st edition, 1937).
Weber, Max
    1919   "Politics as a vocation." Pages 77–128 in *From Max Weber: Essays in Sociology*, edited by Hans Gerth and C. Wright Mills. New York: Oxford University Press, 1958.
    1922   *The Theory of Social and Economic Organization*, edited by Talcott Parsons. New York: Free Press, 1964.
Werthman, Carl
    1969   "Delinquency and moral character." Pages 613–632 in *Delinquency, Crime, and Social Process*, edited by Donald R. Cressey and David A. Ward. New York: Harper & Row.
Wolfgang, Marvin E.
    1958   *Patterns in Criminal Homicide*. New York: Wiley, 1966.
Wolfgang, Marvin E., and Franco Ferracuti
    1966   *The Subculture of Violence: Towards an Integrated Theory in Criminology*. London: Tavistock, 1967.
Yablonsky, Lewis
    1962   *The Violent Gang*. New York: Macmillan.
Zimring, Franklin E.
    1971   *Perspectives on Deterrence*. Washington, D.C.: Center for Studies of Crime and Delinquency, National Institute of Mental Health.

2

Social Control in Illegal Markets*

PETER REUTER

Those engaged in conventional legal commerce enter into contractual arrangements under the protection of a variety of state institutions. Legislatures enact laws that specify limits on both the nature of agreements into which participants may enter and the manner in which they may resolve disputes arising from these agreements. Courts and a number of other facilities are available for settlement of disputes that arise. Various state entities, generically "police," help ensure that court-mandated settlements are carried out.

None of these resources is available to those engaged in illegal activities. They must decide, either as a group or in transaction-specific subgroups, on the rules under which they will conduct their affairs. They must find alternatives to the court for settlement of disputes. And if they do develop nonviolent adjudication systems to substitute for the court, they must also find a substitute for the police to ensure compliance with adjudication decisions.

*The research reported here was supported by grants from the National Institute of Justice. Major support for the writing of this chapter was provided under the Organized Crime Research Agreements Program, administered by Temple University Law School. During my work on this chapter I was a consultant to the Center for Research on Institutions and Social Policy. The chapter draws on empirical work done earlier at the Policy Sciences Center, also with National Institute of Justice funding. The opinions expressed are solely the responsibility of the author.

TOWARD A GENERAL THEORY OF SOCIAL CONTROL
Volume 2: Selected Problems

This chapter is concerned with all three of these problems for participants in large-scale organized[1] markets for illegal goods and services, such as heroin and bookmaking. I pay particular attention to the nature of the mechanisms that may be developed to substitute for the police and the courts in relation to disputes in these markets. I pay less attention to the substitutes developed for the legislative function simply because I have been unable to make much progress, either conceptually or empirically, in that area.

Conceptual Issues

DISPUTE SETTLEMENT WITHOUT THE STATE: PRIMITIVE SOCIETIES

The provision of substitutes for centrally provided courts, legislatures, and police is an issue that has been considered a great deal in contexts other than illegal markets. There is a large anthropological literature[2] describing the mechanisms developed for dispute settlement in primitive societies that lack, in all other senses, the machinery of government. This literature provides a useful starting point for a discussion of the problems faced by participants in illegal markets.

Many societies have existed that lacked the formal mechanics of law-making but nonetheless had adjudication and enforcement processes. Thus, for example, Redfield describes dispute settlement among the Ifugao of North Luzon:

> These people [are] without tribal organization and settlement of claims is effected simply by means of negotiations between the parties. But among the Ifugao the negotiations are carried out not by the parties themselves but by a compromiser, or go-between, selected for the purpose by the parties. The go-between has no authority and no force behind him; there is nothing to support his efforts to secure a settlement by acting for both parties except the fact that the only alternative to settlement is a long drawn-out feud, which is wanted by neither party and nobody else [1967: 10].

---

[1]The term *organized* is used only to convey the notion that trade is continuous, that the entities involved are not all isolated individuals, and that there is enough homogeneity of commodity that prices may be compared and the market defined.

[2]A useful collection of readings on this subject is provided by Bohannan (1967). A more recent collection of essays (Nader and Todd, 1978) provides material on disputing processes in societies with varying degrees of central government dispute-settlement facilities.

Examples from North America include the Comanche Indians (Hoebel, 1967) and the Yurok Indians (Kroeber, 1925), and numerous others have been described in South America, Africa, Asia, and Oceania. What Redfield and other anthropologists fail to explain, however, is how a general perception of the negative consequences of violence in disputes between parties translates into the creation of an effective mandatory system of nonviolent resolution. Yet this process seems to occur whenever there is no government to internalize the collective costs of violence.

A sophisticated effor to provide a general explanation of the emergence of nonviolent dispute settlement mechanisms in primitive societies is that of Posner (1981: chap. 7). He begins with a characterization of the organization of primitive society, noting that each person in a primitive society is a member of a larger collective entity generally based on kinship relations. These collectives serve many functions, perhaps the most important being the provision of insurance in food supplies; each member of the collective has an obligation to distribute his or her surplus to other members who are in deficit. Membership in the collective is not voluntary but is determined entirely by blood or marriage.

The kin group serves as a restraining influence on the use of violence by individual members, for there is collective responsibility for the consequences of that violence. Moreover, the kin group may urge individual members to submit to mediation or arbitration; otherwise, the kin group of an offended party may take action against the group as a whole. Posner's emphasis on the role of the kin group is critical to an understanding of the distinction between primitive societies and illegal markets.

> The importance of the kin group in the enforcement of primitive tort law derives from the absence of effective government. Where the threat of retaliation is the only deterrent to misconduct, it is important that the threat be credible, and often it would not be if there were only one potential retaliator. Even after compensation is substituted for retaliation, there must still be a credible threat of retaliation in the background to coerce payment of the compensation. The need to maintain a credible retaliatory capability is another reason, besides the need for a risk pool, why the recognized kin group is larger in primitive than in modern societies [1981: 194].[3]

Posner also explains why the kin group is the relevant collectivity for dispute settlement, which may be of some interest in considering the

---

[3]This statement explicitly concerns tort law, which in modern societies pertains to "civil wrongs" such as defamation and negligence. However, Posner properly uses the same reasoning in his discussion of dispute resolution generally.

role of ethnicity in illegal markets. First, kinship provides a low-cost method of determining eligibility. It also ensures homogeneity and mutual obligations on other grounds that make the collective function more smoothly. Third, it limits the size of the group, which might otherwise become dominant and effectively function as a state.

Having satisfactorily accounted for the emergence of nonviolent dispute settlement and for the social forces leading to compliance (i.e., the substitutes for courts and police), Posner admits to little understanding of the process generating the norms of procedure and substance. There is no central body that can function as a legislature. Settlement agents can reap no return from the issuance of their opinions as precedents, since in preliterate societies there can be no ownership of intellectual product. That leaves only "custom" as the source of applicable norms. The relevant characteristics of custom are its slow rate of change and inflexible precision of penalties.

In light of these observations, how much understanding of the mechanisms for dispute settlement generated in illegal markets can be obtained by consideration of primitive societies? The centrality of kinship collectives suggests the major difficulty. Although the extended family is an important bond for some groups within the illegal economy of contemporary America,[4] many others belong to no such "kinship collective." Indeed, some participants in illegal activities have no other relatives involved in the same activities. Even those who have relatives involved rarely have the entire family group as coparticipants. Hence, if collectives are to operate in illegal markets to restrain the violent actions of individuals and ensure the routine nonviolent settlement of disputes, they must reflect some other grouping principle. Both for sociological and economic reasons, it is difficult to identify a similarly broad principle that would ensure that the vast majority of participants were members of groups that assumed collective responsibility for the individual's actions.

It is also important to note that custom is likely to be a less powerful force for such markets. The obvious set of customs for participants in these disputes are the norms embodied in the common law of the legitimate society in which they are imbedded. It is, after all, readily available to them in great detail. It minimizes the demands on the rule-making

---

[4]Aronson (1978) provides an interesting case study here. He describes the operation of a criminal gang based almost entirely on extended family ties. The gang was able to coordinate exceptionally violent acts over a long period of time without concern about internal informants. The demise of the group came about because of the inclusion of one nonfamily member in the inner core. He turned informant rather than serve a lengthy prison term, as family members had.

powers of any institutions they may develop themselves. Given the heterogeneity of their backgrounds, the common law can also substitute for the more localized customs that they may individually seek to use, without giving any obvious advantage to one group.[5]

Nonetheless, the adoption of the common law is an unlikely result. First, the participants entered their illegal activities in defiance of some part of the laws of the surrounding legitimate society. They might therefore look askance at efforts to make them conform to the remainder of the corpus of law. In addition, an understanding of the law is likely to be differentially distributed across identifiable groups within the population of criminals, so that an effort to promote the use of the common law may be seen as an effort to promote the interests of some groups over others.

It is also important to note that the illegal economy is not autonomous. It must accept restraints arising from the existence of legitimate institutions of society. In particular, participants in the illegal economy can always decide that the costs of appealing to those institutions may be less than accepting the rules of the illegal economy in a given instance. Disputants who believe that they are being treated unfairly within the dispute settlement system may attempt to overthrow the results by becoming informants to the state.[6] The possibility of appeal limits the powers of the illegal economy, viewed as a society, over its population.

The following two sections present an alternative approach to the problem discussed earlier, using the notion of a "market" for dispute-settlement services. Factors leading to a *demand* for such a service are first identified, followed by a discussion of certain characteristics of the *supply* of dispute settlement services for participants in illegal activities.[7]

---

[5]Another reason might be suggested, namely, the efficiency of the law developed by common law institutions (Posner, 1977). This motivation for adaptation, however, depends on the perception of the adaptors, not generally legal sophisticates.

[6]Many of those in the Federal Witness Relocation Program, designed to protect witnesses from retaliation, entered it because of fears that their criminal associates were planning to kill them. Ironically, in some cases the associates mistakenly assumed that these persons had already become informants; in fact, only the associates' threats made them informants (see Graham, 1977).

[7]There is a related literature that ostensibly has some relevance but that can be quickly dismissed. Becker and Stigler (1974) have considered the privatization of the police function but only with respect to detection of violations of law. Landes and Posner (1975; 1979) have considered the possibility of private provision of judicial services. In both cases, however, the more fundamental institutions of lawmaking and rule enforcement are provided by the state. Their results concerning the feasibility and desirability of the private alternatives to state-provided detection and court services do not carry over to the enforcement and legislative functions.

REPUTATION AND THE DEMAND FOR ARBITRATION

Why might participants in illegal market transactions seek nonviolent third-party dispute resolutions? They have, after all, another alternative, namely, the use of force or intimidation. Sorting out the consequences of violence for dispute resolution, and the circumstances under which it may be optimal, may clarify aspects of the demand for arbitration.

There are costs to the use of violence. First, wherever violence is contemplated, there is some uncertainty about the outcome. Each disputant may be unsure about the resources that the other commands. In particular, each may be uncertain whether the other is a member of an organization that will regard a dispute with a member as a dispute with the organization. Second, there are costs incurred in actually executing threats; time must be devoted to the effort, and others may have to be paid to assist the disputant. Finally, there is a reputational cost, namely, the cost of acquiring the reputation for intimidating transactional partners. This last deserves detailed examination, because it provides the most powerful motivation for avoiding the use of violence across markets and disputes.

I start with the assumption that illegal markets are not characterized by monopoly control. This assumption reflects research reported in Reuter (1983: chaps. 2–5). The degree of competition is irrelevant for this discussion; it may be oligopolistic or perfectly competitive. The critical issue is that no transactor can compel others to transact with him or her because they have alternative suppliers or customers available to them. Hence, acquisition of a reputation for being an unreliable transactor, along any dimension, will impose costs on the participant: Other participants will be reluctant to do business with that person.

Note also that disputes are more likely to arise in illegal than in legal markets. The lack of formal written contracts, or indeed of any written documents at all, as well as the additional uncertainties created by law enforcement efforts lead to more frequent occurrence of situations in which two parties may have a genuine disagreement about the obligations of each party at some point in the development of the transaction.

The first factor (competition) ensures that there is a cost to acquiring a reputation for "unfairness" in the resolution of disputes that may arise in the course of transactions. The second factor (lack of written contracts) suggests that this cost may be substantial, for such disputes are likely to be frequent. The lack of court enforceability of contracts may make the reputation for attempting to find reasonable resolutions for the disputes that inevitably arise in the course of business even more important than in legal markets.[8] Macaulay (1963) reports that in legitimate markets the preservation of such a reputation is considered in the decision to litigate a contractual disagreement.

The emphasis on reputation in illegal markets is also justified by the absence of the symbols of reliability and quality that facilitate impersonal operation of legitimate markets. For example, there is no equivalent in the marijuana market to Department of Agriculture grading of meat. The marijuana purchaser must resort to self-testing to the extent that he or she doubts the representations of the seller; accurate testing to determine the THC content of marijuana is expensive relative to the value of a low-level transaction.[9] Similarly, a potential creditor cannot turn to a Dun and Bradstreet report or bankruptcy court record in order to determine the reliability of a possible debtor.[10] Yet bettors and bookmakers routinely extend each other short-term credit;[11] the basis for that decision is word-of-mouth information about the reliability of the other party and about the likelihood that, in the case of a genuine dispute, he or she will resort to use of violence or force.

If a concern with reputation is critical to the demand for nonviolent dispute resolution, then there may be substantial variation between markets in the extent to which disputes are arbitrated. There are two components to reputation, both of which can vary between markets and even between levels within one product market. The first component is the value ascribed, by others, to the expectation of "honorable" con-

---

[8]Posner (1981) makes a similar point: "I conjecture that in trades where, because of cost or other reasons, legal sanctions for breach of contract are ineffectual, businessmen will be extremely sensitive to accusations of sharp dealing because reputation is the only surety of faithful performance between contracting partners [p. 143]."

[9]Tetrahydrocannabinol (THC) is the hallucinogenic ingredient in marijuana. High-quality marijuana is characterized by high THC content, which can be determined only through complex chemical testing, and low percentages of seed and twigs. Sampling by smoking is an alternative that is feasible only in certain transactional settings.

[10]The examples may be generalized as follows. The Department of Agriculture example concerns provision of a public good. Absent any low-cost method for charging all users of marijuana for this service, there will emerge no illegal market instrumentality to serve that function. The Dun and Bradstreet example concerns private-market provision of information. In this case, it is the hostile role of government to the flow of information in illegal commerce that creates difficulty. An illegal market Dun and Bradstreet service would place all reporting enterprises at risk.

[11]A large bookmaking enterprise in New York in the mid-1970s might handle $1 million per week in bets during the football season. With accounts settled on a weekly basis and all bets being placed by telephone, the bookmaker frequently has $100,000 in short-term credit extended to customers as a group. He may also owe a number of individual bettors as much as $5000 each (Reuter, 1983: chap. 2).

duct. The second is the ease with which adverse information can be credibly disseminated.

Consider first the market value of reputation. As mentioned earlier, bookmakers place a high value on reputation because the nature of the business requires frequent credit transactions with customers; the only alternative is joint escrow accounts, which create risk of legal exposure and have significant transaction costs. At the other end may lie heroin importers. The cost of testing the quality of a package of heroin is almost invariant to its size.[12] There is no credit relationship in the importer–dealer transaction.[13] Hence, the dealer has little concern with the reputation of the importer for honest dealings, for only a trivial fraction of the gross profits need to be invested in ascertaining the relevant fact, namely, the quality of the heroin.

Similar considerations bear on the second component, namely, the extent to which adverse information is credibly disseminated in the market. The participants in bookmaking, for instance, subject to only slight penalties following arrest, may readily exchange information with others about particular transactions and operators. Indeed, my impression, from discussions with police and participants,[14] is that each participant has a strong awareness of the reputation of numerous others and that relevant information is rapidly disseminated. Heroin dealers, faced by grave threats against life and property from both police and competitors, may be much less willing to exchange reputationally relevant information with other dealers, at least at the higher levels.

These examples suggest some of the variables that may determine the importance of reputational considerations to a participant. The level of legal penalty, the cost of product testing relative to purchase price, the discreteness of transactions, and the variability of financial flows between parties all have a potential influence. Market power is also a relevant variable. The less competitive the market, the smaller is the elasticity of demand with respect to reputational loss, because shifts to alternative suppliers will lead them to increase their price. All may vary

[12]Heroin quality is a function of purity and the nature of the adulterants used, both accurately determinable with only moderately sophisticated scientific tests.

[13]A credit relationship is feasible. The infrequency of high-level deals, however, makes such credit less essential, whereas the great dangers faced by the dealer in disposing of the goods and the importer's less detailed knowledge of the dealer's business would lead the importer to charge a risk premium higher than the dealer's subjective evaluation. Moreover, it would give the dealer an additional incentive to inform against his importer, because incarceration hinders debt collection.

[14]The Appendix to this chapter provides a brief description of these sources. More detail is provided in Reuter (1983: chap. 1 and appendix).

not only between product markets but also between levels within any one market. High-level heroin dealers, facing higher legal risks and lower percentage testing costs, are likely to have less reputational concern than lower-level dealers have.

If reputation is the prime motivation for seeking or accepting arbitration, then the demand for these services should vary across markets. *Those markets in which reputation is highly valued and in which adverse information is rapidly disseminated are the markets in which arbitration*[15] *will be most frequently sought to resolve disputes.* This is not to say that in any market at any level there will be arbitration of all disputes. Apart from any irrationality on the part of participants, surely to be expected in these markets when disputes frequently involve matters of "face" or honor, the value of the disputed property has an influence. The higher the value of the disputed property, the greater is the reluctance of the party holding the property to permit its distribution through arbitration. Reputational loss may reasonably be assumed, all else constant, to rise less than proportionately with the value of the disputed property, for it will be optimal to sacrifice some of one's reputation if the value of the property, discounted by the difference between the subjective probability of holding that property in a nonarbitrated dispute and receiving it through arbitration, exceeds a certain level.

SUPPLYING ARBITRATION SERVICES

Having identified sources of demand for arbitration services in the cost of violence and the value of reputation, I now turn to the much more complex question of their supply. I shall treat here just two aspects of the supply side: the relationship of adjudication and enforcement and the competitive structure of the arbitration services market.

Even where both parties have sought adjudication in order to avoid loss of reputation, decisions are not necessarily self-enforcing. Both parties may seek the adjudication, but one (or both) may reject its terms once the decision has been made. Consider an instance in which A is in possession of the disputed property. He is convinced that an impartial adjudicator will award him the property on the merits of the argument. He is also confident that he could retain the property without adjudication, having a superior command of violence, which he prefers not to invoke for reputational reasons. If the adjudicator decides against him

[15]Arbitration is defined here as having two components: adjudication and enforcement of the adjudicated ruling.

(A may have misperceived the merits of B's case),[16] then it may be optimal for him to resist implementing the judgment. That will depend on the value of the disputed property, the expected reputational loss, and the expected cost of retention.

Adjudicators then must also provide some credible evidence of an ability to enforce their decisions,[17] that is, an ability to use force to obtain or protect the disputed property. The contract for the arbitrator's services will need to cover, presumably through the initial payment, both adjudication and contingent enforcement. Reputational concerns of the arbitrator will ensure that he carries out his enforcement obligations in case of noncompliance.

This need to maintain an enforcement capability suggests precisely why the arbitration market might not be competitively structured.[18] The greater the arbitrator's reputation for effective intimidation, the lower the enforcement cost for a single decision will generally be. If the arbitrator has overwhelming force at his disposal, then decisions will be essentially self-enforcing, as decisions in criminal court are for the state.[19] The arbitration market should then be characterized by a small number of enterprises that are large relative to enterprises in the client markets.

Can we go further and argue that the arbitration market is likely to be monopolized? Nozick (1974: chap. 2) has argued for this result in a related setting. Starting with a simplified "state of nature," Nozick suggests that the possibility of disagreement between individuals will lead to the creation of "mutual protective associations" in the absence of a state. He goes on to argue that there will emerge a single protective association (possibly out of a federation of associations) or a series of

[16]Alternatively, the arbitrator may have been corrupted by B. Indeed, if arbitrators did not operate in a market where their reputation for integrity was an asset, it appears that the arbitrator could appropriate most of the value of the disputed property through bribes. But if reputation matters in product markets, then *a fortiori* it matters in the market for adjudicators: An adjudicator who acquires a reputation for corruption will get few cases.

[17]It is possible that adjudication and enforcement services are provided by separate enterprises; the end result is, in terms of structural relations, essentially the same.

[18]This is not inconsistent with the Landes-Posner (1979: 237) claim of perfect markets for adjudicative services, for they are concerned with settlements for which the state serves as the ultimate enforcement authority.

[19]They are self-enforcing in that the state devotes no resources specifically to a single decision. On the other hand, it is necessary for the state to invest in the creation of a police force in order for this to occur. The term *self-enforcing* might be more appropriately reserved to situations where there is no investment for either general or specific deterrence, as with voluntary associations.

localized monopolies, for overlapping associations will have to work out dispute resolution systems for their own disputes. Such "meta-disputes" can be resolved only through monopoly or confederation.

In Nozick's analysis, the protective associations have a purely coercive role. The associations, in dealing with one another, may have a concern for perceived fairness; the individual disputants from different associations do not. That is a critical difference from the situation we are considering, where the demand for adjudication and enforcement arises from a concern with fairness. Disputes are not between arbitration enterprises, the equivalent of protective associations, but are brought to a single arbitration enterprise to be resolved in a manner that preserves the reputation for integrity of the two disputants.

It is not clear that a monopoly will emerge in this case. The argument for the emergence of a small number of large arbitration enterprises was the fact that larger arbitration enterprises could more cheaply offer effective enforcement of adjudication, not that they needed to maintain a certain size relative to one another, as in Nozick's situation. The market may be large enough to accommodate a number of minimum-cost arbitration enterprises. Whether in the absence of antitrust authorities they will merge to form a monopoly depends on many factors: the elasticity of demand, the difficulty of joint leadership of an illicit enterprise in which the command of force is an important attribute, and the problems of providing credible assurance to one entrepreneur involved in a takeover that he will in fact receive promises of future compensation once he has lost command of the enterprise. It would take us too far afield to examine these factors, which are discussed in detail in Reuter (1983: chap. 6). Even if each arbitration enterprise is only an oligopolist, it should be able to extort a portion of excess profits from client illegal entrepreneurs. Not only does the arbitrator have monopoly power, but also that power is based on a reputation for violence, and the arbitrator is, through the nature of the service he provides, able to obtain information about the workings of client enterprises. Although the "discovery" rules for arbitration proceedings in illegal markets are no doubt highly restrictive; that is, each disputant will attempt to limit severely the amount of information obtained by the other, the arbitrator must surely acquire significant data on the workings of the two disputants. The potential for using these powers to restructure the final markets for illegal goods and services seems substantial. Indeed, the monopolist in dispute-settlement service markets appears to acquire substantial elements of the power of government. With this in mind, I now turn to consideration of the Mafia as a provider of dispute-settlement services.

The Mafia as a Dispute-Settlement System

The material presented here comes from a larger study of the organization of illegal markets in New York (Reuter, 1983). That research, depending heavily on interviews with participants in the markets, has led me to accept the views of the police with respect to at least one aspect of the role of the Mafia, namely, its monopoly of the provision of dispute-settlement services. I have recorded a number of instances in which Mafia members are employed by others to settle disputes nonviolently. There are markets (e.g., high-level heroin distribution) in which the members of the Mafia are prominent and disputes are rarely subject to nonviolent third-party resolution. There are others (e.g., high-level marijuana distribution) in which the Mafia is unimportant and there is little use of violence. But I have been unable to find any instances in which anyone other than a Mafia member sold dispute-resolution services.[20] The evidence is not overwhelming; it is briefly discussed in the Appendix and in more detail in Reuter (1983: appendix). For the remainder of this chapter, I shall assume that the Mafia does have the monopoly, but here I first provide a brief suggestion as to why this has occurred.

I believe that the critical factor accounting for the Mafia's monopoly on dispute-resolution services is its reputation, itself a function of the durability and stability of the group. The explanation for these can be found in part in the distinctive culture of immigrant Sicilians and in part in an accident of timing.

It is a commonplace of discussions of the Mafia, both in Sicily and the United States, to stress the historically based suspicion of Sicilians toward government. Ruled for centuries as a colony, often by very distant kings, its natives never acquired legitimized political power. Loyalty was to the family and village rather than to the abstract state. Initial contact with the police of major American cities, predominantly Irish and German when the major wave of migration reached the United States from 1890 to 1920, reinforced that suspicion. Criminal gangs were at least tolerated and frequently provided important organizations in dealing with external political authority (see Ianni, 1972: chaps. 1–3).

The accident of timing was Prohibition, which occurred just as the major wave of Italian migration was coming to its end. Already deeply involved in the provision of illegal wine to the Italian community, the gangs were young, homogeneous, and ambitious. They were scattered

---

[20]Some nonmembers may earn revenues as intermediaries in obtaining adjudication services for others.

throughout the major cities of the nation, an important asset when the relevant market was truly national, as it was for bootleg liquor.[21]

Once having acquired a unique reputation for control of violence and political connections, the Mafia had an asset that could be exploited in a number of ways. Corrupt police sought to form alliances with the group that was most likely to be able to coordinate extortion effectively. Newspaper reporting was biased toward reporting the activities of the Mafia, the only group that readers could be expected to recognize. And other participants in criminal activities, less organized and unable to obtain any better information about the resources the Mafia actually commands than were newspaper reporters or corrupt police, accorded them certain powers of government, in particular the right to provide dispute-settlement services whose efficient provision is based on a reputation for command of coercion. It is in fact my conjecture (Reuter, 1983: chap. 7) that the Mafia is a "paper tiger." It is now reaping the return for having had dominant violence in the past, without incurring the expense of maintaining the forces to carry out its threats. That, however, is not critical to the following discussion.

THE MAFIA

In the next section I present a series of six stylized accounts about the settlement of disputes by Mafia members in the greater New York City area. The "tales" are intended to illustrate the variety of dispute-settlement processes and the quality of available information. In order to give a context to these examples, I should begin with a brief, also stylized, description of the Mafia in the New York area.[22]

The Mafia appears to consist of a set of "families" that have a moderately clear hierarchical structure. Only males of Sicilian or southern Italian background may belong. The lowest level members are called "buttons" or "soldiers." Each button is responsible, in a limited sense, to a "lieutenant" or "capo." The family is headed by an individual who is referred to as a "don" and who has an "underboss" as his deputy. I again must emphasize that the terminology is variable; I have generally adopted the police terminology for purposes of consistency and familiarity.

The nature of the relationships between levels of hierarchy in a family is unclear. Some capos appear to have almost complete autonomy.

---

[21]Gangs in different cities gained through cooperation in exchange of various kinds of liquor, whose optimal entry points and distribution routes were determined by external production location.

[22]This account is based largely on conversations with police and criminal informants.

Whether payments are made by capos to the don is uncertain; my own guess is that the economic and command relationships are quite variable between families. There is no existing account of how or why individuals rise within the family. There are occasional reports of demotions, generally arising from specific failures. Some members refuse promotions.[23]

New York is reputed to have five families; another is located in New Jersey and interacts with the New York families. It is the only metropolitan area with more than one family, at least according to the accounts of law enforcement officers. No informant with whom I have had contact claims detailed knowledge of other cities.[24]

The relationship between the New York families appears to be essentially amicable.[25] There is some degree of specialization, both with respect to territory and function, by the families. Certainly individual gangs within each family specialize in a few activities in a limited area. Often the territorial definitions are very tight. All the territory in Brooklyn from Fifth Avenue down to the docks, and with well-specified east-west coordinates, apparently is identified with a gang headed until recently by a Gambino family capo named Tudo. This is not to say that other Mafia members do not occasionally do business there or that the gang can tax all illegal ventures there. It simply means that most of the gang's activities are there and that, within that territory, the hierarchical structure does serve some tax function; that is, lower-level members must coordinate certain activities such as numbers and bookmaking with, and make some payments to, their immediate superiors in the hierarchy. The gang probably also has some degree of political protection there, lacking in other areas, but examination of that will take us too far afield.

Family members may do business with members of the other fami-

[23]It is difficult to explain this, for there is no clear account of what additional responsibilities a member assumes when he rises in the hierarchy. Promotion may mean that more time is devoted to essentially bureaucratic functions. Alternatively, members may believe that promotion will bring increased police attention or provide greater exposure in interfamily conflict.

[24]This is itself a significant indicator of how localized are Mafia activities. Valachi, the major source for the standard account of the Mafia, showed great ignorance of activities outside of New York City (Hawkins, 1969).

[25]Since 1960, there appear to have been only two major interfamily conflicts. One is the rather celebrated Gallo–Profaci wars, which actually revolved around the efforts of an ambitious faction in one family to acquire autonomy. The other began with Joseph Bonnano's plan to remove the more senior heads of three other families in the New York area. It is difficult to obtain accurate accounts of either of these wars, but the number of dead may have been about 10 in each case. Some information about the Bonnano incident is provided in Zeiger (1975).

lies. There are enduring enterprises that involve partnerships between members of two different families. There are short-term ventures involving members from more than two families. Wars between families have occurred, but the enduring relationship is one of complicated interdependence. The interesting question here is whether this translates into cartel behavior with respect to arbitration services or whether there is effective competition between Mafia members or families in the selling of adjudicatory and enforcement services. We shall resume this discussion after consideration of the examples.

EXAMPLES OF DISPUTE SETTLEMENT

Incident Number 1. This incident concerns the sale of stolen liquor and took place shortly after World War II when imported liquor was very difficult to obtain. Harry (Jewish) owned a bar and was a minor bookmaker. He contracted to buy from Tony (Italian), the narrator of the incident, 20 cases of Scotch. The Scotch had been stolen from the docks and was priced at $150 per case, which was substantially below market price.

When Tony's trucker delivered the Scotch, Harry gave him only $1500. The trucker called Tony and asked for instructions. Tony told him to return the money and bring back the liquor, which he did.

The next day Tony went to Harry's bar. He pulled a gun on Harry and demanded $300 for the risk and inconvenience that Harry had caused the trucker. Harry said Tony did not need the gun and that he would give Tony more than $300, which he did. The incident was watched by a police lieutenant who was Harry's protector.

The following day Tony was summoned by a Mafia member (Frank) whom he regarded as his mentor. An adjudication was being arranged because Harry had complained, through a senior Jewish gangster (Hymie) who was close to another senior Mafia member (Joe). All five parties were present at the "sit-down." Tony told his version of the incident. Harry's Mafia representative, Joe, was incensed at Harry's behavior. He ordered Harry to refrain from any actions against Tony. Indeed, even Hymie apologized to Tony and said that he had not been told the full story.

Comments: The story was told 30 years after the incident. Although Tony was a very minor figure and not a Mafia member, his mentor was a very prominent member of a major Mafia family. Harry was a minor figure who very soon after this incident achieved a temporary importance in the bookmaking business. His indirect Mafia representative was also a prominent member but of a different family.

Incident Number 2. Seymour (Jewish) was a bookmaker in Brooklyn. He incurred very large debts to a number of individuals. The creditors ranged from a taxicab driver, who mortgaged his car in order to lend to Seymour at 2% per week, to a very prominent mafioso, whom he owed $20,000 at 1% per week. His debts may have totaled $750,000, and there were at least 20 separate creditors.

Seymour eventually decided that there was little likelihood of meeting his obligations, even though he now had the business running smoothly. He simply left New York. This, as one might expect, led to consternation on the part of many of his creditors.

Seymour had a brother, Dick, who was an important figure in the garment district. One of his sources of income was the creation of phantom companies. These would pay bookmakers by check, in exchange for money, so that they could declare some apparently legitimate income for tax purposes. As a favor to Dick, who was greatly embarrassed by Seymour's behavior, a senior mafioso, who was not one of the creditors, arranged a meeting of the known creditors. At that meeting the mafioso set the terms for partial payment of the creditors, with the profits from continuing operation of Seymour's bookmaking enterprise as the source of payment. The creditors, as a group, accepted the payment schedule, and apparently no effort was made to pursue Seymour.

Comment: The incident was narrated by one of Seymour's agents who later took over the operation on behalf of the creditors. Curiously enough, he started stealing from the operation, despite the substantial reputations of some of the main creditors now receiving monies from the business.

Incident Number 3. This incident also concerns a failing bookmaking operation. It is far more complex, however, and the following is just a distillation of a tangled web of events.

Ruby, Milty, and Bob (all Jewish) were involved in various bookmaking partnerships, though Ruby was primarily a loan shark. Their joint enterprise had its ups and downs. Debts were incurred by Bob on behalf of Milty and himself, and it became clear after a while that Milty had no intention of honoring his share of those debts.

Ruby and Bob were quite closely associated with a major Mafia figure, Andy. Milty had a close, but ambiguous, relationship with another mafioso, Jimmy. In each case the mafioso had been involved in the financial affairs of the various bookmaking partnerships. Andy and Jimmy belonged to different families. Both were very senior and had considerable autonomy.

After various efforts to resolve the problem of indebtedness without involving the two mafiosi, Ruby and Bob made an approach to Andy.

He agreed to meet with Jimmy and resolve the matter. The agreement reached was that Milty had to make some payments to Bob and his creditors, but the total was less than the amount actually owed because Milty was apparently in poor shape financially. In return Bob and Ruby were to stop threatening Milty and were not to take any action against him. Because Milty could not make the necessary payments immediately, Jimmy made a substantial initial payment (perhaps to be charged to Milty as a loan-shark debt) and the rest was to be paid according to a schedule worked out between Bob and Milty. They worked out such a schedule, but Milty soon fell behind. He suffered no adverse consequences.

Comments: The involvement of the two mafiosi is complex. Both of them had some financial relationship with the participants, but how they were affected by the settlement is unclear. The narrator was Bob.

Incident Number 4. Tony, the narrator of the first tale, was involved in a jewelry theft with three other persons. He had been informed that there was a particularly valuable piece of jewelry in the apartment and had a good description of it.

The theft was successful, in that a great deal of jewelry was located and the thieves (all Italian) made off without any problems. The piece of jewelry they were expecting to find, however, was not included. Tony suspected that one of the others, Joe, had quietly pocketed it. In the car after the theft he asked Joe whether he had it. Joe said he did not. Tony then had one of the others hold a gun against Joe while he searched him. He found the piece of jewelry and then gave Joe a beating before throwing him out of the car. Joe made a complaint to a mafioso, Allie, who was a member of the Profaci family. Because the complaint concerned activities that took place around 4th Avenue in Brooklyn, Allie asked that the dispute be adjudicated by members of the Gambino family, which was the dominant family in that area.

Tony and his two partners were called down to meet with four mafiosi, all in the Gambino family. One was Tony's mentor, Frank. The other three included two who were probably neutral toward him and one who was quite friendly. Tony told his side of the story and was then sent out of the room. Joe was not present at any time during the proceedings. Tony was then called back in and was told that Joe would be rebuked and would not receive any of the proceeds of the robbery. He had alleged that he had been wrongfully deprived of his share.

That evening Tony took $2500 to Ralph, one of the adjudicators neutral to him. He suggested that Ralph keep $1000 and give the other three adjudicators $500 each.

Comments: Tony claims that he initiated the payment decision; his other two partners were willing to pay their share once he suggested it. Ralph did disburse the monies as requested, and Tony was treated with markedly more friendliness after this incident.

Incident Number 5.[26] Michael Hellerman (Jewish) was a successful, young stock manipulator. He maintained a long-term relationship with Johnny (Dio) Dioguardi, a major mafioso in the Lucchese family, whose main source of income seems to have been labor racketeering.

Hellerman had been involved in an unsuccessful swindle that had lost money for two minor mafiosi, Fusco and Burke, members of the Colombo family. He now began a new one and offered to let them share in the proceeds so as to compensate them for the former failure. The swindle required that Hellerman control all the sales of a certain stock. The other party, Stein, who had initiated the deal, now tried to cheat Hellerman through some undisclosed sales. Hellerman found out about this and confronted one of Stein's associates at a meeting in Miami.

Stein arranged for Fusco and Burke to be informed that he was being backed by a mafioso of the Bonnano family, Evola. Stein, in the course of negotiations about arranging an adjudication, insulted Fusco. Fusco obtained permission from his own boss, Aloi, and Stein's mentor, to give Stein a beating for failure to show respect.

A meeting was arranged involving all the principals and their mentors. The other participants had not believed that Hellerman would be able to obtain Dioguardi's explicit help and had arranged that Hellerman would end up as the loser, being required to compensate everyone else. When Dio actually turned up at the meeting, Hellerman moved from being the least protected to the most protected, for Dio was the most senior of the mafiosi present.

Dio ordered Stein to work out an acceptable arrangement with Hellerman; this yielded a total of $78,000 to be divided by the numerous parties. The division was extremely complicated. Hellerman ended up as the prime individual beneficiary, with $15,000. Dio, who had risked no money and invested minimal time, also received $7,500, however. Aloi and his associates, who had invested a great deal more time, received about $1500 each.

Comments: The story is narrated by Hellerman, who later became an important witness against some of the participants. In particular, he was the major reason for Dio receiving a long prison sentence. It is possible that his narrative overemphasizes the involvement and power of Dio.

Incident Number 6.[27] Joe Valachi is perhaps the most prominent Mafia

[26]This incident is taken from Hellerman and Renner (1977).
[27]This incident is taken from Maas (1969).

informant. His account of the Mafia has provided the basic framework for the official version since 1963.

Valachi was a member of the Genovese family. His immediate superior within the family was Tony Bender. At the time of this incident, 1946, he owned a restaurant in partnership with another mafioso, Luciano. Luciano belonged to the Mangano family.

Valachi suspected that Luciano was stealing from the restaurant, which was making about $2500 per week, in order to finance substantial gambling losses. One night he discovered Luciano removing money from the cash register. Luciano did not deny that he was taking the money to pay off his gambling debts, and Valachi lost his temper. He systematically beat up Luciano, even though he knew that there was a strong prohibition against beating other members without formal permission.

Luciano initially made some threats, then apparently backed down. He did, however, complain to his superior within the Mangano family. A meeting was arranged at which were present Valachi, Bender, Luciano, and Anastasia. Anastasia, a member of the Mangano family representing Luciano only because Luciano's immediate superior was ill, was the most senior.

The result of the meeting was dictated by Anastasia. He ruled that Valachi had acted improperly but that Luciano was clearly at fault. Luciano was forced to compensate Valachi for the money taken and the two were to dissolve the partnership. Neither was to use force against the other. Both abided by the agreement.

IMPLICATIONS OF THE EXAMPLES

More examples of dispute settlements could be presented, drawing on both published materials and informant interviews. It is clear even from the few presented here, however, that there is a great range of variation in both the procedural and substantive aspects of settlement. The available examples do not permit anything approaching a full delineation of the variations. I shall use the six presented here to suggest some general characteristics.

First, each participant has a single representative for dispute settlement, and the relationship between them antedates the occurrence of the dispute. I have found no instance in which a participant, faced with a dispute, has gone into the market to hire a representative for just that purpose.[28] It is also interesting to note that representation is not spe-

[28]More precisely, I have no instance in which a participant attempted to do this. Perhaps it is possible but not attempted because of time constraints; the Mafia member would need time to verify the status of his client.

cialized to a subset of disputes. At one stage I conjectured that representatives might have market specialities, so that a group of participants might retain an arbitrator to deal with disputes arising in the course of a particular line of business.[29] It appears, though, that reputation is not product–market specific. Representation seems to be exclusive in that a single individual is represented by only one arbitrator.

Second, there is no set of substantive rules that govern settlements, even within one family. The results of settlements are not widely disseminated, so that uniformity would be surprising. Indeed, even the occurrence of an arbitration is likely to be known only to small networks. One, not unexpected, exception is a rule prohibiting the use of violence between members of the Mafia. Such violence, without prior sanction from more senior members, needs clear justification. Preservation of the group *qua* group requires this, given the difficulty of closure following use of violence. Apart from this, it would appear that cases are settled in ways that reflect the relative power of the representatives and the "merits" of the parties' positions.[30] The assertion about the merits of the cases is highly subjective and conjectural; the reader may make his or her own judgment of the six examples.

Third, arbitrators and participants regard the decisions as self-enforcing. The expectation is generally correct. When one party does not fulfill the conditions of the judgment, there is no simple procedure for ensuring that enforcement efforts are made. The third incident provides an example of this problem.

Fourth, adjudication is not a specialized function. All the persons who were involved as adjudicators also had involvement in a range of criminal activities. Older members probably obtain a higher percentage of their income as a result of payments by lower-level members and associates, but the bulk of representatives are active participants in illegal markets.

Fifth, each family recognizes the legitimacy and hierarchy of the other families. In the last example, Anastasia outranks Bender and is allowed to dictate the terms of settlement, though he comes from a different

[29]I have only one possible example. A group of numbers bankers during the early 1960s may have had an agreement to use their own resources both to adjudicate any internal disputes and to enforce the adjudication decisions.

[30]It is important to note here that the disputes tend to be about rather simple contractual arrangements. The facts may be difficult to determine, but the obligations of the two parties under each asserted state are relatively clear. This is perhaps surprising in view of the fact that the contractual arrangements are oral and hence take account of a limited set of contingencies. The explanation is probably to be found in the irreducible risks of being in illegal commerce, which restrict the range of contractual alternatives considered.

family. In that case he decided in favor of the member of the other family. In the case of Dio (fifth incident), again it was recognized by the other family that he had the right to dictate the terms of settlement, in this instance in favor of his client. Disputes that involve different families are not treated as matters of family concern; that is, the dispute is not automatically raised to a higher level.

This last observation suggests the possibility that the five families, if not the entire set of families in the nation, operate as a single entity with respect to this provision of arbitration services. Hierarchy within a family is recognized in other families precisely as it is recognized across divisions of government or corporations. This makes a prima facie case for the Mafia acting as monopolist–extortionist in the market for arbitration services. It is to this contention that I now turn.

The Mafia, Arbitration, and Extortion

Arbitration services appear to be available to many participants in illegal markets. Persons such as Ruby, Bob, and Hellerman are able to obtain continuing access to these services, though they are not members of the Mafia; indeed, they come from a different ethnic group. Whether all participants can acquire access is an open question. On the basis of very incomplete information, I am inclined to believe that any participant who can establish a substantial business relationship[31] with someone else who is a mafioso or a "subscriber" himself will be able to gain access.

In order to analyze the effectiveness of the Mafia monopoly over arbitration services, there are two questions to be considered. First, take a market in which the Mafia is known to be active, either directly or through a number of subscribers. What are the consequences of not being a member or subscriber for a participant in such a market? The extent to which a nonsubscriber is constrained provides a measure of the rents available to the Mafia from an arbitration monopoly.

Second, can a subscriber shop for the best price–seniority[32] combination, or do the families coordinate their offers? To the extent that different family members are able to price their services independently, the

[31] A series of repeated business transactions involving something other than purchase of final goods or services.

[32] As one might expect, the seniority of a representative within a family determines the effectiveness with which he can represent his clients' interests. That is, the more senior the representative, the more likely it is that his client will prevail in a case where the merits are unclear.

Mafia fails to extract the available rents. If there is no coordination then, given the number of members in the New York area (perhaps 2000), there may be a moderately competitive market for arbitration services.

NONSUBSCRIBERS

The bookmaking market again provides interesting examples. There is considerable evidence that Mafia members have an involvement as bettors and financiers (both for equity and loan capital). Various persons who are closely associated with the Mafia own and manage operations in the market. No one who is an active participant in the market can fail to be aware that the Mafia has an intimate involvement and that many participants can appeal to a Mafia member for protection in the case of a dispute.

Despite this, there appear to be bookmakers[33] who choose not to establish ties with any Mafia member. They neither enter into a partnership arrangement nor make payments that, by implication, are designed to ensure that the member will accept some responsibility for the continued physical and financial security of the bookmaker when involved in a dispute with another participant.

One predictable consequence of a bookmaker not becoming a subscriber is that he will act cautiously in extending credit to persons whom he believes may make use of Mafia ties to default on accrued betting losses.[34] Informant comments verify this directly. One informant, Bob, the source of two of the dispute-resolution examples, provided such information about a bookmaker named Sol. Sol has carefully avoided any long-term ties with the Mafia. He is constantly attempting to screen his customers to ensure that he has none who might defraud him. This effort has not been entirely successful. On a number of occasions he has in fact failed to collect from some large bettors who turned out to be, in the common argot, "wise guys." He has accepted his inability to intimidate or persuade them and has written off the losses as bad debts. The informants clearly believe that he could become a subscriber if he so desired, but an extreme concern with the secrecy of his actions has led him not to subscribe.

Bob, in his descriptions of various participants in the bookmaking and loansharking business, cited numerous examples of participants

[33]In this case the term covers bookmakers, runners (commission agents), and professional bettors.

[34]The nonsubscriber bookmaker will not attempt to coerce a Mafia member or subscriber.

who had problems in getting paid and were unable to do anything about it, whereas others have made very direct use of Mafia connections to resolve a credit problem.

There are even some examples that suggest that a subscriber can obtain adequate protection against the predatory efforts of a member. Steve was a Jewish bookmaker who had a relative by marriage, Sy (also Jewish), once a major figure in the rackets. Sy, though semiretired, still retained his contacts with many Mafia members. At one stage Steve was approached by two Mafia members, Angelo and Johnny, with an offer of partnership. Steve was interested, because they both had good customer lists.[35] Before entering into the partnership agreement, however, he asked Sy to find out if his partners could be trusted. Sy determined through his Mafia friends that the purpose of his partners was to cheat Steve and then, when Steve found out about the cheating, to intimidate him with their Mafia credentials. Steve informed Angelo and Johnny of his relationship to Sy, previously unknown to them. Angelo agreed to continue the partnership but did not cheat Steve. Johnny, who had initiated the predatory notion, decided that the relationship to Sy would make it impossible to cheat Steve successfully and that he was no longer interested. He withdrew from the venture.

It is possible then to participate in a market where the Mafia is an important influence without becoming a subscriber to the Mafia for dispute-resolution services. The cost of doing so is an increased exposure to the risk of one-time swindles by participants who do have Mafia protection. There is no evidence to suggest that an unprotected bookmaker will be subject to long-term extortion by a Mafia member. Indeed, the frequency of incidents involving nonsubscribers writing off debts because of the inability to collect makes it clear that some bookmakers prefer to adopt that strategy rather than become subscribers.

IS THE MAFIA A CARTEL?

There is evidence of poor coordination among the families with respect to the sale of "subscriptions." For example, Bob discussed a bookmaker named Arnie who was associated with a Mafia gang headed by Sal. Arnie felt that he was getting poor service from the gang; in fact, he suspected they were extorting him. To solve this problem he went to another Mafia gang (presumably from a different family, but the account

---

[35]That is, there were a number of bettors, making frequent large wagers and promtly honoring their obligations, who would place bets with a bookmaker designated by Angelo or Johnny.

is unclear) and borrowed $75,000 at the prime rate, about 1% per week. He did not need the money but wanted to create a relationship with this new Mafia group. It is unclear whether he used this relationship to help him in his bookmaking activities, but it did apparently prevent Sal's gang from further extortion.

The more general evidence comes from tales that indicate the unawareness of other market participants about the connections of their colleagues. Hellerman surprises his partners when he brings Dio into the scene. Steve, in the bookmaking partnership incident described earlier surprises his partners when he tells them of his relationship to Sy. Without exchange of information there cannot be coordination. Some relationships are well known. Others only surface when there is some reason for the relationship to be known. Some subscribers appear to make deliberate efforts to tie themselves to a number of families, relying on the natural discretion of participants for segmentation of the knowledge.

SCOPE OF MAFIA JURISDICTION

As has been suggested earlier, the Mafia does not provide arbitration services in all illegal markets. There are at least two classes of markets in which disputes appear to be settled by other means, even if violence is not used.

In certain product markets, Mafia members are almost completely absent, either as participants or as providers of arbitration services. Marijuana importation and distribution is the most notable example.[36] The explanation for their noninvolvement in the activity itself is not obvious. The low penalties levied on participants, even at the higher levels of trafficking,[37] the great diversity of the customer population,[38] and the ease of concealment of the sales transactions and their infrequency no doubt all play a role.

There is, nonetheless, some reason to expect that participants require a dispute-settlement system. Many higher-level transactions involve use of credit. There is even said to be sale on consignment. Although the major participants do not have records of criminal violence or any apparent involvement in the financial frauds that are the common avocation of

[36]Although I believe this statement applies to large cities generally, I can assert it confidently only for New York.

[37]Impressionistically, reports about large marijuana seizures suggest that they occur primarily at the importation point. Those arrested rarely include the American importer.

[38]Survey data, probably an underestimate, show 16 million current users in 1977 (Petersen, 1980: 6).

participants in other narcotics and gambling markets, it would be naive to assume that they are men of singular virtue. Yet, as a matter of observation there appear to be few, if any, disputes that lead to the use of violence[39] and nothing to suggest that the Mafia serves a dispute-settlement role.

One possible explanation, though it must be regarded as extremely speculative, is that there is an element of genuine collegiality in this business that makes reputation a critical asset. It appears that there are close working relationships between numerous participants at the same level of the business.[40] A participant who chose to cheat someone else in an egregious fashion might find it difficult to continue in the business with the same set of partners, and finding a new set may be a costly undertaking. This, of course, only covers the case where one participant sets out deliberately to defraud another. Genuine disputes, where the dispute is the result of a misunderstanding or unforeseen event, pose a different problem. The simple answer may be that in a business where the dominant participants make no routine use of violence, such disputes lead to a coolness between the disputants that may or may not be resolved over time but that permits them to continue working with their mutual acquaintances—just as in legitimate markets.

The other limitation of the Mafia's jurisdiction, as suggested by the six examples, is ethnic. I have no examples of Mafia resolution of disputes involving balcks or Hispanics, though members of these groups appear to be major providers of gambling, narcotics, and loansharking services to their own communities. This limitation is puzzling, for both black and Hispanic organizations had close relationships, in these markets, with Mafia members, at least until 1970.

Various *ad hoc* explanations suggest themselves. Interethnic attitudes may very well play a role. Whereas Jewish and Irish gangs have offered the Mafia critical and distinct resources (managerial sophistication, money, and political connections), the newer urban ethnic groups were essentially clients for a long time. There may have been an unwillingness on the part of the Mafia to offer them the semblance of equality that "subscription" represents. And, at the risk of making broad generalizations about ethnic behavior, there may also have been a greater willingness in the black and Hispanic gangs to make use of violence, seen as a very critical symbol of individual worth. The relative indifference of

[39]In southern Florida such violence is common, but because many of the involved marijuana importers are also involved in the cocaine traffic, the source of the violence is unclear.

[40]Partnerships to finance or distribute a single shipment seem to be reasonably common.

police, for many years, to violence in these communities also suggests that participants may have worried less about the consequences of violent acts.

Concluding Comments

The quality of the available information limits our capacity to draw definite conclusions about the Mafia as a provider of dispute-settlement services. I am uncomfortably conscious of the number of times I have had to qualify an assertion with "appears to be."

Nonetheless, the evidence supports a claim that the Mafia has a monopoly on dispute-settlement services in the New York City region. Only persons who are Mafia members may sell such services, though some nonmafiosi undoubtedly obtain monies from acting as brokers for nonmembers seeking the services of a Mafia member.

There is little else about the dispute mechanism that lends itself to easy characterization. I am unable to detect consistency in procedure or substance. My assertion earlier that the merits of the case are determinative in those instances where they are clear needs to be refined by testing against a large body of detailed case descriptions, which I do not presently have. I am particularly concerned also with the lack of cases indicating consistent enforcement when judgments are flouted. I have some in which there is no enforcement; these are surely inconsistent with the continued use of Mafia dispute-settlement services by nonmembers.

The Mafia's failure to coordinate the efforts of its members to ensure that they extract the available monopoly rents is a matter of interest in its own right. The explanation is surely to be found in the problems of sharing information in an illegal organization. Coordination for the purpose of systematic extortion by a large group requires the sharing of information, which enables each member to put numerous others at risk. The Mafia has strong sanctions against detected informants. How effectively these work is unclear, for there seem to be numerous instances of members providing at least limited amounts of information to the police over long periods of time without penalty. In any event, there are enough instances of a member providing information in a trial that it is understandable if members are cautious about providing information about their activities to other members with whom they are not closely allied.

The homogeneity of the Mafia ought to provide a screening mechanism for protection of the integrity of the group. Mafia members still are recruited from first- or second-generation migrants from southern Italy and Sicily, growing up in homogeneous communities in which the forces of authority are regarded as hostile. Some members develop ties to the broader community,[41] but most do not. Ianni (1972) presents evidence of the upward mobility of Mafia children, which possibly serves to weaken the paternal allegiance to the criminal group. The most recent of the prominent Mafia informants (DeMaris, 1980) suggests that there has occurred an "Americanization" process within the Mafia, leading to an erosion of old ethnic loyalty.[42]

There is another factor impeding the flow of information necessary to coordinate the activities of individual Mafia members in their dispute-settlement role. Property rights are not well defined within the organization. Valachi, for example, reports a constant concern that his superiors would appropriate enterprises that he had created. The taxation function of the hierarchy was easily transformed into expropriation. This threat of expropriation leads to concealment within gangs.

How does one account for the failure to develop property rules that would permit the organization as a whole to tax client criminals more effectively? It is not as though participants believe that the organization will not endure and thus seek to appropriate rents that will exist only in the short-run; members, even those now hostile to the organization, exhibit strong faith in its continued existence.

I think that the answer may be found in the absence of internal market forces within the Mafia. I argued that individual members refrained from extortive behavior in illegal markets because it would greatly reduce the set of other participants willing to transact with them. This restraint does not apply within the Mafia itself. Senior members who aggressively seek opportunities to take clients from less senior members incur a reputational loss within the family, but those serving under them cannot transfer to some other group. Junior members may provide less support to their seniors in response to such aggressive behavior, but there is a limit to the damage they can inflict in this way, consistent with retaining family membership.

Finally, let me emphasize again that the empirical material all comes from New York, which, as was mentioned earlier, is unique in that it has

----

[41]It is tempting to suggest that these are the ones most likely to become informants. John Roselli, apparently murdered because of his possible testimony concerning the role of the Mafia in the assassination of President Kennedy, provides one example. Frank Costello, rumored to be a longtime FBI informant, is another. Both moved easily among professionals outside of the extended Mafia community.

[42]It should be noted though that this is a long-standing complaint of aging members of the Mafia, the same claim can be found in the conversations of De Carlo during the early 1960s (Zeiger, 1975).

numerous autonomous Mafia families. In other cities the single family may be able to coordinate its activities as a supplier of arbitration services, and hence exert some effective control over client markets. For those other cities, we lack even the weak evidence available for New York. But my own expectation is that, except where there is a very strong family leader, the problems of coordinating activities in an atmosphere of suspicion and impeded information flows leads to a substantial degree of effective competition.

Within a narrow sphere the Mafia has acquired one of the attributes of government, namely, monopolization of third-party dispute arbitration. This monopoly seems to be based on the group's reputation for superior coercive powers within the set of illegal markets. Its weakness relative to the government of the legitimate society in which it is imbedded, however, leads to a rather crude and ineffective system of dispute settlement. It may be able to reduce to some degree the level of violence and instability that would characterize participation in mass illegal markets, but it provides little in the way of effective and predictable justice.

Appendix: Data Sources

There exists no substantial body of published information about dispute settlement in illegal markets. A few incidents are recounted in various gangster autobiographies,[43] usually of dubious credibility, and in the reminiscences of former law enforcement officers.[44] There is also some interesting information in two sets of wiretap transcripts that were published in the mid-1960s when the FBI's legal powers for electronic surveillance were broader than they have been since 1969.[45]

The preceding discussion draws somewhat on these accounts, though it draws more heavily on interviews with informants and police in the course of research on illegal markets in the New York area (Reuter, 1983). The informants were involved in a variety of activities; most information was obtained on bookmaking, numbers, and loansharking,

---

[43]The most convincing of these autobiographies are Maas (1969), Teresa (1973), and Hellerman and Renner (1977).

[44]The best such accounts of incidents in the criminal world are provided in Daley (1978) and Villano (1977).

[45]The surveillances were placed in the homes of Sam De Cavalcante and Angelo De Carlo, both prominent New Jersey Mafia figures. In each case partial transcripts were released to the public as the result of challenges by the defense prior to a trial. The De Cavalcante tapes are adequately summarized in Zeiger (1973). There is a very fine account of the De Carlo tapes in Zeiger (1975).

with smaller amounts concerning fencing and marijuana and heroin distribution. Some police wiretap transcripts were also obtained.

All of these sources have potentially serious biases. Published memoirs reflect law enforcement views about what is important. Former law enforcement officers report what they have been led, at least partly by institutional ideology, to believe is important. They emphasize the Mafia. Publishers are interested in publishing the "memoirs" of Mafia members and associates because there is an established public interest in the group.

Even the interview materials are not free of this taint. The informant is eager to produce materials that he thinks are likely to interest the person paying him. Whether he believes in the unique importance of the Mafia, he is sure that the researcher or police officer does. I hope that I have managed to persuade informants that my views are more agnostic than that, but I cannot be sure of my success.

References

Aronson, Harvey
    1978 *Deal*. New York: Ballantine.
Becker, Gary, and George Stigler
    1974 "Law enforcement, malfeasance and compensation of enforcers." *Journal of Legal Studies* 3: 1–27.
Bohannan, Paul (editor)
    1967 *Law and Warfare*. Garden City, N.Y.: Natural History Press.
Daley, Robert
    1978 *Prince of the City*. Boston: Houghton Mifflin.
De Maris, Ovid
    1981 *The Last Mafioso*. New York: Times Books.
Graham, Fred
    1977 *The Alias Program*. Boston: Little, Brown.
Hawkins, Gordon
    1969 "God and the Mafia." *The Public Interest* 4: 24–51.
Helleman, Michael, and Thomas Renner
    1977 *Wall Street Swindler*. Garden City, N.Y.: Doubleday.
Hoebel, E. Adamson
    1967 "Law-ways of the Commanche Indians." Pages 255–262 in *Law and Warfare*, edited by Paul Bohannan. Garden City, N.Y.: Natural History Press.
Lanni, A. J. F.
    1972 *A Family Business*, New York: Russell Sage Foundation.
Kroeber, Alfred
    1925 *Handbook of the Indians of California*. Washington, D.C.: U.S. Government Printing Office.
Landes, William, and Richard Posner
    1975 "The private enforcement of law." *Journal of Legal Studies* 4: 1–45.
    1979 "Adjudication as a private good." *Journal of Legal Studies* 8: 235–284.

Maas, Peter
    1968   *The Valachi Papers*. New York: Bantam Books.
Macaulay, Stewart
    1963   "Non-contractual relations in business." *American Sociological Review* 28.
Nader, Laura, and Harry F. Todd (editors)
    1978   *The Disputing Process—Law in Ten Societies*. New York: Columbia University
            Press.
Nozick, Robert
    1974   *Anarchy, State and Utopia*. New York: Basic Books.
Petersen, Robert
    1980   "Marijuana and health." Pages 1–53 in *Marijuana Research Findings: 1980*, edited
            by Robert Petersen. Rockville, Md.: National Institute of Drug Abuse.
Posner, Richard
    1977   *Economic Analysis of Law*. Boston: Little, Brown.
    1981   *The Economics of Justice*. Cambridge, Mass.: Harvard University Press.
Redfield, Robert
    1967   "Primitive law." Pages 3–24 in *Law and Welfare*, edited by Paul Bohannan.
            Garden City, N.Y.: Natural History Press.
Reuter, Peter
    1983   *Disorganized Crime: The Economics of the Visible Hand*. Cambridge, Mass.: MIT
            Press.
Teresa, Vincent (with Thomas Renner)
    1973   *My Life in the Mafia*. Greenwich, Conn.: Fawcett.
Villano, Anthony
    1977   *Brick Agent*. New York: Ballantine Books.
Zeiger, Henry
    1973   *Sam the Plumber*. Bergenfield, N.J.: New American Library.
    1975   *The Jersey Mob*. Bergenfield, N.J.: New American Library.

3

Social Control under Totalitarianism*

JAN T. GROSS

The thoughts on totalitarian systems of social control presented in this essay were stimulated by archival research in the Hoover Institution with a unique collection of documents: autobiographical statements by people who experienced the imposition of Soviet rule in southeastern Poland from September 1939 to June 1941.[1] One finds in these depositions the image of a Communist revolution, as it were, in a variety of

*Parts of this chapter appeared in an article entitled "A note on the nature of Soviet totalitarianism," in *Soviet Studies* 34 (July 1982): 367–376.

[1]In September 1939 the Soviet Union, bound by a treaty with Hitler's Germany, occupied over 50% of the territory of the Polish state. During the 21-month long rule in the area—from the Red Army's aggression against Poland on September 17, 1939, to the outbreak of the Russo-German war on June 22, 1941—the Soviet authorities had deported about 1.25 million Polish citizens (roughly 9% of the local population) into the Soviet Union. The social and ethnic composition of the deportees reflected the entire spectrum of social classes and nationalities making up prewar Polish society. After Hitler's attack on the Soviet Union, Polish-Soviet diplomatic relations were reestablished, and a pact was signed between the two countries. One of the stipulations of the Polish-Soviet agreement called for the release ("amnesty") of all Polish citizens detained in the Soviet Union and for the establishment of a Polish army in the territory of the Soviet Union. In 1942, about 120,000 people—soldiers of the newly created Polish army and their families—were evacuated to Iran. They had all gone through the experience of Soviet occupation of their homeland before they were deported into the Soviet Union. In Iran they were asked to give depositions about their lives under the Soviet regime, and about 20,000 of these

59

social settings that usually leave no trace in history, except as a round number in official statistics. People who are often written about but rarely heard from have left in these documents detailed accounts of their lives: There are statements from peasants telling about the organization of Soviet rule in their villages and hamlets, about the confiscation of large landholdings and their distribution to the village poor, about taxation that was imposed on everybody, and about collectivization. Craftsmen of all sorts and small merchants tell how they fared under the new regime. Civil servants, policemen, foresters, school teachers, and other petty officials tell what happened to their jobs after the revolution. Workers describe new working conditions in the workers' state. Many of these respondents are barely literate and have no stimulating insights to offer, but they know names and biographies of their neighbors, they know who did what and sometimes can also tell why, and they remember trivial details, gossip, and scraps of conversations. Through these biographies we can observe the application of the Soviet power to what it can do best—namely, carry out a social revolution. There is, however, a common theme in these otherwise different accounts. And what one sees as a recurrent pattern in the way political power was exercised under the Soviet regime is rather paradoxical and runs against the standard interpretation of totalitarianism. The Polish case thus suggests a new model of social control under totalitarianism in general.

The Polish Case

A familiar photograph appears in *Pravda* every so often, showing a Red Army soldier engaged in a conversation with a group of people. The soldier, somewhat bigger than everybody else in the group but not overwhelming, and rather friendly, is holding a few papers in hand,

---

protocols were preserved in the Polish Government Collection (PGC), the Anders Collection (AC), and the Poland Ambassada USSR Collection in the Hoover Institution (HI) at Stanford University, as well as in the archives of the Sikorski Institute and the Underground Poland Study Trust in London.

The Hoover Archives sources are used as primary reference material in this essay. There is, however, another corpus of data of comparable quality about the Soviet regime—the Smolensk Archives (Fainsod, 1963). I have not worked with original documents of the Smolensk Archives, and I shall use them primarily as cross-references in the form in which they have been presented by Merle Fainsod in *Smolensk under Soviet Rule*. The Smolensk documents cover the period from 1917 to 1938, that is, several phases of the Soviet regime following the stage of revolutionary takeover. As such, they complement the Hoover Archives sources and offer, jointly, a sound basis for generalizations.

maybe a copy of a newspaper, while his interlocutors, dressed in traditional peasant costumes or simple garments of working people, listen intently. The iconography of the Soviet propaganda is well established. But for the facial features of the crowd one could not tell that a photograph taken in 1979 in Afghanistan was separated by a 40-year interval from an almost identical one taken in 1939 in Poland. Apparently wherever it goes, whether to Afghanistan or to the western Ukraine, the Red Army's orders are the same: Its soldiers meet to speak with the local population. And this is what they say: "For twenty years you lived under the masters' yoke, who drank your blood, and now we have liberated you and we give you freedom to do with them as you please [Hoover Institution (HI), Poland Ambassada USSR Collection, Box 48]." A Soviet officer thus addressed the inhabitants of Świsłocz village in Wołkowysk county of the Białystok viovodeship. And according to another survivor:

> After the Red Army entered the village [Maszów in Luboml county of the Wołyń voivodeship], lieutenant Minkov, battery commander Velov and the commander of the 234th regiment of heavy artillery from Kiev ordered everybody together and pronounced a fiery speech that they brought freedom and equalization to all classes. They said that they authorize people to go and take away what rightfully belongs to them and to avenge pains of twenty years of exploitation— kill and take the property and those who filled their pockets and barns with your blood. [Poland regained its independence in 1918, after the First World War, and remained independent until 1939. This was frequently called the Twenty Years.] If you are not going to succeed on your own, the Red Army will assist you [HI, Anders Collection (AC), 7426].

In the Horodziej village of Nieśwież county of the Nowogród voivodeship, a "Commissar" Danilov climbed on a makeshift platform and addressed the population that was brought to the marketplace: "If someone has a grudge against somebody else, he can do with him what he wants: take his property or even life [HI, Polish Government Collection (PGC), 5137]." Michał Garus from Łososin hamlet in Kosów Poleski county of the Polesie voivodeship writes,

> As soon as the Red Army entered into the nearest village Różana Grodzieńska, immediately their so-called politruks started visiting neighboring hamlets and began their so-called agitation against the entire Polish State, against the government, they kept saying who was murdering you during the Polish times you can now go to him and do to him whatever you want [HI, PGC, 5531].

Even though the rapporteurs of these first encounters with the Red Army lived far away from one another, in several different voivodeships of southeastern Poland, one is struck by the similarity of their ex-

periences. Throughout the occupied territory the conquering army de-
creed a period of lawlessness: "What's the matter with you? Let them
play a little," answered a local Red Army commander to a forester who
complained about robberies and killings in Kalnica, in Wilno voivodeship (HI, AC, 7758). For several days a general dispensation was granted
to do as one pleased: "After the Red Army came the Soviet authorities
permitted the local communists to avenge themselves on the local Polish
population. I was informed about this by a local communist Dimitri
Gavriluk, a Ukrainian, from Korsynie village in Kowel county [HI, PGC,
2823]." People were told that they could "square accounts" with their
enemies (HI, PGC, 2413), and for a few days countless acts of violence
were committed throughout the occupied territory. They were, so to
speak, inflicted by the local inhabitants on themselves. Furthermore,
even though most violence was directed against Polish settlers brought
to the area in the interwar period or against wealthier landowners, also
mostly Polish, one would be mistaken in describing this phenomenon as
an incidence of class warfare. What motivated people was ethnic hatred
(to which, incidentally, the Soviet invaders made direct appeals) rather
than class antagonisms. But more specifically still, because these were
local events, carried out quickly, without prior organizational prepared-
ness or ideological mobilization, they were acted out predominantly
along the lines of personal enmities. Indeed, as the preceding quotes
indicate, it was personal hatred that the Soviet speakers evoked when
they first addressed the inhabitants of occupied villages and hamlets.
The victims and their tormentors knew one another personally; their
names are recorded in numerous depositions (HI, PGC, 2611, 3134,
3356, 4032, 8032, 9222).

Even though the spontaneous terror of the early days was curtailed
by the Soviet authorities after a short time (about three days, it appears),
with local militias or village committees taking over the enforcement of
"law and order" in the territory, the personal mode of dispensing coercion continued to be the main feature of the newly established regime.
Volunteers flocked into local committees and militias, and they were
very often the same people who responded enthusiastically to the initial
appeals of the Soviet officers and agitators to take justice into their own
hands. Thus, not surprisingly, to the local inhabitants the establishment
of Soviet rule in the area was characterized by, one is tempted to say, a
certain *privatization* of the instruments of social control:" The so-called
temporary authorities [in September and October 1939, village and town
committees bore the word *temporary* in their official names] began their
functioning from squaring personal accounts," wrote a student living at
the time in Kosów Huculski in Stanisławów voivodeship (HI, PGC,

7648). Soon after the setting up of temporary committees, "arrests and searches began, often motivated by personal enmities," recalled a painter from Kiwerce in Wołyń (HI, PGC, 6673). Similary, in Łuck a high school teacher reports that arrests very often resulted from local militiamen's actions motivated by personal hatred (HI, PGC, 9905). Indeed, a number of people from different localities (e.g., HI, PGC, 2376, 2999, 7654, 8892) confirm a pattern of behavior whereby law enforcement agents and other representatives of the state settle private disputes while carrying out their official duties; more precisely, *settling private disputes appeared to be their principal mode of carrying out official duties and establishing their own authority.* And this feature was not necessarily characteristic of the transition period, from Polish to Soviet rule in the area. Here is a glimpse into the interior of the Soviet state: Over a decade after the October Revolution, as collectivization was being carried out in the Smolensk Oblast of the Soviet Union, a secret police report dated February 23, 1930, noted:

> Middle and even poor peasants were being arrested by "anybody"—by raion [the smallest unit of territorial administration] emissaries, village Soviet members, kolkhoz [collective farm] chairmen, and anyone in any way connected with collectivization. People were being transported to militia prisons without the slightest grounds or evidence. . . . Some poor peasants and "activists" were blackmailing the richer peasants, taking bribes for removing them from the confiscation or deportation lists [Fainsod, 1963: 246].[2]

There is some evidence that the new administrative personnel in Soviet-occupied Poland were occasionally censored by Soviet superiors or local Red Army commanders, but these were exceptions to the rule and are reported as unusual circumstances.

In principle, then, the new apparatus was motivated by particularistic interests—avenging personal wrongs or satisfying greed for material objects and hunger:

> The poor ones were invited to join the so-called rural militia and were being promised big financial rewards, and that they might take for themselves without pay-

[2]The Smolensk Oblast was no exception in this respect. In May 1933, Stalin and Molotov sent a letter to all Party and Soviet workers and to all organs of the secret police (OGPU):

> The Central Committee and the Sovnarkom are informed that disorderly mass arrests in the countryside are still a part of the practice of our officials. . . . Arrests are made by all who desire to, and who, strictly speaking, have no right to make arrests. It is not surprising that in such a saturnalia of arrests, organs which do have a right to arrest, including the organs of the OGPU and especially the militia, lose all feeling of moderation and often perpetrate arrests without any basis, acting according to the rule: "First arrest, and then investigate" [Fainsod, 1963: 185].

ment, meat, crops, and other things from the neighboring estates and from
wealthier peasants [HI, PGC, 6689].

The militia and the local comittee didn't do much; they were mostly drinking hooch
and eating robbed geese, turkeys, pigs, and lambs. I remember how they robbed a
pedigreed ram from Mrs. Szyrynowa, and they couldn't agree what to do with it
because three of them wanted it. In the end, they killed it and six of them ate it in
one night [HI, PGC, 3660].

And there were numerous such depositions from all over the occupied
area (e.g., HI, PGC, 2131, 6105, 9926) illustrating how local militias and
temporary committee personnel were appropriating material objects for
their personal use while carrying out apartment or house searches, al-
legedly for hidden weapons, or while preparing inventories of confiscated real estate or commercial property. The spread of this practice and
its duration—beyond the few initial days of anarchy—preclude one from
interpreting this phenomenon as errant behavior or abuse of and departure from officially issued instructions. The Soviet local administration
was encouraged to act in pursuit of its personal interests while discharg-
ing functions of representatives of the Soviet authority. Thus, for instance, the Smolensk OGPU (Secret Police) reported on February 28,
1930, on the progress of collectivization in the Oblast:

In many villages "certain members of the workers' brigades and officials of lower
echelons of the Party-Soviet apparatus" deprived members of kulak [rich peasant]
and middle peasant households of their clothing and warm underwear (directly
from the body), "confiscated" head-wear from children's heads, and removed
shoes from people's feet. The perpetrators divided the "confiscated" goods among
themselves; the food they found was eaten on the spot; the alcohol they uncovered
was consumed immediately, resulting in drunken orgies. In one case a worker tore
a warm blouse off a woman's back, put it on himself with the words, "You wore it
long enough, now I will wear it." The slogan of many of the dekulakization [i.e.,
expropriation of larger peasant landholdings] brigades was: "Drink eat—it's all
ours." One commune in search of more and richer "confiscations" commenced to
dekulakize kulaks of the bordering village soviet. As the kulaks in question were
administratively under the "jurisdiction" of another kolkhoz, a struggle ensued
between the communards and the kolkhozniks. The communards under the direction of their party secretary absconded with much of the money and property of the
kulaks before the kolkhoz could act. In the process, even eyeglasses were torn from
the peasants' faces; kasha [buckwheat] was "confiscated" straight from the oven
and either eaten or used to smear the ikons [holy pictures] [Fainsod, 1963: 245–246].

That privatization of the state was an official policy finds a striking
confirmation in yet another kind of evidence. We discover the following
when we scrutinize the personnel records of local authorities sponsored
by the Soviet Union in occupied Poland: "These are the names I remember: three Furman brothers and their sister nominated to the Red Militia

and to the village council, also the Samosenko couple [HI, PGC, 3356]" (Dederkały, Krzemieniec county in Wołyń); in Żurawica (Łuck county in Wołyń), Jakub and Dymitr Maksimczuk were running the village committee (HI, PGC, 3107); in Świsłocz (Wołkowysk county of the Białystok voivodeship), the gmina (the smallest unit of territorial administration) committee was headed by Piotr Kordosz assisted by his daughter Luba and his brother Aleksander (HI, PGC, 8791); in Chołojów (Radziechów county of Tarnopol voivodeship) a Ukrainian named Szulba and his two sons "took the power" (HI, PGC, 5285): in Wolica Derewlańska (Kamionka Strumiłowa county of the Tarnopol voivodeship) Jan and Bazyli Baka, Jan and Teodor Szczur, and Stefan and Łać Bohonos were on the village committee (HI, PGC, 2827); in Bratkowce (Stanisławów voivodeship), among the "activists" of the local committee were Iwan Żyrdak and his brother Jarosław and Teodor Chiczyj and Irena Kaczor, Teodor's daughter (HI, PGC, 4032); in Więckowice (Sambor county of the Lwów voivodeship), Michał, Grzegorz and Jan Hołowa were in the village militia (HI, PGC, 2837); while in Złotkowice (Mościska county of the Lwów voivodeship), Mikołaj and Józef Sydorowicz were running the local committee (HI, PGC, 10273); in Kirżana village (Wilejka county of the Wilno voivodeship), the Hryszkiewicz family, Jan, Onufry. Tymoteusz and Eustachy, were in charge (HI, PGC, 704); while in another village of the Wilno voivodeship, in Szaniowce in Dzisna county, Jan and Józef Izojtko presided over the village committee (HI, PGC, 10264).

The preceding is merely a sample list with villages drawn, for purposes of illustration, from several different voivodeships, but it shows conclusively that throughout the occupied territory the newly introduced Soviet authority was vested in a network of families that held executive power—power of life and death—over communities in their jurisdiction. The state had been, as it were, franchised to these individuals, for, strictly speaking, they were the state: They were allowed to carry weapons and to use them with impunity, or, in a Weberian phrase, they were given the monopoly of legitimate use of coercion in this territory. From time to time they were ordered to deliver a quota of foodstuffs, to parcel a landowner's property, or to mobilize local inhabitants during election day. But how they executed these tasks was left to their own discretion. They could use for their own benefit whatever had not been claimed by the hierarchically superior organs of the state. They could redistribute the burdens in the community so as to punish personal enemies and benefit friends.

In the Smolensk Archives sources we find corroborating evidence concerning the organization of the kolkhozes. In the 1930s, the frontier of sovietization, so to speak, was here, and, given the occupational structure in the Soviet Union, the majority of its population lived on collective farms whose management represented the Soviet authority. As Fainsod reports:

> This management had its perquisites, illegal and quasi-legal, and many kolkhoz chairmen sought to protect them from exposure by installing their own clique in strategic positions in the kolkhoz, by absorbing the chairman of the village soviet, the store manager, and other leading village personalities into a common network of shared privileges, and by bribing the relevant raion officials where possible to keep quiet. Sometimes the ruling clique was literally a close-knit family group, [as in] a kolkhoz near the village of Vasinichi where the wife was chairman of the kolkhoz, the husband the accountant, and the father the business manager. . . . Nor was this case an isolated exception. . . . In Dorogobuzh raion [in] a kolkhoz (named after Voroshilov) the son of the chairman was the accountant, the wife the milkmaid, the mother the receiver of milk, and the father the guard of the kolkhoz [1963: 270–271; see also p. 239].

The pattern of recruitment (entire families drafted into state service) and the guiding principle of conduct ("squaring personal accounts") conform to the characterization of the Soviet rule suggested earlier. This strategy of social control might be labeled the *privatization of the state*. One can thus see how nepotism is not merely a distortion of socialist development that might come about decades *after* the takeover, and *after institutionalization of a Communist ruling class and its privileges. In fact, as this evidence from occupied Poland reveals, privatization of the state is introduced during the revolution itself as a principal instrument to destroy the previously existing authority structure and to implement coercion.*

The Privatization of the State

It is fundamentally important to realize that the privatization of the state under totalitarianism extends further, beyond the group of state employees exercising social control over the rest of society. Indeed, it extends, in a way, to all citizens. I would argue that although the standard interpretation of totalitarianism is correct—an interpretation viewing it as a system of rule obliterating the distinction between the private and public domains, where the state pervades, or mediates, all relationships between individuals[3]—we have misunderstood the mechanism

[3]See, for example, Juan Linz's discussion of literature on totalitarianism in his "Totalitarian and authoritarian regimes" (1975: 175–411). He thus concludes his brief review of current definitions of totalitarianism: "Explicitly or implicitly those definitions suggest a

that brings it about. It is not surprising that we did so, for the prima facie evidence supported the standard interpretation. What we saw was the process of *Gleichschaltung*, destruction of all voluntary associations and institutionalized forms of group life that preceded or were independent of the new state. Then it was seen that new organizations, all state controlled, were sponsored and that everybody had little choice but to join them. All spheres of life came to be regulated by the state, and so *it appeared that the private domain was sequestered by the state*. What must be corrected is the second part of this diagnosis. Although indeed obliteration of the distinction between private and public domains takes place under totalitarianism, it occurs not exclusively as a result of the sequestering of the private domain by the state (though such is its institutional or formal appearance) but, primarily, because of the privatization of the public domain. I have already introduced some evidence supporting this point, and, in addition, it is possible to show that the rank-and-file members of society have a relationship to the state similar to that of the state's functionaires; that is, they can and do use the state freely for the settlement of private disputes. This is because *everybody has immediate access to the apparatus of the state and uses it frequently against other members of society*. Privatization of the public domain is the dominant feature of totalitarianism, and only by reference to it can one explain a variety of phenomena that would otherwise appear as oddities in a presumably monolithic, all-encompassing, all-powerful, and omnipresent totalitarian state.

Consider the following personal accounts:

Soviet authorities conducted searches and arrests . . . directly in response to denunciations by neighbors who had personal accounts to square [HI, PGC, 1167].

Accusations, denunciations, and personal animosities could lead to arrest at any moment. People were officially encouraged to bring accusations and denunciations [HI, PGC, 2229].

Whoever had a grudge against somebody else, an old feud, who had another as a grain of salt in his eye—he had a stage to show his skills, there was a cocked ear, willing to listen. Posters encouraged people to bring denunciations [HI, PGC, 3062].

The local population was frequently motivated by personal matters in denouncing its brothers in the NKVD [Secret Police] [HI, PGC, 3362].

There is no person in the world who can please everybody, and so one person's enmity caused another person's arrest [HI, Poland Ambassada USSR, Box 46].

---

tendency toward the destruction of the line between state and society and the emergence of 'total' politicization of society by political organizations, generally the party and its affiliates [p. 188]."

A friend of mine by the name of Bolesław Szlamp had a personal enemy from his school days who accused him of preparing to escape across the frontier. Soviet authorities had no other proofs and sentenced and deported him for ten years to the USSR for forced labor [HI, PGC, 5966].

Once again, the preceding is merely a sample of observations and recollections from a variety of voivodeships—from Białystok, Lwów, Nowogród, and Stanisławów. And what they evoke is familiar to students of Soviet totalitarianism: People, motivated by personal enmities, were denouncing one another to the secret police.[4] What is more, under Nazi rule the *modus operandi* of the police was identical. Reinhard Mann, who studied Gestapo files from Düsseldorf, found that:

In the majority of cases, denouncements were generated by private conflicts, . . . they were to operate to "solve" these conflicts, i.e., the complainant tried to eliminate his enemy indirectly by means of the Gestapo. Quarrels between spouses, differences between landlords and tenants, conflicts within a neighborhood, rivalries in professional spheres, failed love affairs—all produced denouncements [1979: 233].

The commonly accepted insight into the essence of totalitarianism reveals how an individual loses his or her separate identity, how he or she becomes subsumed under, and blended with, the state. The separation between private and public spheres gets abolished under totalitarianism, in the sense that it becomes a state prerogative to decide about the most intimate matters affecting a human individual. Collective interest supersedes individual rights: One cannot refuse the state anything on

[4]During the 1935 Party purge, 455 people were expelled from the Smolensk City and Raion Organization. "In achieving this grand total the Smolensk Party authorities had enjoyed the benefit of no less than 712 oral denunciations" (mainly in speeches at Party meetings) and "200 written declarations with compromising materials on members of the CPSU(b) [Fainsod, 1963: 230]." And a year later, when the sequence of great purges began, "a holocaust of denunciations swept through Party ranks [Fainsod, 1963, 233]." The victims of the 1935 purge were classified, in a report of the Smolensk Party Organization, into 16 different categories. Thus 7 "Agents of the Enemy" were purged (cat. 1), 12 "White Guardists" (cat. 2), 32 people "corrupt in a moral and ethical sense" (cat. 14), and 9 "who left other parties, changing only on surface" (cat. 4). But by far the most numerous category of victims was defined in even vaguer terms, and it is hard to imagine how anyone could defend himself or herself against an accusation, no matter how arbitrary and unfounded, that he or she did "not inspire political trust and betrayed the interests of the party" (cat. 8, 127 victims) (Fainsod, 1963: 230: see also p. 191). There are volumes of diaries and memoirs from the Stalinist period and equally voluminous folklore—camp songs—illustrating how personal motivations brought people to denounce one another. But we have overlooked somehow the theoretical implications of this strategy of social control.

the ground of protection of individual rights. The fate of each individual is placed "in the hands" of the collectivity. The state—the party—may dispose of anyone according to what it deems to be in the group's best interest. The individual becomes a tool for the construction of a collective destiny.

The principal mechanism that accounts for the penetration of the state into the private domain is the practice of denunciation. An act of effective denunciation (i.e., followed by state reprisals against the denounced) can be seen, paradoxically, both as a service rendered *to* the state (providing it with sought-after information) and as a service rendered *by* the state (providing an individual citizen with a prompt settlement of a private dispute in his or her favor). Since private enmity has been the primary motivation for bringing denunciations to the authorities, we are best able to understand totalitarianism's all-pervasiveness and awesome power *not* as a consequence of its being well informed and efficient. On the contrary, the evidence suggests that it is both dismally ill-informed and mismanaged. *The real power of a totalitarian state results instead from its being at the disposal, available for hire at a moment's notice, to every inhabitant.* The absence of the so-called rule of law in a totalitarian regime finds its concrete expression also in that every citizen has direct access, unmediated by lengthy and complicated procedures, to the coercive apparatus of the state. *Everybody can use the political police against everybody else*— quickly, without delays or undue formalities. The ubiquity of terror as well as terror's random quality, instilling all Soviet citizens during the Stalinist period with the constant fear of arrest, has its roots in the privatization of the state that I have described: "A young writer, who in 1938 was five years old, said to me recently, 'May I ask you something? How was it that you survived?' What could I say? . . . I shall never know [Ehrenburg, 1966: 429]"—this is the famous writer Ilya Ehrenburg reminiscing, certainly not an enemy of the Soviet regime.[5] Of course,

---

[5]Once again, the Smolensk Archives provide an insight into Soviet reality that may be illuminating. In 1931, during deportations from the Oblast, an atmosphere of panic and resignation spread in the area. Nobody knew when or where he or she would be taken away. An OGPU "report cited a 'characteristic' case where one citizen came to the raion procuracy and begged to be deported together with the kulaks, reasoning that he would at least have a chance to start a 'less hectic life' [Fainsod, 1963: 248–250]." In occupied Poland, many people were accused under the famous Article 58 (Aleksandr Solzhenitsyn said that one's whole life could be subsumed under this article), which stipulated, in one of its paragraphs, that aiding and collaborating with a bourgeois state is harmful to the interests of the Soviet Union and, therefore, a crime. Thus, for instance, a defense attorney from Lwów was accused of having supported interests of a bourgeois state on account of his having been a lawyer in Poland and a reserve officer in the Polish army. "This formula of accusation is absurd," he commented in his deposition, "and it contradicts fundamental

the vulnerability of Soviet citizens did not originate in the fact that everybody was engaged in anti-Soviet activity and that the state knew all about it. The overwhelming majority of Soviet citizens practiced obedience to the party line, but that did not inspire them with a sense of security—not because they were all afflicted with paranoia. *They had reasons to be afraid because the decision about their freedom or incarceration was left to the discretion of anyone at all from among their fellow citizens.* One could get arrested because a neighbor took a liking to one's apartment or one's wife or husband, because of envy on the job, or the desire to get even for some injury that one had caused to somebody else long ago.

There was little a Soviet citizen could do to protect his or her innocence once the state was let loose on him or her but to use what Merle Fainsod (1963) has called the "right of petition." One could write letters to higher authorities, not infrequently to Stalin himself, laying out one's sorrows and grievances in the hope that the abuse one suffered at the hands of local authorities (local "masters,"[6] one should say) would be brought to an end by an intervention from high above. And it sometimes was. The all-powerful distant ruler—the Obkom (Oblast Committee of the Communist Party) secretary, for example, as shown in the documentation from the Smolensk Archive—would occasionally take the case of a little man and destroy speedily a local clique that made the little man's life miserable. The point is, however, that even though activated to uphold some general sense of right, or justice, of the grieving individual, the mechanism at work was no different from the case of

---

principles of penal and international law which preclude one state to bring accusations against citizens of another state for having fulfilled their citizenship duties [HI, PGC, 4094]." In an identical case, a more inquisitive accused got a clarification from his Soviet prosecutor: "To my question—why do you put me on trial for having fulfilled my obligations as a Polish citizen—he replied that the entire world belongs to them and that everybody will be tried [HI, AC, 4411]."

[6]Here are two episodes for purposes of illustration: In a letter to the second secretary of the Smolensk Obkom, a group of kolkhozniks complained about unbearable conditions that they have had to suffer. The chairman of the kolkhoz was to blame, and nothing could be done about it—"If a kolkhoznik tells Pyalov [the chairman's name] the truth, he answers: 'I am the master, I do what I want' [Fainsod, 1963: 272]." The second episode took place in the town of Augustów in Białystok voivodeship of occupied Poland. The witness who reported it was standing in line inside a cooperative store that had just received a shipment of socks. Suddenly, a local Soviet official walked into the store through the back door, looked over a few pairs of socks, and then decided to purchase the whole supply. The salesman, pointing out to the waiting crowd, hesitantly objected: "And what about the people, comrade nachalnik?" To which the nachalnik, with arrogance superior even to that of Louis XIV, the Sun King, when he uttered his famous "l'état c'est moi," replied, "I am the people" and walked away with all the socks in stock (HI, PGC, 6466).

a denunciation. Whether through denunciation or through a petition, an individual was pulling in the state in a highly personalistic fashion, as it were, directly to settle his or her problems. "Now, Ivan Petrovich," wrote a desperate petitioner to the Smolensk Obkom secretary, "there is only one hope—you [Fainsod, 1963: 399]," or as in another personal plea to Rumyantsev, the Obkom secretary, "I trust you implicitly, and whatever your opinion will be on this problem, it will be law for me [Fainsod, 1963: 229]." Thus, the mechanism that reestablished momentarily a sense of justice in the experience of Soviet citizens was also predicated on the principle of privatization of the public domain. Even though in each concrete case the successful application of the "right of petition" restored belief in the existence of principles of justice binding on all, in a more general sense the mechanism merely served to perpetuate and reinforce the strategy of social control that I have identified as the underlying structural feature of totalitarianism.

A peculiar variation of the "right of petition" had been used in western Ukraine and Belorussia shortly after the Soviet invasion. It characterized the "revolutionary," that is, early, period of Soviet rule. Local people in good standing with the regime—outspoken sympathizers, collaborators, or those who were as poor, or poorer, than anybody else around—could certify that an arrested, or about to be arrested, person did no harm to anybody in the past and was no exploiter. Very often such a voucher was as good as a "not guilty" sentence of a court of law, though the procedure was used exclusively in an agricultural setting, in villages and relatively small communities, and was not without risks for the sponsors themselves (HI, PGC, 8461). But the point is that effective release, or exemption from arrest, by petition of some loosely defined group of local citizens who felt entitled to file was, once again, institutionalized arbitrariness. It was, simply, "reverse denunciation." The same people's word was just as good to send anyone to jail as it was to pluck someone out of it. And, in all honesty, it did the former much more frequently.

Good and evil were meted out in the Soviet system in the same fashion, without slow procedures of institutional mediation but in response to individuals' pulling in the state when they felt like it, driven, as the case may have been, by greed, maliciousness, jealousy, or despair. That "justice" was occasionally dispensed in this way only reinforced the very mechanism that exposed Soviet people to the whims of their co-citizens, for it offered occasional proof that the system "works," and, as we know from social psychology, an intermittent reinforcement schedule perpetuates behavioral patterns more than any other (Tarpy, 1975: 151–154).

Strange as it may seem, in Stalinist Russia the decision about *who* would actually go to jail was left largely to the discretion of ordinary Soviet citizens. And because anybody could cause anybody else's arrest, the Soviet terror acquired its awesomely random quality that rendered it so effective—there were as many "reasons" for being sent to jail as there were different motivations inspiring individual denunciations. The famous *uranvilovka*—equalization—of Soviet citizens was real despite the built-in stratification of the Soviet society in which access to goods depended on one's position in the bureaucratic hierarchy. It was real because everybody shared the power to bring down and destroy anybody. This ability to get anybody arrested was the great equalizer. It was an unusual power, however, a power to destroy but not to protect. Nobody was able to provide for the security of one's own person, whereas anybody was able to ruin anybody else's life. Hence, also, arose the well-known process of social atomization under totalitarianism. In the end, *what brings social atomization is less the outlawing of voluntary associations than the mutual fear and distrust induced into people's minds by a system of social control in their society that operates so that they can only cause harm to one another and are at the same time defenseless against such attempts by others.*

A Note on Totalitarian Language

Even a most rudimentary discussion of social control under totalitarianism must include some observations on its rules of language usage. Language is a primary tool of social intercourse, and one can imagine neither extensive coordination nor continuity in social action without its benefits. The imposition of strict rules on discourse is an integral part of totalitarian social control.

One must realize from the outset that totalitarian rules of language usage are fundamentally different from, for instance, restrictions placed on public utterances by government censorship in nontotalitarian despotisms or, in any country, in times of national emergency. Totalitarian rules do not aim simply at *preventing* some information (considered adverse to the state's interests) from being disseminated. Instead, totalitarianism puts a radical imprint on the entire structure of the language, modifying its syntax and semantics. Consequently, the effects it obtains are very profound. Wrote Ernst Cassirer in 1945: "If nowadays I happen to read a German book published in the last ten years . . . I find to my amazement that I no longer understand the German language. I find many terms which I have never heard before and the old and familiar terms have won a different and strange connotation. The ordinary words are charged with feelings and violent emotions [1979: 254]." The author of a dictionary of *Nazi-Deutsch* published in New York in 1944 commented: "The ambiguity of this para-logical language serves not only to deceive the enemy but also as an instrument of social control. . . . The language that is spoken in totalitarian countries . . . is more than a vehicle of communication. It is a vehicle of command which helps shape the pattern of a social structure [Paechter, 1944: 5]." The most parsimonious list of features of totalitarian language would include the following characteristics:

1. Totalitarian language has a rigorous, strictly prescribed canonic form. Its ideal and most perfect embodiment is a slogan (Paechter, 1944: 6; *Język propagandy*, 1979: 7,8). A sequence of slogans constitutes a perfect text.
2. Totalitarian language is highly rhetorical. It is saturated with figures of speech; it is, literally, a figured-out language.
3. Totalitarian language abolishes the distinction between prescription and description, between what is and what ought to be. It is, in the words of Roland Barthes, "a language expressing value judgments . . . in which definition, that is to say separation between Good and Evil, becomes the sole content of all language, [in which] there are no more words without values attached to them, so that finally the function of writing is to cut out one stage of the process: there is no more lapse of time between naming and judging [1967: 24]."

The ritualization of speech, the imposition of strictly prescribed canonic forms on the usage of key words and phrases especially in matters relating to public life, endows a totalitarian regime with an extremely effective mechanism of social control. It furnishes the regime with a sensitive monitoring device by which to detect all departures from binding orthodoxy. The regime does not even have to monitor the content of writings and speeches—the mere reordering of word sequence, a change in adjectives routinely following a given noun, identifies a potential free thinker (*Język propagandy*, 1979: 61, 62). Simultaneously, the regime does not have to explain or justify in any way the changes in its own policies; instead, it simply invokes a formula of condemnation and applies it to a policy or a person. The whole variety of the world is reduced in this ritualized language to only one piece of information: whether a given item (an individual, a social movement, a state, an idea, a policy, or whatever) is approved or rejected. One may recall, for visual illustration, a row of grim faces on the reviewing stand during a national holiday in Stalin's Moscow or Mao's Peking—it was precisely the order of appearance that mattered there and how it compared with the order the last time these people appeared together in public. All it revealed was the degree of approval by the Great Helmsman—why some were discarded and others promoted; what they argued about no one knew, was supposed to know, or should be interested in finding out.

Saturation of totalitarian language with rhetoric introduces into it what some linguists have called "loose semantics" (*Język propagandy*, 1979: 3). How does one defend against an accusation of being a "running dog of imperialism," for example? When do production difficulties turn into "wrecking"? Khrushchev is an "Elder Brother" one day in China and "a rotten egg, . . . the biggest bad egg on earth" the next (Pasqualini, 1973: 295). All of this is quite confusing to ordinary people, for they often do not know why anything should be one way or the other and could never have figured it out for themselves without being told. The figurative language provides a handy tool for segregating all human experience into that which is approved and ennobled and that which is rejected and damned. Everything a person does is somehow related to the supreme goal of the community: It either promotes or hinders its realization. There is no space for prosaic pursuits and detached simple discourse. Metaphor reigns supreme, and even the most natural, commonplace activities acquire new meanings: In Nazi Germany, for example, women no longer bear children, instead "they fight the battle of births (*Geburtenschlacht*) [Paechter, 1944: 14]." "In ordinary speech our words have a double function: a descriptive and an emotional function. They express human feelings, or they describe objects or relations of objects. . . . In the language introduced by the political myths . . . the whole emphasis is laid on the emotional side; the descriptive and logical word is transformed into magic word [Cassirer, 1979: 253–254]." As a result, language fails in its primary function, which is to be "a prerequisite of our representation of empirical objects, of our concept of what we call the 'external world' [Cassirer, 1979: 148]." This failure, I believe, constitutes the perfect fulfillment of a totalitarian strategy of social control. It is in the "destruction" of language (*Język propagandy*, 1979: 27–28: Paechter, 1944: 13) that, literally, the destruction of the public domain takes place, because language *is* the public domain and taking it away from a community constitutes a supreme act of privatization.

Totalitarian language fails miserably as an instrument of persuasion. Cynicism and mistrust of any public message are widespread in communities subjected to totalitarian rule; nor is it a good instrument for processing information. But, at the same time, it is most effective as an instrument of social control. This seeming paradox is resolved when we realize that totalitarianism is not a polis but its opposite. That which permits totalitarianism is, precisely, what renders social interaction and human community impossible. Thus, totalitarian language functions as an instrument of social control by depriving human beings of the opportunity to check their ideas against empirical evidence derived from experience. Consequently, those in charge of totalitarian language can say whatever pleases them and cannot be proven wrong—as in the famous watchword of Italian fascism *Mussolini ha sempre raggione* (Mussolini is always right)—whereas those subjected to it may spare no effort collecting evidence and may stand ready to play by the rules but still cannot chart a course of behavior that will assure them well-being and security.

When in the middle of forced collectivization and widespread famine and at the peak of the purges Stalin utters his famous "Life has become better, life has become happier," it is a statement totally divorced from evidence provided by the surrounding reality of collective life. No one else could have made such a claim but he who had a copyright on Soviet reality. After all, basically the same "evidence" lent itself just as likely to an opposite generalization, also proclaimed by Stalin, that class struggle intensifies as socialism is being built. Simply put: Even though the prevailing norm, more or less accepted by everybody, was to follow the "party line," no one could tell for sure how it would be drawn from one day to another. Even the most respected leaders of the revolution and subtle Marxist theoreticians one after another failed to fathom this "party line" and perished. People could no longer pass judgment about the outside world if they were deprived of their language: It was appropriated by a ruling elite that adopted a peculiar manner of speech, one from which the criterion of truth or the context of objective reality was eliminated.[7] Each of its statements was a definition and an act of creation; it produced "the thing" and the truth about it. In the ideal blueprint of a

[7]Lest I be suspected of being carried away by my own writing and literary imagination, here is what one suspects ought to represent the pedestrian, down-to-earth, unimaginative, practical assessment of the Soviet mentality—a diplomat's report from Moscow, written in 1944.

But there is a second, and even more daring, *tour de force* which the American mind must make if it is to try to find Russian life comprehensible. It will have to understand that for Russia, at any rate, there are no objective criteria of right and wrong. There are not even any objective criteria of reality and unreality.

What do we mean by this? We mean that right and wrong, reality and unreality, are determined in Russia not by any God, not by any innate nature of things, but simply by men themselves. Here men determine what is true and what is false.

The reader should not smile. This is a serious fact. It is the gateway to the comprehension of much that is mysterious in Russia. Bolshevism has proved some strange and disturbing things about human nature. It has proved that what is important for people is not what is there but what they conceive to be there.

The diplomat was George F. Kennan (1967: 562–563), and the report apparently made no great impression on Washington.

totalitarian society where people can neither pass judgment nor draw conclusions about the world around them, they cannot act as independent subjects. They can only obey orders.

Speaking of totalitarian language, one should mention yet another form of invasion into the public domain: its drastic curtailment that occurs when totalitarianism disenfranchises a historical nation of its past, of its historical tradition. A ban imposed on whole patches of collective memory is no less than an appropriation, by a ruling elite, of a shared common property. This too is a kind of privatization.

Conclusions

In summary, it may be fruitful to identify privatization of the public domain as the most important structural feature of social control under totalitarianism. It offers a single perspective by which to analyze a variety of phenomena that have been separately discussed in the past. Thus, the ubiquity and randomness of totalitarian terror may be understood as direct consequences of each citizen's being able to use directly, without institutional mediation of law courts or bureaucratic regulations, the state repressive organization in his or her private disputes. Equality and social atomization under totalitarianism are direct derivations of the same process. Furthermore, the pervasive corruption under totalitarianism (a subject I have not discussed here)—the "second economy"—appears to be neither a curious aberration of the system nor a feature independent of the system's essential mode of functioning. It appears simply as another manifestation of the privatization of the public domain—corruption may be defined as the use of public office for private gain (Scott, 1972: 3–4)—as characteristic of the totalitarian organization of a society as is terror or the destruction of language. To conclude: This strategy of social control deprives the individual of the means to associate or compromise with other individuals. As a result, he or she is left alone in an atomized society, to be a master or a slave, all-powerful and helpless at the same time.

References

Barthes, Roland
    1967   *Writing Degree Zero. Elements of Semiology.* Boston: Beacon Press.
Cassirer, Ernst
    1979   *Symbol, Myth, and Culture: Essays and Lectures of Ernst Cassirer 1935–1945.* New
           Haven, Conn.: Yale University Press.

Ehrenburg, Ilya
  1966 *Memoirs, 1921–1941*. New York: Grosset & Dunlap.
Fainsod, Merle
  1963 *Smolensk under Soviet Rule*. New York: Random House.
Język propagandy
  1979 *Zeszyty Towarzystwa Kursów Naukowych*, edited by Stefan Amsterdamski *et al.*
  Warsaw: Niezależna Oficyna Wydawnicza.
Kennan, George F.
  1967 *Memoirs*. Bantam Books.
Linz, Juan J.
  1975 "Totalitarian and authoritarian regimes." Pp. 175–412 in *Handbook of Political
  Science*, edited by Nelson Polsby and Fred Greenstein. Reading, Mass.: Addi-
  son-Wesley.
Mann, Reinhard
  1979 "Everyday life in National Socialist Germany: Popular protest and regime sup-
  port." Paper presented at the Third Annual Meeting of the Social Science
  History Association, Columbus, Ohio, 1978. Reprinted in *Zur Soziologie des
  Widerstands in nationalsozialistischen Deutschland*. Köln: Universität zu Köln.
Paechter, Heinz
  1944 *Nazi-Deutsch. A Glossary of Contemporary German Usage*. New York: Frederick
  Ungar.
Pasqualini, Jean (Bao, Ruo-Wang)
  1973 *Prisoner of Mao*. New York: Coward, McCann & Geoghegan.
Scott, James C.
  1972 *Comparative Political Corruption*. Englewood Cliffs, N.J.: Prentice-Hall.
Tarpy, Roger M.
  1975 *Basic Principles of Learning*. Glenview, Ill.: Scott, Foresman.

4

Social Control in Suburbia*

M. P. BAUMGARTNER

In recent decades, a substantial body of work in social science has addressed the question of how social control varies with the settings in which it occurs. Aside from numerous studies of law in modern society, much research has been devoted to informal social control in tribal and other traditional communities (for representative collections, see Bohannan, 1967; Aubert, 1969; Black and Mileski, 1973; Nader and Todd, 1978). Largely ignored, however, has been informal social control in modern settings (but see Suttles, 1968; Felstiner, 1974; Merry, 1979; Thomas-Buckle and Buckle, 1982). Because it is clear that most conflict is handled without recourse to law, this omission means that little is actually known about normative life under the distinctive conditions prevailing in modern societies.

Against this background, this chapter presents findings from an ethnographic study of social control in a suburb of New York City. It focuses on how middle-class adults exercise social control against their friends, neighbors, and acquaintances in everyday life. (For these purposes, it excludes from consideration matters within families and between strangers and business associates. These are discussed in Baumgartner, 1984; forthcoming.) The central theme of the analysis is that

*This chapter is a revised version of a paper presented at the Annual Meeting of the American Sociological Association, New York City, August 1980.

middle-class people in the suburb studied favor the use of nonconfrontational strategies of conflict management in dealing with their personal
associates, and that this pattern is related to the social organization of
their relationships. In particular, it is argued that the atomization, transiency, and fragmentation of social ties that characterize middle-class life
encourage unusually restrained responses to grievances, including tolerance, avoidance, conciliatory approaches, and secret complaints to
official agents of social control.

The Setting

The findings reported here derive from an investigation of day-to-day
social control in a town that, for these purposes, will be given the
pseudonym of Hampton. Hampton is a suburb of New York City and as
such is part of one of the largest and most developed metropolitan areas
in the United States today. It is an outlying suburb, located some distance from Manhattan. At the same time, it is also a suburb of another,
smaller city to which it is geographically closer. Hampton covers 4
square miles and is inhabited by approximately 18,000 people.

The community is not a new one but rather is a mature and settled
place. At first an isolated small town, then a summer retreat for a handful of wealthy New Yorkers who built lavish country homes there,
Hampton was transformed into a suburb by successive waves of immigration from nearby cities during the present century. The town grew
especially quickly in the 1920s and in the post–World War II period.

About two-thirds of the men in the labor force—and virtually every
adult male younger than 65 is employed—hold middle-class jobs, over-
whelmingly upper middle class in nature. They work, for instance, as
physicians, lawyers, engineers, architects, college professors, bankers,
stockbrokers, and corporate executives. (Some of the last group are
high-ranking officers in major American corporations.) Ethnically, most
of the men and their wives are of northern European extraction—Anglo-
Saxon, German, Scottish, French, Scandinavian, and Irish backgrounds
are all common. Most are Protestant, a sizable minority are Catholic,
whereas only a few are Jewish. As a group, this segment of the population is highly educated and affluent.

The remaining third of the town's men are employed for the most
part in working-class jobs. They serve as skilled laborers and craftsmen,
operatives, and service workers of various kinds. A few people, largely
from working-class families, have opened small shops. (Only a small
proportion of the men are engaged in traditional lower-middle-class,
white-collar jobs. The town is thus essentially polarized into two social

categories: the majority upper middle class and the minority working class.) Members of the working class are mostly Italian-Americans, part of an ethnic community founded by immigrants who were employed as groundskeepers and maids on the estates of the wealthy a century ago. There is also a small black community, accounting for about 3% of the total population, with a status and history similar to that of the Italian-Americans.

Apart from status differences, there is another way in which the classes stand apart in this suburb: in the morphology of their social relationships. Although far from constituting a traditional peasant community, working-class residents have considerably more stable and dense interpersonal networks than do their middle-class counterparts. They move less often and are more frequently surrounded by relatives, friends, and associates assembled into enduring social circles. Middle-class residents, on the other hand, are highly mobile geographically, and their pasts and futures in the town are much shorter than those of their fellow citizens. They tend to be isolated and atomized, separated from members of their larger families and only loosely integrated into neighborhood and friendship groups (which they supplement, in some cases, by participation in clubs and associations). In general, theirs is a world of "weak ties," in which people have scattered "contacts" rather than intimate relationships with those beyond their immediate families (on weak ties, see Granovetter, 1973). It is this aspect of middle-class life that appears to be expressed most prominently in the patterns of social control discussed in this chapter.

Method

Information about conflict management in the suburban town of Hampton was gathered over a period of 12 months during 1978 and 1979. Since that time, contacts with some of the citizens have been maintained, and several additional visits to the town have been made. In the course of this investigation, diverse data were collected through the complex of techniques known as "participant observation"—direct observation, informal interviewing, and the perusal of written materials available to the public at large. Such methods seem especially suitable for eliciting detailed and accurate information on the sensitive topic of interpersonal conflict (see Glaser, 1965; 436; see also Becker and Geer, 1957). Nearly two dozen formal interviews were also conducted with such social-control specialists as police officers, elected officials, the municipal judge and prosecutor, juvenile authorities, administrative officers, and members of the clergy.

Although it was possible to observe nearly all of the matters heard in the municipal court over many months, in general the cases uncovered in this study constitute only a small sample of the town's conflicts. As has been true of other field studies of conflict management, the investigation clearly yielded a disproportionate amount of information about dramatic disputes and sanctions, including, in this instance, a particularly large number of cases brought to law (see Koch, 1974: 23–24). Even so, in other respects the cases included in the sample should constitute a reasonably representative collection of conflicts and settlement strategies; they are drawn from all segments of the community and reflect input from a wide variety of sources.

During the course of the study, detailed information was obtained on 89 cases of conflict between unrelated acquaintances who were not involved in commercial or official dealings with one another. Of these, 27 were heard in the municipal court, representing the great majority of matters between such people handled by the judge in the course of a year. (Law cases involving relatives are discussed in Baumgartner, 1984.) The remaining 62 cases were either observed in the community or described by participants and third parties. In addition, 7 cases were collected involving at least one person who, although not formally acquainted with the other, was known to him or her by sight or through gossip. One of these cases was brought up in court. About 60% of the total cases, and somewhat more of those gathered outside the court, involved middle-class disputants, mostly in conflict with other middle-class people. Besides information about these incidents, fragmentary descriptions of dozens of other grievances and conflicts were also recorded and taken into account in the present report. They included, for instance, material on isolated sanctions whose larger context was unclear and on grievances not pursued by those who harbored them. Finally, pertinent generalizations about patterns of disputing and social control were made by many townspeople—officials and ordinary citizens alike—and were duly noted for purposes of the study. In the following pages, it is the cases, fragments, and generalizations pertaining to adult middle-class normative life that are of particular concern.

Social Control without Confrontation

Across a variety of settings and grievances, the middle-class residents of Hampton most often pursue indirect strategies of social control. Aggressive confrontations, formal legal actions, and exhaustive mediation sessions are relatively infrequent among them. An observer from a more urban setting is likely to be struck by the apparent tranquility and harmony of day-to-day life in the town, and residents are quick to note that, unlike New York City, theirs is a community in which people "get along" and "don't kill each other." Social control outside the household is rarely of a kind to attract much notice from anyone who is not directly involved.

It is nonetheless the case that grievances arise with regularity. This is so even though tensions seem to be minimized in the first place by the extensive freedom of association and the pervasive privacy that characterize suburban—and especially middle-class suburban—life, features that allow people to restrict many of their dealings to those with whom they feel compatible. (On the use of the regulation of space and attendant privacy to control conflict in the suburbs, see Perrin, 1977: chap. 3.) Barking dogs, rambunctious children, untended yards, perceived insults and encroachments, and a variety of other annoyances and offenses are endemic throughout the town. No one can escape experiences of this kind completely.

In reports, both detailed and fragmentary, about specific middle-class complaints and conflicts, and in general observations about conflict management made by the town's residents, a few responses to such grievances stand out as the most typical. They include tolerating conduct perceived as deviant and taking no counteraction, simply avoiding the offender, approaching the offender in a conciliatory fashion and seeking an accommodation, and, less often, making a secret complaint to an official. These actions, which singly or in combination are used to handle the great majority of middle-class grievances, have at least one characteristic in common: They entail little or no open confrontation, proceeding instead through stifling, truncating, or denying hostility. In this regard, they differ sharply not only from the violent retaliations seen in the feuds and wars of many groups—such as the Melanesians described by Pospisil (1958) and Koch (1974), the South American Indians described by Harner (1972) and Chagnon (1977), and the Africans described by Evans-Pritchard (1940) and Lewis (1961)—but also from the full airings of mutual dissatisfactions seen in the moots and negotiation sessions of the Kpelle of Liberia (Gibbs, 1963), the Tiv of Nigeria (Bohannan, 1957), the Arusha of Tanzania (Gulliver, 1963), the Tibetan nomads (Ekvall, 1964), and numerous others.

TOLERATING DEVIANT BEHAVIOR

When an offense occurs in Hampton, doing nothing more than grumbling privately to family members or close friends is the most common strategy of conflict management. During the course of the present investigation, dozens of idle complaints unaccompanied by any positive action were heard or mentioned by informants. Other investigators have labeled this type of response "lumping it" (Felstiner, 1974: 81; Galanter, 1974: 124–125) or "endurance" (Merry, 1979: 903), though in Hampton many absorbed grievances seem to be quickly forgotten rather than suffered by being lumped or endured. In any event, most middle-class people, most of the time, bear with inconveniences and, as a result, avoid the risk of becoming embroiled in conflict. Rather than take strong measures, they will absorb much conduct that greatly annoys or offends them, as well as that which is less bothersome.

Thus, for example, a woman did nothing about her next-door neighbor's huge stacks of rotting and fungus-encrusted wood, even though she found them both unsightly and unhealthful. She remarked to relatives, however, that "Barney [the neighbor] has a mental illness about wood" and described in detail the diseases she felt she might contract because of him. In another neighborhood, most people also took no action at all against a man living a block away on a working-class street who periodically burned chicken feathers and droppings accumulated in his poultry shop, although the stench created—like that of burning hair—was extremely offensive to them and persisted for hours at a time. One family simply absorbed the exhibitionistic antics of a middle-aged man who lived next to them, even on one occasion when he arrived at their door completely naked, rang the bell, and announced that he just wanted to return some mail of theirs mistakenly delivered to his address. Another family learned that their neighbors had been silently aggravated for years by spotlights they had installed—which shone into the neighbors' homes—only when this complaint came out in a zoning-variance hearing that they themselves had initiated in an unrelated matter. People also bore with such annoyances as persistent loud rock music, a trumpet student's dissonant practices, an unchained St. Bernard that ran loose and slobbered on those it encountered, a dogbite inflicted on a child by a friend's pet, and injuries to children caused by other children, among assorted problems.

Because so many ultimate differentials in social control are determined by the decision whether to take action of any kind against offenders, the considerable willingness of middle-class people in Hampton to put up with annoyances is an especially consequential feature of their normative life. The rarity of confrontation does not arise only because numerous deviants are allowed to escape sanctioning, however. Even when people do take action against offenders, they are likely to so do obliquely rather than directly. Avoidance is a favorite tactic of the middle-class residents in this suburban town.

AVOIDANCE

The transition from inaction to avoidance is nearly imperceptible in most cases, for the latter tactic generally begins with little or no fanfare. Middle-class people are rarely thrown together with friends or neighbors in the course of daily events; most time is spent either in the home or at the workplace. Even very amicable neighbors commonly pass days without encountering one another, and people who consider themselves good friends may likewise see one another only occasionally. A person or family who hardly knows the neighbors and has few friends does not attract much attention, and such isolation may not be noticed at all. If it is, and if it is commented on, others are likely to say simply that the party in question "minds his [or her] own business." Where interaction is so loosely structured, it is an easy matter to avoid dealing with an offender.

In Hampton, avoidance means that people are not greeted when encountered or greeted perfunctorily, not invited to visit or visited in turn, and not offered small favors or asked to do them. Effort is made not to run into them at all. Middle-class people consider it a mark of maturity and responsibility to rely heavily on avoidance as a way of dealing with bothersome people. It might be added that in the few cases in which individuals appeared in the municipal criminal court to press grievances against neighbors or other acquaintances, the judge usually recommended avoidance as the optimal way to manage the conflict, regardless of the social class of the parties involved (e.g., "If you people can't get along, just try to stay out of one another's way").

Because middle-class neighborhoods and friendship networks are so atomized, avoidance in Hampton is rarely exercised collectively in the form of a boycott. When a person or family is avoided by several other people, it is generally the product of individual actions or the actions of small groups of friends, and little or no resentment is voiced about those who continue to associate with the offender. (In many cases, in fact, people are not even aware of who has dealings with whom.) In one neighborhood, for instance, most people chose to have nothing to do with an older couple who frequently sat drinking on their front porch, lacing their loud conversations with profanity. In another, a family whose home was considered "filthy" was avoided by several neighbors. In a third, an eccentric old woman who accosted neighbors and chattered incessantly and aimlessly, and who also had such unusual habits as throwing dishes out the window and striking matches for no apparent reason, soon alienated most of her neighbors and was left alone by all of them.

Avoidance is sometimes triggered by a single offensive incident. In one case, for example, a young man and his parents were convinced that a friend of the former's had stolen a stereo tape deck from his car. The circumstantial evidence was considerable, and they were also aware that the friend had been in trouble with the authorities on several occasions for theft. Rather than call the police or seek to recover the tape deck forcibly, however, the victim—with the strong encouragement of his parents—simply began to avoid further contact with the suspected offender. In another case, a middle-aged woman infuriated a friend by remarking, in the context of a discussion about incest, that she thought the friend secretly desired such a relationship with her own son. The insulted woman responded with avoidance. And in still another case, a family began to avoid a neighbor who had criticized their daughter's boyfriend.

It is consistent with the way in which middle-class people react to conflict that avoidance outside the family does not usually elicit intervention by third parties. To the contrary, people generally feel that those who do not get along *should* avoid one another. They also feel that it is improper and unwise for outsiders to become embroiled in conflicts that do not directly concern them. In practice, this even means that it is not uncommon for one spouse to continue interacting amiably with a person whom the other spouse is avoiding. Several such cases came to light during this investigation and appeared to arouse no special interest in the townspeople who knew of them. Because middle-class people are often hesitant to press a conflict openly, whether to escalation or to resolution, avoidance is an acceptable outcome that freezes hostilities and allows the parties involved to direct their attention to other concerns.

CONCILIATORY APPROACHES

Although avoidance seems to be the favored mode of sanctioning among the middle class in this suburb, in some cases people opt to approach offenders in order to seek an accommodation from them. Such a reaction is more forceful than tolerating a grievance or relying exclusively on avoidance, but it is still remarkable in the extent to which it is managed without open conflict. Indeed, it is common for the request to be made in such a way that the aggrieved person not only adopts a posture of reason and moderation but also appears to be asking a favor of the offender.

This tactic is best described by example. In one case, a man built a small ornamental pond in his yard and stocked it with goldfish but was disturbed to note that the fish died shortly after he bought them. He replaced the fish, but the second batch proved no hardier than the first. The man soon decided that the fish were being injured by the many neighborhood children who came to the pond to look at them and, on occasion, to poke at them with sticks or to throw rocks at them. He put up a "no trespassing" sign and asked his own children to discourage the visitors, but the pond continued to be an attraction and the fish continued to die. After some time, the man opted for a new tactic. He instructed his children to ask the names of all those found at pondside, whether they appeared to be injuring the fish or not, and then called the parents concerned. In these conversations, he explained his problem at some length and noted that he was on the verge of giving up on the fish altogether. He remarked that he did not know exactly which children might be causing the damage and observed that in any case it was probably inadvertent rather than malicious. Finally, he asked the parents if they could possibly discourage their children from visiting the pond. The reactions of those he called were generally sympathetic, and the parents did instruct their youngsters to stay away from the man's yard.

The same strategy was employed by an aggrieved man who lived across the street from a family with several teenaged boys. These young people, along with their friends, tended to congregate in a parking area at the back of their house, where they talked, played music, and occasionally drank beer. The traffic in and out of the driveway to the parking area was heavy by neighborhood standards. Furthermore, many of the boys drove somewhat unrespectable vehicles—motorcycles, sports cars, "souped-up" trucks, and so on—and they also tended to drive fast and noisily, roaring in and out with their radios blaring and tires squealing. After doing nothing about the situation during the first summer in which the boys were his neighbors, the man enjoyed a respite in the winter. But the following spring the problem resumed. Finally, the man approached the boys' father one day when both men happened to be outside. He remarked that his daughter would soon be home from college and that he was concerned that she or a friend of hers might be hit by one of the vehicles speeding in or out of the driveway across the street. He asked the man if he would mention the problem to his sons and urge them to drive more slowly in the future. The encounter was amiable, and the boys' father did in fact bring up the matter with his sons. They, for their part, despite observing that the neighbor's daughter must attend a "retard school" if she did not "know enough to get out of the way of a car," responded favorably to his request and asked their friends to be more conservative in their driving as well. After this, the two families became, if anything, more friendly with each other, and the boys shoveled their neighbor's snow as a favor the next winter.

Although they may grumble privately about receiving such complaints, most people approached in this way are willing to accommodate the aggrieved parties. When they are not, the complainants usually fall back on tolerance or avoidance. When one of the many people subjected to the odor of burning chicken feathers described earlier finally remarked jovially to the offender that she "hated the smell of burning chicken-do," the man to whom she voiced her complaint responded, also lightheartedly, "too bad." The woman then dropped the matter and continued to be friendly toward the offender. (In a study of a suburb of Philadelphia and Trenton, it was observed that humor is a frequent vehicle through which complaints are aired; Gans, 1967: 177.) Because those approached are generally cooperative, and because when they are not, aggrieved middle-class persons tend not to press the issue, verbal altercations outside the family are uncommon.

SECRET COMPLAINTS

In a relatively small number of cases, middle-class people in Hampton take their grievances to an official third party for action of some kind. The police, court personnel, zoning officers, sanitarians, and elected officials are all prepared to receive and process complaints from townspeople about one another. What is especially noteworthy in this context is not only that this tactic is less common than the others already discussed but also that when it does occur, the complainants are very often at pains to remain unknown to the offenders. In many cases they refuse to divulge their identities to the officials whom they contact.

Middle-class people make anonymous complaints despite a guarantee of confidentiality by the agency involved, as is the custom at the Zoning Office and the Board of Health. The police also take calls made anonymously and will often protect the identities of complainants who are known to them. (To the police, conflicts in Hampton are "touchy matters" to be handled with the utmost discretion.) Unlike the zoning officers and sanitarians, however, the police may inform a citizen that they can take no action against an offender—beyond warning him or her—unless the aggrieved party steps forward publicly and signs a written complaint. This formality is necessary, by their account, for any misdemeanor—or minor crime—not witnessed by an officer. As a result of this policy, a large proportion of middle-class complainants abandon their efforts to invoke the law and fall back on such tactics as inaction or avoidance. They would rather suffer their problems than confront the offenders openly. (On the anonymous use of urban police in neighbor conflicts, see Black, 1980: 116.) Some of these citizens voice resentment toward the police. One man, for instance, was still expressing indignation a year later that the officers who responded to his complaint about neighborhood youths lighting firecrackers had asked him "to sign his life away" before they would take formal action.

Elected officials may also be notified about interpersonal conflicts outside the family. Like the sanitarians, zoning officers, and police, they normally keep information about who calls them—if they have it—to themselves. Some people refuse to reveal their identities to these officials, even when pressed to leave their names so they may be informed of what actions were taken on their behalf. Only the court, for purposes of its formal hearings, requires that complainants come forth publicly. It may be partly for this reason that the court is so underutilized as a tactic of social control (see Baumgartner, 1984).

Because the identities of complainants can be learned not only from the officials but also from clues provided by the circumstances surrounding a mobilization, factors other than guarantees of confidentiality appear to influence patterns of complaint. Thus, middle-class people are far more willing to contact an official about problems that affect an entire neighborhood indiscriminately—loud music, for example, or roaming dogs—than about annoyances especially linked to themselves. In cases of this kind, it is difficult for offenders to deduce who has complained against them. Such was true, for example, when a man called the police about the noise one of his neighbors was making with a power saw, when a woman complained to the police and the mayor about music emanating from a nearby church, and when a man complained to a town council member and the zoning officer about the unauthorized conversion of a private home in his neighborhood into several rental units. It was also true when someone made three separate complaints about a particular dog running loose on several occasions. In this instance, the dog's owner became increasingly frustrated because she could not pinpoint who the disgruntled neighbor was, something she wanted to know, she said, so that she might make peace with him or her.

Secret complaints, in which the offenders are left unaware of who has invoked officials against them, both stifle and obscure hostility between the parties involved. People visited unexpectedly by a police officer, a zoning officer, or a sanitarian may be extremely angry, but as long as they are unable to direct their anger at a specific target they are generally unable to take any counteractions. Few retaliations, threatened or executed, can be aimed at neighborhoods in general. (It might be noted, though, that in one case a working-class man unhappy with his neighbors for several reasons announced that he was going to move and, as revenge for his alleged mistreatment, sell his house to a black family—something he did not actually do.) In any event, an individual who complains secretly generally avoids a confrontation with the offender and escapes the consequences of his or her action, while the chagrin felt by the target of the complaint dissipates without further rancor or harm. The complainant is even able to continue amicable dealings with the offender as if nothing had happened, while the hostility that generated the complaint remains hidden beneath an outward appearance of good will.

INFREQUENT TACTICS

The distinctive character of day-to-day social control in Hampton is determined in large part by omission, or what is not done when people have grievances against their associates. Especially noteworthy by their absence are tactics of social control entailing aggressive confrontation between the parties involved. In comparison with the case in surrounding cities, assaults, serious threats, tire slashings, and analogous incidents are rare. Very few people carry and fewer use such dangerous weapons as guns, switchblade knives, and razors, and no homicide involving friends or neighbors has occurred in the town in memory. Violence and property destruction are especially uncommon among middle-class adults who, for all intents and purposes, never resort to them; the most aggressive action by such a person recorded during the study happened when a man, in a dispute with a neighboring youth, intentionally put his fingers on the latter's freshly waxed car. As noted earlier, even heated altercations are uncommon, and the few that do occur are the subject of much gossip by those who learn of them.

Equally infrequent are gatherings of concerned individuals devoted to the negotiation or mediation of disputes. Nothing more elaborate than the conciliatory approaches described earlier is seen with any regularity, and people rarely convene in any forum to have a complete airing of disagreements or to arrive at explicit reconciliations. There are no places—like the beerhalls of Bavaria (Todd, 1978), coffeehouses of the Near East (Rothenberger, 1968: 160), or the homes of prominent citizens in rural Ireland (Arensberg and Kimball, 1968: 184–186)—where middle-class individuals have their grievances weighed and processed informally by groups of interested associates. Nor do individuals seek to hold meetings for such a purpose; moots such as those found in Europe during the tribal period (see Berman, 1978) or in parts of Africa (Gibbs,

1963) do not exist. Similarly, members of the clergy report that they are rarely called on to mediate conflicts between nonfamily members. Even extensive dyadic negotiations involving principals alone are infrequent, with people apparently hesitant to invest so much in conflict. This applies in friendships and even more so in other relationships.

Also uncommon are attempts to impose psychotherapy or other help on offenders. In other words, middle-class people exercise little therapeutic social control outside their families (on therapeutic social control, see Black, 1976: 4–6; Horwitz, 1982). In one of the few cases of this kind uncovered during the present investigation, neighbors mobilized the social workers at the Board of Health to obtain help for a woman who was, in their opinion, abusing children left in her care during the day. In another case, involving a working-class deviant, a group of women sought to convince an Italian immigrant to accept money from their club to send his 12-year-old son to camp. They argued that the boy was suffering emotionally from spending as much time as he did with his father, whom he accompanied on the job whenever possible. (The father was a sexton at a church in town.) When the man grew angry and insisted that the women leave him alone, they backed off, although they commented among themselves about his rudeness and the damage he was inflicting on the boy. The infrequency of efforts to impose therapeutic help is all the more noteworthy because middle-class people do privately interpret some of their conflict in psychological terms. Thus, for instance, a woman subjected to the exhibitionist discussed earlier remarked to her family that they "really ought to see about getting that poor man some help," the woman disturbed by her neighbor's rotting wood piles believed the offender to suffer some obsessive mental disorder pertaining to wood and fires, and a young woman began to avoid a friend who had developed, in her opinion, into a "drug-addicted nymphomaniac."

Finally, formal legal contests between middle-class persons are rare as well. During 40 weekly sessions of the town's municipal criminal court held in 1978 and 1979, just 6 cases were initiated by middle-class friends or neighbors. Because private prosecution is the norm in this court (see Baumgartner, 1984: forthcoming), the bringing of legal actions ordinarily involves a great deal of confrontation. Middle-class people appear to be more at ease when the police and prosecutor handle their complaints, but the circumstances under which anyone is likely to receive this service—notably when predatory strangers such as burglars are apprehended and tried in a higher court—are very uncommon. On the civil side, only one case was uncovered involving two middle-class associates.

In sum, one side of the predilection for indirect strategies of social control found among these middle-class suburbanites is an aversion to confrontative tactics, even in the form of moots. This pattern contrasts with the situation in low-income housing projects, for example, where conflicts are more openly aired and more forcefully prosecuted (see Merry, 1979). Not all people in Hampton, however, are as adverse as middle-class adults are to confronting offenders openly. It is useful, in seeking to explain middle-class patterns of social control, to observe that other segments of the population in the same town exercise more confrontation in the face of grievances.

A NOTE ON CONFRONTATION, AGE, AND SOCIAL CLASS

To a large extent, young people and working-class people in Hampton favor the same strategies of social control as middle-class adults do, so that overall, normative life appears more similar than different across the town. Nonetheless, it is possible to discern clearly a tendency in both of these other populations toward greater reliance on confrontation. Age and social class interact in this regard, so that working-class youths are the most likely of all Hamptonians to adopt an aggressive posture toward their adversaries. In fact, it is only in this group that hostile confrontation achieves a measure of prominence as a strategy of social control.

Young people, particularly those from working-class families, make occasional use of forceful self-help of various kinds. Physical aggression—though virtually never of a sort to cause serious injury, and virtually never with weapons—occurs with some frequency. For example, weekend nights at the local bars commonly see brief altercations between drunk patrons, who are usually known to one another before the fights occur. Bar employees and other customers typically handle these incidents by themselves, without the help of the police. Fights occur spontaneously in other settings as well, whereas some violent encounters are prearranged and have an almost-ritualized character.

Young people make more personal threats than do older people, and they engage in more harassment and more property destruction as forms of punishment. In one case, for instance, a young person drove his car onto a neighbor's lawn during the course of a conflict; in another, a group of young friends retaliated for an affront to one of their number by driving past the offender's house late at night, blowing their car horns; in a third case, young people left a bag of manure on the doorstep of an unpopular neighbor. When a man called the police to disperse a group of young neighbors who were sitting in cars drinking and listening to music, they responded by spraying the sides of his house with black spray paint during the middle of the night. In fact, much "vandalism" in Hampton is property destruction undertaken by young people as a form of social control.

Moreover, the young people of this suburban town are disproportionately represented in the ranks of those who press some kinds of formal complaints, particularly those heard in the municipal criminal court. It is also relevant to note that the only civil action involving friends or neighbors uncovered in this investigation occurred when one youth sued another to recover a $400 debt—an action that was criticized by older people who learned of it.

Working-class adults are also more likely than middle-class adults to opt for confrontation when they have grievances. Violence, although less common than among youths, is still found. Several incidents involving fights and property destruction in the working-class community were recorded during the study. In one case, for instance, an altercation broke out between two groups of men when one faction installed a "spite fence" down the middle of a shared driveway. During this encounter, a person sustained a broken nose and several car windows were smashed. In another instance, two friends and co-workers exchanged blows over a disagreement about who should win a union election. Fisticuffs and auto-glass destruction occurred in other cases, and in one unusual encounter, two women scuffled after mass one Sunday until separated by a priest. The intial aggressor in this matter accused her opponent of having an affair with her husband. (All of this seems consistent with the observation that in Levittown, a Philadelphia and Trenton suburb, working-class people are more likely than middle-class ones to report quarrels between their neighbors; Gans, 1967: 160.)

Formal complaints of most kinds are dominated by working-class people too. As discussed in more detail elsewhere (Baumgartner, 1984), working-class individuals, though they comprise but a third of the town's population, generate the greatest share of business handled by the municipal court, the zoning office, and the sanitarians at the Board of Health. They also make more complaints to the police and to elected officials. And in contrast to complaints made by middle-class people, theirs are less often secret.

The greater willingness of young and working-class people to confront offenders directly (and in some cases aggressively) suggests that the extreme aversion to confrontation seen among middle-class adults is related to features of their social situation that are not altogether shared by these other groups. In the following section, the middle-class propensity to avoid confrontations is analyzed in terms of the distinctive morphology of social relations found among middle-class people in this surburban town.

Social Control and Weak Ties

Two characteristics most sharply distinguish middle-class people and reverberate across many dimensions of their lives. These are their high social status and the structure of their personal relationships. One apparent effect of social status on normative patterns is that it discourages the submission of conflicts to the judgment of third parties: Because few outsiders are of sufficiently superordinate status to command deference and respect, few are consulted about interpersonal tensions. Higher-status people in a number of settings have been found less willing than others to invoke a variety of third parties. Thus, among the Zapotec Indians of Mexico:

> Certain classes of people avoid using the courts. For example, the families of the *principales*, the leading government advisers, rarely utilize the town court. . . . For any member of such a respected or respectable family to be found in court would be considered a shame, and any wise member of such a family hesitates before involving the name of his family in a public hearing [Nader, 1964: 413].

In a contemporary Bavarian village, it was similarly found that comparatively high status people—those with secure incomes and standing in their community— initiated suits against peers in the court or the formal "reconciliation agency" far less often than low-status "marginals" did (Todd, 1978). When Louis XIV of France attempted to discourage dueling by setting up a "court of honor" where aristocrats could air their grievances against one another and receive judgment, his experiment failed because nobles refused to use the court (Baldick, 1965: 61). (For a more detailed discussion of this point, see Baumgartner, 1984; forthcoming; see also Black and Baumgartner, 1983: 112–114.) Yet in explaining the general aversion to confrontation of all kinds, not just legal, among the middle class of this suburban town, social status alone seems inadequate.

The annals of history and anthropology contain many references to a propensity for frequent and forceful prosecution of grievances by assorted high-status groups. Thus, for example, in at least one area in India, disputes among high-caste individuals are said to have been "frequent, bitter, and often violent. . . . These fights would often be over questions of land, but more frequently would arise over insults [Cohn, 1959: 88]." Among the Nuristani of Afghanistan, informants report that aggression and attendant mediation are more common among high-status people than among lower status ones, who are said to be less likely to quarrel (Jones, 1974: 109). Similarly, in a contemporary Lebanese village, members of the highest stratum "have more disputes than the other social classes," partly because they are "quick to take affront for any real or imagined slight to personal or lineage honor or position [Rothenberger, 1978: 170–171]." And in medieval Europe, the nobility often answered offenses, which they too were quite ready to perceive, with violence. In one instance, "Périgord [a part of France] ran with blood because a certain lord thought that one of his noble neighbors looked like a blacksmith and had the bad taste to say so [Bloch, 1940: 296]." Thus status, though an important influence on normative life, does not by itself ensure a propensity for indirect strategies of conflict management.

A factor that seems more clearly to influence the predominance of nonconfrontation in the normative life of the suburban middle class is the morphology of their social relationships. As noted earlier, these people tend to be socially anchored only loosely into atomized and shifting networks of weak ties. Their high rate of mobility means that bonds between persons are frequently ruptured and replaced with new and equally temporary ones, so that relationships often have short pasts and futures. Even relatives (other than nuclear family members) are likely to reside elsewhere, at a distance too far for easy contact except by telephone. Middle-class lives are also highly compartmentalized. Relationships tend to be single stranded, restricted to a single dimension of interaction, and partly as a result, middle-class social networks are not interconnected and are not formed into dense webs of common associates. Ties are scattered through many towns and regions.

This culture of weak ties seems to undermine confrontation in several ways. In the first place, it renders forceful action against offenders less compelling by holding out the likelihood that a subsequent departure of either party will take care of the problem in the normal course of events, and it makes avoidance a feasible option in the meanwhile. It makes bitter enmities and resentments difficult to sustain and limits the ability of people to accumulate damaging information about one another. (Both of these points are also discussed in Baumgartner, 1984: forthcoming.) A system of weak ties lessens involvement in any single relationship and leaves people little time to manage conflict within it. And finally, it

deprives people of cohesive bands of supporters to assist them in pressing grievances, whether through violence or negotiation. Each of these
implications is elaborated in the following pages.

THE TRANSIENCY OF PROBLEMS

For members of the middle class, the town where they live is often
only a temporary place of residence. Many are asked by their employers
to transfer to other locations; some leave for personal reasons, usually to
improve on their dwellings or neighborhoods. Still others take up new
homes on retirement, perhaps near one or more of their scattered children, or in a warmer climate. Only a few middle-class people seem
committed to spending the rest of their lives in the same town, much
less in the same neighborhood or house.

When a grievance arises, therefore, many people are able to look
forward to eventual separation from the annoying situation. Even if the
aggrieved individual himself or herself is not likely to move, the chances
are good that the offender will. That ordinary changes of residence in
fact truncate conflicts is clear in a number of cases collected during the
study. Thus, in one instance, a middle-class woman about to move to
another state (because her husband had been transferred) remarked that
one of the best things about the move was that it would enable her to get
away from a friend with whom she had been having intermittent disagreements for some time. In the case of the exhibitionist noted earlier,
the problem ultimately resolved itself when the offender moved. And in
a further example, a neighborhood terrorized by an unruly St. Bernard
was relieved when the dog's owners left town. The possibility of a
graceful exit from a tense situation makes confrontation less compelling.
People can opt for a holding pattern of tolerance or avoidance without
having to resign themselves to a permanent source of displeasure.

At the same time, the loosely woven texture of daily life makes avoidance an easy alternative should an aggrieved person choose to take any
action at all against an offender. There is little pressure to associate with
particular individuals, and few occasions are likely to bring together
those who would rather stay apart. If tensions escalate, the parties can
simply ignore one another without disrupting a larger network of associates. In many cases, their avoidance will not even be noticed.

Evidence from other societies indicates that transient and atomized
people everywhere are comparatively unlikely to confront offenders directly. The alternative of avoidance defuses many conflicts. Thus, for
instance, accusations of witchcraft are less common in fluid and tran-

sient societies where people can simply move away from one another (Douglas, 1970: chaps. 4–8). Violence, too, seems less likely where avoidance is possible; in one case, for example, there was a dramatic increase in rates of violence among a traditionally nomadic people, the Chenchu of the Indian subcontinent, after they were confined by the British to a single enclosed camp (Fürer-Haimendorf, 1967: 17–24). It has been hypothesized that mediation and adjudication will also be relatively undeveloped where it is possible for people to avoid their antagonists (Felstiner, 1974), and a decline of law under contemporary conditions has been projected on the basis of the decreasing lifespan of relationships and a corresponding decrease in the lifespan of disputes (Black, 1976: chap. 7). The patterns of social control in suburbia are consistent with these hypotheses.

THE SCARCITY OF INFORMATION

Confrontation is further undermined by the relative poverty of social knowledge involved in middle-class relationships. Of special interest in this context is the difficulty in accumulating information about any individual's past misdeeds, and the implications this has for the dynamics of reputation, or "normative status" (Black, 1976: 111). Direct experience with the same offender is apt to be limited by the tendency of people to move away from one another and by the low intensity of social bonds. Beyond this, the structure of relationships greatly reduces the amount of secondhand information people are able to acquire about one another. When people move, their knowledge and opinions move as well. And even on a day-by-day basis, the low cohesiveness of middle-class networks discourages the pooling of grievances and the sharing of compromising information. Accordingly, when a friend, neighbor, or associate annoys an individual, the problem is likely to appear as a first or second offense committed by a person with no particular reputation for good or ill.

The relative absence of reputations in suburban life is quite significant, for first and second offenders everywhere appear to fare better than those who are seen as chronic deviants (see Black, 1976: 118–119). First offenders are tolerated more readily and, if sanctioned, proceeded against more leniently than are repeat offenders. This trend exists across diverse societies and arenas of social control (see, e.g., Rattray, 1929: 37; Hoebel, 1954: 88–92; Werthman and Piliavin, 1967; Farrell and Swigert, 1978). One anthropologist explains litigiousness in an African society with the accumulation of grievances between parties over time (Gluckman, 1967: 21–22). Another explains execution, banishment, and witch-craft accusations in certain simple societies with the ability of the inhabitants to assemble "community dossiers" on one another; where social conditions make such dossiers impossible, these sanctions are not prevalent (Colson, 1974: 53–59; see also Black, 1976: 137). At the same time, where information about people is restricted, victims are under little pressure to preserve their "honor" by taking action against offenders anyway (Christie, 1977: 6). It is consistent with all of these observations that middle-class suburbanites, provided with so little information about one another, are remarkably disinclined to take forceful action in the face of grievances.

THE DIVISION OF SOCIAL ATTENTION

Because of the fragmentation of their social networks, the middle-class people of a suburb experience little continuity of concern from one interaction to the next. A husband and wife with whom another couple exchanges visits is unlikely to have the same configuration of contacts and interests as a bridge partner, a fellow club member, or a neighbor. Accordingly, each relationship provides its own activities and entails its own demands. Because people thus divide their social attention many ways, comparatively little time and effort can be devoted to any one concern.

This fragmentation of social attention constitutes an empirical basis for the frequent middle-class claim that people are "too busy to be bothered" or "have no time" to pursue a grievance and that they "have more to do than worry about" some offending associate. Other involvements, including those that are work related, draw aggrieved individuals outside the social context within which given annoyances arise. The more this is so, the less time remains to plan and execute sanctions against any offender and the more conflicts are perceived as unwelcome intrusions that might interfere with additional involvements. The middle-class situation in this regard may be contrasted with that prevailing in small, bonded groups. There, little is likely to be of more interest to everyone than interpersonal tensions between two or more members. With no outside involvements to distract their attention beyond the group, conflict can readily become a consuming preoccupation. It can also become a source of entertainment for both the parties and the onlookers, a relief from the unchanging interactions and unvarying routines. Among suburban people, however, the drama of conflict and confrontation is not needed to spice daily life, and it is little appreciated.

THE LACK OF SUPPORT GROUPS

Another way in which weak ties minimize confrontation is by depriving people of powerful support groups. When tensions erupt, individuals must generally proceed on their own. Extended family members, who might otherwise be expected to lend their assistance, are usually living some distance from the aggrieved party and are, in any case, caught up in their own networks and concerns. Spouses and young children are typically the only relatives present, and they too have other preoccupations (besides being, in the case of children, of limited value in confrontations). Friends, neighbors, and associates are near to hand but are rarely intimate enough to be counted on to provide assistance. Even advice is difficult to obtain from those who know little or nothing about the offense or the offender, and many middle-class people are reluctant to give it under any circumstances (believing it better to "stay out" of others' conflicts altogether).

Without supporters to help in the management of conflict, people seem likely to stay away from direct confrontations. Evidence from other settings indicates a close relationship between the availability of support groups and the vigorous prosecution of grievances. In one cross-cultural survey, for example, it was found that societies in which kin members are clustered into tightly knit "fraternal interest groups" sharing many common pursuits experience high amounts of violent retaliation for injuries; those lacking such groups tend to be peaceful (Thoden van Velzen and van Wetering, 1960). The relationship between supporters and other kinds of direct confrontation has also been noted by investigators. Whether, and to what extent, disputes will be negotiated, for example, depends greatly on the ability of aggrieved parties to recruit an "action-set" to help them (Gulliver, 1969; see also Bohannan, 1957: 65). Resort to law also appears to be encouraged by the presence of support groups (see Black, 1976: chap. 4). Thus, in Periclean Athens, fraternities and clubs that assisted their members in legal matters—and to one of which most prominent Athenians belonged—stimulated recourse to professional advocates and facilitated many aspects of lawsuits (Chroust, 1954: especially 352–353). The absence of support groups in a middle-class suburb, then, would be expected to deter many modes of confrontation, and the prevalence of indirect strategies of social control there is partly understandable from this perspective.

In light of the foregoing, the somewhat greater willingness of young and working-class people to resort to confrontation can be understood. Along several morphological dimensions, each group in the town studied differs from middle-class adults in ways that might be expected to generate a more aggressive prosecution of grievances. Young people tend to move within the confines of more closely bonded networks and to develop more intense enmities as well as warmer friendships. With fewer far-flung ties, they are less divided in their interests and commitments and less distracted from conflicts at hand. A striking feature of the youthful response to grievances is the propensity of bands of good friends to rally around one another, so that much hostility passes between groups. (Middle-class adults who, because of their more atomized networks, do not proceed collectively in the face of grievances are made especially uneasy by this fact. They fear that antagonizing one youth will provoke "a gang of kids" to exact vengeance.)

Working-class people, too, are better organized for confrontation. Because they are less transient than middle-class people, their grievances are more permanent. They have greater opportunity to accumulate grudges, and their more cohesive networks are able to store, collate, and disseminate damaging information more efficiently. Like youths, they have less fragmented social lives, and fewer demands that distract them from their conflicts. Moreover, working-class people tend to live near their larger families, and so they enjoy more dependable power bases from which supporters can be recruited to assist in confrontations.

For all these reasons, one would expect Hampton's youths and working-class people to engage in more confrontation than do middle-class adults, which, in fact, is the case. It is important to emphasize again, however, that the degree of variation in social relationships across segments of the town is actually quite limited when seen against the range found throughout human populations. Accordingly, all of the people in this suburb also have much in common when they handle grievances against one another.

Concluding Remarks

If the preceding analysis has merit, it implies that a nonconfrontational style of social control—including such tactics as tolerance, avoidance, and conciliatory approaches—will be found wherever social life is characterized by transiency, atomization, and the fragmentation of social ties. Because exactly these traits appear to be increasingly pervasive in modern society, it may well be that nonconfrontation will become an ever more widespread feature of contemporary normative life. Such a development is consistent with recent projections of the future of law and conflict management in modern society (e.g., Felstiner, 1974; Black,

1976: chap. 7). Seen in this light, social control in suburbia may illustrate a pattern now coming to dominate the moral order of the modern world.

ACKNOWLEDGMENTS

For commenting on various aspects of the work presented here, I thank Donald Black, Mark Cooney, Kai Erikson, Richard Lempert, Sally Engle Merry, Frank Romo, Susan S. Silbey, and Stanton Wheeler.

References

Arensberg, Conrad M., and Solon T. Kimball
    1968 *Family and Community in Ireland.* 2d edition. Cambridge, Mass.: Harvard University Press (1st edition, 1940).

Aubert, Vilhelm (editor)
    1969 *Sociology of Law: Selected Readings.* Baltimore: Penguin Books.

Baldick, Robert
    1965 *The Duel: A History of Duelling.* London: Chapman and Hall.

Baumgartner, M. P.
    1984 "Law and the middle class: Evidence from a surburban town." *Law and Human Behavior,* forthcoming.
    forth- *The Moral Order of a Suburb.* New York: Academic Press.
    coming

Becker, Howard S., and Blanche Geer
    1957 "Participant observation and interviewing: A comparison." *Human Organization* 16:28–32.

Berman, Harold J.
    1978 "The background of the Western legal tradition in the folklaw of the peoples of Europe." *University of Chicago Law Review* 45: 553–597.

Black, Donald
    1976 *The Behavior of Law.* New York: Academic Press.
    1980 *The Manners and Customs of the Police.* New York: Academic Press.

Black, Donald, and M. P. Baumgartner
    1983 "Toward a theory of the third party." Pages 84–114 in *Empirical Theories about Courts,* edited by Keith O. Boyum and Lynn Mather. New York: Longman.

Black, Donald, and Maureen Mileski (editors)
    1973 *The Social Organization of Law.* New York: Seminar Press.

Bloch, Maurice
    1940 *Feudal Society,* vol. 2: *Social Classes and Political Organization.* Chicago: Phoenix Books, 1964.

Bohannan, Paul
    1957 *Justice and Judgment among the Tiv.* London: Oxford University Press.

Bohannan, Paul (editor)
    1967 *Law and Warfare: Studies in the Anthropology of Conflict.* Garden City, N.Y.: Natural History Press.

Chagnon, Napolean A.
    1977 *Yanomamö: The Fierce People.* 2d edition. New York: Holt, Rinehart and Winston (1st edition, 1968).

Christie, Nils
    1977   "Conflicts as property." *British Journal of Criminology* 17: 1–15.
Chroust, Anton-Hermann
    1954   "The legal profession in ancient Athens." *Notre Dame Lawyer* 29: 339–389.
Cohn, Bernard S.
    1959   "Notes on law and change in North India." *Economic Development and Cultural Change* 8: 79–93.
Colson, Elizabeth
    1974   *Tradition and Contract: The Problem of Order.* Chicago: Aldine Press.
Douglas, Mary
    1970   *Natural Symbols: Explorations in Cosmology.* New York: Pantheon Books.
Ekvall, Robert B.
    1964   "Peace and war among the Tibetan nomads." *American Anthropologist* 66: 1119–1148.
Evans-Pritchard, E. E.
    1940   *The Nuer.* London: Oxford University Press.
Farrell, Ronald A., and Victoria Lynn Swigert
    1978   "Prior offense as a self-fulfilling prophecy." *Law and Society Review* 12: 437–453.
Felstiner, William L. F.
    1974   "Influence of social organization on dispute processing." *Law and Society Review* 9: 63–94.
Fürer-Haimendorf, Christoph von
    1967   *Morals and Merit: A Study of Values and Social Controls in South Asian Societies.* Chicago: University of Chicago Press.
Galanter, Marc
    1974   "Why the 'haves' come out ahead: Speculations on the limit of legal change." *Law and Society Review* 9: 95–160.
Gans, Herbert J.
    1967   *The Levittowners: Ways of Life and Politics in a New Suburban Community.* New York: Vintage Books.
Gibbs, James L., Jr.
    1963   "The Kpelle moot: A therapeutic model for the informal settlement of disputes." *Africa* 33: 1–10.
Glaser, Barney
    1965   "The constant comparative method of qualitative analysis." *Social Problems* 12: 436–445.
Gluckman, Max
    1967   *The Judicial Process among the Barotse of Northern Rhodesia.* 2d edition. Manchester: Manchester University Press (1st edition, 1955).
Granovetter, Mark S.
    1973   "The strength of weak ties." *American Journal of Sociology* 78: 1360–1380.
    1974   *Getting a Job: A Study of Contacts and Careers.* Cambridge, Mass.: Harvard University Press.
Gulliver, P. H.
    1963   *Social Control in an African Society: A Study of the Arusha, Agricultural Masai of Northern Tanganyika.* Boston: Boston University Press.
    1969   "Dispute settlement without courts: The Ndendeuli of southern Tanzania." Pages 24–68 in *Law and Culture and Society,* edited by Laura Nader. Chicago: Aldine Press.
Harner, Michael J.
    1972   *The Jivaro: People of the Sacred Waterfalls.* Garden City, N.Y.: Anchor Books.

Hoebel, E. Adamson
  1954 *The Law of Primitive Man: A Study in Comparative Legal Dynamics.* Cambridge, Mass.: Harvard University Press.
Horwitz, Allan V.
  1982 *The Social Control of Mental Illness.* New York: Academic Press.
Jones, Schuyler
  1974 *Men of Influence in Nuristan: A Study of Social Control and Dispute Settlement in Waigal Valley, Afghanistan.* London: Seminar Press.
Koch, Klaus-Friedrich
  1974 *War and Peace in Jalémó: The Management of Conflict in Highland New Guinea.* Cambridge, Mass.: Harvard University Press.
Lewis, I. M.
  1961 *A Pastoral Democracy: A Study of Pastoralism and Politics among the Northern Somali of the Horn of Africa.* London: Oxford University Press.
Merry, Sally Engle
  1979 "Going to court: Strategies of dispute management in an American urban neighborhood." *Law and Society Review* 13: 891–925.
Nader, Laura
  1964 "An analysis of Zapotec law cases." *Ethnology* 3: 404–419.
Nader, Laura, and Harry F. Todd, Jr. (editors)
  1978 *The Disputing Process—Law in Ten Societies.* New York: Columbia University Press.
Perrin, Constance
  1977 *Everything in Its Place: Social Order and Land Use in America.* Princeton, N.J.: Princeton University Press.
Pospisil, Leopold
  1958 *Kapauku Papuans and their Law.* Yale University Publications in Anthropology, No. 54. New Haven, Conn.: Yale University Press.
Rattray, R. S.
  1929 *Ashanti Law and Constitution.* Oxford: Clarendon Press.
Rothenberger, John E.
  1978 "The social dynamics of dispute settlement in a Sunni Muslim village in Lebanon." Pages 152–180 in *The Disputing Process—Law in Ten Societies,* edited by Laura Nader and Harry F. Todd, Jr. New York: Columbia University Press.
Suttles, Gerald D.
  1968 *The Social Order of the Slum.* Chicago: University of Chicago Press.
Thoden van Velzen, H. U. E., and W. van Wetering
  1960 "Residence, power groups and intra-societal aggression: An enquiry into the conditions leading to peacefulness within non-stratified societies." *International Archives of Ethnography* 49 (pt. 2): 169–200.
Thomas-Buckle, Suzann R., and Leonard G. Buckle
  1982 "Doing unto others: Disputes and dispute processing in an urban American neighborhood." Pages 78–90 in *Neighborhood Justice: Assessment of an Emerging Idea,* edited by Roman Tomasic and Malcolm M. Feeley. New York: Longman.
Todd, Harry F., Jr.
  1978 "Litigious marginals: Character and disputing in a Bavarian village." Pages 86–121 in *The Disputing Process—Law in Ten Societies,* edited by Laura Nader and Harry F. Todd, Jr. New York: Columbia University Press.
Werthman, Carl, and Irving Piliavin
  1967 "Gang members and the police." Pages 56–98 in *The Police: Six Sociological Essays,* edited by David J. Bordua. New York: Wiley.

5

Two Models of Social Control in Simple Societies*

JANE F. COLLIER

In every society, people's ways of defining and responding to deviant behavior are shaped by the concepts available to them for understanding the nature of their social world and of the humans who inhabit
it. These conceptual frameworks, which exist as "folk models of social
structure" (Barkun, 1968), are in turn shaped by people's experiences,
which are themselves shaped by the social worlds in which people live.
In this chapter, I draw on this line of reasoning to suggest that different
patterns of social control derive from different conceptual frameworks
originating in different forms of social inequality. In the process of setting out this argument, I offer suggestions both for classifying societies
and, through the analysis of two types of simple societies, for understanding the relationship, in any given society, between processes of
social control and the organization of social inequality as the latter is
realized in the organization of production.

The analytical framework used in this chapter is drawn from Max
Gluckman (1965), because he not only argued that the folk models of
social structure people use to define and respond to deviant behavior are

*The research and writing of this chapter were supported by grant no. BNS 76–11651
from the National Science Foundation for "A Cross-Cultural Study of Social Stratification
and Legal Processes."

products of particular social and economic backgrounds (1969: 354) but also offered a framework for classifying societies—"tribal" versus "modern"—and a complex theory of the connections between socioeconomic organization and the legal settings within which folk models are forged. In his analysis of tribal society, Gluckman (1965) suggests that a low level of technology, combined with a lack of durable goods, gives rise to a particular form of social organization that shapes all aspects of the legal system—institutions, norms, and claims—by limiting the degree of political centralization, fostering a normative emphasis on obligations owed between specific people rather than on rights held by individuals, and leading to conflicts more concerned with behavior than with rules. Gluckman does not develop a model of modern society, but his analysis of tribal society implies that had he done so, he would have suggested that a high level of technology combined with an abundance of durable goods gives rise to a type of social organization permitting the development of highly centralized political systems, fostering a normative emphasis on rights held by individuals rather than on obligations owed between specific people, and leading to conflicts more concerned with rules than with behavior. Gluckman's analysis thus suggests both a scheme for classifying societies and an analytical framework for understanding the relationship between productive processes and social control.

Although the analytical framework used here is drawn from Gluckman, I do not follow him in granting analytical priority to technology. I do not deny the importance of technology in shaping both the amount of goods a social group may produce and the division of productive labor, but I am more interested in how society-wide inequality is organized than in either the absolute amount of goods available or the numbers and organization of people who work together. My primary reason for not granting technology analytical priority, however, is that although technology both limits and fosters social inequality, social factors also shape the development or adoption of technology. Thus, for example, capitalist folk wisdom posits that no one will invent a better mousetrap unless the inventor can expect to profit from the effort, and it has often been observed that modern hunter–gatherers, far from welcoming all the technological innovations offered them, accept primarily those items that can be widely distributed and require minimal maintenance, such as steel knives and axes (Sahlins, 1972).

Because I do not grant technology priority as an independent variable, I face analytical problems Gluckman managed to avoid. Technology has the double virtue of being both empirically observable and distinct from human behavior, whereas the organization of social inequality, which is the critical variable in my analysis, exists only in the actions of people and is in no sense independent of the variable I seek to explain: the folk models of social structure that organize patterns of social control. The type of analysis I advocate, therefore, is a dialectical one in which human experience is viewed as shaped by social structure even as structures are realized in the practices of actors pursuing their own subjective ends. Such an approach to explanation, which is very close to the approach advocated by Bourdieu (1977), is also open to the criticisms that have been leveled at his work. DiMaggio, for example, notes that Bourdieu's alternative to empiricism does not inspire confidence. DiMaggio (1979) writes:

> Bourdieu rejects correlational analysis in favor of explanations that are thoroughly systematic. For these he posits a twofold test: that they be consistent with empirical findings; and that they be coherent, circular, inclusive, and, in effect, overdetermined. Such a satisfactory system of proofs, [Bourdieu] confesses, "inevitably appears as a vicious circle, inspired by the spirit of the system, to a positivist epistemology" [p. 1467].

Although I, like Bourdieu, advocate systematic rather than correlational explanations, in this chapter I focus primarily on how social inequality structures the experiences from which people build folk models of social structure; I shall allude only briefly to the role of folk models in structuring the organization of inequality. Hence, I present but a fraction of what is necessarily a more inclusive analysis.[1]

The body of this chapter is divided into four parts. The first discusses the question my analytical framework is designed to address and compares my framework with those used by other anthropologists who have classified societies for the purpose of analyzing their legal systems. The second part discusses my analytical framework, and the third describes two types of simple societies in order to trace the relationship, in those two types of societies, between how inequality is organized, folk models of social structure, and patterns of social control. Finally, the concluding part considers the usefulness of my analytical framework for analyzing more complex societies.

The Question of Meaning

In treating folk models of social structure as the basis for understanding patterns of social control, I am stressing the importance of under-

---

[1]I have developed a fuller analysis of relations between folk models and forms of social inequality in an as yet unpublished manuscript.

standing meaning for interpreting human action. In particular, my analysis rests on the assumption that it is impossible to know what an action is without understanding what an action means to or for those who perform it. Understanding meaning, therefore, is the key to analyzing social practices.

Understanding meaning, however, is not a straightforward process because it is always difficult to steer a course that passes between the Scylla of absolute meaning and the Charybdis of complete relativism. If the subjectivism inherent in trying to understand intentions is avoided by a focus on publicly shared meanings, there remains the problem of avoiding both the rock of absolutism (the position that words mean what *Webster's Dictionary* says they mean) and the whirlpool of relativism (the position that there are as many, if not more, folk models of social structure as there are human languages).

One way to avoid the extremes of absolutism and relativism is to focus on socially organized consequences of action, on the assumption that what actions can mean for actors is structured by their experiences of the social consequences actions produce. This is my strategy. In particular, I focus on how forms of social inequality structure the consequences that acts have for relations between people. A focus on forms of social inequality thus offers a way of understanding both how actions covered by the same English word—such as, for example, instances of *theft* or *adultery*—can mean quite different things in different societies, and how people with different languages, living in different parts of the world, can have quite similar folk models of social structure and so have quite similar ways of defining and responding to deviant behavior.

Because a focus on forms of social inequality requires the construction of ideal type models of different kinds of societies, I shall introduce the two models to be discussed later in this chapter by comparing the kinds of models I am trying to build with other ways anthropologists have classified legal systems. Moore identifies three kinds of classification:

> (1) a dichotomy founded on the basic differences in social organization between technologically simple and technologically complex societies; (2) an evolutionary series focusing on legal concomitants of the development from decentralized to centralized political systems, e.g., enforcement procedures, courts, and codes; (3) a procedural dichotomy, which contrasts dispute settlements hammered out or bargained out between the disputants themselves (often with supporters and allies on each side) and dispute settlements made by a third party having authority over both disputants [1970: 253].

All three classification schemes, from my point of view, run aground on the rock of absolute meaning, but each also offers particular insights.

The analysis presented in this chapter is, as already noted, largely drawn from the work of Gluckman (1965), who, like Maine (1861) and Durkheim (1893), developed "a dichotomy founded on the basic differences in social organization between technologically simple and technologically complex societies [Moore 1970: 753]." Although I differ from Gluckman both in refusing to privilege technology and in postulating more than two types of societies, I share his focus on differences in social organization and, most importantly, his reason for building models in the first place. Because I believe there are many "types" of societies, and because—as will become clear later—I privilege political systems, my classification scheme closely resembles the "evolutionary series focusing on legal concomitants of the development from decentralized to centralized political systems" that Moore (1970: 254) describes as exemplified by the work of Diamond (1935: 1951: 1965) and Hoebel (1954). This resemblance, however, is superficial because I, like Gluckman, Maine, and Durkheim, classify in order to analyze rather than analyze in order to classify. The Diamond–Hoebel evolutionary series differs from the Maine–Durkheim–Gluckman dichotomies in much more than numbers of types postulated. The two classification schemes derive from approaches that are actually mirror images of each other. Diamond and Hoebel propose evolutionary schemes after completing their analyses of many societies, whereas Maine, Durkheim, and Gluckman classify societies in order to begin analyzing relations between economy and social control in specific groups. Diamond and Hoebel focus on variation between types of societies. Maine, Durkheim, and Gluckman focus on relations within societies. The classification schemes proposed by Diamond and Hoebel are intended to describe reality, whereas the classification schemes proposed by Maine, Durkheim, and Gluckman are, like the one proposed in this chapter, analytical tools.

The third classification scheme identified by Moore (1970) focuses on kinds of legal or dispute-handling procedures rather than on kinds of societies. Both Gulliver (1963) and Bohannan (1957; 1965) distinguish what might be called "negotiation" from "adjudication," although both then go on to suggest that these two types of procedures are associated with two different types of societies. More recently, however, other scholars have noted not only that both types of procedures occur in both types of societies (van Velsen, 1969) but also that there are many more ways of managing conflict than negotiation and adjudication. Mediation, avoidance, shaming, denial of reciprocity, fighting, and so on, are other ways of managing conflict that occur in all, or almost all, societies. Because these many different ways of managing conflict occur in all or almost all societies, scholars who begin by classifying procedures usually do so in order to develop hypotheses about the settings within societies that permit or foster use of particular procedures.

Although scholars who focus on explaining the cross-cultural occurrence of particular conflict-management techniques usually recognize that such techniques vary according to the total settings in which they occur, they have no systematic way of taking into account the effects of the wider context. Everyone recognizes, for example, that mediation as practiced by an African elder differs significantly from mediation as practiced in Boston, but if the aim is to identify contexts in which "mediation" is successful, then "mediation" itself is taken as an already given category—one that can be defined with the aid of *Webster's Dictionary*. This theoretical framework does offer conceptual tools for examining many of the differences between African and American mediation—in such areas as recruitment of mediators, types of disputes handled, sanctions available, the role of the public, and so on—but this theoretical framework does not offer tools for questioning the meaning of mediation itself. And yet this question should be asked because the experience of participating in mediation in societies where the process is called by the generic term for settling disputes must be qualitatively different from the experience of participating in mediation in societies such as the United States, where mediation may be regarded as a poor substitute for either the intensive psychiatric treatment that, Americans believe, gets at the root of people's interpersonal problems or the court procedures that, even if they do not get at the root of problems, at least lead to decisions that can be enforced. In summary, there is a sense in which mediation as practiced in Africa and mediation as practiced in Boston are different practices.

My aim in this chapter is to suggest a framework for analyzing the sense in which a social practice, such as mediating (or fighting, or compensating, or shaming, or adjudicating), can be understood as a different practice according to the social system in which it occurs. In noting that mediation can have different meanings, I do not, however, want to suggest that we should abandon English for the riches of alien vocabularies. I have no intention of reviving the controversy between Gluckman and Bohannan "about what is a suitable language in which to describe another people's legal system [Moore 1969: 340]." Like Gluckman, I am firmly committed to using English, if only because I, like most readers find it difficult to understand a text filled with foreign words. Rather, I differ from both Gluckman and Bohannan, because they both imply that translation is a preliminary step to analysis, whereas I treat comparative analysis and translation as inseparable.

The Analytical Framework

Although in this chapter I shall trace only how forms of social inequality structure the experiences from which people build folk models of social structure, such an analysis is necessarily incomplete. Forms of social inequality can never be treated as an independent variable because, in the end, the kinds of claims people can make on one another, which constitute forms of social inequality, are themselves organized by folk models of social structure. Lawyers, for example, are fond of pointing out that there is no right without a remedy, thus revealing the role of remedies (how people define and respond to deviant behavior) in structuring rights (the claims people can make on one another).

In this chapter, I begin by taking remedies for granted because I want to treat forms of social inequality as given, but a consideration of remedies does enter my analysis at the deepest level. In particular, remedies provide the starting point of my analysis because it is on the basis of remedies that I distinguish between what might be called "simple" and "complex" societies: between societies where kinship organizes inequality and those where inequality is organized by state structures. If simple societies are ones in which "the individual and his kinship group [have] the privilege right of prosecution and imposition of legal sanctions [Hoebel 1954: 327]," then an analysis of simple societies must begin with an analysis of kinship structures. When analyzing two types of simple societies in the following section of this chapter, I therefore begin my analysis by describing the nature of marriage in each type of society, because it is marriage—defined, for these societies, as the kinds of claims men can hold in women vis à vis other men—that structures the organization of social inequality. Marriage, however, is not the basis of social inequality in all societies even though marriage is always the basis of kinship. In those societies where "clearly defined public officials representing the society as such [Hoebel 1954: 327]" have charge of prosecuting and sanctioning offenders, it is state structures that impose remedies and so determine the claims that organize social inequality. If an analysis of simple societies must begin with a consideration of marriage as the basis of kinship structures, then an analysis of complex societies must begin with a consideration of the state's role in determining the kinds of rights people can hold in things vis à vis other people.

The two types of simple societies I analyze in the following section of this chapter correspond, more or less, to those commonly identified as "bands" and "tribes"—as distinct from "chiefdoms," "states," and other types of centralized, hierarchical societies (see Service, 1962; Sahlins, 1968). Anthropologists who classify societies tend to disagree both on numbers of types and on criteria for distinguishing between them, but they do seem to recognize particular clusters of traits even if they disagree over where to draw boundary lines or which traits to treat as determining. Because the two types of simple societies I analyze correspond to the distinctive clusters of traits most anthropologists call bands and tribes, I will use these labels as equivalent to my preferred labels of "brideservice societies" and "bridewealth societies."[2] But because I begin by contrasting two ways of marrying rather than two ways of procuring food (foraging and simple horticulture), I not only draw slightly different boundary lines between categories[3] but also, more importantly, offer different explanations for why traits cluster. In other words, I shall be offering alternative explanations for commonly observed differences between bands and tribes in their processes of social control.

People who live in bands, for example, are often described as having few rules, as fighting primarily over sex, as frequently resorting to avoidance or group dispersion as a means for handling conflicts, and as occasionally "fighting it out" in contests, duels, or other forms of regulated combat. People who live in tribes, on the other hand, tend to have many clearly articulated norms, to quarrel over property as well as over sex, to handle conflicts by initiating warfare or negotiations rather than by moving away, and to settle disputes by compensating victims of wrongdoing.

These differences in forms of social control are usually explained as deriving from different forms of social organization that themselves derive from different ways of procuring food. When bands are being analyzed, for example, the nomadism usually associated with a foraging

[2]Labeling the two types of societies *brideservice* and *bridewealth* has caused me many problems because these words already have accepted meanings within anthropology. They refer to kinds of exchanges at marriage and exist within a set of terms that includes *gift exchange, dowry, sister-exchange,* and so on. Because I use the words differently from other anthropologists, I confine my use of them to the single purpose of labeling two types of societies. I use other words when describing actual marriage exchanges.

[3]Because I contrast ways of marrying rather than ways of procuring food, I put many South American tropical forest horticulturalists, such as the Yanomamö (Chagnon, 1968), into the same category with foragers such as the Kalahari Bushmen (Thomas, 1958; Marshall, 1976), Australian Aborigines, and American Great Basin peoples. Similarly, I put the buffalo-hunting Cheyenne (Llewellyn and Hoebel, 1941) in with horticulturalists such as the Jalé of New Guinea (Koch, 1974) and such acephalous African groups as Tiv (Bohannan, 1957), Nuer (Evans-Pritchard, 1940), and Arusha (Gulliver, 1963). My two types also do not distinguish between violent and peaceful peoples. I, for example, put the "fierce" Yanomamö (Chagnon, 1968) in with the "harmless" Bushman (Thomas, 1958) even as I put the violent Jalé (Koch, 1974) in with the Arusha, who deplore violence (Gulliver, 1963). Yet in another sense my two types do correlate with two different ways of handling conflict, which can be labeled "contests" and "negotiation."

way of life is frequently used to explain such commonly noted social features as people's reluctance to accumulate personal belongings, their willingness to share territories with others, a group size that seldom exceeds 100 people, and the fluid character of social life as reflected in a lack of strong lineages or age sets, frequent fluctuations in group membership, and leaders' reluctance to give orders. These social features, in turn, are then credited with explaining the common patterns of conflict management found in bands. The lack of commonly accepted normative rules is explained as resulting from the fact that if people assert few claims in objects or territories, then they seldom need to fight over property. The tendency for most disputes to be about sex is commonly explained as resulting from the fact that if property is taken away as a cause for disputes, then only sex is left. The frequent use of avoidance or group dispersion as a way of handling conflict is explained as arising because if people are nomadic anyway, then both individuals and groups can easily move away from troublesome relationships. And the occasional occurrence of dramatic confrontations, such as duels of various sorts, is explained as occurring because if leaders cannot give orders, then disputants who face one another have no alternative but to fight it out.[4]

Just as the nomadism associated with foraging is often credited with explaining many features of band patterns of social control by explaining band social organization, so the sedentism made possible by simple horticulture is often credited with explaining many of the features that distinguish tribal patterns of social control from those of bands. It is often noted, for example, that the sedentism made possible by simple horticulture allows people to accumulate at least some valued objects, domesticated animals, and stored surpluses of food, just as the practice of horticulture gives people a reason for asserting claims in land. Similarly, horticulture permits larger settlements, often exceeding 100 people, and thus permits the development of more complex social groupings, such as corporate lineages and age sets. These groupings, in turn, give scope for leadership, fostering the recognition of lineage "elders" or the development of local group "big men" who have the power to give orders to junior kinsmen or followers. Patterns of conflict management then are said to reflect these social features. That tribal peoples usually have many well-developed, widely recognized norms reflects

---

[4]I am oversimplifying the explanations of those who attribute differences between band and tribal processes of social control to nomadism and sendentism, respectively. A good example of the kind of explanations I am challenging is provided by Roberts (1979: chaps. 5–6), but I hesitate to criticize his work, because I think his book is one of the best available introductions to legal anthropology.

sedentary peoples' need for norms to regulate social interaction. That tribal peoples fight over property as well as over sex reflects the importance of valuables, domesticated animals, and land. Tribal peoples' preference for facing conflict rather than moving away reflects the difficulties settled horticulturalists encounter in finding new land, seeds, and so on. And, finally, tribal peoples' tendency to settle intergroup conflicts by negotiating compensatory payments for victims—even though armed skirmishes may both precede and follow resort to the bargaining table—occurs because tribal peoples have both the valuables necessary for paying compensation and respected leaders who can order followers to comply with negotiated settlements.[5]

Two Types of Simple Societies

Before offering my alternative explanations for band and tribal processes of social control, I shall briefly list the societies I used in building the ideal types underlying my analyses, and also those societies specifically excluded from consideration. My sources for brideservice (or band) societies include works on the Eskimo (Hoebel, 1954; Chance, 1966; Balikci, 1970; Briggs, 1970), Washo (Downs, 1966), Basin–Plateau peoples (Steward, 1938), and Comanche (Hoebel, 1940; Wallace and Hoebel, 1952) of North America; the Yanomamö (Chagnon, 1968), Mundurucú (Murphy and Murphy, 1974), and Sharanahua (Siskind, 1973) of South America; the Murngin (Warner, 1958; Berndt, 1965) and Tiwi (Hart and Pilling, 1960) of Australia; the Kalahari Bushmen (Thomas, 1958; Marshall, 1976), Pygmies (Turnbull, 1961), and Hadza (Woodburn, 1968)

---

[5]Although I will offer alternative explanations for the commonly observed differences between bands and tribes, I do not intend to deny the importance of technoenvironmental factors for explaining social patterns. Such factors are useful for explaining within-type variations, particularly when combined with historical factors. If, for example, I were trying to explain differences, rather than similarities, between the Venezuelan Yanamamö and the Kalahari Bushmen, I would invoke such factors as Yanomamö horticulture versus Bushman foraging, the Venezuelan tropical forest versus the Kalahari Desert, and historical differences in how Western imperialism affected the Amazon Basin and southern Africa. Similarly, I have no intention of denying that technoenvironmental factors have both a facilitating and a limiting effect on degrees of social complexity. It is easier for horticulturalists in a favorable environment to maintain large settled villages than it is for foragers in a poor environment to do so, but horticulture and a rich environment can explain only the possibility for large villages, not why they do or do not develop. Similarly, foraging and a poor environment can explain why groups are nomadic and why people accumulate few things, but foraging and a poor environment cannot explain why foragers are not extremely possessive about the few goods they do carry with them.

of Africa; and the Ilongot (Rosaldo, 1980) of the Philippines. My sources
for bridewealth (or tribal) societies include my own fieldwork in Zina-
cantan, Chiapas, Mexico (Collier, 1973; 1977; 1979) and works on the
Cheyenne (Llewellyn and Hoebel, 1941; Hoebel, 1960) of North America; the Tiv (Bohannan, 1957), Nuer (Evans-Pritchard, 1940), Arusha
(Gulliver, 1963), and Ndendeuli (Gulliver, 1971) of Africa; and the Jalé
(Koch, 1974) of New Guinea. Other societies I expect can be fruitfully
analyzed using the bridewealth model include the Trobriand Islanders
(Malinowski, 1926; Weiner, 1976); the Kapauku Papuans (Pospisil, 1958)
of New Guinea; and the Kaguru (Beidelman, 1971), Plateau Tonga (Colson, 1962), and Sebei (Goldschmidt, 1967) of Africa. Societies specifically
excluded from the two types discussed in this chapter include the Kiowa
(Richardson, 1940) and Yurok (Kroeber, 1926) of North America; the
Ifugao (Barton, 1919) of the Philippines; and the Kachin (Leach, 1954) of
highland Burma, all of which are ranked societies. Also excluded are the
Barotse (Gluckman, 1955), Tswana (Schapera, 1938), Ashanti (Rattray,
1929), and Soga (Fallers, 1969) of Africa, as well as the Ontong Javanese
(Hogbin, 1934) of Polynesia, all of which are chiefdoms. Finally, I have
excluded all those Eurasian and North African peoples who have long
lived within, or around the edges of, centralized states having organized
coercive power, even if the community or ethnic group actually studied
by an ethnographer was a remote peasant village or in an area over
which a state had little control.

The distinction I draw between brideservice and bridewealth societies, although based on differences in how men acquire wives, is not,
as it might first appear, a distinction between societies where grooms
perform services for in-laws and those where grooms give valuables.
Rather, it is a distinction between two ways of living. This point is
crucial because in both types of societies men work for and give gifts to
kinsmen of women they hope to marry, and because in both types of
societies men who commit adultery with, or steal, a married woman
may give goods to that woman's husband. The distinction between
brideservice and bridewealth societies, therefore, lies not in acts performed by potential husbands and married women's lovers, but rather
in what those acts mean.

In brideservice societies the gifts and services a young man tenders to
his wife's kinsmen represent only his continuing claims in his wife vis à
vis other men. A husband's claims last only so long as gifts and services
continue, and as a result, a man works for and gives gifts to his in-laws
for as long as his marriage endures. In such societies, men who have
been cuckolded often demand or seize property from men who have
cuckolded them, but in such societies the cuckolded husband who de-

mands goods from his wife's lover is not extracting compensation for violated rights. Rather, he is asserting his equality with his challenger by displaying his ability to take something away from the man who took something away from him. In the end, therefore, the gifts and services a young man tenders to his wife's kinsmen represent primarily the husband's willingness to fight any other man who tries to sleep with the woman he claims as his wife (see Collier and Rosaldo, 1981).

In bridewealth societies, in contrast, the young man who works for, or gives gifts to, kinsmen of a woman is "buying" rights in that woman vis à vis both her kinsmen and other men. Once a young man has worked for or given gifts to his in-laws, he expects to receive either his wife or repayment for his goods and services—repayment that can then be put toward obtaining a substitute wife. As a result, young men in bridewealth societies need tender only a finite (although frequently disputed) amount of goods and services to in-laws. Similarly, the young man who tenders gifts and services to a woman's kinsmen obtains rights in the woman vis à vis other men. In many African bridewealth societies, for example, a man's payment of bridewealth is said to "buy" rights in a woman's sexuality, labor, and reproductive capacity. Although it does mean that a husband acquires rights to sleep with his wife, live in the house she maintains, and demand obedience (i.e., labor) from her children, it also means that a man feels entitled to claim repayment in valuables from any other man who sleeps with his wife, enjoys the products of her labor, or marries one of her daughters. In other words, the man in a bridewealth society who gives gifts to and performs services for his in-laws makes an investment that under normal circumstances he can expect to have repaid manyfold in the future. In most bridewealth societies, not only do women and their children produce goods and services for women's husbands (either by directly producing the valuables senior men exchange or by producing subsistence goods so that senior men have the leisure to produce valuables) but also women and their children provide women's husbands with opportunities for claiming goods and services from other men: Married women may commit adultery, women's sons work for their mothers' husbands, and women's daughters can be married to other men in return for valuables. In a bridewealth society, therefore, in contrast to a brideservice one, a man's gifts and services to his in-laws represent his claim in future goods and services rather than only his willingness to fight any other man who tries to sleep with his wife.

An analytically useful, although vastly oversimplified, way of characterizing the difference between brideservice and bridewealth societies is to note that in brideservice societies, goods cannot be exchanged for rights in women,[6] whereas in bridewealth societies, goods (material or symbolic)[7] can be exchanged for rights in women.[8] This difference is analytically useful because it reveals that in brideservice societies, where only a husband's services can validate his claims in a wife, no one except the parents of a daughter[9] can enjoy regular access to another man's services and products. In a bridewealth society, in contrast, where goods can be exchanged for rights in women, a man who has goods can use those goods to help other men acquire wives and so, by acting as a father should act toward his sons, enjoy legitimate rights to claim obedience from more "sons" than happen to be born to his wife or wives. Brideservice and bridewealth societies thus have very different ways of organizing social inequality, even as they also tend to have different amounts of social inequality.

In brideservice societies, where each man "earns" his own wife, men who are securely married have no more need to work for others. They are free from all debts and obligations to other men, although they continue to tender occasional gifts and services to in-laws as proof of their willingness to fight other men who might try to steal their wives. In brideservice societies, therefore, the most salient inequality is that between insecurely married men, who must heed the wishes of those able

[6]In brideservice societies, the only equivalent for one woman is another woman. Such societies are often described as practicing sister-exchange marriage.

[7]The Tiv are a bridewealth society in my terms, yet Bohannan (1957: 72) describes them as having practiced "exchange marriage" before the British colonial government abolished the custom. In precolonial Tiv society, however, young men married by giving female "wards" in exchange for wives—wards that were allocated to juniors by senior men. In Tiv society, therefore, wards played the role valuables play in other bridewealth societies.

[8]Richard Lempert (personal communication) suggested that the difference between brideservice and bridewealth societies is that women are more "alienable" in the latter than in the former. I think this characterization is correct, and, moreover, it highlights the crucial issue of how it is possible for men to hold rights in women—a question I tackle in my longer manuscript noted in Footnote 1. In arguing that women are alienable, however, I want to emphasize that the sense in which women are property in simple societies is very different from the sense in which slaves are property in complex societies with state structures. Because ownership is always a relationship between people rather than a relationship between an owner and the thing or person owned, the meaning of ownership varies according to the social system in which it occurs.

[9]In brideservice societies, a husband who lends his wife to a younger brother can, like parents of a daughter, enjoy regular access to another man's services and products. A husband, however, like the parents of a daughter, can enjoy a woman's lover's services only so long as he can ensure the cooperation of the woman in question. In brideservice societies, only people able to influence a woman's behavior directly can enjoy the services of her lover, in contrast to bridewealth societies, where the man who enjoys another man's services need not concern himself with the behavior of the woman his "dependent" acquires with the valuables provided.

to influence the behavior of desired brides, and securely married men, who need heed no other man.

In bridewealth societies, by contrast, even securely married men have to work for those who can help them acquire valuables because fathers (or uncles in matrilineal societies) who lack the goods that sons (or uterine nephews) need to marry lose their dependents—that is, workers—to more successful elders. In bridewealth societies, therefore, there are two salient inequalities: one inequality between juniors who must work for seniors and seniors who usually have juniors working for them, and an inequality between those seniors who have acquired many dependents to work for them and those seniors who have lost their dependents to other households. In bridewealth societies, all young men start out with equal "needs," but only some young men turn into respected elders or renowned "big men." Other seniors lead more humdrum lives, and still other seniors turn into pitied "poor" who live by accepting charity from generous political leaders.

Although the models of brideservice and bridewealth societies I am about to present were developed from analyses of several historically specific groups, I shall illustrate the two models with examples drawn primarily from ethnographic accounts of only two nineteenth-century buffalo-hunting tribes of the American Plains: Comanche for brideservice, and Cheyenne for bridewealth. These two societies were selected for several reasons. First, they had very different folk models of social structure and so assigned very different meanings to what an outside observer might view as similar behaviors. A contrast between Comanche and Cheyenne thus reveals the importance of knowing what an action means for understanding what an action is. Second, not only have the legal systems of Comanche and Cheyenne been well described by Hoebel (1940) and Llewellyn and Hoebel (1941), respectively, but also both were described by the same ethnographer: E. A. Hoebel. Hence, differences between the two societies cannot be attributed to differences in ethnographers' concerns or abilities. Finally, because both Comanche and Cheyenne were nomadic buffalo hunters, a comparison of these two societies calls into question the adequacy of explanations that attribute differences in social control to differences between nomadic and sedentary ways of life.[10]

[10]Although a comparison of the Comanche and the Cheyenne calls into question the adequacy of explanations based on differences between nomadism and sedentism, such a comparison cannot be used to refute explanations that attribute differences in dispute-handling mechanisms to differences in economies or subsistence strategies. The Comanche and Cheyenne have been described as sharing similar "geographical environments," "economic systems," and "familial structures" (Hoebel, 1954: 130), but, in my

BRIDESERVICE

Brideservice, as noted earlier, is not a way of marrying but a way of life. It makes sense to analyze a simple, egalitarian society in brideservice terms *not* when grooms are culturally required to perform services for in-laws (although such cultural requirements may exist), but rather when the services and gifts a groom tenders to his in-laws represent only his continuing claims in his wife vis à vis other men. The kind of brideservice I am describing is realized in an organization of production that is found, to my knowledge, only among groups subsisting either by foraging or by simple horticulture combined with hunting. In such groups, men distribute their meat widely, usually according to rules favoring seniors, whereas women feed families from foodstuffs they gather, grow, or obtain when meat is distributed by men. In Comanche society, for example, "a man who returned to camp with meat was obliged to share it with all who came for some [and] had to give the best part to his wife to take to her father [Hoebel, 1940: 119]." Although there may be a simple sexual division of labor in brideservice societies, marriage does not involve an equal or balanced exchange of products between a husband and wife. Little of a man's meat may end up in his wife's pot, and women acquire meat from returning hunters who are not their husbands. As a result, marriage has very different implications for women and men. Women do not need to marry in order to gain access to male products. But a man must marry if he wants to eat regularly or to escape having to cook for himself.

This organization of production shapes male and female life cycles in brideservice societies. Because a young man's parents cannot provide him with the means of obtaining a wife—as parents can in bridewealth societies—bachelors usually leave parental homes to search for brides. Bachelors thus lead wandering lives. They live on the outskirts of groups, eat irregularly, and get blamed for causing trouble when they seduce other men's wives. In Comanche society, for example, adolescent boys were expected to spend most of their time away from camp seeking spiritual visions, hunting, or raiding for horses. Comanche boys

---

opinion, these similarities are superficial. The Comanche and Cheyenne both lived on the Great Plains, but their geographical environments were different in that the Comanche lived south of both the large buffalo herds and the main routes of the fur traders. The Comanche and Cheyenne both hunted buffalos, but their economic systems were different in that the Cheyenne, but not the Comanche, produced buffalo products for the world market. Finally, the Comanche and Cheyenne familial structures were alike in that both lacked clans, but the Comanche lived in nuclear or polygynous families, whereas the Cheyenne lived in extended, uxorilocal households called camps.

formed gangs and probably ate irregularly because "as their fathers stole stock, they rustled food from the camp [Wallace and Hoebel, 1952: 130]."

The culturally marked inequality in brideservice societies is, as already noted, the distinction between securely married men and unmarried or insecurely married men, but it rests on a deeper inequality between men's and women's obligations.[11] Because women are obliged to feed families, married men live very different lives from bachelors, even though all hunters have the same obligation to share their meat widely. Whereas bachelors are condemned to live on the outskirts of groups and eat irregularly, married men can live in the center of camp and enjoy a regular diet. Once a man has a wife to sleep beside him at night and provide sexual services on demand, other married men no longer regard his presence as threatening. And once a man has a wife to keep his fire and build his shelter, he acquires a place in the camp that permits him to become an effective social actor. With a wife, a man can play the role of host and invite other men to share the food, the shelter, and occasionally the sexual services provided by his wife. A man with a wife can expect to be heard in public gatherings because, as a man with something to lose, his words carry more weight than the words of a bachelor. And because a man with a wife has all his daily needs provided, he can devote his time to building the exchange networks that enhance social influence.

Although the inequality between bachelors and married men is culturally marked, marriage is actually a slow process rather than an event because girls resist settling down. For girls, marriage brings restrictions without new privileges, because a girl who begins living with her husband does not acquire any greater access to male products than she enjoyed while living with her parents,[12] and she acquires a husband who not only expects to be fed every day but also resents her sexual

---

[11]Men's and women's productive obligations are unequal because although both sexes provide needed foods, women must feed families every day of their adult lives, whereas men do not hunt every day, and more of a man's meat becomes available for exchange, gift, or the manipulation of social relations as his parents-in-law grow old and die. Men and women are also unequal because women in brideservice societies are "never in a position to fail [Siskind, 1973: 128]," and therefore never in a position to be recognized as successful. Women are never "dependent" like bachelors, but, on the other hand, they can never become "independent" like securely married men.

[12]As mothers-in-law, women do enjoy privileged access to the products of sons-in-law. It seems no accident, therefore, that women exhibit the least resistance to marriage in Australian societies where women acquire same-age or older sons-in-law (husbands of their unborn daughters) at the time they begin living with their own (often aged) husbands.

affairs with other men. Hoebel reports, for example, that Comanche brides often resisted marriage by refusing to work or by running off with lovers (1940: 73). Because girls in brideservice societies resist assuming adult responsibilities, men actually marry by obtaining the cooperation of an eligible girl's kin. Marriage thus begins as a relationship between a groom and his wife's relatives, in which a groom justifies being around his bride by doing what his in-laws tell him and by bringing gifts to his wife's kin. In Comanche society, for example, suitors brought gifts to an eligible girl's brother, father, or guardian, and "in a few cases a boy was known to work (hunt or raid) for the family of the girl he wanted for a wife for as much as one, two, or three years [Wallace and Hoebel, 1952: 134]."

Although men in brideservice societies never stop tendering gifts and services to the parents of women they claim as wives, relations between a man and his wife's parents change over time, because a groom gradually becomes less dependent on his in-laws as his marriage becomes secure. The relation between a man and his in-laws thus undergoes gradual changes as a man passes from being dependent on his in-laws' consent to remain near his bride, through the point at which a man no longer needs his in-laws' approval to stay with his wife, to a final stage when a man's parents-in-law are either dead or dependent on his good will to remain near their daughter. This final stage usually coincides with the period when a man's own daughters are attracting suitors, and so it marks the high point of a man's social influence. Women's power also peaks at this stage of the life cycle, for it is as mothers-in-law that women gain privileged access to male products. A Comanche man may have been obliged to give the best part of his meat to his wife's father, but I suspect his wife delivered the meat to her mother.

This organization of production explains three facts Fried notes about the political systems of "egalitarian" societies:

1. "It is difficult, in ethnographies of simple egalitarian societies, to find cases in which an individual tells one or more others, 'Do this,' [whereas] the literature is replete with examples of individuals saying the equivalent of 'If this is done, it will be good,' possibly or possibly not followed by somebody else doing it [1967: 83]."
2. "While men in these societies do not seem to display any drive for universal dominance within their groups, they do display a considerable drive to achieve parity, or at least to establish a status that announces 'don't fool with me' [1967: 79]."
3. "Sexual tensions are the cause of much of the conflict" that occurs (1967: 75).

Put into the theoretical framework being used in this chapter, Fried's observations touch on the amount and kind of power available to leaders (the ability to give only advice, not orders), social values (a drive to achieve parity), and "causes" of conflict (sexual tensions). Each of these will be considered in turn.

SOCIAL CONTROL IN BRIDESERVICE SOCIETIES

Political leaders in brideservice societies have little power[13] except over their own insecure sons-in-law. Mature polygynous men with several sons-in-law may serve as focuses for group cooperation, but such leaders cannot give orders because they have no means of either rewarding or sanctioning other men who are securely married. At the same time, the power mature men have over insecure sons-in-law is purely negative in that fathers-in-law cannot reward obedience but can only punish disobedience by sending erring sons-in-law away. It is little wonder, therefore, that leaders in brideservice societies appear so reluctant to tell others what to do. Hoebel, for example, reports that Comanche peace chiefs played an active role "in situations where the problem was a question of what *ought* to be done," but peace chiefs lacked the power to give orders (1940: 19).

The unavailability of power in brideservice societies may explain why men "do not seem to display any drive for universal dominance within their groups," but the unavailability of power cannot entirely account for why men should "display a considerable drive to achieve parity [Fried, 1967: 79]." An examination of the male life cycle, however, suggests that the parity for which men strive is the position available to securely married men whose wives feed them and whose in-laws cannot send them away. Such men need never ask for anything because their wives furnish all their daily requirements, and although such men continue to provide gifts and services for in-laws, the fact that in-laws can no longer send them away causes the gifts and services to take on a different meaning from the gifts and services tendered by bachelors and

---

[13]The concept of "power" I use is drawn from Emerson (1962), who defines power as a relationship in which the power available to one party is a function of another's "need." I find Emerson's formulation useful because it suggests that the amount of power generally available in a social system is a function of the efficiency of those mechanisms that act to put some people into the position of needing what others can provide. In brideservice societies, little power is available to leaders because securely married men need nothing. Leaders in bridewealth societies, in contrast, have more power available to them because even securely married men need valuables in order to collect dependents in their households.

insecurely married men. The gifts of a man who cannot be sent away testify to his generosity, whereas the gifts of an insecurely married man testify only to his need. The parity for which men strive is thus a state of independence that takes its meaning from the visible dependence of bachelors and insecurely married men.

"Sexual tensions" appear to lie at the heart of most conflicts between men because the parity for which men strive is, in the end, the status of being securely married. In a social world where a man needs a wife, and nothing else, to achieve the most culturally valued status available in his society, relations among men are organized through men's claims in women. All conflicts between men—whatever their precipitating cause—can thus be interpreted as being over women, because only men's relations with women have consequences for relations among men.[14] Hence, in brideservice societies people fight primarily over sex.

Although all conflicts between men, whatever the precipitating cause, can be interpreted as being over women, what is at stake in such conflicts is not so much the contestants' claims in any particular woman as the ability of each contestant to maintain a status that announces "don't fool with me." In brideservice societies, a man's ability to enjoy the parity all men desire depends on his having a wife to feed and care for him, but because both marriages and health are frail, a man's ability to maintain equality with other men is experienced as resting less on his ability to claim any particular woman than on his ability to defend any claims in women he cares to make. The man who develops a reputation for letting others "fool" with him becomes vulnerable to having whatever woman he tries to claim seduced by others, whereas the man who maintains a reputation for fighting to keep whatever he claims as his can afford to give away troublesome, adulterous, or lazy wives because others believe he can keep any woman he wishes to keep. Conflicts between men are thus experienced as status challenges, a fact clearly expressed by Hoebel when he notes that for the Comanche, "adultery and taking another man's wife were direct attacks upon the prestige of the wife's husband . . . , which could not be ignored by the man who would maintain enough face to make life liveable [1940: 50]."

Because conflicts between men are experienced as status challenges, a challenged man's actions are interpreted as revealing his ability to maintain a status that announces "don't fool with me." Hoebel, for example, reports that "cowardly" Comanche cuckolds responded very differently

[14]In brideservice societies, there are many kinds of disputes, including quarrels between spouses and fights between women over men, but only men's disputes over women receive the public attention accorded cases that potentially involve major social realignments.

from "brave" ones (1940: 51–53), but the point is not that "cowards" and "brave" men responded differently to being cuckolded. Rather, it is that Comanche classified men as "cowardly" or "brave" on the basis of actions they took when other men challenged their claims in women. In brideservice societies, the cuckold who would maintain a status that announces "don't fool with me" must assert parity with his challenger by confronting his challenger man to man or by taking from his challenger the equivalent of what his challenger took from him.

It is in this light that I understand the reported prevalence of "contests," or forms of regulated combat, in brideservice societies. Not only do leaders lack power to impose settlements but also status, not women or goods, is the central issue. In brideservice societies, contests are ideally encounters both sides can win. Contests should permit both men to show the aggressiveness necessary for each to establish a status that announces "don't fool with me," because contestants must be proclaimed equal if there is to be any hope of future peace. Were one man to "lose" a contest, for example, peace would be impossible because that man must strive to achieve parity by demonstrating his capacity for violence. Therefore, in brideservice societies, leaders' interventions frequently take the form of ensuring that both sides fight fairly (see Chagnon, 1968: 95).

Because conflicts between men in brideservice societies are experienced as status confrontations, *the conflict-management procedures of such societies do not provide a forum for the development and articulation of social rules.* When conflict erupts, people focus their attention on the relative bravery or aggressiveness of contestants, not on the abstract merits of their cases. They come to understand their world as one where relations between people are based on personal prowess. Hoebel, for example, reports that among Comanche "personal power was the recognized basis of social relations between men [1954: 137]." It is little wonder, therefore, that ethnographers describe bands as having few social rules. Not only are people in bands unable to recite lists of rules to visiting ethnographers but also, when asked about particular conflicts, people are more likely to report on the prowess of contestants than to talk about rights and wrongs.

Because people in brideservice societies tend to picture themselves as living in a world where prowess, not rules, determines social relations, they also tend to picture themselves as living in a world where what each person has must be acquired alone and defended with violence if need be. For example, Hoebel writes that among Comanche, *"ability* to possess was 'nine points of the law' [1940: 66]." It is no accident, therefore, that people in brideservice societies are described both as willing to give things away and as reluctant to assert claims in things or land. In a world where defense of any claim may involve violence, no sensible person asserts more claims in things than he or she is willing to defend.

Finally, it is in this context that I understand brideservice people's frequent use of avoidance or group dispersal for handling conflicts. In a world where people experience conflict as leading inevitably to violence, people are naturally reluctant to fight with, and perhaps kill, others they care about. In brideservice societies, people who feel angry go off by themselves; spouses who quarrel separate; and kinspeople who cannot get along together move apart. *People in brideservice societies would rather separate than fight* (Turnbull, 1968).

Although ethnographers who write about the dispute-handling procedures of brideservice societies tend to focus on dramatic contests and avoidance practices, brideservice peoples have at least two other widely reported mechanisms for avoiding or handling conflicts: *Individuals practice restraint, and people intervene in the quarrels of others.* The Kalahari Bushmen of southern Africa, for example, are famous for restraining themselves because they fear anger will "burst out of all control" and lead to fights with poisoned arrows, for which they have no antidote (Marshall, 1976: 280). Brideservice peoples in general, however, tend to fear showing anger or taking any action that might provoke resistance from others. Brideservice peoples not only give away objects to avoid having to defend them but also avoid making requests of others for fear others will refuse, and they avoid taking actions that might circumscribe another's freedom of choice for fear of provoking resistance. Hence, leaders seldom give orders, and little or no public recognition is accorded to the point at which a man and woman begin living together as husband and wife.

People in brideservice societies also actively intervene in the quarrels of others. When a man is angry, others may shun him, thus leaving him by himself, or they may hide his weapons to prevent him from harming anyone. And when a fight does break out, other people intervene, either to separate the fighters or to make sure they fight fairly. Angry men in brideservice societies can thus reach for their weapons with the reasonable assurance that other people will prevent them from having to kill their opponents. The very conflict-management procedures of brideservice societies thus permit men to act out the violence that lends credence to their folk belief that conflict leads inevitably to bloodshed.

BRIDEWEALTH

Although men in many societies validate their marriages by presenting gifts to brides' kin, the kind of societies I call bridewealth lack social mechanisms for passing advantages down generations (as happens in ranked societies) or for maintaining a system of statuses with unequal economic prerogatives (as happens in chiefdoms with "offices"). In particular, the kind of societies I call bridewealth are ones in which production takes place within households that vary in numbers of working adults and hence in productivity. In nineteenth-century Cheyenne society, for example:

> The general custom of matrilocal residence gave rise to an extended domestic family . . . consisting of a man and his wife, their married daughters and husbands, their unmarried sons, their daughters' children, and any adopted or dependent relatives. The Cheyenne called such a group a "camp" and usually named it after the male head of the family. While each elementary family in the camp occupies a separate lodge, the camp represents an economic unit. The sons-in-law assist in the hunting and work; food is prepared in the mother's lodge, each daughter taking her share to her own lodge where each elementary family eats as a unit [Eggan, 1955: 61].

Although there is no evidence to suggest how widely Cheyenne production units varied in size, there is evidence that Cheyenne camps varied in prestige (Hoebel, 1960: 29). And it seems reasonable to assume that the most prestigious camps were those with many workers, because parents of several working children would find it easier to maintain the well-stocked central lodge Hoebel describes as characteristic of a "good" family (1960: 29), and to exhibit the continuous generosity expected of a Cheyenne peace chief.

In bridewealth societies, adolescents and young adults work for household heads because such heads control the valuables young people need to validate their marriages, and so to set up households of their own.[15] Young men, in particular, tend to work for seniors who can negotiate for them with senior kin of eligible brides. This need for marriage-validating goods shapes men's and women's life cycles. In bridewealth societies, young men do not wander in search of brides. Rather, they work within the households of seniors (usually parents) who first can help them marry and then can negotiate with their in-laws for the return of unhappy brides who flee to natal kin. In most bridewealth societies, young couples spend the first few years of married life living with and working for those seniors who negotiated their marriage, but young adults gradually experience a growing freedom from seniors' control as those seniors who supported them grow old and die and as a couple's own growing children consume more of their produce. Finally, as they receive valuables from senior kin of daughters' suitors and com-

---

[15]This account of why juniors work for seniors is both oversimplified and ultimately wrong, but it is adequate for the limited purposes of this chapter.

mand the labor of young men who hope for help in marrying, parents of adolescents and young adults become creditors and managers instead of debtors and workers. Because in bridewealth societies, marriage-validating valuables pass directly between the senior kin of bride and groom, juniors have no means of acquiring valuables except by working for seniors and seniors acquire the valuables they need for rewarding juniors who work for them.

Although most people in bridewealth societies pass from working for others through a stage of growing independence finally to become household heads who direct the labor of juniors, not all young people turn into equally successful elders. Rather, young people become differentiated according to ability and luck long before they become household heads. Those juniors who work hard, have luck, and show intelligence attract attention and favors from seniors, whereas those who are lazy, unlucky, or lacking in intelligence receive little notice. Extra support from seniors, in the form of valuables, enables hardworking young men to acquire more desirable, and more, brides, to obtain specialized ritual knowledge,[16] and to begin lending valuables to people in other households. Over time, then, some men acquire many wives and children to work for them, learn how to perform rituals for personal and community benefit, and acquire many debtors in other households. Such men become community leaders because, in contrast to less successful elders, their large households, extensive ritual knowledge, and many debtors enable them to gather together the large quantities of goods and large numbers of people needed to stage important ceremonies, conduct organized warfare, and engage in interregional trade.[17]

This organization of production explains three characteristics commonly noted about acephalous tribal societies: (a) the existence of re-

---

[16]In many, if not most, bridewealth societies, acquiring ritual knowledge is like acquiring a bride in that both are validated with gifts of valuables, and both permit their possessor to later claim valuables from others. In bridewealth societies, religion, like kinship, acts to ensure the neediness of juniors and the ability of seniors to provide the valuables juniors need. Legal systems also have the same effect, in that unmarried juniors commit most of the wrongs (elopements, seductions, and adulteries), thus ensuring their need for valuables to compensate victims who, as fathers and husbands, are already married men.

[17]Sahlins (1963) suggests that "big men" in Melanesia gain access to many goods by giving away fewer goods than they receive from others. Sahlins thus locates inequality in the sphere of exchange. I, on the other hand, locate inequality in the sphere of production. In my view, big men acquire goods not by finessing the ideal of reciprocity between kin, but rather by collecting many workers in their household production units. Similarly, big men's power is limited, not by the revolutionary proclivities of cheated exchange partners, but rather by the fact that household production units dissolve on the death or senility of their founders. In bridewealth societies, wealth cannot be inherited.

spected leaders variously described as "lineage elders," "notables," "big men," "faction leaders," or even "chiefs"; (b) "generosity" as the prime qualification for political leadership; and (c) conflicts centering on valuables and women, often discussed in terms of "debt." These observations touch on the amount and kind of power available to leaders, social values, and causes of conflict.

SOCIAL CONTROL IN BRIDEWEALTH SOCIETIES

In bridewealth societies, leaders can give orders as well as advice because leaders have the ability to reward others for compliance. Young men need valuables in order to marry, and middle-aged household heads also need valuables in order to help their dependents marry and acquire ritual knowledge. Sahlins describes Melanesian "big men" as faction leaders who, in competition with other leaders, acquire followers by "providing informal private assistance to people of a locale [1963: 291]," and this description fits leaders in all bridewealth societies, even those called by terms suggesting an ascribed status or office, such as "lineage elder," "peace chief," or "village headman." At the same time, leaders in bridewealth societies may be recognized as ritual specialists who, like Cheyenne peace chiefs, "know" how to run the universe and so have recognized authority to tell others what to do. But leaders in bridewealth societies, like their counterparts in brideservice ones, lack the power to punish others. Leaders cannot inflict bodily harm on others or deprive others of what they require to survive because, in a political system where "leadership is a creation of followership [Sahlins, 1963: 290]," all followers (except a few publicly recognized "bad lots") can obtain aid from rivals of former patrons.

Generosity is the most valued behavior in bridewealth societies because it is visibly how leaders become leaders by collecting followers. Successful leaders accumulate working juniors in their households by "generously" providing the valuables necessary for validating juniors' marriages, and successful leaders acquire followers in other households by "generously" lending household heads the valuables those heads need to provide for resident juniors. For example, Hoebel describes the personal requirements for chiefly status in Cheyenne society as

> an even-tempered good nature, energy, wisdom, kindliness, concern for the well-being of others, courage, generosity, and altruism. These traits express the epitome of the Cheyenne ideal personality. In specific behavior this means that a tribal chief gives constantly to the poor. "Whatever you ask of a chief, he gives it to you. If

someone wants to borrow something of a chief, he gives it to that person outright"
[1960: 37].[18]

In Cheyenne society, as among Comanche, the most valued behavior could be practiced only by men who had achieved the highest status available in their society, for just as Comanche men aspired to the parity enjoyed by securely married men, so Cheyenne men aspired to the generosity that could be exhibited only by men who headed production units large enough to produce more goods than were needed for supporting household members. And just as the parity desired by men in brideservice societies takes its meaning from the visible dependence of bachelors and insecurely married men, so in bridewealth societies the generosity exhibited by political leaders takes its meaning from the inability of youths and heads of small households either to give valuables away or to return equivalent valuables for those received from parents or patrons. In bridewealth societies, exchanges of valuables publicly establish the relative status of, and the relationship between, giver and receiver. To receive "outright" without hope of making any return is to admit social failure—an inability to initiate or maintain social relationships. To receive as a child receives from a parent is to accept a child's obligation to obey the parent. And to receive with the expectation of making a direct, equivalent return is to accept only temporary inferiority. In most bridewealth societies there is no clear distinction between gifts and loans because it is often in the interest of those who transfer valuables to others to define such transfers as gifts, thus defining the receiver as one who is either a social failure or a child who owes unquestioning obedience. Receivers, in contrast, often define such transfers as loans, thus defining themselves as owing only a finite amount of goods or a specific set of services.

Men in bridewealth societies quarrel over both women and valuables because the system of social inequality rests on the need of young men for valuables to validate their marriages, and so to acquire, vis à vis other men, rights in the labor and products of women and their children. In bridewealth societies, valuables and men's rights in women are not just interchangeable but actual equivalents, because it is through exchanges of valuables that men validate rights in women just as it is by establishing rights in women that men justify claiming valuables from other men

[18]From *The Cheyennes: Indians of the Great Plains,* 2nd ed., by E. Adamson Hoebel. Copyright © 1960 by Holt, Rinehort and Winston, Inc. Copyright © 1978 by Holt, Rinehart and Winston. Reprinted by permission of Holt, Rinehart and Winston.

who enjoy those women's sexual, domestic, or reproductive services. In bridewealth societies, all conflicts between men, whatever their precipitating cause, can be phrased as being over rights in women or valuables because all relations between men are organized in terms of exchanges. It is the inability of never-married men to claim rights in either women or valuables that puts them in the position of owing obedience to seniors who provide for them, just as it is ever-married men's expectation of acquiring both valuables and rights in future daughters that enables them to define others' "gifts" as "loans" that will be repaid. In other words, men's conflicts over women in bridewealth societies, like men's conflicts over women in brideservice ones, are less about men's relations with women than about men's relations with other men.

Brideservice and bridewealth societies, however, have very different idioms for understanding men's relations with other men. In brideservice societies, a man experiences his ability to enjoy parity with other men as resting on his ability to maintain a status that announces "don't fool with me," whereas in bridewealth societies, a man experiences his ability to establish relations with other men as resting on his control of valuables. In bridewealth societies, conflicts are understood not as challenges to the status of some individual man, but rather as calling into question the nature of a *relationship* between two or more specific people. In particular, the act of taking something, especially a woman, from another man has a very different meaning in brideservice and bridewealth societies. In brideservice societies, adultery and wife stealing call into question the *victim's* ability to maintain a status that announces "don't fool with me." In bridewealth societies, adultery and wife stealing call into question the *offender's* ability to initiate or maintain relationships with others because, in taking something from another person, the offender establishes a relationship with his victim in which the victim, as someone who has given something to someone else, has claims on the body or valuables of the offender. This contrast in what similar acts mean is dramatically illustrated by differences between Comanche and Cheyenne expectations of who should take action in cases of adultery or wife stealing. In Comanche society a cuckold "was under social obligation to take action against the offender. For a man not to do so was not looked upon as an act of social grace; indeed, such behavior was a social disgrace. A man so acting was stamped not as magnanimous, but as lily-livered [Hoebel, 1940: 50]." In Cheyenne society, in contrast, offenders were expected to make the first move. A man whose wife had been stolen by another was expected to wait patiently until approached by an "emissary, usually a tribal chief [who] came from the aggressor bearing the [peace] pipe and, (a) bringing horses or other goods acceptable to a man, or (b) asking the husband what he desired in the way of settlement [Llewellyn and Hoebel, 1941: 201]." In both Comanche and Cheyenne societies, then, the person whose ability to establish relationships with others had been cast into doubt was expected to initiate settlement procedures. In Comanche society this person was the victim, whereas in Cheyenne society it was the offender.[19]

This contrast between Comanche and Cheyenne procedures for handling cases of adultery and wife stealing also illustrates that in brideservice societies, where conflicts are experienced as status challenges, contestants must confront one another or be labeled "cowards," whereas in bridewealth societies, where conflicts are experienced as incomplete exchanges, conflicts can be—and ordinarily are— handled by people other than the disputants themselves, usually by seniors who have the valuables necessary for completing exchanges.[20] In Cheyenne society, for example, dispute-handling procedures usually involved "the sacrifice of wealth and gain of prestige by an interceding person [Llewellyn and Hoebel, 1941: 125]."

Many anthropologists who write about bridewealth societies report that people in them recognize "collective responsibility," in which all members of an offender's kin group become liable for a wrong committed by one. The point, however, is less that kin group membership defines liability than that liability defines kin group membership. In bridewealth societies, whoever pays compensation to the victim of another's wrong can, by claiming to have assumed a father's responsibility toward an offender, claim obedience (i.e., labor) from the offender. Just as in brideservice societies all of a cuckold's actions are interpreted as revealing his ability to maintain a status that announces "don't fool with

[19]There are other striking differences between the conflict-management procedures of brideservice and bridewealth societies. People in bridewealth societies, for example, usually distinguish between elopements and adultery, with elopement being an offense against the bride's kin and adultery being an offense against her husband. People in brideservice societies, in contrast, recognize only adultery. If a girl runs off with her lover, nothing is done unless a man who has been giving gifts to the girl's parents decides to take offense. It seems no accident, therefore, that Hoebel (1940) reports no elopement cases for the Comanche, whereas several are reported for the Cheyenne (Llewellyn and Hoebel, 1941). Similarly, people in bridewealth societies usually have recognized procedures by which a man whose wife has returned to her natal kin may negotiate with his in-laws for her recovery. In brideservice societies, the return of a bride to her natal kin precipitates a case only if her husband treats her desertion as adultery, either by accusing his in-laws of incest or by challenging the man he suspects of planning to move in with his wife.

[20]The Comanche "champion-at-law" is a famous figure in legal anthropology, but in Comanche society, the man who accepted help from a champion publicly admitted his own cowardice.

me," so in bridewealth societies all actions taken by an offender and his kin are interpreted as defining relationships within the offender's kin group. An offender able to compensate his own victim can avoid being placed in the position of a son who owes obedience. A senior who cannot pay compensation to a dependent's victim risks losing his dependent to another senior. And an offender for whom no one will pay compensation becomes an outcast, for he or she is, by definition, a person without kin and thus a person whom others may kill or enslave without risk of vengeance.

It is in this context that I understand the observation that *people in bridewealth societies tend to handle disputes by initiating warfare or negotiations rather than by moving away.* Not only are leaders able to initiate warfare or negotiations because they have the followers and valuables necessary for doing so, but because conflicts are defined as incomplete exchanges people experience conflicts as enduring until exchanges are completed. *Moving away is no solution to conflict in bridewealth societies,* as it is in brideservice ones. Rather, people who move away are viewed only as waiting for the appropriate moment to attack or initiate negotiations— even if the waiting lasts for generations.[21]

Because conflicts in bridewealth societies are viewed as incomplete exchanges, the conflict-management procedures of bridewealth societies provide a forum for the development and articulation of social norms. In the process of justifying resort to warfare or of negotiating settlement terms, leaders must discuss the relationship between what was done and what is owed. As a result, *bridewealth peoples tend to have well-developed sets of norms, covering both the obligations owed between people in long-standing relationships and the compensatory payments owed for particular wrongful acts.* The well-developed norms of bridewealth societies, however, are not rules that determine the content of settlements. Rather, such norms serve only as counters for negotiating settlement terms, which, in the end, reflect not norms but rather "the distribution of bargaining power between the two parties [Gulliver, 1963: 300]."

[21]Readers familiar with Llewellyn and Hoebel's (1941: 136) description of Cheyenne chiefs as constituting a "High Court" in murder cases may be surprised by my portrayal of the Cheyenne as having handled conflicts by initiating warfare or negotiations between opposed kin groups. In my opinion, the Cheyenne resembled other "tribes without rulers" (Middleton and Tait, 1958) in that homicides within the jural community (i.e., the Cheyenne tribe) were settled by payment of compensation, even if a victim's kin distributed compensatory goods to the poor (see Llewellyn and Hoebel, 1941: 12–13), whereas homicides committed by people outside the jural community (i.e., by members of other tribes) provoked vengeance killings. In my opinion, Cheyenne chiefs were not judges; they were ritual leaders like the Nuer leopard-skin chief described by Evans-Pritchard (1940).

Reconciliation rituals, in which disputants and their supporters publicly affirm acceptance of settlement terms, are a particularly dramatic feature of conflict-management procedures in bridewealth societies. Llewellyn and Hoebel, for example, were deeply impressed by Cheyenne concern for obtaining unanimous consent to decisions and for rehabilitating offenders (1941: 336). These features, however, are common to most bridewealth societies. In such societies, all offenders are "rehabilitated" except for the very few who have so alienated everyone that no one steps forward to compensate their victims, and "unanimous consent" is required if settlement terms are to be accepted as ending a dispute. Because all acts of hostility are justified as counteractions to balance a previous wrong, only settlements publicly accepted by both sides can be interpreted as forestalling further conflict. Were only one side to accept settlement terms, the other could interpret those terms as having been imposed on it, and therefore either as a direct breach of norm or as a counteraction that is not justified because the action being countered was itself a counteraction for a previous breach. In other words, only a reconciliation ritual can end a potentially endless cycle of actions and counteractions (see Bohannan, 1957: 211), although, in reality, the ongoing processes of social life—as juniors struggle to free themselves from needing seniors' support while trying to support those junior to them—tend to unravel any particular settlement. In bridewealth societies, people often distinguish between "hearts" and "mouths" because experience teaches them that although "mouths" may speak of reconciliation and forgiveness, "hearts" tend to harbor thoughts of vengeance.

Ethnographers who write about the conflict-management procedures of bridewealth societies tend to focus on warfare, negotiations, and reconciliation rituals, but people in bridewealth societies do, like their counterparts in brideservice societies, practice self-restraint. When people in bridewealth societies practice restraint, however, they say they do so not because they fear offended others will react with violence, but rather because they do not want to establish undesirable relationships.

Finally, *gossip is often reported to be an important mechanism of social control in bridewealth societies.* In all societies people tell stories about the misdeeds of people who are not present, but gossip, like all social practices, has different consequences in different types of societies. In brideservice societies, gossip has few consequences for its male victims because personal prowess, as established in direct confrontations, determines the relationship one man has with others. In bridewealth societies, however, gossip can seriously harm its victim because if others believe the victim of gossip has committed some wrongful act, then those others may seek vengeance or compensation if they believe themselves harmed or they may break off relations with the victim if they believe the victim lacks control over the allocation of his or her labor and its products. In either case, gossip undermines its victim's ability to enter into, or continue, advantageous relationships with others. People in bridewealth societies thus justly condemn gossip as harmful activity—one for which compensation may be demanded—even as they actively practice it. In societies where experience teaches that "hearts" harbor desires not voiced by "mouths," sensible people both seek out and pass on to allies all the information about others they can obtain.

Conclusion

In this chapter, I have traced the relationship between the organization of inequality and processes of social control in two types of simple societies in order to illustrate my thesis that in any society people's ways of defining and responding to others' behavior are shaped by "folk models of social structure," which in turn are in turn shaped by people's experiences of the consequences their actions produce. In particular, I have suggested that *people who live in brideservice societies have few rules, fight primarily over sex, frequently resort to group dispersion, and occasionally stage contests,* not because people in brideservice societies lack things to fight over or find it easy to move away, but rather because such people have a social system in which young men earn wives for themselves and so need to incur no debts or obligations to other men once they are securely married. In brideservice societies, men experience their ability to enjoy parity with other men as resting on their capacity to maintain a status that announces "don't fool with me," and so people in brideservice societies interpret others' behavior as statements about individual bravery or prowess. Similarly, I suggested that *people in bridewealth societies have many rules, quarrel over both valuables and sex, handle conflicts by negotiations or warfare, and settle disputes by compensating victims,* not because such people lead more settled lives and have more material possessions to fight over, but rather because the need of young men for valuables to validate their marriages permits successful seniors to accumulate many working juniors in their households. In bridewealth societies, therefore, people experience their ability to initiate and maintain advantageous relationships with others as resting on their ability to be generous, and so people in bridewealth societies interpret others' behavior as statements about who owes what to whom.

Because this chapter focused on simple societies, where marriage organizes social inequality, perhaps I should conclude by briefly contrasting two folk models of social structure in complex societies where state structures are involved in the organization of inequality. In 1963, I spent 9 months in a small Spanish village, and for the past 4 years I have been cursorily analyzing "conflict diaries" written by students in my classes on legal anthropology at Stanford University.[22] Although I have not done serious research on conflict management in either Spain or California, I noticed that Spanish villagers in 1963 seemed more interested in actors' acts than intentions, whereas California college students barely mentioned acts but devoted considerable diary space to analyzing intentions, particularly their own. Put simplistically, Spanish villagers talked about conflict within the Mediterranean value system of "honor and shame" (Pitt-Rivers, 1966), in which family honor is assessed on the basis of family members' acts rather than their intentions, whereas California college students wrote about conflict within a value system of moral individualism, in which individuals—not families—are judged by their intentions rather than by acts (except as acts are taken as evidence of intentions). Spaniards and California college students thus used very different folk models of social structure for defining and responding to the behavior of others, as well as for justifying their own.

The different folk models of social structure used by Spanish villagers and California college students correlate with their experiences of social inequality. In 1963, the Spanish village was an inegalitarian community[23] in which each person's occupation and life-style depended on how much land had (or had not) been inherited from parents. People thus experienced their status relative to other villagers as resting on *who* they were: Challenges to a woman's chastity were challenges to her children's status as legitimate heirs, even as a system of partible inheritance ensured that, in practical terms, seducing a girl was equivalent to claiming a portion of her family's land. In the Spanish village, a family's ability to keep its land was experienced as resting on its ability to preserve its women's virtue, and that ability was judged on the basis of

---

[22] I am grateful to Laura Nader, who suggested having students keep conflict diaries. I presented a preliminary analysis of these diaries at the 1980 meetings of the American Anthropological Association.

[23] Actually, the Spanish village was a quite egalitarian community in 1963. It had neither hovels nor mansions, neither beggars nor large landowners—partly because the largest landholders lived elsewhere. The villagers also spoke of themselves as all belonging to one family, as all equally members of the "pueblo." Nevertheless, villagers experienced profound status differences. On occasion, poor villagers spoke bitterly of the "five rich families," and the community was, in fact, divided into three fuzzy-edged status groups: landless day laborers, people who worked their own land, and landowners who employed day laborers.

each family member's overt behavior—women's modest demeanor and men's quickness to sense and avenge insults—rather than on people's intentions.[24] California college students, in contrast, live surrounded by equals. American housing patterns ensure that most students grew up in economically homogeneous neighborhoods, and on campus only radical students make serious efforts to talk with janitors, kitchen help, security guards, or secretaries.[25] Students thus experience whatever differences they notice between themselves and others as resting on *what* they are: Differences in activities and possessions reflect differences in how individuals choose to allocate time and money, whereas differences in grades or other success, such as getting into medical or law school, are said to reflect differences in either innate intelligence or time spent studying, depending on whether success or failure is being justified. Because college students experience observed differences in activities and possessions as reflecting individuals' past choices, they quite logically try to predict future behavior by ascertaining individuals' intentions.

Although the daily experiences of Spanish villagers in 1963 and of California college students today correlate with their very different folk models of social structure, there is no sense in which their different conceptual frameworks can be viewed as original to the people I interviewed. Concern for family honor was once (and still is) widespread in Eurasia and northern Africa, and moral individualism is hardly a product of college campuses. A recent distinction by Wallerstein (1979: 5) between two types of complex societies may offer a framework for understanding how these two different folk models were forged. Wallerstein contrasts "world-empires," in which the state allocates economic resources, thus setting up status groups with differential privileges, with "world-economies," in which no single state controls the allocation of economic resources, thus leading—at least in modern times—to a system of states in which "core" countries enjoy "developed" economies, "peripheral" countries sink into "underdevelopment," and "semi-peripheral countries" mediate between the two. Because Wallerstein's "world-empires" and "core" countries in the modern world-economy correlate with Lenski's (1966) categories of "agrarian" and

[24]Spanish villagers did discuss people's intentions, but they did so in the context of deciding whether to feel pity for someone who was suffering the just and inevitable consequences of his or her acts, or of acts committed by another family member.

[25]In my classes, I introduce students to componential analysis by asking, "What kinds of people are there at Stanford?" Only one class, so far, has gone beyond listing kinds of students to include professors, administrators, secretaries, and librarians, but even that class did not include janitors, kitchen help, or gardeners.

"industrial" societies, respectively, Lenski's analysis of stratification processes in those societies can be used to understand how the organization of inequality shapes experiences in each. In particular, Lenski's (1966: 290) observation that downward mobility is the primary experience of people in all classes of agrarian societies suggests why people in such societies should be so concerned with "hanging on" to what they have—a concern for which family honor, as realized in a concern for female chastity, is a powerful metaphor. Similarly, that upward mobility has been the primary experience of people in all classes of industrialized core countries (Lenski, 1966: 415) suggests why individuals in such societies should be so concerned to discover their own and other's capacities and preferences. Finally, Foucault's (1977) analysis of how "judging the crime" gave way to "judging the criminal" in modernizing Europe provides a rich framework for understanding Spanish villagers' concern for acts and California students' concern for intentions, even as his analysis also illuminates the complex ways in which conceptual frameworks, and their associated power structures, organize processes of social control. It thus appears that the general approach I have followed in my analysis of simple societies has other possible applications.

ACKNOWLEDGMENTS

This version of the chapter has benefited from the comments of Donald Black, John Comaroff, Richard Lempert, Sally Engle Merry, Laura Nader, Michelle Rosaldo, June Starr, and Barbara Yngvesson.

References

Balikci, Asen
  1970 *The Netsilik Eskimo.* Garden City, N.Y.: Natural History Press.
Barkun, Michael
  1968 *Law without Sanctions.* New Haven, Conn.: Yale University Press.
Barton, Roy F.
  1919 *Ifugao Law.* Berkeley, Calif.: University of California Press, 1969.
Beidelman, Thomas O.
  1971 *The Kaguru.* New York: Holt, Rinehart and Winston.
Berndt, Ronald M.
  1965 "Marriage and the family in North-Eastern Arnhem Land." Pages 77–104 in *Comparative Family Systems,* edited by M. F. Nimkoff. Boston. Houghton Mifflin.
Bohannan, Paul
  1957 *Justice and Judgement among the Tiv.* London: Oxford University Press.
  1965 "The differing realms of the law." *American Anthropologist* 67 (pt. 2): 33–42.
Bourdieu, Pierre
  1977 *Outline of a Theory of Practice.* Cambridge: Cambridge University Press.

Briggs, Jean
    1970   *Never in Anger.* Cambridge, Mass.: Harvard University Press.
Chagnon, Napoleon A.
    1968   *Yanomamö, the Fierce People.* New York: Holt, Rinehart and Winston.
Chance, Norman
    1966   *The Eskimo of North Alaska.* New York: Holt, Rinehart and Winston.
Collier, Jane F.
    1973   *Law and Social Change in Zinacantan,* Stanford, Calif.: Stanford University Press.
    1977   "Political leadership and legal change in Zinacantan." *Law and Society Review* 11: 131–163.
    1979   "Stratification and dispute handling in two highland Chiapas communities." *American Ethnologist* 6: 305–328.
Collier, Jane F., and Michelle Z. Rosaldo
    1981   "Politics and gender in simple societies." Pages 275–329 in *Sexual Meanings,* edited by S. Ortner and H. Whitehead. New York: Cambridge University Press.
Colson, Elizabeth
    1962   *The Plateau Tonga: Social and Religious Studies.* Manchester: Manchester University Press.
Diamond, A. S.
    1935   *Primitive Law.* London: Watts.
    1951   *The Evolution of Law and Order.* London: Watts.
    1965   *The Comparative Study of Primitive Law.* London: Athlone Press.
DiMaggio, Paul
    1979   "Review essay: On Pierre Bourdieu." *American Journal of Sociology* 84: 1460–1474.
Downs, James
    1966   *The Two Worlds of the Washo.* New York: Holt, Rinehart and Winston.
Durkheim, Emile
    1893   *The Division of Labor in Society.* Glencoe, Ill.: Free Press, 1960.
Eggan, Fred
    1955   "The Cheyenne and Arapaho kinship system." Pages 35–98 in *Social Anthropology of North American Tribes,* edited by F. Eggan. Chicago: University of Chicago Press.
Emerson, Richard
    1962   "Power-dependence relations." *American Sociological Review* 27: 31–40.
Evans-Pritchard, E. E.
    1940   *The Nuer.* Oxford: Clarendon.
Fallers, Lloyd
    1969   *Law without Precedent.* Chicago: University of Chicago Press.
Foucault, Michel
    1977   *Discipline and Punish.* New York: Random House.
Fried, Morton
    1967   *The Evolution of Political Society.* New York: Random House.
Gluckman, Max
    1955   *The Judicial Process among the Barotse of Northern Rhodesia.* Manchester: Manchester University Press.
    1965   *Politics, Law and Ritual in Tribal Society.* New York: Mentor, 1968.
    1969   "Concepts in the comparative study of tribal law." Pages 349–373 in *Law in Culture and Society,* edited by Laura Nader. Chicago: Aldine Press.

Goldschmidt, Walter
    1967   *Sebei Law.* Berkeley, Calif.: University of California Press.
Grinnell, George B.
    1923   *The Cheyenne Indians,* vol. 1. New Haven, Conn.: Yale University Press.
Gulliver, Philip
    1963   *Social Control in an African Society.* Boston: Boston University Press.
    1971   *Neighbours and Networks.* Berkeley, Calif.: University of California Press.
Hart, C. W. M., and A. R. Pilling
    1960   *The Tiwi of North Australia.* New York: Holt, Rinehart and Winston.
Hoebel, E. Adamson
    1940   *The Political Organization and Law-Ways of the Comanche Indians.* American Anthropological Association Memoirs, No. 54.
    1954   *The Law of Primitive Man.* Cambridge, Mass.: Harvard University Press.
    1960   *The Cheyennes.* New York: Holt, Rinehart and Winston, 1978.
Hogbin, H. I.
    1934   *Law and Order in Polynesia.* London: Christophers.
Koch, Klaus-Friedrich
    1974   *War and Peace in Jalémó.* Cambridge, Mass.: Harvard University Press.
Kroeber, A. L.
    1926   "Yurok law." Pages 511–516 in *Proceedings of the 22nd International Congress of Americanists,* Rome.
Leach, E. R.
    1954   *Political Systems of Highland Burma.* New York: Beacon Press, 1965.
Lenski, Gerhard
    1966   *Power and Privilege.* New York: McGraw-Hill.
Llewellyn, Karl, and E. Adamson Hoebel
    1941   *The Cheyenne Way.* Norman, Okla.: University of Oklahoma Press.
Maine, Henry Sumner
    1861   *Ancient Law.* London: Murray.
Malinowski, Bronislaw
    1926   *Crime and Custom in Savage Society.* London: Routledge & Kegan Paul.
Marshall, Lorna
    1976   *The !Kung of Nyae Nyae.* Cambridge, Mass.: Harvard University Press.
Middleton, John, and David Tait
    1958   *Tribes without Rulers.* London: Routledge & Kegan Paul.
Moore, Sally Falk
    1969   "Introduction." Pages 337–348 in *Law in Culture and Society,* edited by Laura Nader. Chicago: Aldine Press.
    1970   "Law and anthropology." Pages 252–300 in *Biennial Review of Anthropology, 1969,* edited by Bernard Siegel. Stanford, Calif.: Stanford University Press.
Murphy, Yolanda, and Robert Murphy
    1974   *Women in the Forest.* New York: Columbia University Press.
Pitt-Rivers, Julian
    1966   "Honour and Social Status." Pages 19–77 in *Honour and Shame,* edited by J. G. Peristiany. Chicago: University of Chicago Press.
Pospisil, Leopold
    1958   *Kapauku Papuans and Their Law.* Yale University Publications in Anthropology, No. 54. New Haven, Conn.: Yale University Press.
Rattray, R. S.
    1929   *Ashanti Law and Constitution.* Oxford: Clarendon.

Richardson, Jane
  1940   *Law and Status among the Kiowa Indians.* Monographs of the American Ethnological Society, No. 1. New York: J. J. Augustin Publisher.
Roberts, Simon
  1979   *Order and Dispute.* New York: St. Martin's.
Rosaldo, Michelle Z.
  1980   *Knowledge and Passion.* New York: Cambridge University Press.
Sahlins, Marshall
  1963   "Poor man, rich man, big-man, chief: Political types in Melanesia and Polynesia." *Comparative Studies in Society and History* 5: 285–303.
  1968   *Tribesmen.* Englewood Cliffs, N.J.: Prentice-Hall.
  1972   *Stone Age Economics.* Chicago: Aldine Press.
Schapera, Isaac
  1938   *A Handbook of Tswana Law and Custom.* London: Oxford University Press.
Service, Elman
  1962   *Primitive Social Organization.* New York: Random House.
Siskind, Janet
  1973   *To Hunt in the Morning.* London: Oxford University Press.
Steward, Julian
  1938   *Basin-Plateau Aboriginal Sociopolitical Groups.* Bureau of American Ethnology Bulletin, No. 120 (U.S. Govt. Publication).
Thomas, Elizabeth M.
  1958   *The Harmless People.* New York: Knopf.
Turnbull, Colin
  1961   *The Forest People.* New York: Simon & Schuster.
  1968   "The importance of flux in two hunting societies." Pages 133–137 in *Man the Hunter,* edited by Richard Lee and Irvin DeVore. Chicago: Aldine Press.
van Velsen, J.
  1969   "Procedural informality, reconciliation, and false comparisons." Pages 137–152 in *Ideas and Procedures in African Customary Law, edited by Max Gluckman.* London: Oxford University Press.
Wallace, Ernest, and E. A. Hoebel
  1952   *The Comanches.* Norman, Okla.: University of Oklahoma Press.
Wallerstein, Immanuel
  1979   *The Capitalist World-Economy.* Cambridge: Cambridge University Press.
Warner, W. Lloyd
  1958   *A Black Civilization.* 2d edition. New York: Harper Brothers (1st edition, 1937).
Weiner, Annette
  1976   *Women of Value, Men of Renown.* Austin, Tex.: University of Texas Press.
Woodburn, James C.
  1968   "Stability and flexibility in Hadza residential groupings." Pages 103–110 in *Man the Hunter,* edited by Richard Lee and Irvin DeVore. Chicago: Aldine Press.

6

Social Control and Corporate Organization: A Durkheimian Perspective

ALBERT BERGESEN

In this chapter I want to discuss some general theoretical ideas about social control with particular attention being paid to the Durkheimian tradition of understanding the social functions of crime and religious ritual in maintaining social solidarity. I want to propose a general explanation for the activation of social control institutions in those situations where everyone agrees that no real crime has been committed. To do this I want to examine one of the most dramatic examples of the use of social control mechanisms in the absence of real crime: Political witch-hunts. First I will discuss some of the common characteristics of political witch-hunts and then propose an explanation that links Emile Durkheim's understanding of the social functions of crime and punishment with his understanding of the religious functions of rite and myth. The principal independent variable will be the organization of collectivities as corporate actors, and the heart of the argument will be that the more corporate the collectivity, the more it activates its institutions of social control for ritual persecutions.

The political crimes of interest here involve accusations of *plotting* to overthrow the government, *conspiring* with *foreign agents* and *disloyal elements* to "deliver the nation into the hands of the enemy," and engaging in *seditious* and *treasonous* activities of all kinds—in short, subversive activity. Crimes of this sort are accompanied by a sense that the society

141

TOWARD A GENERAL THEORY OF SOCIAL CONTROL
Volume 2: Selected Problems

is in some way *contaminated* and *polluted* (Douglas, 1966) and that a *collective cleansing* is required to *purify* the fabric of social life. As Inkeles observes, "When the inner taint is 'discovered' [referring to subversion], there is no solution but to cut out the infested part root and branch, to destroy the tainted carrier himself lest he soon infect all. Furthermore, the taint may be manifested not only in people, but by institutional forms, ideas, and systems of ideas [1968: 75]."

This collective outrage over *inner contamination* has taken different historical forms: the Jacobins during the French Revolution discovered a "Foreigners' Plot"; the Soviets during the 1930s discovered wreckers, saboteurs, and other counterrevolutionary elements and, like the Jacobins before them, proceeded to cleanse their society through purging purported subversive elements. Other examples would be the Chinese during the Great Cultural Revolution, who discovered their revolutionary society tainted by "bourgeois elements," "revisionists," and "capitalist roaders" (see Bergesen, 1978), or the Americans of the McCarthy era discovering their society polluted and contaminated with subversives.

Most sociological explanations deal with individual witch-hunting incidents, but not with the general process that might underlie them all. Although witch-hunts appear in quite diverse societies, from eighteenth-century France to twentieth-century United States, they all seem to share certain common characteristics, which provide a base for conceptualizing them as a singular social phenomenon and explaining them with a general explanation.

1. It appears that crimes of treason and sedition are not evenly distributed over the history of a nation. They seem to come in sudden dramatic outbursts. Although one-party socialist states seem recurrently to discover all sorts of subversion, it is by no means a steady rate of crime. There may be various sorts of minor purges occurring at all levels of the Party in a society such as the Soviet Union, for example, but the appearance of the large number of "traitors," "saboteurs," and "Trotskyites" during the Stalin purges represents a dramatic upsurge in the number of political deviants found. Similarly, the Cultural Revolution in China represents a dramatic increase in the volume of deviance in a society that seems to have experienced large numbers of political deviants to begin with. This sporadic nature of political witch-hunts is not limited to one-party socialist states, however. The American experience of McCarthyism or the discovery of a Foreigners' Plot during the French Revolution is very similar to the outbursts of subversion experienced by the Soviets and Chinese. In all these cases the society suddenly finds itself infested with all sorts of subversive elements. What this suggests is

that something out of the ordinary happens to these societies that results in the dramatic discovery of enemies from within.

2. These outbursts of deviance also seem to be accompanied by a great concern for the necessity of taking some action, as a pressing urgency seems to grip societies at this point. This urgency is quite similar to the definition of crime waves Erikson used in his study of witch-hunting in the Massachusetts Bay Colony: "In the sense that the term is being used here, 'crime wave' refers to a rash of publicity, a moment of excitement and alarm, a feeling that something needs to be done. It may or may not mean an actual increase in the volume of deviation [1966: 69]." This characterization is particularly appropriate for instances of "political crime waves," where a great sense of urgency is intimately connected with the feeling that the survival of the whole political community is at stake.

For example, the purported problem with Communist leanings, tendencies, sympathies, and so on, among university professors during the McCarthy period was not that they could have used their time better, or they wasted state funds, but rather they were subserting or undermining the values—and possibly the physical existance—of the nation as a whole. Similarly, the failure to meet economic plans by factory managers in socialist states (Bendix, 1956) is not just a matter of inefficiency, losing money, or poor planning, but a question of "sabotage" and an attack on the interests of the state and nation itself. The danger is always to national existence itself, and as such, of the utmost severity and urgency.

3. This discovery of seditious, treasonous, or disloyal elements that seems to come in waves and accompanied by a generalized alarm and fear that the goals and interests of the nation itself are being undermined is also accompanied by the identification of the most diverse, and at times seemingly nonpolitical, acts and actors as subversive. This is traditionally seen as a consequence of the hysterical nature of witch-hunts, where the hunting of enemies gets "out of control" and innocent groups come to be accused, tried, and punished for crimes they never committed.

This aspect of political witch-hunts is perhaps the most popularized and well known, and only a few examples are needed to make the point. For instance, during the French Reign of Terror "intelligence with the enemy" was a crime, but because much of the enemy was composed of émigrés living abroad, all sorts of innocuous correspondence with those who fled the country was defined as constituting treason. Antirepublican opinions were also considered seditious, and the discovery of royalist songs or material symbols such as a bust of Louis XVI, fleurs-de-lis, or white *cocardes* was taken as irrefutable evidence of anti-republican sentiment. Furthermore, complaints about the new regime or praise of the old order constituted seditious activity (Greer, 1935). Similarly, McCarthyism found threats to the country in the wording of a Girl Scout handbook (Bell, 1960), a play exploring thoughts of a conscientious objector, interest in the United Nations, civil liberties, and American foreign relations (Lazarsfeld and Theilens, 1958).

4. Finally, these outbursts seem to be handled with a maximum amount of social ritual. The concern is not with mere apprehension, or the thwarting of conspiratorial plots, but with the *dramatization of their danger*. One of the distinguishing characteristics of political witch-hunts is the public ritual dramatizing both the presence of danger and the apprehension and punishment of subversion. Public trials, printed confessions, investigating committees, and other degradation ceremonies are all elements in the drama of the modern witch-hunt. The presence of dramatic "show trials" during the Stalin purges, the televised McCarthy hearings, and the roving bands of Red Guards authorized to purify the party bureaucracy in China lead one to believe that the central concern of a witch-hunt is more with demonstrating the presence of danger to national security than in actually ferreting out real enemies.

Some Explanations of Political Witch-Hunts

The largest body of literature links the purge and political terror of one-party states to various theories of totalitarian regimes. Most discussions of the political purge examine particular cases such as the Cultural Revolution (Bridgham, 1967, 1968, 1970; Gray and Cavendish, 1968: Lifton, 1968; Baum and Bennett, 1971) or the various Soviet purges (e.g., Brzezinski, 1956; Conquest, 1968).

Theories of totalitarianism begin with the assumption that these states have a ruling elite intent on massive social transformations that require the total control of institutional life. The purge is thus seen as part of the "arsenal of the state."

PURGES AND THE MAINTENANCE OF
A RULING ELITE

The most general explanation centers on the function of the purge in maintaining the security and power of elites by eliminating real enemies and terrorizing potential enemies through the punishment of imaginary conspirators. For Brzezinski (1956), the more totalitarian a system, the more isolated the ruling elite, and this isolation leads to suspicion of potential enemies, which in turn results in periodic purges. The purge also becomes a rational instrument for the "atomization" of the general society, preventing alternative sources of power from developing and keeping the general population in a state of constant fear. Purges, according to this reasoning, provide scapegoats for regime failures. The lack of institutional procedures for political succession and the lack of pluralistic institutional power arrangements that could impede the acquisition of total power are often mentioned as reasons for elite insecurity and the subsequent use of the purge to maintain political power.

POLITICAL TERROR AND SOCIAL MOBILIZATION

A second explanation roots the purge in the more or less rational intent of political elites to achieve massive social change (Dallin and Breslauer, 1970). Here it is thought that rapid industrialization or the collectivization of agriculture generates a certain amount of resistance, with the purge serving as a means for eliminating this blockage.

RELEASE OF STRAIN

It has also been argued by Inkeles (1950) that one of the latent functions of the purge is to provide an institutional mechanism for the release of strain that builds up in a closely regulated society. Self-criticism and public confessions by party and government bureaucrats give the people some sense of having control over their public officials and as such function as a device for releasing tension and channeling aggression. Purges, it is further suggested, act as a functional equivalent of elections by providing the periodic removal of party or government officials. The mobility built into more democratic systems, it is argued, is in some way attained through the instrument of the political purge.

McCarthyism and Status Politics

The theory of status politics, as an explanation for various American protest and reform movements, such as the Progressive (Hofstadter, 1955), Temperance, and Prohibition (Gusfield, 1963) movements and the "radical right" of the early 1950s (Lipset, 1955; Bell, 1964), has also been applied to the McCarthy period (Bell, 1960). The argument is that these movements represent responses to the transformation of America from a basically rural, agrarian, and politically decentralized nation to an urban, industrial, and politically centralized state. This social transformation created strains for different groups that found their "status position," as opposed to their economic or class location, being undermined and replaced by new groups and new standards. These status groups share little else except their common predicament of being, in Bell's words, "dispossessed." They range from small businessmen resenting increased government controls to small-town Protestant America, which found its values giving way to urban life and metropolitan culture.

The application of this reasoning to McCarthyism has been made by Bell, who argues that the anti-Communism theme of these movements represents symbolic objects on whom displaced status groups can vent their anger. The fear of Communists and their suspected location in the State Department, or in elite universities such as Harvard symbolize the larger social transformation to an urban metropolitan society. The status-politics argument, though, centers on explaining why various groups support anti-Communist movements rather than focusing on the question of why the nation as a whole should be so preoccupied with rooting out subversion. Because much of the witch-hunting was initiated by the state (House Un-American Activities Committee, Senator McCarthy), explanations that do not include these political agencies miss a good part of this hysterical anti-Communism.

Toward a New Theory of Political Crime

Before advancing an alternative explanation, I want to comment briefly on some of the shortcomings and difficulties with the formulations I have just reviewed.

The common theme running through both the explanation of the totalitarian purge and McCarthyism is that these events are irrational outbursts or paranoid fabrications by isolated ruling elites and "dispossessed" status groups. The supposed presence of traitors, "Communists," "revisionists," "capitalist roaders," "royalists," and other political heretics becomes reduced to the projections and fantasies of various groups under some kind of strain. The burden of explanation is shifted to accounting for why particular groups would engage in such irrational behavior, giving us theories about changing status institutions (the status-politics explanation) and the structural isolation of ruling elites (the totalitarian explanation).

These perspectives leave two aspects of political witch-hunts untouched. First, why does the society as a whole experience a sudden increase in political deviance? To answer this means turning away from viewing political hysteria as the property of particular groups or as the creation of a political elite and focusing on the national collectivity as a whole. Second, the substance of these crimes must be taken seriously and explained sociologically, not just dismissed as fabrications useful for political persecution or paranoid projections. The ritual, pomp, hysteria, drama, and terror of witch-hunts are their defining characteristics, and as such require a substantive explanation.

The Boundary Crisis Hypothesis

One such explanation derives from Emile Durkheim's (1893) understanding of the social functions of crime and moral deviance. For Durkheim, crime is not a social problem but a "normal" aspect of society. The designation by the community (society) of some action as morally deviant has the positive function of drawing the community together and reaffirming its social solidarity. "Crime brings together upright consciences and concentrates them. We have only to notice what happens, particularly in a small town, when some moral scandal has just been committed. They stop each other on the street, they visit each other, they seek to come together to talk of the event and to wax indignant in common [Durkheim, 1893: 102]." For Durkheim, crime was behavior that "offended the common conscience," and hence the collective reaction by the community and its agencies of social control. The function of designating behavior as crime is to redefine ritually the substance of the moral order that those acts transgress. This interpretation of crime and social control has become the cornerstone for a sociological analysis of moral deviance, particularly "victimless crimes" such as drinking, homosexuality, prostitution, and drug use.

The Durkheimian perspective on the normality of deviance and its positive functions in reaffirming the social order has been advanced by Kai Erikson (1966) in two important ways. He suggests that (a) if the designation of certain actions as deviant serves a positive function, then—other things being equal—we should expect a relatively constant volume of deviance within a community; and (b) if there is a sudden increase in the volume of deviance, we can assume that it is the result of some crisis in the community's sense of collective identity. Specifically, if the community experiences a threat to its social boundaries, what he calls a "boundary crisis," we should expect the community to manufacture a certain volume of deviance (persecuting people for crimes they did not commit) to reestablish the impaired, blurred, or threatened social boundary.

This formulation represents a significant advance over the original Durkheim proposition, which we can better understand by examining the relationship between three variables: human behavior, moral rules, and societal reactions (usually in the form of action taken by institutions of social control). In the original Durkheim position, the moral rules remain fixed and are transgressed by human behavior, which then results in these acts being defined as criminal or deviant. The society reacts when someone violates its moral rules, and the reaction is a means of reaffirming the moral rule in question, as punishment points out to the community just what the moral order is about. As such, punishment, and hence institutions of social control, functions to reaffirm collective moral sentiments.

Erikson next adds a new dimension: The process does not begin with some behavior transgressing a fixed moral rule, but the moral rule itself shifts to include activities that were not themselves a real threat to moral boundaries. Following Durkheim, Erikson reasoned that if crime is normal, then why could not society create deviants to fit its own needs, rather than waiting for individuals to transgress preestablished moral bounds? The causal process has been altered. The emergence of deviance is no longer dependent on the independent action of some transgressor; rather, the moral rule shifts to include behavior that had existed all along. *Being defined as a deviant now depends on the boundary shifting to include the action in question, not the action crossing the fixed moral boundary.* If it is no longer behavior violating moral boundaries but shifting boundaries, what causes these boundaries to shift? The answer remains somewhat vague in Erikson (1966), but it is suggested that when the community experiences a crisis, some threat to its collective identity or corporate existence, the societal community collectively reacts by activating its institutions of social control to persecute people (manufacture deviance) as a means of reaffirming the community's corporate identity.

By charging, arresting, imprisoning, or executing people for a variety of crimes against the collective purposes of the nation, those very collective values and sentiments are renewed. The dramatization of opposition to collective sentiments through the activation of social-control institutions is one means to reaffirm a threatened sense of collective identity.

This explanation for the activation of social-control mechanisms to create a large volume of deviance involves three steps: First, there is an exogenous *threat* to a collectivity's existence (the sense of itself as a bounded entity). Second, these events lead to a "boundary crisis," a loss, say, in the meaning of collective existence, a sort of national identity crisis. Third, the threatened collective identity is reconstituted and redefined by activating institutions of social control to *identify and create social deviants*. For Durkheim, the threat to the moral order comes from within (people violating the collective conscience), but for Erikson, it comes from without, with the community reacting and manufacturing "crime" and deviants within its own midst. This theoretical framework is frankly organic and functionalist, viewing institutions of social control (police, prisons, the state) as agents of the collectivity as a whole and not as agents of particular elites or class interests. Although we do not as yet fully understand this boundary-crisis-leads-to-deviance process, there appear to be at least there stages.

STAGE 1: THE THREAT

There is an almost unlimited number of crises a society might experience—economic depression, rapid growth with industrialization and urbanization, going to war, or suffering military defeat. The question is, which would result in a collective identity crisis? Or, would different threats create different types of crises, or maybe threaten different kinds of boundaries? At present there are no firm answers, but by examining some of the incidents mentioned by Erikson and by considering general social conditions prior to political witch-hunts, we can make some preliminary distinctions that may be theoretically relevant.

In discussing the condition of the Massachusetts Bay Colony prior to the discovery of witches in Salem village, Erikson notes three general matters preoccupying the colony. The first centers around relations between the mother country and the colony, as Charles II notified the Bay Colony of his renewed interest in colonial affairs and dispatched four commissioners to look after his royal interests. Charles then ordered the Bay Colony to allow the establishment of an Anglican church in Boston and finally revoked the charter under which the colony was established, sending a royal governor to represent his interests. The second matter involved a war with an Indian confederacy led by Chief Phillip, and the third involved a number of personal feuds and land disputes that were preoccupying the courts.

Assuming some or all of these matters may have created the boundary crisis that resulted in the Salem witchcraft mania, how do we decide which one? Or, an even simpler task: What do these events suggest in terms of sociological variables that might constitute a general threat to any collectivity? Relations with England seem the most significant as they involve the colony as a corporate collectivity. Internal turmoil, such as the property disputes, may create crises, but these seem more problems for the society as an aggregation of individuals and organizations, rather than as a corporate entity. Relations with England, though, involve a change in the status of the colony as a sovereign political entity. The revoking of the charter and the sending of commissioners and a royal governor can be seen as direct threats to the colony's independent political status. Along with this direct threat to independent collective experience, a second source of problems of group identity centers on the very process of becoming a corporate group (Swanson, 1970), which involves more than merely establishing the requisite structural arrangements for taking corporate action. A collective identity is also required. Moreover, the problems of creating new national identities are well documented (see Apter, 1963; Lipset, 1963). The claim often voiced by developing countries that they are possessed by subversives may in fact be an integral aspect of the very emergence of a national collective identity. In these cases witch-hunts may have more to do with establishing a collective identity in the first place than with a threat to national existence, making some degree of witch-hunting a constituent component of nation-building.

Another source of boundary crisis can be seen in the demands placed on the United States in its new role of world leader after 1945. Here an entirely new social order is not being constructed, but a new international situation places demands on the nation. Changes in the larger context in which a collectivity is embedded can place particular importance on its collective identity, an importance that may generate a certain volume of deviance as a means of ritually reaffirming national goals. Because it is the corporate nation—through the state—that is the basic actor in the international state system, changes or alterations in that system, or in a nation's position in that system, can also create various degrees of boundary and identity crises. In effect, you need not be directly attacked to wonder who you are and exactly what you are about.

In sum, then, there appear to be at least three sources of crises for collective identities:

1. Some crises involve a direct threat to a society's collective existence. This suggests that problems between states—defeat in war, threats from other states, expulsion from treaty organizations, or diplomatic humiliations—could constitute a crisis in the corporate identity or existence of national collectivities.
2. Some collective-identity problems might arise from the very processes of creating a new corporate community. This sort of argument was not part of the original Erikson formulation but is implied in his analysis of the Antinomian heresy (1966: 71–107), for

there seemed to be no other problem facing the community except the construction of its social institutions and collective identity.

3. A change in contextual relations, such as the placing of new responsibilities on a collectivity or the requiring of action that it is not equipped to provide, can constitute grounds for generating deviance as a source of new collective identities. The strain and adjustment involved in the rise of the United States to world hegemony after 1945 suggests this.

STAGE 2: THE BOUNDARY CRISIS

The problem of determining just what constitutes a threat is also present in determining just what is meant by the term *social boundary*. Erikson's discussion of the boundary-maintaining capacity of social groups remains quite general, as he refers to "a symbolic set of parentheses" that establishes the "margins of the group" and gives a community its "distinctive shape" and "unique identity" (1966: 3–29).

In any society there are numerous groups, some encompassing others and some overlapping others. The emergence of different kinds of deviance—sexual, political, religious—will depend on the particular boundary that faces difficulty. What this means is that there is no such thing as a single unidimensional volume of deviance. With multiple boundaries, there can obviously be multiple "crime waves," each repairing their relevant boundary. For instance, the ritual labeling of different kinds of sexual activity as morally deviant probably reaffirms a different social boundary than does the discovery of antirepublican, anti-communist, or anti-American subversives.

In the case of political deviance, the task is somewhat simplified. It seems reasonable that the various political witch-hunts I have been referring to probably do not function to strengthen the boundaries defining sex roles but rather are related to some aspect of the community's political order. The "royalist agents," "clandestine clergy," "foreign spies," "Hebertists," "Brissotins," and others who formed part of Robespierre's vast Foreigners' Conspiracy were intent on overthrowing the new French republic; the "revisionists" and "captialist roaders" in China and the "Trotskyites" and "saboteurs" in the Soviet Union were intent on destroying the "Revolution" and its new political order; and the "Communist sympathizers," "fellow travelers," and "card-carrying members" were intent on undermining American national security during the McCarthy period. In each of these cases the question was the very existence of the corporate political community in which collective existence is realized—the nation-state.

If, as suggested earlier, societies exist as communities with multiple sets of boundaries, and if different kinds of deviance relate to different boundaries, then the political deviance we are concerned with suggests that the boundaries in question are also political. Purported attacks against "the Republic," "the Revolution," and "the Nation" suggest that the boundary in question is the identity of the community as a sovereign political entity.

STAGE 3: THE CRIME WAVE

The crime wave refers to the manufacturing of deviance by society's various institutions of social control, which simply means arresting, putting on trial, and imprisoning people for political crimes they have not committed. In a more general sense, almost any institutional structure can function as a means of social control to the extent that it participates in labeling individuals, groups, or cultural artifacts (art and literature) as politically subversive. One of the major problems with the boundary crisis theory is a tendency at present toward a circularity in its reasoning, and it is nowhere more apparent than in the problem of identifying a boundary crisis independent of the subsequent outbreak of deviance. That is, if there is no subsequent crime wave, how is it known whether a boundary crisis has transpired? Is it possible to have a boundary crisis without an accompanying increase in community-designated deviance? At present there is no way of knowing, and this indeterminacy suggests that we do not fully understand the nature of threats, boundary crises, or the resultant deviance. Fundamental questions about why particular types of crimes or certain groups and activities should be identified as morally deviant still remain. The boundary-maintenance perspective predicts merely the presence of deviance, but its substantive character and distribution are not predictable from the model as it is presently formulated. Erikson, however, does suggest an association between a society's values and the character of the deviance it will experience: "Societies which place a high premium on ownership of property, for example, are likely to experience a greater volume of thefts than those which do not, while societies which emphasize political orthodoxy are apt to discover and punish more sedition than their less touchy neighbors [1966: 19]." To analyze more systematically the activation of social control institutions to manufacture political deviance we shall need a more precise definition of political crime.

POLITICAL CRIME

Sociologically, what does it mean to say an activity constitutes a political crime? Is it political because the control agencies making the designation use it for political purposes, as in the conventional interpretation of political crime in totalitarian states, or does political crime have some distinguishing characteristic separating it from other forms of social deviance? The answer, I think, is that those activities that are usually termed political crimes share a common property.

Political crimes are acts defined by agencies of the state as opposing or subverting the interests and purposes of the corporate national collectivity—the nation-state. In some sense all deviance involves an attack on the interests of society, this being the central thrust of Durkheim's analysis of why certain actions illicit collective responses of disapproval and punishment. But not all deviance is understood to involve attacks on a collectivity's distinctly *corporate interest.* Political crime distinctly involves issues of *national* security and *national* interests.

The most obvious crimes against the national interest are *treason* and *sedition,* including accusations of *plotting* and *conspiring* to overthrow the government or give aid to the enemy for the same purpose. Actually, anything that is considered subversive represents an attack on the nation as a corporate collectivity. Political crimes need not always be so straightforward as treason, for anything that involves an attack on, or subversion of, the national interest represents a political crime.

Consider, for example, the deviant activities of "economism" and "bureaucratism" that appeared during the Chinese Cultural Revolution. Although these deviant acts do not seem political or in any way to involve the interests of the collectivity, they both center on opposition to the corporate interests of the polity. The essence of economism and bureaucratism is the charge of placing individual interests in front of the larger political purposes of revolutionary China, the corporate national collectivity.

Economism involves the separation of economic issues from their larger political significance, and more specifically the practice of giving primacy to the free working of price mechanisms and material incentives. In a highly politicized society such as China, the larger collective purposes of building socialism and destroying the remaining vestiges of capitalism are infused into the activities of everyday life. Consequently, economic decisions that we would understand as having significance solely for the exigencies of running a factory are filled with transcendent political meaning. The giving of material incentives is not merely a matter of plant policy but involves political ideology, and not because each daily activity is really linked to national goals, but because this society finds its collective goals infusing the fabric of its institutional life. Individuals are supposed to possess the "collectivist spirit," meaning daily activity should be motivated by a desire to serve the higher purposes of the nation rather than one's personal self-interest. Hence, activities that "corrupt the masses revolutionary will" and lure them to seek only "personal and short-term interests in disregard of the interests of the state and the collective" are nothing but "out-and-out counterrevolutionary and revisionist."

Bureaucratism is similar to economism, except instead of the advancement of individual interests, it refers to the advancement of institutional interests. Whenever decisions are made that advance the private interests of the party or bureaucracy, the larger mass interests are infringed on. Bureaucratism is also similar to the deviations of being *expert* and not *red* and of *bourgeois individualism.* "National construction" (a collective goal) requires not merely the presence of technical skill, being an "expert," but also the proper commitment to the "ideology of collectivism" and the placing of one's skills "wholeheartedly at the service of the people." Those who are not "red," but are merely "expert," do not offer themselves wholeheartedly "to the people and socialist construction" but think instead in terms of "individual narrow interests." Examples of "harmful individualism" cited in the Chinese press include research personnel who in their pursuit of personal fame "refuse to conduct research in certain problems of production," professors who "regard knowledge as their own private property," and engineers who avoid the study of functional work and choose instead to "play the connoisseur, with resulting damage and loss of national construction [Lee, 1966: 55]."

Political crimes, whether treason, economism, or bureaucratism, all share the characteristic of constituting a threat to the national interest. Again, It is not a matter of determining whether the accused deviant is in any sense a real threat to the political authorities. No matter how trivial or farfetched it may seem, any activity defined by that society as constituting a threat to its corporate interest is a political crime.

THE INSTITUTIONAL ECOLOGY OF SUBVERSION

Perhaps the most perplexing aspect of the crime of subversion is the great variety of acts that can be so arbitrarily defined as subversive. It seems as if people from all walks of life, doing any sort of activity, can be labeled subversive. Traditionally, we view this as part of the paranoia of those conducting, say, the purge, or groups experiencing status stress. But these are not really satisfying explanations, for mostly they just dismiss the "who gets charged with what" aspect of witch-hunts as paranoia or fabrication. There certainly is paranoia and fabrication during a witch-hunt, but is this the best way to explain the ecology of subversion? That is, why do so many different kinds of activity and so many different kinds of people get labeled subversive? Societies also seem to vary in terms of where they discover subversion. Not all discover danger in the same institutional sectors. Practically all societies—if they discover subversive elements in their midst—find subversion in the various branches of government, with the state bureaucracy appearing as the most popular location. The Soviets and Chinese, for instance, hunted "imperialist agents" and "capitalist roaders" in the Party and governmental bureaucracy, and the United States in the 1950s activated its social-control apparatus to look for "Communists" in the State Department. In many societies economic institutions are also infested and corroded, as when the Soviets found "wreckers" and "saboteurs" in their factories, Americans found "Communists" in labor unions, and Chinese found "capitalist roaders" on agricultural communes.

This activation of social-control mechanisms to search for imaginary enemies seems to *spread* from one institutional area to another. The dispersion of subversion across and within institutional space is a *variable*, for some, all, or most of their institutional areas are experienced as infected: not just the state apparatus and the economy but also schools, universities, the military, artists, writers, and religious institutions. For others, only a few areas are tainted, and for still others virtually no areas become contaminated. For example, one-party socialist states (Soviet Union, China, etc.) seem to find enemies throughout the fabric of social life. Anyone, in any walk of life, doing almost anything, seems capable of being charged with some sort of "counterrevolutionary" or "anti-state" activity. Others, like the United States, also experience waves of subversion, like the Palmer raids of the 1920s or McCarthyism of the 1950s, but here the subversive elements seem to be discovered in fewer institutional areas. Finally, many multiparty European states seem to have little problem with "the enemy within" or "dangerous thoughts" in their art and literature.

To explain this ecology of subversion we need a theoretical account of why in some states more areas of life become corrupted and morally corroded with subversive activity. The explanation offered here will center on the notion of immanence as used by Guy E. Swanson (1964; 1967; 1971) in his comparative studies of sacred and transcendental forces.

Immanence

The idea of immanence refers to situations where "people discover that which they believe of highest value is itself incorporated, is immanent, in persons, organizations, or various objects in the natural world [Swanson, 1967: 1]." The notion of immanence, whether in the form of spirits residing in totems and other sacred objects or the body of Christ being immanent within the eucharistic bread and wine, can also be applied to peoples' experiences with transcendent political values penetrating and permeating their daily existence.

The idea of immanence is derived from Durkheim's theory of religious symbols (1912). Whereas totems, gods, spirits, and other forces are symbolic representations of society, the national interest and images of "the People," "the Masses," "the Proletariat," and "the Nation" are the relevant symbolic representations of the corporate reality of the modern nation-state.

When we speak of the collective reality of society itself, we mean its existence as a corporate actor. Corporateness is contained "in a legitimated procedure through which participants can undertake collective actions and in a legitimated sphere of action to which this procedure may be applied—a sphere of jurisdiction [Swanson, 1971: 611]." For modern national societies, this procedure for taking collective action is represented by what we commonly call government.

MEASURING CORPORATENESS

The explanation offered by Swanson is based on the notion of a constitutional system, which represents the means by which a collectivity formally organizes itself as a corporate actor. Constitutional systems vary from general agreements allowing all the members of the collectivity to act as its agents to formalized roles that are the sole legitimate representatives of the collectivity. In modern societies, the state acts as the legitimate agency of the corporate nation.

Constitutional systems vary in the extent to which constituent as opposed to corporate interests are given a role in the making of collective decisions. Every collectivity exists both as an aggregation of constituent groups and as a corporate actor, and when functioning as a corporate actor, the collectivity must decide what role the interests and purposes of its constituent parts (versus its corporate interest) should play in making collective decisions.

Following the Durkheimian view that ultimate beliefs are a symbolic representation of the reality of the social order, Swanson suggests:

> Corporate purposes and choices would be more likely to be experienced as present and compelling in the acts of those societies in which the constitutional system—the collective apparatus for making authoritative choices—provided a legitimate role for corporate interests and traditions in the formulation of action, at the same time excluding the special interests and traditions of component groups and individuals in the society [1971: 621].

For the modern nation-state, political party systems represent the institutionalized mechanism for the representation of both constituent and corporate interests in government. *A typology of party arrangements, therefore, also gives us a measure of various degrees of corporateness.*

Nation-states offer a particular advantage when it comes to classifying their constitutional systems, for in the very process of their development they face and resolve our central theoretical concern: To what extent should various constituent interests be given a formal role in the making of collective decisions? In effect, the process of nation-building (Bendix, 1964; Rokkan, 1970) represents a movement toward constituting modern societies as corporate actors, with the state representing the agency endowed with the authority to take legitimate corporate action.

Most contemporary societies are constituted as nation-states, regardless of their level of social or political development, and most nation-states organize their politics through some form of party system. Whether one thinks of the developing states in Africa, Asia, or Latin America, the socialist states of the Soviet Union and China, the past Fascist and Nazi polities, or the plural party systems of Anglo-America and Europe, the political party is, as LaPalombara and Weiner (1955) comment, "omnipresent."

Students of political parties also agree that one of the most important functions of parties is organizing group interests and representing them in governmental structures, as the relationship between various constituent groups and their political institutions is mediated by party systems (Lipset, 1960: Kirchheimer, 1966; Rokkan, 1966).

PROPORTIONAL REPRESENTATION SYSTEMS:
MULTIPARTY STATES

Proportional representation (PR) systems represent the *most extensive incorporation of constituent interests* and hence should be the *least immanent* of all states. PR is an electoral procedure worked out in the nineteenth century that attempts to ensure a correspondence between the proportion of votes a party receives and the number of legislative seats it is awarded. There are numerous specific formulas that have been devised (see De Grazia, 1951; Rokkan, 1966; Rae, 1971), but these are of no particular interest here. PR systems are employed extensively in Europe and are associated with multiparty states.

PR is indicative of the incorporation of constituent interests into central decision making, because each party, no matter what share of the vote it receives, will be assigned exactly the same share of legislative seats. This plan is in direct contrast to plurality systems, where smaller parties, if they do not win the election, do not gain representation in the legislature. The emergence of PR systems was a response to three crises involving the prospective role of different constituent interests in unified national legislatures during the nineteenth century.

First, in the process of nation-building, some of the most ethnically heterogeneous European countries found entrenched linguistic, ethnic, or religious minorities threatening to disrupt the emerging national community if majority representation, which would deny them representation, persisted. Hence, some of the most heterogeneous countries were the first to adopt proportional representation: Denmark in 1855; the Swiss cantons in 1891; Belgium in 1899; Moravia in 1905; Finland in 1906 (Rokkan, 1966). The construction of nation-states involved working out institutional arrangements determining how corporate authority was to be exercised, with particular attention paid to the role various groups were to play. This same argument has also been advanced in terms of the possibilities of national integration in extremely hetereogeneous African states (Lewis, 1965).

Second, the extension of sufferage to ever-widening circles of the populace led to the development of strong working-class parties that desired representation in national legislatures. The majority principle, though, often made the barrier against entry extremely high (the German rule of absolute majority establishing the highest barrier, as it was necessary to obtain 50% of the vote or go without representation), leading working-class parties to push for the adoption of PR.

Finally, given this pressure from growing working-class parties, older bourgeois parties felt threatened and "demanded proportional representation to protect their position against the new waves of mobilized voters created by universal suffrage [Rokkan, 1966: 12]."

In all three cases, whether to give representation to religious and ethnic or working-class interests, or to protect the interests of older parties, PR represents a form of constitutional system where group interests (in the form of Catholic, agrarian, working-class, etc., parties) are given more of a formal role in the making of collective decisions (that is, a place in national legislatures).

PLURALITY SYSTEMS: TWO-PARTY STATES

The second category is another type of electoral arrangement that includes both majority and plurality electoral rules. But because the majority formula is rare, as it is difficult for a single party to obtain more votes than its combined opposition, we will discuss plurality arrangements. Plurality, or simple majority systems require a party to obtain more votes than its nearest competitor to win an election. This type of electoral arrangement is associated with the Anglo-American states of Canada, New Zealand, Australia, Britain, and the United States.

Because constituent interests are allowed less penetration of the agency for collective decision making than in PR systems, we expect these societies to experience more immanence than PR states. Plurality formulas, as the basis of selecting members to national legislatures, place restrictions on the representation of numerous group interests. The requirement of winning an election provides an advantage to larger parties and prevents smaller ones, who represent specific interests or ideological perspectives, from being represented.

The important dimension of constitutional systems is not the mere inclusion or exclusion of constituent interests, but the corresponding inclusion of the corporate interest, and for the following reasons plurality systems involve a greater inclusion of corporate interests than do PR systems.

First, the requirement of winning an election in order to gain entrance into the legislature places pressures on parties to appeal to various groupings that may not regularly share the perspective of the party. Appealing to or representing the interests of one single group is not sufficient to win elections, and parties must appeal to the *common* interests of the community. The interests and purposes that various groups share, rather than those specific to each group, are what is represented (Lipset, 1960).

Second, this community of common interests is often a political community and therefore already an agent of the larger corporate order. Where PR can appeal to more functional groupings, created by the presence of stratificational, ethnic, religious, and territorial cleavages, plurality systems lead parties to represent the interests of politically defined areas, such as states, counties, cities, and electoral districts. For instance, in the United States questions of interest representation are defined in terms of the interests of the "people of California" or the "citizens of San Mateo County" rather than stratificational groupings of class and wealth or ascriptive solidarities of race and religion. The point here is not that these dimensions are not factors in elections, or that issues are not defined in their terms—particularly in heterogeneous societies like the United States—but that one participates in collective decision making (some form of legislature) representing the interests of a politically defined community. One represents New York, Florida, or the Seventeenth District; one is not formally authorized to represent solely the interest of Catholics, Protestants, workers, or farmers.

The differences between PR and majority–plurality systems also reflect different community decisions about how the nation is to exist as a corporate actor, particularly in terms of the role to be given the interests of the whole community and its political subdivisions in relation to the interests of other nonpolitical groupings. Electoral laws reflect collective arrangements about how the corporate existence of the society is to be organized and what role the various interest groups are allowed formally to play.

We have moved from states where constituent interests were given a maximum amount of representation (multiparty, PR states) to systems where broader interests, crosscutting the interests of numerous groups, are formally represented (two-party, plurality states). Our final category represents constitutional systems where only corporate interests are present and where constituent interests are formally excluded.

ONE-PARTY STATES

Single-party states, because there is only one party representing the interests of the society as a whole, should be the most immanent. In one-party states, government is often subordinated to the party. The party takes over the role of representing the corporate interest that is usually left to government. The party acts both as the representative of the interests of the nation as a whole and as the agency for carrying out those interests and purposes. This function is not found in either multiparty PR or two-party plurality systems. By definition, then, in single-party states there is only one larger interest represented in government. This is the national interest, the corporate interest of the nation as a collective whole.

As noted earlier, modern political party systems represent the social arrangement by which any number of constituent group interests, versus the corporate interest of the national collectivity, are formally included in the structural apparatus for making collective decisions and taking collective action—government. Following Swanson's theoretical lead, we expect an association between increased inclusion of the nation's corporate interest and increasing degrees of immanence, which in modern societies translates into being a more politicized society. Or, to put it the other way, we expect increasing politicization (immanence) the more the corporate interest of the collectivity is represented at the expense of constituent interests. In terms of party systems and electoral arrangements, this means that we should expect multiparty states to be, on the average, the least politicized and one-party states the most, with two-party systems somewhere in between. Here immanence is a variable, and in theory modern states could be placed along a continuum from high to low degree of immanence. In practice, though, the most dramatic and clear-cut examples of immanence are found within one-party states.

To better grasp this idea of immanence we can consider a few of the more dramatic examples of the infusion of transcendent political purposes and images of the corporate nation-state into the substance and structure of concrete daily existence. One of the most straightforward examples is where a leader's individual qualities become identified with the collective purposes of an entire nation (Rustow, 1967). Where it is said, "Ghana is Nkrumah and Nkrumah Ghana," or "Hitler is Germany and Germany is Hitler," we see examples of situations where the image of the corporate political community is understood to *reside* in, or merge with, national leaders. It is a traditional characteristic of one-party states, where Castro, Stalin, Mao, Nkrumah, and others have at various times been considered the *embodiment* of national existence. This is exactly what Swanson would mean by immanence if he were studying *The Birth of the Gods* (1964) in modern societies.

Another example of immanence is what Inkeles (1968) terms the *nationalization of affect*. He refers to the tendency to interpret the expression of affect in terms of larger political goals. Individual emotions of love, hate, desire, and ambition can become infused with transcendent political significance: "You do not have children for the pleasure they give you, but so that Hitler and Mussolini may have more workers and soldiers to effect the high purposes for which they were put on earth. Friendship is not important for the gratification it gives, but because comrades may join in carrying out the greatest task of all [Inkeles, 1950: 78]."

Some of the most dramatic recent examples of a high degree of immanence have been in China. Chairman Mao, and particularly the "thought of Chairman Mao," stood as a collective representation of the Chinese polity. During the Cultural Revolution (1966–1969) corporate purposes, symbolized by "the thought of chairman Mao," became dramatically immanent within Chinese society. The famed "little red book" carrying the thoughts of Mao was carried and quoted with a sacred reverence. An article by a military athlete on the psychological and physical benefits of Mao's thought demonstrates the extent to which Mao's thought is understood as an immanent force in the world:

> For a time I suffered seriously from a nervous breakdown. My head ached in the daytime, I could not sleep at night, and I lacked energy. However, the thought of Mao Tse-tung gave me unlimited strength. It gave me a greater courage to overcome difficulties. . . . I made great effort in studying and training. With such strength I finally surmounted all difficulties, continually raised my technical level, and broke a number of national records [quoted in Lifton, 1968: 77].

Here ideology (the thought of Mao) is not distant but is tangible and incorporated into the substance of this world. To some extent all states have a degree of immanence—the flag representing the nation and national holidays, coronations and inaugurations providing rituals whereby people can commune with the gods and spirits of their nation. After all, what are the organic images of "Public Opinion," "The People," and "The Masses" but our very experiences with the corporate reality of the modern political community. Where primitive people experience ancestor spirits we experience "public opinion" and the moving spirit of "Chairman Mao." There is no difference, except the modern vanity of considering our experience with Durkheimian forces as real and theirs as myth and religion. In more immanent states, ultimate values (democracy, socialism, the revolution, freedom, capitalism, and so forth) will be understood, and experienced, as present and compelling in more areas of social life. The more immanent, the more politicized the society.

INFUSING THE MORAL ORDER WITH
POLITICAL SIGNIFICANCE

I also want to argue that the moral order itself can be infused with these political purposes, a situation that lets us understand the presence of more political crime in more corporate, and hence immanent, states.

Imagine a society's moral order as a sort of neon tube that surrounds and bounds society. On one side is that which is normal; on the other, that which is deviant. For different institutional areas of social life there are separate sets of rules and boundaries defining what is right and wrong, moral and immoral, legal and illegal. In our neon tube conception, imagine the tubes stacked one on the other, like a stack of auto tires behind a store. We can consider the top few tubes as representing the moral order of those institutional sectors that constitute the structural apparatus enabling the nation to exist as a corporate actor. This would be the state apparatus: executive, legislative, and judicial institutions, along with the military. The party in one-party states and the vast public bureaucracy common to all modern states would also be included. On lower levels our neon tubes would represent the moral boundaries of various other institutional areas.

We can also arrange our stacks of moral neon tubes along an immanence continuum: the most immanent societies at one end and the least at the other. Imagine here our stacks of doughnut-shaped neon tubes placed next to each other in a row going from the most to least immanent. At one end would be one-party states, at the other multiparty states, with two-party states in the middle. As we move from multiparty to single-party we expect a greater degree of immanence, meaning more areas of social life should be infused with ultimate political significance. The moral order of these various institutions is also penetrated by ultimate political values, which brings us back to the neon tube imagery. When political significance merges with moral rules (the tubes), we can imagine them lighting up or glowing, as a neon tube would when it was turned on or plugged in. Looking at all the societies along the immanence continuum, we see that as we move toward one-party societies more layers of tubes glow, as the moral order in more areas of life is infused with political significance. The top rungs probably glow for all states, as the state apparatus is the most likely to be infused with at least some political meaning. As we move toward one-party states, more and more tubes glow, as the moral order in more and more institutional areas becomes infused with political meaning. When it is said that all crime is political in certain one-party states, it means that all areas of moral life have political meaning, such that the violation of even the most trivial rule (in our imagery, a glowing tube far from the top) represents a political crime. It is political not because it threatens national values, but because national values are immanent in this minor rule.

We are now in a position to make some more precise predictions about the activation of social-control mechanisms to create political deviance. Remember the earlier discussion of Durkheim and Erikson on crime and punishment. Durkheim centered on individual violations of the moral order and Erikson on the community creation of deviance as a response to outside threats to the society's sense of collective identity or corporate existence.

Let us consider the Durkheim process first. Take an "ordinary" crime, say, theft of tools at an industrial plant. Here an individual has crossed the moral boundary—one should not steal—and the community reacts. He is punished. But exactly how this deviant act is experienced depends on whether the moral boundary in question is infused with political significance—in our imagery, whether the neon tube (the moral boundary) is glowing. Where it is, in highly immanent societies, then the "ordinary" theft is not so ordinary at all and is considered a crime against the state, an act of, say, "sabotage" or "wrecking," or the work of "capitalist roaders" or "imperialist agents." In another society, with a lower degree of immanence, where the boundaries are not infused with transcendent political significance (where the neon tubes are not lit up), the violation of the same moral boundary is experienced as a "normal" crime, a question of petty theft and not political subversion. In both cases the same rule was violated, except one rule was immanent with political meaning and the other was not. What is experienced as an ordinary nonpolitical crime versus a political crime therefore has less to do with what was actually done than with whether the moral boundary in question was infused with political meaning.

Any collectivity can be organized as a corporate actor, from families and informal organizations to giant business enterprises. The collective representations of any corporate group structure can also be immanent in their moral order, which would turn "normal" deviance into acts against the purposes and values of the collectivity as a whole. For instance, Swanson (1971) has created a coding scheme for degrees of corporateness in families, and we would expect here that in more corporate families deviant acts would more often be considered acts against the values and purposes of the family as a whole rather than mere rule infractions. Similarly, there should be higher rates of ritual persecutions of various family members as a means of renewing and dramatizing the family's central purposes. At the most general level, the point is that the more the moral order is infused with collective purposes, the more trivial violations of that order will be experienced as threats and dangers to the collectivity as a whole, whether that be a family or nation-state.

In terms of our earlier use of party systems to measure corporateness, we thus expect one-party states to have the largest volume of political deviance (engage in the most political witch-hunting), followed by two-party and then by multiparty states. It is important to remember that the corporate organization of states is a *variable,* and although the epochs of totalitarianism in Germany and the Soviet Union in the 1930s seem dramatically different from anything before, the more general point is that whereas one-party states may have their purges and show trials, two-party states like the United States have also experienced anti-Communist hysteria. Communists hunting capitalists and capitalists hunting communists are instances of the same general process.

Immanence and Boundary Crises

In the Durkheimian model, it is an individual violation of the moral order that creates crime, and in our elaboration of this, violation of a politicized moral order creates political crime. For Erikson, deviance comes from the labeling process of social-control institutions that are activated to reaffirm the community's corporate identity through the ritual persecution of imaginary enemies. Given a threat to a collectivity's corporate existence (Erikson's "boundary crisis"), institutions of social control are activated to manufacture deviation from the collectivity's central values as a means of reaffirming its threatened collective existence. To this model we now add the idea that these collective values and collective identities can be immanent in daily life, creating more or less politicized societies depending on their organization as corporate actors.

This point brings us to a theoretical synthesis of Erikson and Swanson: If national political values are immanent in everyday life (a politicized society), then the process of manufacturing their opposite (creating subversion through ritual persecution by social-control institutions) will occur in all aspects of ordinary daily life. Seemingly nonpolitical actions will be labeled a threat to the nation, not because they really are—after all, it is a witch-hunt—but because the sense of national existence is present in every nook and cranny of social life.

This extensive diffusion of political meaning into daily life has been captured in the term *totalitarian* and linked with the use of the purge and political terror (Arendt, 1968). The point I wish to emphasize here is that this search for imaginary enemies is not limited to totalitarian states, although they do in fact engage in the most political witch-hunting (Bergesen, 1974; 1977; 1984). As I have argued, politicization is a variable, varying with the extent to which the collectivity gives expression to the corporate social interest rather than to multiple constituent group interests. Therefore the activation of institutions of social control for witch-hunts is also a variable.

If we consider Erikson's proposition that, other things being equal, a community should experience a more or less constant volume of deviance—in conjunction with the notion of immanence—we can generate the following propositions:

Proposition 1   *The more corporate the society, the greater the frequency of political witch-hunts.*

This is the most general proposition linking the social organization of societies with frequency of witch-hunting. Empirical support for this proposition has been found in a study of witch-hunting activity between 1950 and 1970 for a sample of 39 countries (Bergesen, 1977).

Proposition 2   *Of a society's total volume of deviance, in more corporate societies a greater proportion will be political deviance.*

If a society ritually persecutes a certain number of people, then the more the moral order is infused with political significance, the more charges of violating the moral order will involve charges of violating a moral order infused with political significance. Hence, more political deviants will be created.

Proposition 3 *Given a boundary crisis, the more corporate the society, the more the ritually manufactured political deviance will be discovered throughout the society's institutional space.*

It is not just that more subversion is manufactured (Proposition 1), or that more of the total volume of deviance is political in character (Proposition 2), but political deviance is created in more areas of social life. This statement is a theoretical by-product of merging Durkheim's sociology of religion (the immanence of collective representations in the fabric of daily life) and his sociology of deviance (the manufacturing of deviance to repair and renew society's collective identity). With daily life so infused with political purposes, their reaffirmation manifests itself in the creation of deviance in areas of life that have nothing to do with the real interests of the state. In creating the opposite of national purposes, the deviance-manufacturing process centers on more and more areas of life the more national purposes are present throughout institutional space. Hence, more corporate societies find more subversion in more areas, and less corporate states, less in less areas.

We expect that the most common place to manufacture subversion is in the organizational structure through which the collectivity realizes itself as a corporate actor (government). This area should be the most highly immanent and, as such, the place where national identities are reaffirmed. As the society becomes increasingly corporate, more and more institutional areas should become politicized and be experienced as periodically infected with subversive elements. Hence, a boundary crisis in the meaning of, say, being a "loyal American" or a "good revolutionary" will entail the manufacturing of "*un*-American activity" or the ritual discovery of "counterrevolutionaries" in a variety of different institutional areas, depending on whether these areas are infused with political significance. Strong support for this proposition was found in the previously mentioned study (Bergesen, 1974; 1977; 1984), where—holding constant a country's size (population), level of economic development (gross national product), and a measure of state strength (number of internal security forces)—a statistically significant association was found between the nature of the political party system and the spread of witch-hunting across different institutional areas.

Summary and Conclusion

The use of institutions of social control to persecute imaginary enemies is a mechanism whereby collective purposes and national identities are renewed and reaffirmed. When someone actually endangers the
nation, it responds. But it also responds whether a truly treasonous
crime has been committed. Where political values are merged with the
moral order, minor infractions are turned into crimes against the state
and nation. In a very real sense it is not because this sort of infraction is
directed toward the interests of the state, but more because the interests
of the state come to it. Durkheim's view that violations of the moral
order create crime can be amplified by noting that when the moral order
is politicized, its violation creates political crime. Further, when all areas
of social life are so infused, minor rule infractions are experienced as
political deviation. Political crimes are not limited to elites or others near
centers of real power, but anyone, doing anything, is capable of being
charged with some kind of political crime.

Although the preceding description is what is usually meant by total
itarianism, the fundamental point here is that politicization is a variable
and corresponds to the manner in which collectivities organize themselves as corporate actors. The more nations organize their corporate
existence as aggregations of component groups and interests, the less
they will experience daily life as penetrated by ultimate political values.
And, conversely, the more they organize themselves to give expression
to their distinctive corporate interest, the more their daily life will be
politicized and filled with transcendent political meaning. The more
rules are infused with political significance, the more their violation will
be experienced as political crime.

Political deviance may also appear regardless of whether the moral
order is violated. The community may manufacture deviance by creating
imaginary political enemies, which is what is generally meant by a political witch-hunt, where the nation finds itself infested with enemies as a
means of renewing common moral sentiments. Durkheim's observation
that society needs the deviant as well as the normal also implies that
subversion is required along with loyalty. If the gods need their wor-
shipers, they also need their enemies. The sacred requires the subversive.

Outbursts of subversion appear when the gods are in danger, when
sovereign political existence is somehow threatened and the ideology,
image, and purpose of the collectivity are in question. At that moment
there is an organic reaction, as the various institutions of social control
begin ritually to search for the enemy within, and the drama of collective

revitalization begins. The political witch-hunt is underway. Exactly who is persecuted and for what crimes depends on where these ultimate political values are found. If they are part of government, then subversion will be found there; if they are part of farming techniques, then disloyalty will appear on the farm. If, as Erikson suggests, we create deviance by moving our moral boundaries to label people deviant, and if these boundaries are colored with ideological significance, then their movement will create ideological deviants of one sort or another. When the nation is threatened and the national identity needs reaffirmation, the opposite of all the nation stands for will be created wherever that national identity resides. If it is diffused throughout society, including the moral order, then its opposition will be created by moving those rules—no matter how insignificant—to create deviance and thereby reaffirm the nation's collective identity. Practically anything and everything has been at one time or another considered subversive. The mystery of why witch-hunts persecute innocent people is no mystery at all, for what people actually do or do not do is irrelevant. If a society needs a certain volume of political deviance, it will find it.

References

Arendt, Hannah
    1968   *The Origins of Totalitarianism.* New York: Harcourt, Brace.
Baum, Richard, and Louise B. Bennett
    1971   *China in Ferment.* Englewood Cliffs, N.J.: Prentice-Hall.
Bell, Daniel
    1960   *The End of Ideology.* New York: Free Press.
    1964   *The Radical Right.* Garden City, N.Y.: Anchor.
Bendix, Richard
    1956   *Work and Authority in Industry.* New York: Harper & Row.
    1964   *Nation-Building and Citizenship.* New York: Wiley.
Bergesen, Albert
    1974   *The Social Origins of Political Witch-Hunts: A Cross-National Study of Political Deviance.* Unpublished doctoral dissertation, Department of Sociology, Stanford University.
    1977   "Political witch-hunts: The sacred and subversive in cross-national perspective." *American Sociological Review* 42: 220–233.
    1978   "A Durkheimian theory of political witch-hunts with the Chinese Cultural Revolution of 1966–1969 as an example." *Journal for the Scientific Study of Religion* 17: 19–29.
    1984   *The Sacred and the Subversive: Political Witch-Hunts as National Rituals.* Storrs, Connecticut: Society for the Scientific Study of Religion Monograph Series.
Bergesen, Albert, and Mark Warr
    1979   "A crisis in the moral order: The effects of Watergate upon confidence in social

institutions." Pages 277–295 in *New Directions in the Empirical Study of Religion*, edited by Robert Wuthnow. New York: Academic Press.

Bridgham, Philip
    1967   "Mao's 'cultural revolution': Origin and development." *The China Quarterly* 29 (January–March): 1–35.
    1968   "Mao's cultural revolution in 1967: The struggle to seize power." *The China Quarterly* 34 (April–June): 6–37.
    1970   "Mao's cultural revolution: The struggle to seize power." *The China Quarterly* 41 (January–March): 1–25.

Brzezinski, Zbigniew K.
    1956   *The Permanent Purge*. Cambridge, Mass.: Harvard University Press.

Conquest, Robert
    1968   *The Great Terror*. New York: Macmillan.

Dallin, Alexander, and George W. Breslauer
    1970   *Political Terror in Communist Systems*. Stanford, Calif.: Stanford University Press.

De Grazia, Alfred
    1951   *Public and Republic*. New York: Alfred A. Knopf.

Douglas, Mary
    1966   *Purity and Danger*. Harmondsworth: Penguin.

Durkheim, Emile
    1893   *The Division of Labor in Society*, translated by G. Simpson. New York: Macmillan, 1933.
    1912   *The Elementary Forms of the Religious Life*, translated by J. W. Swain. London: George Allen and Unwin, 1915.

Erikson, Kai T.
    1966   *Wayward Puritans*. New York: Wiley.

Gray, Jack, and Patrick Cavendish
    1968   *Chinese Communism in Crisis*. London: Pall Mall Press.

Greer, Donald
    1935   *The Incidence of the Terror*. Cambridge, Mass.: Harvard University Press.

Gusfield, Joseph
    1963   *Symbolic Crusade*. Urbana, Ill.: University of Illinois Press.

Hofstadter, Richard
    1955   *The Age of Reform*. New York: Random House.

Inkeles, Alex
    1950   *Public Opinion in Soviet Russia*. Cambridge, Mass.: Harvard University Press.
    1968   *Social Change in Soviet Russia*. Cambridge, Mass.: Harvard University Press.

Kirchheimer, Otto
    1966   "The transformation of the Western European party systems." Pages 177–200 in *Political Parties and Political Development*, edited by Joseph LaPalombara and Myron Weiner. Princeton, N.J.: Princeton University Press.

LaPalombara, Joseph, and Myron Weiner (editors)
    1966   *Political Parties and Political Development*. Princeton, N.J.: Princeton University Press.

Lazarsfeld, Paul F., and Wagner Theilens, Jr.
    1958   *The Academic Mind*. Glencoe, Ill.: The Free Press.

Lee, Rensselaer W., III
    1966   "The Hsia Fang system: Marxism and modernisation." *The China Quarterly* 26 (April–June): 68–81.

Lewis, Arthur W.
    1965   *Politics in West Africa*. London: Allen and Unwin.
Lifton, Robert Jay
    1968   *Revolutionary Immortality*. New York: Random House.
Lipset, S. M.
    1955   "The radical right: A problem for American democracy." *British Journal of Sociology* 6: 176–209.
    1960   "Party systems and the representation of social groups." *European Journal of Sociology* 1: 50–85.
Rae, Douglas
    1971   *The Political Consequences of Electoral Laws*. New Haven, Conn.: Yale University Press.
Rokkan, Stein
    1966   "Electoral systems." Pages 6–21 in *International Encyclopedia of the Social Sciences*, edited by David Sills. New York: Crowell-Collier-Macmillan.
    1970   "Nation-buliding, cleavage formation and the structuring of mass politics." Pages 72–144 in *Citizens, Elections and Parties*, edited by Stein Rokkan. New York: David McKay.
Rustow, Dankwart A.
    1967   *A World of Nations*. Washington D.C.: The Brookings Institution.
Swanson, Guy E.
    1964   *The Birth of the Gods*. Ann Arbor, Mich.: University of Michigan Press.
    1967   *Religion and Regime*. Ann Arbor, Mich.: University of Michigan Press.
    1970   "Toward corporate action: A Reconstruction of elementary collective processes." Pages 124–144 in *Human Nature and Collective Behaviors*, edited by Tamotsu Shibutani. Englewood Cliffs, N.J.: Prentice-Hall.
    1971   "An organizational analysis of collectivities." *American Sociological Review* 36: 607–623.

7

Social Control and Social Formation: A Marxian Analysis

DREW HUMPHRIES
DAVID F. GREENBERG

It is our hope to show in this chapter how Marxian theory can contribute to the development of a general theory of social control. The framework we develop will be used to discuss changes in the scope, ideology, and methods of social control that occurred in England and the United States in the transition from mercantile to industrial capitalism.[1]

Class and Social Control

Marxian theory begins with the social relations of production. When direct producers are separated from the means of production, and distribution is not collective, society is divided into antagonistic classes. The class that does not product but expropriates the surplus produced by others is characterized as an exploiting class, whereas the producers, deprived of the use of their full product, are regarded as an exploited class. As several modes of production (e.g., capitalist, feudal, slave,

---

[1]Elsewhere (Humphries and Greenberg, 1980) we extend our analysis to deal with the monopoly stage of capitalism.

171

TOWARD A GENERAL THEORY OF SOCIAL CONTROL
Volume 2: Selected Problems

petty commodity production) may coexist in a single social formation (Marx, 1858: 106–107), there is typically a multiplicity of classes.

Because antagonistic classes are postulated to have opposing interests with regard to the use of the means of production and distribution of the product, a source of instability is present in all antagonistic modes of production. It follows that exploitative modes of production do not reproduce themselves through economic means alone. An exploited class will seek to reduce or eliminate its exploitation. On the other hand, an exploiting class will attempt to preserve exploitative class relations. To do this, the exploiting class will make use of political and ideological measures, including social control. It will thus define as deviant and attempt to sanction those actions that threaten its interests. For example, it will seek to eliminate forms of appropriation that are inconsistent with the mode of production in question, as well as any behavior that threatens the process of social reproduction. It may do this *directly*, as when capitalists penalize workers for absenteeism. Or it may call on the state to exercise social control on its behalf *indirectly*, through criminal legislation.

An exploited class need not necessarily accept the definitions of the exploiting class about such matters. What an employer defines as employee theft and seeks to eliminate through legal or extralegal measures may be defined by employees as justifiable appropriation in the face of an inadequate wage. Indeed, a subordinate class will define as deviant and attempt to control the behavior of the exploiting class that injures its own interests. Lacking the financial and political resources of the exploiting class, however, it may be compelled to rely on extralegal or illegal methods of social control, such as strikes and industrial sabotage. The exploiting class will in turn try to frustrate these attempts through its own measures, such as criminal prohibitions, injunctions, and job dismissals. We thus have a dynamic picture of social control as both the subject of class conflict and the instrument of class control. As class conflict evolves, so will the scope and forms of social control employed by both exploiting and exploited classes.

Marxist theory does not exclude the possibility that the factual premises from which a class defines deviance and formulates social-control strategies may be in error. Marx (1894) emphasizes that the appearances to which capitalism gives rise obscure its dynamics to capitalists no less than to workers. As a consequence, social control cannot be a simple reflection of the "objective" needs of a class. Indeed, the Marxian notion of contradiction makes explicit the possibility that a dominant class will not be able to implement the social control that it needs to perpetuate its domination.

We must also note that the reproduction of class relations may require that a dominant class control *its own members*, as well as the members of subordinate classes. As Miliband (1977: 67–68) remarks, the assertion in the Communist Manifesto that "the executive of the modern state is but a committee for managing the common affairs of the whole bourgeoisie" implies that the bourgeoisie has affairs that are not common and that may lead to *intra*class conflict. For example, the survival of individual capitalists would be jeopardized if a single capitalist gained dominance over an entire sector of the economy and used this position to raise prices to other capitalist purchasers or to undersell competitors. To prevent this, capitalists may support antimonopoly legislation. It is likewise important to individual capitalists that no single capitalist gain influence over the state to the detriment of all others. Capitalists may thus support political measures that restrain the state (e.g., checks and balances between branches of government and popular elections).

The same is true of the working class. Its members have a common interest in the social control of those workers who may be tempted to sacrifice the interests of the class for personal advantage—hence the reprobation attached to strike breakers, rate busters, and informers, as well as to thieves and narcotics merchants.

It need not be the case that classes will differ with regard to every issue involving social control. Thus, Engels (1878) notes that once movable property exists, *all* classes regard theft as immoral. It is so because workers no less than capitalists have an interest in retaining possession of their belongings. It is only where class interests diverge that we should expect a divergence in social-control goals. In pursuing one interest, a class must not jeopardize more important interests. Hence, slaveowners do not punish slaves with imprisonment, for to do so would be to lose the use of their investment. Consequently slaves in the American South were disciplined primarily with summary corporal punishment (Sellin, 1976). To prevent slaveholders from provoking slave revolts by treating their slaves with excessive brutality, however, southern legislatures dominated by slaveowning interests passed legislation protecting slaves from their masters in limited ways.

To win broad support, a rising class must appeal to interests wider than its own. Marx (1844a: 55–56) therefore emphasizes that no class can become a ruling class unless it can make itself the representative of *general, universal* interests. No doubt this is an overstatement; a class need not gain universal enthusiasm to rule. But it must accommodate the interests of other classes and thus cannot introduce forms of social control that allied subordinate classes strongly oppose. As the slave South illustrates, there are even limits to the forms of control that can be imposed on exploited classes if class rule itself is not to be jeopardized. Engels notes in this connection that it is rare for a code of law to be

> the blunt, unmitigated, unadulterated expression of the domination of class—this in itself would offend the "conception of right." Even in the Code Napoleon the pure consistent conception of right held by the revolutionary bourgeoisie of 1792–96 is already adulterated in many ways and insofar as it is embodied there, daily has to undergo all sorts of attenuation, owing to the rising power of the proletariat [1890: 404].

The Ideology of Social Control

Although our discussion has been couched in terms of interest, advocacy of change in social control is often posed in other terms. Indeed, the phenomenon of the reformer who purports to be altruistic has often been noted in historical research. It has become fashionable to regard claims of altruistic intent as cynical cover-ups for the pursuit of self-interest. At times this cynicism may be warranted, for the language of humanitarianism could be a ploy to gain support from other classes. Yet there is often a problem of evidence. Where hidden motivation cannot be documented, the motivation has generally been inferred from the sometimes repressive consequences of the reform. But if consequences cannot always be anticipated because the relevant actors have a limited and perhaps mistaken understanding of social process, such inferences may be in error.

Marx's own writings do not require us to assume that all action springs from economic interest. When Marx (Marx and Engels, 1846: 246) proposes that "life is not determined by consciousness, but consciousness by life," and that consciousness arises on the foundations of a society's economic structure (Marx, 1859), he is not reducing consciousness to interest (or life to economics). Marx's conception of human nature certainly allows for sentiments of solidarity but argues that these sentiments and the forms in which they are expressed are themselves socially conditioned.

Even when ideas do advance the interests of a class, their proponents are not necessarily aware of this. Engels thus comments:

> The reflection of economic relations as legal principles is necessarily also a topsy-turvy one: it goes on without the person who is acting being conscious of it; the jurist imagines he is operating with a priori propositions, whereas they are really only economic reflexes, so everything is upside down. . . . It seems to me obvious

that this inversion, which so long as it remains unrecognized, forms what we call *ideological outlook* [1890: 404].

In these terms, many ideas about social control, and proposals for change in social control, have been ideological. This is not to say that they are mistaken, or that they are disseminated for the purpose of deceiving anyone. Ideology is not propaganda. Rather, ideology consists of ideas that originate in social experience—particularly the experience of class relations—but without the thinker being aware of it. In short, it is not bourgeois interests but bourgeois society that is the source of bourgeois ideas. These ideas may contain or express class interest but cannot be reduced to class interest.

Nonclass Actors

Thus far we have assumed that the only actors relevant to social control are classes, but this is obviously not true: Other groups have been responsible for many social-control measures as well. Marxian theory, however, views class consciousness as variable. Subjective classes—classes whose members are aware of common class interests and share political goals—form over time through struggle. The obstacles to the formation of subjective classes are many (and in some of Marx's writings were seriously understated). When class consciousness is weak, we can expect to see other entities, such as class fractions or groups that cut across class lines, as more important in establishing social control. Occupational groups are especially likely to be important because communication within an occupation facilitates the dissemination of conceptions of occupational interest and proposals regarding social control policy.

Marxian theory suggests that the state is also relevant. Although Marx and Engels sometimes wrote as if the state could be viewed as a simple tool of a single class, and therefore not an independent actor in its own right, on other occasions they recognized that this was an oversimplification (Engels, 1893). More recent work in Marxian theory has emphasized the partial autonomy of the capitalist state from the direct control of the capitalist class. State office holders may utilize this "partial autonomy" to advance their own immediate interests, or to gain political support by advancing the interests of other social groups such as classes. The financial resources of the modern state, its ability to gain exposure for its views in the mass media, and its near monopoly on the means of violence give it an enormous influence over social control.[2]

The mobilization of both class and nonclass actors has often been the work of individuals or small groups who construct conceptions of deviance, devise strategies of social control and decontrol, and organize support for these strategies. Because this ideological and political work is ordinarily too time-consuming to be undertaken by those directly involved in material production, it is often carried out by others[3]—hence the prominence in nineteenth-century American and British reform movements of clergy, members of the landed gentry, and the wives and daughters of wealthy men. As Embree (1977) notes, though, the mere existence of these "entrepreneurs" is insufficient to guarantee the movements' success. Groups seeking change in social control constantly appear, but not all of them achieve their goals. The success of entrepreneurial efforts to change social control hinges on the ability of the entrepreneur to frame conceptions of deviance and devise strategies of control that mesh with the subjective interests and world view of class or nonclass actors with resources sufficient to carry through an initiative and overcome possible opposition.

Social Control outside the State

Some Marxians (e.g., Althusser, 1971) have recently called attention to the role of institutions that are not units of production, such as the family, the school, and the church, in disseminating ideologies needed for the reproduction of captialist social relations.[4] Just as the state exercises social control in order to manage conflict between and within classes, these nonstate institutions[5] exercise social control to contain conflict between their own members. Generally, Marxian theory directs our attention to the source of conflicts within these institutions in the ensemble of class-based social relations (e.g., marital conflicts that originate in the sexual division of labor in capitalism) and the influence of these relations on the scope and methods of social control employed. As the

[2]As will be seen in our discussion of the mercantile state, this was not always so.

[3]Marx and Engels (1846) note this division of labor within the bourgeoisie.

[4]We note that the partial autonomy of these institutions from the ruling class (more for some institutions than others) implies that the socialization performed need not always be consistent with the needs of the ruling class. When it is not, the state may be called on to do *more* rather than less.

[5]Althusser himself labels the family, church, school, and so on, "ideological state apparatuses," but most Marxists reject this unconventional use of the word *state*.

organization of production and distribution change, so does the social control within socializing institutions.

We note that social control in these institutions can be affected by social control on the part of the state as well. For example, if the state prohibits parents or teachers from disciplining children or students in specific ways, it may reduce the ability of the former to exercise social control within the family or classroom. On the other hand, we may presume that the more effectively these institutions secure the behavioral requirements of the mode of production through socialization, the less the state will need to handle them formally. There is thus reciprocal influence between different forms of social control within the overall framework of the mode of production, as well as between the economic sphere and the socializing institutions. Marx and Engels said little about such matters, and only recently have Marxian scholars begun to carry out empirical investigations of such institutions as the school and the family. For this reason, our treatment of the history of social control within the family and school will be scant by comparison with the treatment we give the state.

Although the preceding Marxist-inspired considerations do not by themselves constitute a theory of social control, they provide a mode of analysis that can be useful in the larger understanding of social control. To illustrate the utility of the approach, we consider social control in England and the United States during the transition from mercantile to industrial capitalism.

Mercantile Capitalism

By the beginning of the sixteenth century, the dissolution of feudalism was well advanced. Almost all serfs had been manumitted. The bulk of the population resided in stratified, agricultural village communities. Apart from a small number of freehold yeomen, most peasants were tenants living on small plots rented from large landowners (gentry and nobility). Some of the poorer peasants also worked part time for wages doing agricultural labor. Artisans and craftsmen engaged in petty commodity production and, to an increasing extent, worked in domestic industry organized by merchant capitalists. Price controls, the prohibition of usury, restrictions on the export of grain, and the regulation of the quality of manufactured goods protected the consumer and prevented competition from eroding the solidarity of merchants and artisans.

The "commercial revolution" of the sixteenth century greatly undermined communal solidarity. As landlords began to produce for market, they were no longer restrained by sentiments of obligation toward their tenants, expelling them when they were no longer needed on the land. Vagrancy thus became a serious problem.

SOCIAL CONTROL AND SOCIAL REPRODUCTION

Lacking most of the administrative resources of a modern bureaucratic state, the Tudor monarchs responded to these developments by trying to stabilize society through the use of formal social control measures. Tudor vagrancy legislation was a major component in this effort. Fearing that the depopulation of the countryside would weaken England militarily, the crown took steps to stop vagrancy. Although the crown encouraged parish relief on a voluntary basis, the gentry-dominated Parliament adopted more sanguinary measures (though these proved to be difficult to enforce). The Tudor monarchs, on the other hand, repeatedly enacted legislation that limited and attempted to reverse the enclosures. This was an attempt to defend the *long-run* interests of landlords, including the crown, in the preservation of the existing social order by defending tenants against landlords who pursued narrow short-run interests too far. As the crown's administrative apparatus was still weak, however, enforcement had to be left to the local justices of the peace. Themselves drawn from the landowning gentry, they frustrated the enforcement of the legislation.

In these efforts, the crown acted with partial independence from the landed classes. In seeking to stabilize its own position, the crown defended the interests of subordinate classes as best it could given its fiscal and administrative weakness, within the limits of the existing hierarchical social order.

MERCANTILISM AND SOCIAL CONTROL OF
THE ECONOMY

To enhance the autonomy of the crown, the Tudor monarchs took steps to increase their revenues and to strengthen the military position of the kingdom. The economic policies put into effect by the Tudor monarchs on behalf of these goals later came to be known as *mercantilism*. Some of them remained in effect well into the eighteenth century. Mercantilism entailed the regulation of the economy in order to maximize the flow of bullion into the realm. Regulation was now oriented toward merchant and manufacturing interests, as well as the crown, instead of the entire community. To encourage the export of manufactured goods, prices were kept down; on the other hand, the export of raw wool was discouraged in the interests of the English textile industry (Buck, 1942: 33, 37; Webb and Webb, 1963: 66). To maintain a favorable balance of trade, consumption was also regulated. Thus, tariffs were imposed to reduce the importation of foreign luxury goods, raising the price of these commodities to the wealthy, and sumptuary legislation was adopted to encourage domestic industry, such as the manufacturing of woolen cloth (Heckscher, 1931: 265; Hurstfield and Smith, 1972: 63–64). Although these measures were undertaken to benefit manufacturing, the Tudor state was no tool of manufacturing interests. Some of the standards imposed on producers were adopted over their explicit opposition, at times because they were technically unworkable.[6]

The social control of labor was another component of mercantile policy. Because manufacturing and agriculture were highly labor intensive, wages had to be held down if English commodities were to be competitive on the world market. Legislation to accomplish this was adopted but was shaped by the broader Tudor program of stabilizing society. Thus, wage controls were imposed, but these were intended to keep wages from falling too low as well as to prevent them from rising too high (Cunningham, 1912: 169). Although a legal obligation to work was created, and penalties were imposed on employees who left their jobs before the end of the year, employers were equally penalized for dismissing their employees prematurely. Sixteenth-century wage-control measures, then, involved more than wage control. They reflected a preoccupation with the decline of tillage and the growth of vagrancy, uneasiness over the spread of impersonal, commercialized social relations, and a fear of masterless men (Cunningham, 1912: 25–44; Bindoff, 1961; Lockyer, 1964: 140; Clarkson, 1972: 168; Powell and Cook, 1977: 185). The legislation provided some benefits to all classes, though more to some than to others.

[6]Because the state was inexperienced at regulation, it often did not know how to achieve its goals. Clarkson notes—concerning efforts to regulate middlemen in the leather trade, undertaken in response to rising shoe prices—that

> it was generally assumed that middlemen were the cause of increasing prices, but the government was ignorant of the structure of the leather industry, even to the point of knowing whether curriers, who processed leather after tanning, were actually leather workers or merely dealers in leather. Between 1548 and 1563 six acts alternately allowed curriers to and prevented them from buying and selling leather. These rapid reversals of policy were the outcome of intensive lobbying by the two London companies of curriers and cordwainers [shoemakers], each trying to obtain exclusive control of the leather trade and both arguing that their particular proposals would achieve the government's aim of keeping prices down [1972: 175].

THE BOURGEOIS REVOLUTION

The bourgeois revolution in mid-century left Parliament and local government in the hands of the gentry and town merchants. Faced with a threat from below during the English Civil War, the propertied classes closed ranks, achieving a high degree of unity and domination of the state. In the last half of the century, the expansion of the economy reduced unemployment, thus diminishing the threat of popular disturbances. With the disappearance of a threat from below, the state shifted its attention from the protection of consumers and subsistence farmers toward the defense of property (Hill, 1961: 152–154, 202).

The content and scope of social control reflects this shift. Thus, during the reign of William (1689–1702), criminal legislation protecting private property tended to become harsher. For example, shoplifting and the stealing of furniture by lodgers became capital offenses. On the other hand, where property was not at stake, penalties were reduced (Hill, 1961: 289; Beloff, 1963: 9–10). These trends continued throughout the eighteenth century (Radzinowicz, 1948; Thompson, 1975). New statutes prohibiting forgery and counterfeiting were adopted to protect transactions involving the paper instruments of credit required as the economy became national (Ignatieff, 1978: 17). As merchant capitalists reorganized production through the "putting out" system, they gained the adoption of embezzlement laws to prevent workers from keeping scraps of raw material left over from the production process and thereby impairing the profits of the merchants who supplied the raw materials and sold the finished product.

To force wages down on behalf of employers, the state adopted measures to expand the supply of laborers. So long as one could survive without working for wages by begging, gambling, or cultivating waste, or by using the commons, forests, ponds, and game preserves to gain a livelihood, it was possible to avoid becoming a wage laborer (Thompson, 1975: 240–241). To foreclose these possibilities, Parliament enacted severe penalties for poaching, stealing fruit from trees, taking fish from ponds, and gathering wood from forests (Thompson, 1975; Ignatieff, 1978: 26–27).[7] The criminal law thus became a means for separating potential laborers from the means of production, leaving no other possible source of income except a wage.

---

[7]That Parliament was indeed concerned with just this issue is apparent from the preamble to one of the eighteenth-century game laws:

> Whereas great mischief do ensue by inferior tradesmen, apprentices and other dissolute persons neglecting their trades and employments who follow hunting, fishing and other game to the ruin of themselves and their neighbours, therefore, if any such person shall presume to hunt, hawk,

At the same time, state control over the bourgeoisie was being reduced. The growth and commercialization of the economy had created a mass of small manufacturers and merchants, who began to campaign against the legally enforceable monopolies, patents, and licenses granted to large merchants by the cash-starved Stuarts in the early seventeenth century. In response to these pressures, as well as the difficulties of regulating an expanded economy, industrial and commerical monopolies were repealed, and restrictive regulations concerning guilds and apprenticeships fell into desuetude during the course of the seventeenth century. Although wage controls remained in effect, the fixing of wages had become exceptional in London by the mid-eighteenth century. Unevenly but surely, the development of the mercantile economy was eroding the state's regulation of the economy.

Hamilton (1978) has argued that the dissolution of the household as the unit of production and the unequal position of men and women in the commercialized economy gave rise to the Puritan ideology of the family in this period. The greater economic resources of husbands enhanced their capacity to exercise social control over their wives; at the same time, the state intervened on behalf of husbands by making it possible for husbands to commit "lewd wives" to houses of correction (Sellin, 1976: 73).

THE MECHANISMS OF SOCIAL CONTROL

The mercantile era saw the introduction of three new forms of state-imposed social control: the house of correction, galley slavery, and transportation. Rusche and Kirchheimer (1939) have argued that each of these innovations and its subsequent employment was shaped by the state's desire to regulate the labor market—that is, to force laborers into the labor market when labor was scarce and contain surplus labor in periods of unemployment. In the mercantile period, this goal required teaching work skills and making labor available as needed in connection with overseas commerce and colonization (see also Sellin, 1976; Ignatieff, 1978: 12). Nevertheless, these efforts often failed: The houses of correction, for example, were rarely able to turn their inmates into productive laborers (Ignatieff, 1978: 32–33).

---

fish or fowl (unless in company with the master of such apprentice duly qualified) he shall . . . be subject to the other penalties [i.e., varying terms in the house of correction] [cited in Ignatieff, 1978: 26].

MERCANTILE IDEOLOGY AND SOCIAL CONTROL

The medieval conception of society as naturally hierarchical retained its validity in the mercantile era. There seems to have been no need to legitimate social control with a new ideology of social class. Rank was explicitly recognized in law (legal privileges often varied by class) and determined the form of punishment imposed on criminals (beheading for nobles, hanging for commoners). The impact of mercantilism on other components of ideology, however, was greater. Roman Catholic doctrine had always prohibited usury on religious grounds, for example. Mercantile doctrine favored state action to keep interest low, but in order to stimulate investment, a secular rationale was needed. Although Luther had reiterated the Catholic condemnation of usury, Calvin tolerated moderate interest on loans, essentially adopting doctrine to the exigencies of business. This ideological shift was quickly reflected in English law: The 1552 act that prohibited interest taking on scriptural grounds was repealed in 1571 by legislation that permitted interest up to 10%. Under the impact of commercial capitalism, major components of morality were becoming privatized. When economic activity is organized on a profit-making basis, interest charges come to be seen as a normal feature of economic activity.

In the Middle Ages, the irregular rhythms of agriculture left serfs and peasants idle for parts of the year, whereas clerics and lords refrained from production altogether. In Catholic doctrine, the poor were loved by God and to give alms was a religious duty. As agriculture became profitable and industry made labor continuously useful, the acceptance of poverty, charity, and idleness was eroded. Charity was criticized as socially harmful because it permitted recipients to stay out of the labor market. To curb vagrancy, the state attempted to suppress begging and indiscriminate private alms giving. The prime carriers of this new ideology were the "industrious sort of people"—the small independent farmers, artisans, craftsmen, and merchants who provided the backbone of the Puritan movement, and who depended on their own industriousness to advance in a competitive economy. This ideology was not primarily a disguise for ruling-class interests; in fact, it became the basis for a radical critique of the great merchants and gentry who lived a life of idleness on income derived from investments. Yet the interest of the middle class as employers is evident in this version of the work ethic, for it was argued (with some basis in fact, and fully consistent with mercantilist doctrine) that the poor would work hard and regularly only if wages were low. High wages, it was said, would lead only to sloth and drunkenness. This line of reasoning provided the rationale for wage-control legislation (Heckscher, 1935: 165–168).

Industrial Capitalism

The "industrial revolution" transformed the forces and relations of production in the late eighteenth and nineteenth centuries, first in England and then in Europe and the United States. Technical innovations led to a more complex division of labor and increased labor productivity. Factory production replaced domestic industry, wage labor largely supplanted remuneration in kind, and the capitalist mode of production became dominant,[8] with petty commodity production persisting as a subordinate mode of production (along with slavery in the American South until 1865).

REDUCTION OF SOCIAL CONTROL OVER THE ECONOMY

The political victory of the middle class in 1832 moved England closer to a true laissez-faire policy. The Corn Laws were repealed, tariffs were reduced, land became a commodity, slavery was abolished throughout the empire, legislation prohibiting the emigration of workers and the export of machinery was repealed, and the welfare payments that interfered with the free play of market forces ended. The flow of "factors of production" was to be governed not by punitive legislation but by the impersonal regulation of supply and demand in the marketplace. With a working class cut off from all legal access to the means of production by state intervention in the mercantile era, capitalists no longer needed the state to force laborers to work for wages (Marx, 1867: 271). The state's involvement in the economy was now to be restricted to the enforcement of "voluntary" contractual agreements and maintenance of the currency.

The bourgeoisie favored this restriction on the role of the state because it prevented the state from giving any individual capitalist a competitive advantage over the others, and because the supply of labor was now sufficient to keep wages down; but laissez-faire policy had wider backing. Working-class support for the repeal of the Corn Laws was won by the promise of cheaper bread, whereas the middle class supported repeal in the hope that wages could be reduced if the cost of workers' subsistence were to decline.

In practice, the state was never as limited in its social-control functions as laissez-faire theory required. Thus, in England, child labor was

[8]The capitalist mode of production entails not only the production of commodities (this is also characteristic of mercantile capitalism and petty commodity production), but, in addition the other factors of production (labor, land, capital) are also purchased as commodities.

restricted by the Factory Act of 1819 and subsequent legislation, factory inspection was begun in 1833, and hours legislation was passed in 1844. These protective measures were achieved, despite the opposition of most manufacturers, by an alliance of workers, artisans hostile to the factory, paternalistic Tory gentry resentful of the industrialists' victory in 1832, physicians and public health professionals, Anglican clergy concerned with retaining the loyalty of working-class worshippers, and even a handful of industrialists who were afraid that the working class would fail to reproduce itself unless working conditions were improved (Marx, 1867: 270; Perkin, 1969: 363, 401; Ward, 1970). The abundant supply of labor from the countryside, however, made the latter consideration irrelevant to most industrialists of the early nineteenth century.[9]

ALCOHOL, SEX, AND SELF-CONTROL

In limiting state interference with the economy, the petty bourgeoisie secured one of the structural conditions it needed for its survival as a class. But individual entrepreneurs needed something more. In an individualistic, competitive economy, success required the possession of appropriate character traits. Entrepreneurs had to be self-motivated to take advantage of market opportunities. It was crucial for entrepreneurs who operated their businesses on thin margins to work hard for long hours and to eliminate the distraction and costs associated with unnecessary personal consumption (Howe, 1976). With labor costs comprising a large fraction of the cost of doing business, it was equally important for employers to minimize the wages paid to employees. The positive emphasis placed on the cultivation of self-mastery, assertiveness, industriousness, thrift, frugality, and abstemiousness and the stress on avoiding laziness and ostentatious consumption in literature written for middle-class male audiences in the early nineteenth century reflected the needs of the individual entrepreneur quite accurately.

As the weakening of community and extended kinship ties had reduced the effectiveness of external sources of social control, and the increased industrial production of low-cost goods multiplied temptations to spend one's earnings, powerful *internal* sources of discipline were required. An internalized sense of duty had to supply what neither formal nor informal external sources could continue to provide.

The preoccupation with middle-class traits is already evident in sev-

---

[9]By 1861, many of the manufacturers who had staunchly opposed factory legislation a few decades earlier now admitted that it had not had the pernicious consequences they had anticipated, and they were now happy to have it (Ward, 1970).

enteenth-century Puritan literature. Although imported to America by the Puritans, this extraordinary emphasis on self-control failed to spread beyond New England to the rest of the colonial population because the structural basis for it did not exist in the agricultural, mercantile economy of the colonies. Not until the early nineteenth century, when the United States was on the verge of its own industrial revolution, did these "Puritan" themes play an important role in influencing social control outside the Puritan colonies themselves. This development can be seen in nineteenth-century thought concerning inebriacy and sexuality. Levine (1978) has noted that attitudes toward the consumption of alcohol shifted drastically at the end of the eighteenth century and in the early part of the nineteenth. The American colonists (including the Puritans) valued alcohol for the contributions it made to health and conviviality. It was widely consumed by all social classes. Work discipline for artisans and craftsmen in the petty commodity mode of production was not rigorous and included drinking rituals as part of a noncompetitive work culture. As the competitive capitalist mode of production became dominant, these rituals disappeared among the middle class, and work discipline was tightened—though drinking remained an important element of male working-class culture. Within the middle class, fear that drunkenness would lead to the loss of self-control led to a rejection of alcohol consumption. Temperance societies were formed to encourage moderation in drinking and, later, abstinence: heavy chronic drinking came to be explained as the consequence of a pathology entailing the loss of self-control. The hysterical tone of much Prohibition literature reflected the precariousness of middle-class status and the danger to that status that uncontrolled drinking posed.[10]

A similar shift in attitudes toward sexuality took place.[11] Eighteenth-century marriage manuals celebrated the pleasures of sex and portrayed female sexuality in a positive light. Beginning in the 1830s, however, middle-class male sex reformers began to find a ready market for their manuals urging husbands to restrict the frequency of marital coitus (often to no more than once a month) and then only for purposes of

---

[10]Gusfield (1963: 36–44) points out that in the first two decades of the nineteenth century, temperance was promoted by Calvinist ministers and Federalist lay leaders concerned with the cultural dimensions of their own displacement by the new middle classes. They had been unable, however, to gain wide popular support for temperance.

[11]Comparable developments were manifested somewhat earlier in England, at the beginning of the eighteenth century, but progressed more slowly because of the strength of the less restrictive aristocratic culture, which was absent in the United States. By 1800, however, the British aristocracy was becoming bourgeoisified, and its sexual ideology closely resembled that of the middle class (Cominos, 1963).

procreation. Female sexuality was denied, and male sexuality was to be suppressed so as not to reduce the energies available for production (Hare, 1962; Cominos, 1963; Engelhardt, 1974; Haller and Haller, 1974; Neuman, 1975; Barker-Benfield, 1976; Bullough, 1976: 542–549). Sexual control was to be exercised by individuals over themselves, and by parents over their children. Restraining devices to aid in this task sold well in England and the United States during the nineteenth century (Bullough, 1976: 549, 561), and surgery was also employed (Barker-Benfield, 1976).

Whereas temperance doctrine originated in the actual danger that uncontrolled drinking posed to a precarious middle-class status, but exaggerated that danger (Levine, 1978), Victorian sexual ideology had a weaker practical basis. Although sexual self-restraint may have had some value to the middle class by reducing the birth rate in an economy that no longer required an endless supply of farmhands and in which the increasing costs of educating children were borne privately (Reed, 1978),[12] the continued prohibition against disseminating information about contraception suggests that the translation of this goal into behavior was mediated by a doctrine of sexual abstinence. This doctrine was derived from class experience of a nonsexual nature. The metaphors through which male sexuality was conceptualized were those of the competitive marketplace (e.g., semen was "spent" in orgasm). Like the capital of the entrepreneur, bodily energy was in constant danger of being depleted.[13]

As women in the United States were being excluded from the public economy in the Jacksonian era, they were not exposed to the same competitive pressures as men, and their sexual ideologies differed. The target of the female sex reformers in this period was not masturbation

[12]The birth rate fell steadily throughout the nineteenth century.

[13]For the Jacksonian sex reformers, who left the farms of western New York and New England to enter the middle class in the commercial cities of the Northeast, the transition to the new competitive order was especially acute. Smith-Rosenberg (1978) suggests that sexuality itself had become more problematic for them at this time because the decline of the apprenticeship system meant that adolescent males remained living with their family of origin instead of boarding out. At the same time, fathers' reduced ability to transmit property or occupation to sons weakened family control of adolescent boys. Preoccupation with uncontrollable, virile young men was thus rooted in the effect that the structural transformation of the economy had on family structure (see also Neuman, 1975).

We note in passing that the high demand for child labor weakened parental control over their children throughout the nineteenth century, because children could leave home and be self-supporting at an early age. At the same time, low wages for industrial labor rendered parents dependent on the contributions their children could make to family income (suggested by Steven Dubnoff).

but the double standard: Their concern was not with self-control but with the young woman who was seduced and abandoned in a community where informal social pressures could no longer force men to marry their pregnant sexual partners (suggested by Carroll Smith-Rosenberg).

Following the Civil War, industrialization shifted the emphasis of these petty bourgeois reform movements away from an exclusive preoccupation with self-control. The expansion of the capitalist mode of production gave the large corporation an increasingly prominent role in the economy, and the industrial proletariat, made up to a large extent of immigrants, grew rapidly. Upwardly mobile fractions of the working class adopted the abstinence patterns of the middle class they aspired to join, and in some cases even became active prohibitionists. Middle-class women, now fully excluded from the public economy, gave Prohibition strong support. Given women's financial dependence on men, male drinking jeopardized their own class position to the same extent that it jeopardized the position of men. The association between prostitution and the saloon posed a potential threat of venereal disease. And, as an exclusively male preserve, the saloon symbolized male prerogative and privilege (Levine, 1979). Much of the leadership of the post–Civil War movement came from these women, as well as from evangelical clergy who were able to draw on the organizational resources of their churches to mobilize lower-middle-class support for the cause, and whose own involvement may have been sparked by their declining occupational status (Hofstadter, 1955: 150–153).

With the backbone of the movement remaining a middle class that was being squeezed economically and politically between labor and capital, antiliquor agitation began to embody the concerns of the middle class vis à vis other classes. The liquor trust, denounced for profiting by promoting human misery, became a symbol of capitalist greed (Isaac, 1965: 123; Blocker, 1976). Middle-class prohibitionists also linked alcohol with working-class crime, labor militancy,[14] industrial efficiency and accidents, the level of wages (it was hoped that if workers stopped drinking, wages could be lowered and class conflict reduced), and political corruption (the saloon played a major role in the urban ethnic political machines). Alcohol control thus became joined with class control (Ostrander, 1957; Gusfield, 1963; Timberlake, 1963). Many states

---

[14]Within months of the great Chicago riot of 1877, the middle classes had initiated "a broad movement of reform, directed toward temperance legislation and Christian missions and charity societies and the public school system, all oriented toward converting workingpeople to middle class notions of work and thrift, sobriety and respectability [Kann, n.d.]." In addition, they strengthened the police force and state militia.

adopted Prohibition legislation, and ultimately Prohibition was established on a national basis.[15]

INDUSTRIAL IDEOLOGY AND SOCIAL CONTROL

The campaign to reduce state regulation of the economy in late eighteenth- and early nineteenth-century Britain was waged in the name of a theory that claimed general social benefits for laissez-faire. As individuals pursued private gain, an "invisible hand" would maximize social well-being—provided all exchanges were consensual. External interference with the terms of these mutually agreeable exchanges could only be detrimental. In a formal sense, this ideology is radically democratic, for it grants equal legitimacy to every individual's preferences for goods and services and is grounded in the realities of the marketplace, where what counts is cash, not the personal attributes of its possessor.

Laissez-faire philosophy provided a new rationale for the existence of the state and its apparatus of social control. Because the rational pursuit of gain would lead individuals to acquire wealth through nonconsensual taking, the state was needed to prohibit and penalize unwilling private exchanges. The entrepreneurial balancing of potential costs and gains thus provided both the theoretical explanation for the existence of crime and for its repression. As individuals enter the theory only abstractly (through their possession of the abstract faculty of rationality) and therefore equally, the sanctions for such exchanges were to be formally equal as well. To avoid unnecessary costs in repressing crime, penalties were to be limited to what was necessary to outweigh the potential gain from the offense. These ideas were first developed by some of the leading figures of the French Enlightenment—Montesquieu, Voltaire, Helvetius, Diderot, d'Alembert—whose thinking had been influenced by the growth of commerce and industry. Generally loyal to the aristocracy or monarchy, they wanted to rationalize and depersonalize state administration. Cesare Beccaria (1764) gave this "classical school of criminology" its most coherent and influential formulation.

Scion of an old noble family, Beccaria in his writings expressed the ideology of that fraction of the aristocracy that had begun to engage in capitalist agriculture and was thus allied with the "new bourgeoisie," consisting of small commercial and industrial (mainly textiles) capitalists producing outside the guilds, and with the modernizing administration of the Austrian Hapsburgs, who wanted to revive the economy of Lombardy so that taxation could pay for the costs of administering the terri-

---

[15]Humphries and Greenberg (1980) extend this discussion to narcotics legislation.

tory (Canderloro, 1956). Theirs was an ideology that simultaneously affirmed de facto privilege in the form of property ownership while denying de jure privilege in the form of legally recognized rank. It was a utopian response to a feudal order that was disintegrating politically and economically. Later this formal equality was embraced by middle-class reformers as a way of legitimating the social-control apparatus against criticism, but it is doubtful that this was a major consideration for Beccaria, for the lower classes posed no threat in northern Italy at this time. The tenets of classical criminology seem to be less a defense of class interests than an indication of how deeply bourgeois modes of thinking were penetrating the analysis of a variety of social problems among all classes.

The writings of the classical criminologists enjoyed great popularity in the United States around the time of the War of Independence. Then, as capitalism became established as the dominant mode of production, explanations of crime began to shift away from abstract rational calculation toward attempts to differentiate criminals from noncriminals on the basis of distinguishing personal traits. For many writers, criminals were incapable of restraining themselves when faced with temptation (Boostrum, 1974). Some attributed this inability to parental overindulgence and the subsequent failure to develop internalized self control. Thus, the upbringing of a man released from a New York prison in 1831 after serving a sentence for attempted rape is characterized as follows: "Lived with his parents who indulged him too much for his good; was a very wild unsteady boy; fond of company and amusements; when he could not get his parents' consent, would go without it [quoted in Rothman, 1971: 70]." These writings tell us little about crime but say much about bourgeois preoccupations over such matters as raising children, resisting impulses in the face of temptation, and working-class movements for higher wages.

Other writers paid more attention to other causes of weak self-control, ranging from an inherited deficit to a pathological social environment. Eclectic and empirically unsupported though these explanations tended to be, they mark the beginnings of an attempt to account scientifically for crime and other phenomena (such as insanity) deemed to require social control. The striking advances in technology made possible by the physical sciences gave impetus to those who sought a comparable understanding of socially troublesome populations.

The individualism of nineteenth-century explanations of crime (and insanity, pauperism, etc.) may have reflected the atomism of the physical sciences, but it is perhaps more plausible that both reflect the social importance of the petty bourgeoisie and the individualizing tendencies of competitive capitalism. The greatest conceptual borrowings, however, came from biology. Lamarckian doctrine (the hereditary transmission of acquired characteristics), hereditary degeneracy, and Darwinian biology shaped explanations of crime in the nineteenth century. As immigration and the sharpening of class conflict in the latter part of the nineteenth century increased the social distance between working-class criminals and middle-class citizens, explanations of crime gave greater prominence to the role of biological defects, but without totally slighting environmental factors. Although increasingly cast in scientific form, it must be kept in mind that little of the nineteenth-century literature on crime met minimal scientific standards of methodological adequacy. For the most part, prescientific concepts of causality and elements of lay morality were simply cast in a scientific framework until well into the twentieth century.

Methods of Social Control under
Industrial Capitalism

THE POLICE

Throughout the eighteenth century, poor harvests, the abolition of usufruct rights to land, forest, and stream, the discharge of soldiers at the end of wars, the export of wheat during times of shortage, forestalling and engrossing on the part of landowners and merchants, fluctuations in the supply and demand for manufactured goods, and the introduction of labor-saving machinery led to periods of rising food prices, unemployment, and social dislocation for the laboring poor. The weakening of paternalistic regulation of the economy exacerbated these problems (Rose, 1961; Thompson 1963; Shelton, 1973). Excluded by property qualifications from voting or holding office, and therefore from utilizing lawful political methods to deal with these developments, agricultural and industrial laborers rioted to enforce the "just price" of the vanishing "moral economy" (Thompson, 1971; Stevenson, 1975) and, in the latter part of the eighteenth century, as capitalist social relations became more firmly established, for higher wages (Shelton, 1973: 8). So long as their aims remained limited, riots were not treated as major threats; indeed, members of the upper classes encouraged, manipulated, and at times led them (Thompson, 1963: 74; Silver, 1967; Shelton, 1973).[16]

[16]According to Shelton (1973), landowners and industrialists channeled popular discontent toward middlemen, who were made scapegoats for economic hardship. As long as riots were directed against middlemen, the holders of major wealth were not threatened.

When riots got out of hand and threatened landed estates or houses of industry, magistrates called out associations of gentry with their servants (in essence, another mob) to put them down—a form of social control based on personal authority. At times the militia and army were also used; however, magistrates mistrusted the loyalty of the militia, for its members' social backgrounds were similar to those of the mob. And the large landowners feared that a standing army would strengthen the centralized state, weakening their own political power (Silver, 1967; Shelton, 1973). When first proposed in the late eighteenth century, a permanent, salaried civilian police force was unacceptable to the gentry because it would have tended to undermine the personal authority of the gentry. Already weakened by the effects of the commercialization of rural society, the patrimonial authority of the gentry was sustained by its personal domination of law enforcement: By pardoning criminals and declining prosecution, the propertied classes could win popular gratitude (Hay, 1975).

Personal forms of enforcement had drawbacks, however, as well as advantages. The hostilities generated in putting down riots continued to divide communities afterward when the parties to the conflict all resided in the community. Calling out the army was too much an all-or-nothing affair; it risked the unnecessary escalation of events and the exacerbation of conflict. As the expanded reproduction of capitalism drew more and more of the population into capitalist social relations and exposed increasing numbers of the lower classes to the vicissitudes of the marketplace, labor militancy and radicalism grew. Conspiracies sprang up. Fear of a revolution, intensified by the French example, ultimately led the landowners to accept the creation of a regular police force, for the army would have been incapable of coping with a domestic uprising if it had had French support (Shelton, 1973; Stevenson, 1977). Merchants and industrialists concerned about riot and theft also supported the establishment of a police force. As Spitzer and Scull (1977a) note, riot was extremely disruptive to the marketplace. Farmers and middlemen traders would tend to avoid rural markets threatened by mob action. In addition, owners of factories threatened with destruction by displaced craftsmen wanted protection (Shelton, 1973).

Beyond the threat of riot, however, merchants wanted to reduce the costs of theft. Colquhoun (1795; 1800), the leading turn-of-the-century police reformer, bemoaned the enormous losses due to theft suffered by merchants in the rapidly growing commercial centers. As the geographical extent of trade grew, private protection on an individual basis became less feasible. Yet, as Spitzer and Scull (1977a) point out, the "free rider" problem—many benefitting at the expense of a few—made collective *private* arrangements unfeasible.[17] The existing system of enforcement, which relied heavily on rewards to informers, recovery of stolen goods for a fee paid by the victim, and private prosecution, had sprung up unplanned as the commercial revolution eroded the traditional enforcement arrangements based on communal solidarity, but it was ineffective and may have encouraged crime. A tax-supported, salaried police patrol was thus adopted as the only feasible solution to the problem of riot and theft in rural market and industrial towns and commercial cities in the final stages of the transition from a mercantile to a competitive capitalist economy. Despite the clear and widely discussed advantages of a public police to capitalist interests, for several decades only minimal steps to strengthen the existing system of enforcement were taken (Donajgrodzki, 1977); not until 1829 was the Metropolitan Police Force finally established in London. Opposition came not only from those who feared the restoration of absolutism but also from elements of the nascent working class and from London officials who resisted the loss of patronage jobs that abolition of the watch and ward system would entail (Manning, 1977), Sir Robert Peel, a Tory politician and landowner and son of a large textile manufacturer, was perfectly positioned to weld the alliance of landowners, manufacturers, and fractions of the petty bourgeoisie that finally succeeded in establishing a bureaucratic police force in England. The establishment of a salaried, preventive patrol was significant not merely as a more efficient way of carrying out social control. Policing represented two qualitatively new developments: rule through impersonal, bureaucratically administered, general law, and a deeper, more finely tuned penetration of formal control into everyday social life (Spitzer, 1979).

The establishment of a bureaucratic mode of enforcement had become possible in a politically decentralized society because economic change had partially weakened patrimonial sources of authority in the countryside, while exacerbating class conflict to the point where the propertied classes realized that they needed a new form of social control, particularly one that was depersonalized. The landowner, who as magistrate dispersed the mob, was too readily identified with the interests he defended.[18] A salaried police force, it was felt, could more

---

[17]Attempts along these lines were made. For example, manufacturers in eighteenth-century industrial towns formed associations to finance the prosecution of laborers accused of offenses connected with the "putting out" system (e.g., embezzlement of raw materials) (Shelton, 1973: 71).

[18]Conversely, the lower gentry who as parish judges sympathized with the rioters and did little to suppress them failed to serve the interests of property (Shelton, 1973: 95). The local militia posed much the same problem. When called on to put down rioters who were

effectively claim to represent a law that embodied general interests rather than those of a particular class, for it would not be a direct party to the disputes that erupted into riots. The creation of the new police thus had an important ideological dimension having to do with the legitimation of social control. Reformers argued that those who were punished would acknowledge the fairness of their punishment and feel guilty only if it was evident that the law was enforced impartially (Ignatieff, 1978: 70–75). By remunerating the police with wage payments, bureaucratization also enhanced the legitimacy (as well as efficiency) of enforcement, for abandonment of the "service for fee" system made it possible for the laboring classes to file complaints—an opportunity they utilized to a substantial degree (Philips, 1977: 125–128). The creation of a police force also permitted the state to adjust its response to the magnitude of a perceived threat with greater precision. The establishment of the police represented an attempt to bring the social control machinery itself under greater control.

As a proactive force, the police were to *prevent* crime rather than merely respond to it after it had occurred. This was to be done by bringing a visible personification of the law into working-class communities on a regular basis.[19] Traditional popular working-class culture, a source of resistance to the discipline of the factory, was reinterpreted as a generating milieu of crime, and the police were called on to eliminate it.[20] The bureaucratization of enforcement made this possible, for the police could arrest and prosecute without regard to the wishes of com-

---

their own family and neighbors, their loyalty could not be trusted. The reformers who urged the creation of a police force hoped that full-time employees salaried by the state would be more loyal than was a militia of community residents who were not paid by the state.

[19]The fathers of the English police saw the force not merely as a deterrent to crime. The police were also to engage in moral exhortation and lead the poor to adopt middle-class morals and living habits (Donajgrodzki, 1977).

[20]Thus Philips notes: "Studies of the introduction of new police forces into communities suggest that one immediate effect which they produce is a marked increase in prosecutions for minor public order offences—brawls, drunkenness, disorderly conduct in public, etc. [1977: 84–87]." In the Black Country the establishment of a "new" police force led to:

> a general campaign against drunkenness, disorderly behavior and fighting in the streets, and against the hitherto tolerated blood sports [bullbaiting, prizefighting, cockfighting and dogfighting]. Middle class opinion had moved decisively against such "barbarous" sports. . . . The new police played an important role in stamping out these sports. . . . The police sought them out, broke them up, arrested and prosecuted the participants [p. 86].

The police carried out similar campaigns against working-class culture in Boston (Lane, 1975), Salem (Ferdinand, 1972), and other northeastern industrial cities in the United States (Harring, 1980).

plainants. The assault on working-class culture would have been unthinkable outside the context of bureaucratized enforcement.

The circumstances surrounding the establishment of police departments along the Eastern Seaboard in the United States prior to the Civil War were quite similar to those in England. Riots were a frequent occurrence in preindustrial Boston, New York, Philadelphia, Baltimore, St. Louis, and Cincinnati (Lane, 1975; Richardson, 1970; Walker, 1977). As riots in these cities took on social and political overtones in the decades preceding the Civil War, proposals for establishing a police system something like that of London were adopted. Again, it took some years before reformers could overcome fears that the police would be used to establish a tyranny, and also the opposition of local political leaders reluctant to lose patronage jobs.

As Harring (1980) has noted, the mere establishment of police forces in preindustrial American cities did not necessarily have much practical consequence, because often little more was involved than a formal reorganization of existing watch systems under a single agency, with little administrative change. Prior to the invention of the telegraph and telephone, administrative decentralization was a technological necessity. Moreover, budgetary constraints limited the growth of police departments. It was the post–Civil War strife that overcame capitalist reluctance to pay for increased protection with higher taxes. Together with petty bourgeois shopkeepers and professionals, industrial capitalists lobbied successfully for appropriations to increase the size of urban police forces and helped to develop new strategies of development in response to strife involving factory workers and their employers.[21] In times of crisis, the police could be called on to intervene on behalf of owners.

The extent to which a police force actually carries out class-based social-control functions is always limited by organizational and political factors. In nineteenth-century American cities, bribes paid by saloon keepers, who were important figures in urban politics, substantially nullified the enforcement of laws against saloons and vice, though not necessarily against drunkenness.[22] One might expect that the widening of suffrage would have limited the use of the police against the working

[21]Policing in the industrial Black Country of northern England was reorganized in the nineteenth century in much the same way (Philips, 1977: 57–60).

[22]The necessarily decentralized character of police patrol always reduces the organization's ability to gain officers' compliance with organizational policy. In this period, however, police corruption seems to have been less a case of individual police refusing to enforce the law in return for payoffs than an organizational policy of nonenforcement in return for bribes at the highest levels of the administrative hierarchy.

class. On occasion (e.g., in Boss Tweed's New York), big-city mayors did refuse to use the police to break strikes. The loyalty of the police, who were themselves drawn from working-class backgrounds, could not always be guaranteed in actions against strikers. But in the large cities, the conservatism of the larger middle class and the inability of unnaturalized immigrants to vote limited the ability of the working class to influence policing policy. The national divisions that separated the police from the policed, along with a variety of organizational strategies designed to preserve the loyalty of the force, generally sufficed to ward off large-scale political defection (Harring, 1980). In smaller industrial towns, on the other hand, the working class was proportionately larger and often had middle-class support during strikes. Under those circumstances, the small local police forces could not be utilized to repress strikers, and capitalists consequently relied more heavily on private forces (Gutman, 1963: Spitzer and Scull, 1977b).

PROPORTIONALITY IN PUNISHMENT

Proposals to abolish the death penalty in England for most offenses and to establish a rough proportionality between the gravity of the offense and the severity of the penalty reflected concerns for both the legitimacy and the effectiveness of law. The carnival-like atmosphere at executions, as well as occasional riots and defiance on the part of the condemned, seemed to erode respect for the majesty of the law (Cooper, 1974; Linebaugh, 1975: Ignatieff, 1978). Eighteenth-century juries apparently refused to convict petty thieves in order to avoid sending them to the gallows, and frequent pardons reduced the certainty of punishment. Insisting that these conditions jeopardized property by undermining the deterrent effect of the law,[23] in the second decade of the nineteenth century the petty bourgeoisie and capitalists from all over England flooded Parliament with petitions urging a reform of sentencing (Rustigan, 1981). In alliance with reforming Tory landlords who were equally concerned with the legitimacy of the law, this middle class successfully pressured Parliament into eliminating the death penalty for most offenses. By the time Parliamentary reform gave the middle class formal political representation in 1832, much of this reform had already been carried out, though business interests continued to press for further

[23]The merchants who petitioned Parliament blamed the upswing in crime after 1815 on the weakness of law enforcement, but with little basis. The increase is now generally attributed to the difficulty that soldiers discharged at the end of the Napoleonic Wars had in finding employment.

reductions in capital punishment in succeeding decades (Cooper, 1974: 41).

The early nineteenth-century argument for reducing the use of the death penalty was posed on humanitarian as well as pragmatic grounds. Rusche and Kirchheimer (1939) attribute this humanitarianism to the industrial revolution, which increased the demand for labor and thus raised the social value of a human life. There is probably some truth to this explanation. The death penalty had been much less used in the American colonies than in England in the eighteenth century, possibly reflecting the comparative scarcity of labor in the colonies, though perhaps more plausibly reflecting the absence of a panicky landed gentry. But this is to take too narrow a view of the matter. The humanitarianism of the reformers was part of a shift in religious ideology associated with their upward mobility. The break from the Calvinist doctrine of predestination, in favor of the belief that anyone could be saved, came as petty bourgeois Dissenters prospered and became well-to-do capitalists. Their humanitarianism was a response to the contradiction between an ascetic, self-denying orientation to the world adopted by a lower middle class and sustained by religious doctrine and the economic success that those who adhered to this doctrine had achieved. Instead of using wealth for personal enjoyment, they used it for public service. Humanitarian reform was a way of expressing a common humanity with the poor and outcast. At the same time, the class position of the reformers gave a strong social-control component to their paternalistic humanitarianism (Ignatieff, 1978: 58).[24]

Pashukanis has argued that there is a deep structural connection between the principle of proportionality in punishment advocated by eighteenth- and early nineteenth-century criminal law reformers and the development of industrial capitalism:

> Deprivation of freedom, for a period stipulated in the court sentence, is the specific form in which modern, that is to say bourgeois capitalist, criminal law embodies the principle of equivalent recompense. This form is unconsciously yet deeply linked with the conception of man in the abstract, and abstract human labour measurable

[24]A similar combination of pragmatic and humanitarian concerns seems to have been responsible for the campaign against the death penalty in the United States just after the War of Independence. In New York, for example, the campaign of businessmen was led by Thomas Eddy, a prosperous Quaker merchant (Lewis, 1965: 4). For evidence concerning a similar shift in religious doctrine in the United States and a discussion of the effect of this shift on the way crime and punishment were viewed, see Davis (1957) and Griffin (1960).

in time. Industrial capitalism, the declaration of human rights, the political economy of Ricardo, and the system of imprisonment for a stipulated term are phenomena peculiar to one and the same historical epoch [1929: 180–181].

Here Pashukanis asserts not that imprisonment for fixed periods was in the interest of capitalists, but rather that the reduction of human labor to abstract, interchangeable labor time in the industrial phase of capitalism leads members of a capitalist society toward specific notions of appropriateness of sanctions based on the metaphor of commodity exchange. It was therefore in the nineteenth century when the capitalist mode of production became fully established that imprisonment for fixed periods of time proportional to the injury caused by the crime became a major form of criminal punishment.

Yet it is important not to lose sight of the fact that public sentiment regarding punishment was translated into new penal practices only insofar as it could be manifested politically: through acquittals of defendants (made possible because of popular participation in the administration of justice through the jury system—a precapitalist survival), petitions to Parliament and representation in Parliament after 1832. The gentry who enacted the so-called Bloody Code in the eighteenth century, and whose political authority was reinforced by gaining pardons for clients, had to be defeated politically before the new system could be established.

THE PENITENTIARY

The prison system devised by these English reformers reflected the same concerns that informed their campaign against the death penalty. To legitimate punishment, all prisoners had to be treated equally regardless of social rank. This equality required the elimination of prisons operated privately under contract from the state, for in these, a prisoner's standard of living was governed by the payments the prisoner made to the jailkeeper (Sheehan, 1977). Like the police, the prison was now to be administered through a system of formal rules impartially administered by a bureaucratic government agency. Abuses of authority were to be prevented by opening the prison to public inspection (Ignatieff, 1978: 77–78).

Based on a vision of reconciliation between classes that economic and social change had driven apart, the prison was to reform miscreants, not demolish them (Ignatieff, 1978: 210). Because crime was attributed to indolence, avarice, the decline of authority, and irreligiosity (that is, to

the vices of the laboring classes), the new prison discipline was to consist of a regimented daily routine, hard labor, an abstemious alcohol-free
diet, submission to authority, and religious exhortation. Because popular working-class culture was believed to sustain crime, prisoners were
to be cut off from the outside world and from one another, visitors and
correspondence were restricted, and the cellular system and rule of
silence were imposed to prevent even the slightest communication
among inmates.[25]

The Federalist merchants (Quaker and other Protestant denomina-
tions) who created the American penitentiary were motivated by somewhat similar concerns. To restore the social order that the conflicts of the
Jacksonian era seemed to be destroying, they built prisons and other
confining institutions, with systems of discipline that British and European administrators were to copy (Lewis, 1970; Rothman, 1971).

The English and American prisons were established as a response to a
crisis in preindustrial capitalism.[26] The form that the prison took, however, was not entirely determined by that crisis but was also governed
by the theories of crime causation then prevalent, and by the organizational innovations being introduced in connection with the industrial
revolution. The failure of the houses of correction to turn a profit for the
out-work masters who were given contracts for the use of inmate labor
had, along with the continuing difficulty of supervising cottage industry, stimulated the development of the factory. Many of the new disciplinary techniques the English reformers introduced into the penitentiary had first been introduced as solutions to administrative problems in
"free" production,[27] as well as in the schools, hospitals, and other institutions the same group of reformers were managing for the poor
(Hartwell, 1971: 77; Ignatieff, 1978: 32, 62; for a similar diffusion of
social-control strategies in the case of French prisons, see Foucault,
1975). Similarly, the example of the Lowell, Massachusetts, textile mills
inspired the introduction of collective labor to Auburn Prison in New
York in 1821.

[25]To achieve this strict control, imprisonment for debt had to be abolished. Because
debtors had not been convicted of a crime, they could not be subjected to the rigorous
discipline of the penitentiary (Ignatieff, 1978: 31). As business indebtedness and bankruptcy were becoming a more normal feature of the capitalist economy, imprisonment for
debt also came under increasing criticism from business classes.

[26]Most of the committals to the Gloucester penitentiary between 1792 and 1809, for
example, involved breaches of labor discipline on the part of agricultural workers and
workers in the "putting out" system. (Ignatieff, 1978: 108–109, 79–83).

[27]Linebaugh (1976) notes that Jeremy Bentham's Panoptican design for penitentiaries
and workhouses was adapted from a plan his brother Samuel Bentham had devised to
stop carpenters employed in a shipyard from pilfering materials.

The requirement that prisoner labor yield a profit had a continuing impact on social control within the institution. For example, prison administrators attempted to impose a silence rule and strict discipline using corporal punishment to control prisoners who worked in the new industries. But in the long run, factory production was incompatible with the rule of silence and with brutalizing discipline. The silence rule eventually disappeared, and discipline within the institution was subordinated to the requirements of production.

As in the case of the police, the prison evolved in a direction that diverged greatly from the plans laid by the founders. In both cases, the explanation lies in economic and political developments connected with the evolution of capitalism—developments that the founders were able neither to anticipate nor to direct.

Discussion

Our purpose has not been to present a history of how social control changed as mercantile capitalism was transformed into competitive industrial capitalism; as such, our work would be woefully inadequate. Instead, our goal has been to present a somewhat schematic interpretation of selected changes in the scope, ideology, and forms of social control in Marxian terms. It is the logic utilized in explaining the events, not the events themselves, that has been our main focus.

Contrary to popular misconceptions, Marxian theory asserts neither that the ruling class manipulates social control at will on behalf of its interests, nor that the economy wholly determines social-control arrangements: "The sum total of these relations of production constitutes the economic structure of society—the real foundation, on which rise legal and political superstructures and to which correspond definite forms of consciousness. The mode of production in material life determines the general character of the social, political, and spiritual processes of life [Marx, 1858: 20–21]." Leaving aside the problems raised by this "base–superstructure" metaphor, we note that it is only the *general character* of social, political, and spiritual processes that Marx asserts to be determined by the mode of material production, not their every detail.

The historical record, as we have reviewed it, seems to confirm this. Broad trends in social control correspond to successive transformations of capitalism. State regulation of the economy is extensive in the mercantile stage but contracts with the coming of competitive industrial capitalism. New forms of social control, such as the police and the prison, are associated with the transition from one stage to another. Explanations of deviant behavior become scientific rather than religious under the impact of capitalist industrialization, and the formal qualities of social control are also transformed.

But there is no one-to-one correspondence between the stages of capitalism and social control. Many aspects of social control are not unique to a single stage. Moreover, we found in our analysis that the explanation of changes in social control could not be restricted to the analysis of the economy narrowly defined but also had to take into account such considerations as the character of the state, the content and degree of adherence to popular ideologies, the level of class consciousness, and the degree and forms of mobilization of *all* classes (not just the ruling class), as well as divisions and alliances among classes and class fractions. This does not mean that political and other factors that are unrelated to economic factors should be added to the theoretical approach as such. On the contrary, they are all influenced by the forces and relations of material production but are simply not totally determined by them (see also Spitzer, 1980).

Taken by itself, a mode of production is too limited a concept to tell us much about social control (Greenberg, 1975). One could hardly argue, for example, that the sublimation of energies achieved by Victorian sexual repression was necessary for—and could be deduced from—the imperatives of capitalist industrialization. Yet one cannot understand the appeal of sexual restraint in the nineteenth century without understanding the structural position of the petty bourgeoisie in a competitive economy. Capitalism provides the class experience from which ideologies of social control are developed. Thus, the classical criminology principles of formal equality and proportionality are unquestionably related to a stage in the development of capitalism, but it is doubtful that these principles could be rigorously deduced from the concept of capitalism. The same is true of such social-control methods as the police and the prison.

If one were to borrow the scientific language of "variable" analysis, these observations imply that a general Marxian theory of historical change in social control cannot be framed in such a way that the "mode of production" is treated as the independent variable. Social control must be understood in terms of *social formations* containing an articulated set of production modes, along with associated political and ideological elements. Yet here too the distinction between dependent and independent variables is somewhat misleading, for social control is itself a part of a social formation, and thus the social formation cannot be considered as entirely prior to social control, either logically or empirically. Indeed, the mode of production is not entirely distinct from social control conceptually, for social control can be (though is not always) part of the forces and relations of production (consider penal slavery, prison labor, and factory discipline). We are thus faced with a complex problem involving joint or reciprocal determination rather than unidirectional causality.

A complete theory of Marxian social formations does not exist at present, and consequently a general theory of historical change in social control cannot be formulated at this time. Even in the absence of such a theory, our work has value in calling attention to considerations that must be taken into account in empirical research on historical change in social control. Someone who assumes a priori that subordinate classes can never have an impact on social control will never look for their influence and consequently will never discover it. If ideology is believed to be nothing more than a mask for class interests and carries no weight of its own, then it too can be neglected. As long as the state is thought to be totally dominated by a single class whose will it carries out, then there is no need to examine the constraints on social control imposed by the form of the state, or to take account of its partial autonomy. Research on social control can only be hamstrung by such non-Marxian reductionism. Conversely, if our methodological dicta are kept in mind, empirical research carried out on particular problems involving historical change on social control can contribute to the larger task of developing a general theory.

A somewhat different approach might also prove fruitful. We have tried to show the utility of Marxian concepts in understanding historical change as it actually occurred. Much might be learned, however, by considering historical change as it *might have occurred* had something else been different. This can be done theoretically through *Gedanken* experiments (thought experiments) in which the consequences of alternative conjunctures are theorized. Consider the origins of the police, to take a single example. Earlier we noted the role of Sir Robert Peel in the creation of the British police. Was his role a necessary one? Had he died before becoming prime minister, would there be no police in England today? In a way this is a question about how precarious the alliance was that voted for the police; if not too precarious, perhaps the outcome of the vote in 1829 would have been the same without Peel. Even if a police force had been defeated in 1829, however, the matter would surely have come up again and again. That decades were required to gain acceptance for a police force tells us that the task was not easy politically, so that the creation of the police does not follow in any simple way from the existence of problems to which it was a proposed solution. On the other hand, that all industrial nations, capitalist and communist, have established bureaucratic police forces suggests that some of the detailed political considerations that might be critical to an understanding of why the English police were created in 1829 are actually irrelevant to an understanding of why, in the long run, police forces are created. By focusing on events as they actually occurred, one may end up explaining events that are nothing more than a kind of random noise as far as the long-range, structural transformations of societies are concerned. Questions such as these can be explored by theorizing about what the consequences of not having had a police force would have been for different classes and class fractions, what alternatives they might have favored instead of the police, and what class alliances might have been feasible with regard to these alternatives.[28]

Similar analyses can be carried out for other social-control developments. Although this approach can be checked in part by comparative empirical research, its greatest value is to render the empirically observed patterns of change theoretically problematic, and thus to stimulate theorizing. Marxian theory provides a resource in carrying out this strategy by calling to our attention the various elements whose role should be investigated.

ACKNOWLEDGMENTS

We are grateful to Piers Beirne for helpful comments on an earlier draft.

References

Althusser, Louis
    1971 "Ideology and ideological state apparatuses (notes toward an investigation)."
           Pages 127–186 in *Lenin and Philosophy*, edited by Louis Althusser. New York:
           Monthly Review Press.
Barker-Benfield, G.
    1976 *Horrors of the Half-Known Life: Male Attitudes toward Women and Sexuality in
           Nineteenth-Century America*. New York: Harper & Row.
Beccaria, Cesare
    1764 *Of Crimes and Punishments*. Indianapolis, Ind.: Bobbs-Merrill, 1963.
Beloff, Max
    1963 *Public Order and Popular Disturbances, 1660–1714*. New York: Barnes and Noble.

[28]Spitzer's and Scull's (1977a) analysis of the relationship between the creation of the British police and the structural transformation of English society adopts this methodology.

Bindoff, S. T.
  1961   "The making of the statute of artificers." Pages 56–94 in *Elizabethan Government and Society*, edited by S. T. Bindoff, J. Hurstfield, and C. H. Williams. London: Athlone Press.
Blocker, Jack S., Jr.
  1976   *Retreat from Reform: The Prohibition Movement in the United States, 1890–1913.* Westport, Conn.: Greenwood Press.
Boostrum, Ronald
  1974   The Personalization of Evil: The Emergence of American Criminology, 1865–1910. Unpublished doctoral dissertation, School of Criminology, University of California, Berkeley.
Buck, Philip
  1942   *The Politics of Mercantilism.* New York: Henry Holt.
Bullough, Vern L.
  1976   *Sexual Variance in Society and History.* New York: Wiley.
Canderloro, Giorgio
  1956   *Storia dell' Italia Moderna*, vol. 1: *Le Origini del Risorgimento.* Milano: Feltrinelli.
Clarkson, L. A.
  1972   *The Pre-Industrial Economy in England, 1500–1750.* New York: Schocken.
Colquhoun, Patrick
  1795   *A Treatise on the Police of the Metropolis.* Montclair: Patterson Smith, 1969.
  1800   *A Treatise on the Commerce and Police of the River Thames.* Montclair: Patterson Smith, 1969.
Cominos, Peter
  1963   "Late-Victorian sexual repression and the social system." *International Review of Social History* 8: 18–48, 216–250.
Cooper, David D.
  1974   *The Lesson of the Scaffold: The Public Execution Controversy in Victorian England.* Athens, Ohio: Ohio University Press.
Cunningham, W.
  1912   *The Growth of English Industry and Commerce during the Early and Middle Ages*, vol. 2. Cambridge: Cambridge University Press.
Davis, David Brion
  1957   *Homicide in American Fiction, 1798–1860: A Study in Social Values.* Ithaca, N.Y.: Cornell University Press.
Donajgrodzki, A. P.
  1977   "'Social police' and the bureaucratic elite: A vision of order in the age of reform." Pages 51–76 in *Social Control in Nineteenth Century Britain*, edited by A. P. Donajgrodzki. Totowa, N.J.: Rowman and Littlefield.
Embree, Scotty
  1977   "The state department as moral entrepreneur: Racism and imperialism as factors in the passage of the Harrison Narcotics Act." Pages 193–204 in *Corrections and Punishment*, edited by David F. Greenberg. Beverly Hills, Calif.: Sage.
Engels, Friedrich
  1878   "Herr Eugen Dühring's revolution in science." Pages 270–279 in *Basic Writings on Politics and Philosophy: Karl Marx and Friedrich Engels*, edited by Lewis S. Feuer. Garden City, N.Y.: Anchor, 1959.
  1890   "Letter to Conrad Schmidt." Pages 407–409 in *Basic Writings on Politics and Philosophy: Karl Marx and Friedrich Engels*, edited by Lewis S. Feuer. Garden City, N.Y.: Anchor, 1959.

1893   "Letter to Franz Mehring." Pages 407–409 in *Basic Writings on Politics and Philosophy: Karl Marx and Friedrich Engels*, edited by Lewis S. Feuer. Garden City, N.Y.: Anchor, 1959.

Englehardt, G. Tristram
1974   "The disease of masturbation: Values and the concept of disease." *Bulletin of the History of Medicine* 48: 234–248.

Ferdinand, Theodore N.
1972   "Politics, the police, and arresting policies in Salem, Massachusetts since the Civil War." *Social Problems* 19: 572–588.

Foucault, Michel
1975   *Discipline and Punish: The Birth of the Prison*. New York: Pantheon, 1977.

Genovese, Eugene D.
1974   *Roll, Jordan, Roll: The World the Slaves Made*. New York: Pantheon.

Greenberg, David F.
1975   "On one-dimensional Marxist criminology." *Theory and Society* 3: 610–621.

Griffin, Clifford S.
1960   *Their Brothers' Keepers: Moral Stewardship in the United States, 1800–1865*. New Brunswick, N.J.: Rutgers University Press.

Gusfield, Joseph R.
1963   *Symbolic Crusade: Status Politics and the American Temperance Movement*. Urbana, Ill.: University of Illinois Press.

Gutman, Herbert G.
1963   "The worker's search for power: Labor in the Gilded Age." Pages 38–68 in *The Gilded Age: A Reappraisal*, edited by H. Wayne Morgan. Syracuse, N.Y.: Syracuse University Press.

Haller, John S., Jr., and Robin M. Haller
1974   *The Physician and Sexuality in Victorian America*. Urbana, Ill.: University of Illinois Press.

Hamilton, Roberta
1978   *The Liberation of Women: A Study of Patriarchy and Capitalism*. London: George Allen & Unwin.

Hare, E. H.
1962   "Masturbatory insanity: The history of an idea." *Journal of Mental Science* 108: 1–25.

Harring, Sidney L.
1980   "Policing a class society: Late nineteenth and early twentieth century expansion of the police." Pages 292–313 in *Crime and Capitalism: Readings in Marxist Criminology*, edited by David F. Greenberg. Palo Alto, Calif.: Mayfield.

Harrison, Brian
1971   *Drink and the Victorians: The Temperance Question in England, 1815–1872*. Pittsburgh: University of Pittsburgh Press.

Hartwell, R. M.
1971   *The Industrial Revolution and Economic Growth*. London; Methuen.

Hay, Douglas
1975   "Property, authority and the criminal law." Pages 17–63 in *Albion's Fatal Tree: Crime and Society in Eighteenth Century England*, edited by Douglas Hay, Peter Linebaugh, John G. Rule, E. P. Thompson, and Cal Winslow. New York: Pantheon.

Heckscher, Eli F.
1931   *Mercantilism*, vol. 1. New York: Macmillan, 1955.
1935   *Mercantilism*, vol. 2. New York: Macmillan, 1955.

Hill, Christopher
     1961   *The Century of Revolution, 1603–1714*. Edinburgh: Thomas Nelson and Sons.
Hirst, Paul, and Barry Hindess
     1975   *Precapitalist Modes of Production*. Boston: Routledge & Kegan Paul.
Hofstader, Richard
     1955   *The Age of Reform*. New York: Vintage Books.
Howe, Daniel Walker
     1976   "Victorian culture in America." Pages 2–28 in *Victorian America*, edited by
             Daniel W. Howe. Philadelphia: University of Pennsylvania Press.
Humphries, Drew, and David F. Greenberg
     1980   "The dialectics of crime control." Pages 209–254 in *Crime and Capitalism: Read-
             ings in Marxist Criminology*, edited by David F. Greenberg. Palo Alto, Calif.:
             Mayfield.
Hurstfield, Joel, and Alan G. R. Smith
     1972   *Elizabethan People: State and Society*. New York: St. Martin's Press.
Ignatieff, Michael
     1978   *A Just Measure of Pain: The Penitentiary in the Industrial Revolution, 1750–1850*.
             New York: Pantheon.
Isaac, Paul E.
     1965   *Prohibition and Politics: Turbulent Decades in Tennessee, 1885–1920*. Knoxville,
             Tenn.: University of Tennessee Press.
Kann, Kenneth
             "The Big City Riot in 1877: Chicago." Unpublished paper.
Lane, Roger
     1975   *Policing the City: Boston, 1822–1885*. New York: Atheneum
Levine, Harry Gene
     1978   "The discovery of addiction: Changing conceptions of habitual drunkenness in
             America." *Journal of Studies of Alcohol* 39: 43–174.
     1979   "Temperance and women in 19th century United States." In *Research Advances
             in Alcohol and Drug Problems*, vol. 5. New York: Plenum.
Lewis, W. David
     1965   *From Newgate to Dannemora: The Rise of the Penitentiary in New York, 1796–1848*.
             Ithaca, N.Y.: Cornell University Press.
     1970   "The reformer as conservative: Protestant counter-subversion in the early re-
             public." In *The Development of an American Culture*, edited by Stanley Cohen and
             Lorman Ratner. Englewood Cliffs, N.J.: Prentice-Hall.
Linebaugh, Peter
     1975   "The Tyburn riots against the surgeons." Pages 65–118 in *Albion's Fatal Tree:
             Crime and Society in Eighteenth Century England*, edited by Douglas Hay, Peter
             Linebaugh, John G. Rule, E. P. Thompson, and Cal Winslow. New York:
             Pantheon.
     1976   "The passage from workers' power in the period of manufacture: Samuel
             Bentham, technological repression, and the eighteenth century British
             shipyards." Paper presented at the annual meeting of the American Political
             Science Association.
Lockyer, Roger
     1964   *Tudor and Stuart Britain, 1471–1714*. London: Longmans, Green.
Manning, Peter
     1977   *Police Work: The Social Organization of Policing*. Cambridge, Mass.: M.I.T. Press.
Marx, Karl
     1844a "Introduction to *A Contribution to the Critique of Hegel's Philosophy of Right*."

Pages 55–56 in *Karl Marx: Early Writings,* edited by T. B. Bottomore. New York: McGraw-Hill, 1964.

1844b "Economic and philosophical manuscripts." Pages 61–219 in *Karl Marx: Early Writings,* edited by T. B. Bottomore. New York: McGraw-Hill, 1964.

1858 *Grundrisse: Introduction to the Critique of Political Economy.* New York: Vintage, 1973.

1859 "Excerpt from *A Contribution to the Critique of Political Economy.*" Pages 42–46 in *Basic Writings on Politics and Philosophy: Karl Marx and Friedrich Engels,* edited by Lewis S. Feuer. Garden City, N.Y.: Anchor, 1959.

1867 *Capital: A Critique of Political Economy,* vol. 1: *The Process of Capitalist Production.* New York: International Publishers, 1967.

1894 *Capital: A Critique of Political Economy,* vol. 3: *The Process of Capitalist Production as a Whole.* New York: International Publishers, 1967.

Marx, Karl, and Friedrich Engels
1846 "Excerpts from *German Ideology.*" Pages 246–261 in *Basic Writings on politics and Philosophy: Karl Marx and Friedrich Engels,* edited by Lewis S. Feuer. Garden City, N.Y.: Anchor, 1959.

Miliband, Ralph
1977 *Marxism and Politics.* Oxford: Oxford University Press.

Neuman, R. P.
1975 "Masturbation, madness and the modern concepts of childhood and adolescence." *Journal of Social History* 8: 1–27.

Ostrander, Gilman M.
1957 *The Prohibition Movement of California, 1848–1933.* Berkeley, Calif.: University of California Press.

Pashukanis, Evgeny B.
1929 *Law and Marxism: A General Theory.* London: Ink Links, 1978.

Perkin, Harold
1969 *The Origins of Modern English Society, 1780–1800.* London: Routledge & Kegan Paul.

Philips, David
1977 *Crime and Authority in Victorian England: The Black Country 1835–1860.* Totowa, N.J.: Rowman and Littlefield.

Powell, Ken, and Chris Cook
1977 *English Historical Facts, 1485–1603.* Totowa, N.J.: Rowman and Littlefield.

Radzinowicz, Leon
1948 *A History of English Criminal Law and Its Administration from 1750,* vol. 1. London: Stevens and Sons.

Reed, James
1978 *From Private Vice to Public Virtue: The Birth Control Movement and American Society since 1830.* New York: Basic Books.

Richardson, James F.
1970 *The New York Police: Colonial Times to 1901.* New York: Oxford University Press.

Rose, R. B.
1961 "Eighteenth century price riots and public policy in England." *International Review of Social History* 6: 277–282.

Rothman, David J.
1971 *Discovery of the Asylum: Social Order and Disorder in the New World.* Boston: Little, Brown.

Rusche, George, and Otto Kirchheimer
1939 *Punishment and Social Structure.* New York: Russell and Russell, 1969.
Rustigan, Michael
1981 "A Reinterpretation of Criminal Law Reform in Nineteenth-Century England."
Pages 255–278 in *Crime and Capitalism: Readings in Marxist Criminology,* edited by
David Greenberg. Palo Alto, Calif.: Mayfield.
Sellin, Thorsten
1976 *Slavery and the Penal System.* New York: Elsevier.
Sheehan, W. J.
1977 "Finding solace in eighteenth-century Newgate." Pages 229–245 in *Crime in
England, 1550–1800,* edited by J. S. Cockburn. Princeton, N.J.: Princeton University Press.
Shelton, Walter J.
1973 *English Hunger and Industrial Disorders.* Toronto: University of Toronto Press.
Silver, Allan
1967 "The demand for order in civil society: A review of some themes in the history
of urban crime, police and riot." Pages 1–24 in *The Police: Six Sociological Essays,*
edited by David J. Bordua. New York: Wiley.
Smith-Rosenberg, Carroll
1978 "Sex as symbol in Victorian purity: An ethnohistorical analysis of Jacksonian
America." *American Journal of Sociology* 84: 212–247.
Spitzer, Steven
1979 "The rationalization of crime control in capitalist society." *Contemporary Crises*
3: 187–206.
1980 "'Left-wing' criminology—an infantile disorder?" In *Radical Criminology: The
Coming Crises,* edited by James A. Inciardi. Beverly Hills, Calif.: Sage.
Spitzer, Steven, and Andrew Scull
1977a "Social control in historical perspective: From private to public responses to
crime." Pages 265–286 in *Corrections and Punishment,* edited by David F. Greenberg. Beverly Hills, Calif.: Sage.
1977b "Privatization and capitalist development: The case of the private police." *Social Problems* 25: 18–29.
Stevenson, John
1975 "Food riots in England, 1792–1818." Pages 33–74 in *Popular Protest and Public
Order: Six Studies in British History, 1790–1921,* edited by R. Quinault and J.
Stevenson. New York: St. Martin's Press.
1977 "Social control and the prevention of riots in England, 1789–1829." Pages
27–50 in *Social Control in Nineteenth Century Britain,* edited by A. P. Donajgrodzki. London: Croom Helm.
Tawney, R. H.
1912 *Religion and the Rise of Capitalism.* Harmondsworth: Penguin, 1964.
Thompson, E. P.
1963 *The Making of the English Working Class.* New York: Vintage Books.
1971 "The moral economy of the English crowd in the eighteenth century." *Past and
Present* 50: 76–136.
1975 *Whigs and Hunters: The Origins of the Black Act.* New York: Random House.
Timberlake, James H.
1963 *Prohibition and the Progressive Movement, 1900–1920.* Cambridge, Mass.: Harvard
University Press.

Walker, Samuel
  1977   *A Critical History of Police Reform*. Lexington, Mass.: Lexington.
Ward, J. T.
  1970   "The factory movement." Pages 54–77 in *Popular Movements: c. 1830–1850*,
         edited by J. T. Ward. London: Macmillan.
Webb, Sidney, and Beatrice Webb
  1963   *English Poor Law History*, part 1: *The Old Poor Law*. Hamden: Archon.

8

Social Control and Relational Disturbance: A Microstructural Paradigm[*]

SHELDON EKLAND-OLSON

Relational disturbances take many forms. Mental illness, unemployment, contract disputes, marital infidelity, crime victimization, death, and physical illness all can have varying influences on the stability and structure of interpersonal relationships. The aim of this chapter is to present a microstructural paradigm for the study of such disruptions as well as the mechanisms of social control that result from them.

Assumptions, Definitions, and Propositions

The orienting definitions and assumptions of this paradigm can be briefly stated. *Relational disturbance* is the sociological counterpart of psychobiological stress (Selye, 1976). Like the structural and chemical changes taking place at the body's cellular level when persons are confronted with stressors, changes occur at the level of interpersonal relations when these networks are confronted with a wide range of disturbances. Unlike Selye's (1976) work on stress, where the emphasis is on the nonspecific responses of the body to any demand, the focus here is

*This chapter was presented at the American Sociological Association Meetings, New York, 1980.

TOWARD A GENERAL THEORY OF SOCIAL CONTROL
Volume 2: Selected Problems

on response mechanisms inherent in the reciprocal exchange, normative beliefs, and affective attachments that link actors in networks of interpersonal relationships. These response mechanisms are the primary sources of social control.

Social control is defined as any social mechanism or process whose purpose is to respond to relational disturbance. One important attribute of social control (along with others such as the severity, celerity, and certainty of punishment) is its structure. Structural shifts in control mechanisms take place when interpersonal networks are confronted with relational disturbance. Such shifts may include a redistribution of power,[1] a neutralization of moral constraints, as well as the withdrawal of one or more of the parties. In addition, outside actors are frequently mobilized. The police might be called, an arbitrator chosen, or commitment proceedings initiated.

A microstructural theory of social control should specify factors related to the probability, degree, and pattern of such changes in the core network. The *core network* is defined as that set of relationships most influential in the attitudes, behavior, and well-being of actors in particular situations (McCallister and Fischer, 1978). The probability, pattern, and degree of structural shifts in the core network are here seen as a function of the *resilience, isolation,* and *closure* of the interpersonal network most immediately affected by the disruptive event. These terms are discussed later in the chapter.

Disruptive events and the structure of control mechanisms are not independent. The most important property of the disruptive event, when it comes to the structure of the core network, is its seriousness. *Seriousness* is here conceived in terms of the degree of relational disturbance. This is consistent with Burr's (1973) definition of a stressor event as some event that brings about changes in the boundaries, structure, and processes within the family. It is equally applicable to nonfamilial units such as business relationships. As discussed later, this conception departs from more cultural approaches such as those of Rossi, Waite, Bose, and Berk (1974) and Gottfredson and Hindelang (1979a).

Three implications of these assumptions and definitions should be noted. First, the study of social control is not limited to normative deviance (compare Gibbs, 1972; Black, 1976). Rather, social control as here defined includes the full array of ties (exchange and affective as well as normative) that bind actors in networks of relationships. Social control is not necessarily normative, for it may emerge from utilitarian considera-

---

[1]Power is defined here as the balance of dependencies among actors engaged in exchange relationships (Emerson, 1962).

tions of advantage or emotional outrage as well as moral indignation. Moreover, social control should be judged effective or ineffective according to its impact on networks of relationships, in all their dimensions, not just in terms of whether normative order has been restored.

By connecting social control to relational disturbances of all types we incorporate not only normative deviance, where moral beliefs are violated (e.g., crime), but also disputes where pragmatic judgments of advantage dominate, as well as tragedies where the overriding concern is emotional loss (e.g., death). By so doing we are in a better position to synthesize the parallel research done by those interested in the mobilization of law (Black, 1973; Gottfredson and Hindelang, 1979a), the processing of disputes (Felstiner, 1974; Danzig and Lowy, 1975; Nader and Todd, 1978; Roberts, 1979), and adaptation to familial crises (Hill, 1949; McCubbin, Joy, Cauble, Comeau, Patterson, and Needle, 1980).

Second, it should be noted that the conception of social control as any social mechanism whose purpose is to respond to relational disturbance takes the external nature of the response as a variable rather than as a definitional property of social control (compare Horwitz, 1977). For example, the structure and strength of relationships have an important influence on mobilization of the increasingly external third parties involved in mediation, arbitration, and adjudication (see, e.g., Nader and Todd, 1978). Sources of variation in the structural properties of responses to relational disruptions are of central concern in the following sections.

Finally, the structural interpretation of seriousness should be underscored. Recognized as an important factor for some time, the seriousness of relational disruptions has received a good deal of recent attention, stemming in the case of crime from the work of Sellin and Wolfgang (1964) and in the study of mental stress from the work of Holmes and Rahe (1967). In each instance the seriousness of particular events is established according to aggregate patterns of responses to interviews and questionnaires. Although there is some evidence of consistency on the *ranking* of events according to their stressfulness, there is less uniformity when it comes to estimating the *level* of seriousness for any given event (Miller, Bentz, Aponte, and Biogan, 1974; Rossi *et al.*, 1974). Apparently, the level of seriousness depends in part on the social context in which the event takes place. Within the microstructural paradigm presented here it is useful to conceptualize seriousness in terms of the impact on specific sets of relationships rather than in terms of general public opinion.

Using these assumptions and definitions, the remainder of the chapter deals with factors related to the probability, degree, and pattern of structural changes in control mechanisms. When and under what circumstances are people likely to call the police? Utilize psychiatric or other clinical services? Hire a lawyer? Go to court to settle a dispute? In one sense these situations involve very different issues. In another, they center on a single question: What factors are related to the structural elaboration of social control?

A microstructural answer to this question can be briefly outlined. Networks of interpersonal relationships are seen as a major source of stability. These relationships are sometimes subjected to disruption. In response, social linkages of three basic types—normative, exchange, and affective—are brought into play as sources of support and control. In some instances the reservoir of support and control is exhausted or substantially depleted. When this point of network tolerance is reached, the structure of the response changes. The arena of social control branches out. The pattern of this structural change depends on the structural proximity of alternative sources of social control. The basic proposition is that *social-control mechanisms will be utilized according to their structural proximity to the relational disturbance in question.*

The structural proximity of alternative social-control mechanisms is determined by the resilience, isolation, and closure of the network in question. These network properties are defined as follows:

1. *Network resilience:* Resilience is defined as that property that "determines the persistence of relationships within a system and is a measure of the ability of this system to absorb changes of state variables and parameters, and still persist [Holling, 1976: 83]."
2. *Network isolation:* Isolation is one dimension of network permeability and is defined in terms of the amount of information flow and opportunity for interaction between external networks and the network in question.
3. *Network closure:* Closure is a second dimension of network permeability and is defined by the normative, exchange, and affective attachments between the networks in question and specified alternative networks.[2]

[2]A number of problems arise when measurement strategies are developed to accompany these definitions. Measurement strategies have received a good deal of attention in the network literature. Some of the issues are discussed and summarized in *Sociological Methods and Research* (November 1978). In addition it should be noted that the measurement problems are compounded in the present instance because, in addition to the mapping of network structure, the present set of definitions and propositions calls for a mapping of structural change as networks expand and contract in the process of handling relational disruptions.

A network's resilience, its ability to absorb a shock and go on, is important in the morphological study of social control in that it determines the degree to which immediate relationships among actors can be drawn on as sources of support and control. This reserve energy for adaptation is determined in part by the strength of reciprocal exchange, emotional caring, and common normative beliefs that bind actors together. The relative strength of these social ties remains an open question in any given situation (compare Cahn, 1964; Scott, 1971; Turner, 1976). All else equal, however, multidimensional relationships, that is, relationships characterized by an overlap of mutually beneficial exchange, normative agreement, and shared caring, are more resilient than are more restricted relationships. In addition, network resilience is determined by the degree of involvement, that is, the recency, frequency, and duration of the interaction among actors. The general proposition linking network resilience to the probability and degree of structural elaboration of social control follows:

The greater the network resilience, the lower is the probability and degree of structural elaboration of social-control mechanisms.

Networks also become more or less solicitous, receptive, or vulnerable to external sources of control such as the police, doctors, or mental health professionals, according to the permeability of their boundaries. As defined earlier, network isolation refers to the degree of access, the amount of information about and opportunity to interact with, for example, ministers, rabbis, lawyers, psychiatrists, nutritionists, folk curers, surgeons, and so on.

Network closure, in contrast, refers not to access but to approach ability. Approachability is the subjective dimension of social distance (see, e.g., Simmel, 1908; Kadushin, 1962; Verbrugge, 1977). The degree of approachability between the disrupted network and potential sources of social control depends on the interpretation of available information. Persons will turn to a friend or relative, minister, priest or rabbi, seek a lawyer, call the police, hire a psychiatrist, or file a suit in part according to the subjective social distance from these alternative sources of assistance. This social distance waxes and wanes through progressive collective attempts to define and deal with the "trouble" in question (Emerson and Messinger, 1977). Thus, it is more accurate to speak of network closure and isolation than personal attitudes or resources when it comes to explaining the structural elaboration of social control. This is discussed later in the chapter.

The proposition linking network isolation and closure to the structural elaboration of social control is as follows:

Network isolation and closure will influence not only the probability but also the pattern and degree of structural elaboration in social-control mechanisms.

This proposition along with the previous one dealing with network resilience form the core of our microstructural approach to the study of social control. Two alternative frameworks are frequently encountered.

One alternative focuses on the importance of overarching cultural and macrostructural factors. The second assigns primary importance to attitudes and resources of individuals. Each of these is discussed in a later section. For now it is enough to note that if we limit ourselves to either the individual or macrostructural approaches, we are left with a substantial gap: We know little about how broad structural and cultural factors become operable in particular life situations, and we know little about how individual attitudes and resources intermesh with the broader social environment. It is precisely at this point that the strength and structure of interpersonal networks and their proximity to external sources of social control become important (see, e.g., McKinlay, 1972).

With these general definitions, propositions, and possible alternatives in mind, what evidence is available concerning the structural elaboration of social-control mechanisms? Findings and conjectures dealing with dispute processing, mobilization of the law, and utilization of physical and mental illness professionals and facilities are considered.

Relational Resilience and Social Control

Empirical support for the idea that structural changes in social-control mechanisms are influenced by the resilience of the disrupted network comes from a wide range of sources. Evidence is perhaps strongest from cross-cultural research on the handling of disputes (Nader and Todd, 1978; Roberts, 1979). In the face of disputes, social bonds among actors change in a number of ways. The balance of power may shift as the availability of resources and interest in those resources changes. Affective commitments may be weakened or withdrawn, as well as initiated and strengthened. Norms may be neutralized or sharpened into bold relief. These shifts in the strength and structure of interpersonal networks largely determine the rhythm and flow of dispute processing (Yngvesson, 1978: 74).

When adjustments are restricted to the actors immediately confronted with relational disruption, the reaction takes shape as negotiation. The important structural characteristic of negotiation, as an ideal type, is not the number of parties but that the structure of the control network. In terms of the actors involved, the network remains what it was before the dispute. Parties draw on existing emotional ties, normative beliefs, and patterns of exchange in order to process differences. This reliance on the network's reservoir of support and control yields negotiated resolution most likely in the context of strong, multiplex, interpersonal ties.

The more resilient the relational bond among actors, the higher the probability is of a negotiated settlement in disputes.

Resources inherent in the disrupted relationships are sometimes supplemented. In the case of dispute processing, three alternatives are discussed most frequently: mediation, arbitration, and adjudication. These control mechanisms differ from one another in the extent to which the third party is considered independent of the disrupted relationship (Yngvesson, 1978: 85).

A mediating actor has little if any independence from the relationship troubled by dispute. The mediator becomes part of the disrupted relationship, facilitating communication and sorting out pros and cons for each party to consider. As the control process moves toward arbitration it develops a more distinct third party. Unlike a mediator, an arbitrator is one who can make independent decisions. Arbitration involves working with actors and drawing on common values, just as mediation does, but it also involves an independence of actions that parties agree to support beforehand. Finally, adjudication clearly involves the most independent third party. The adjudicator has legitimacy beyond the relationship in question. Intervention can take place whether or not the parties wish it. Decisions reached are binding. It is this attribute of independence that sets the ideal-typical *legal* actor apart from other third parties (see, e.g., Weber, 1925; Bohannan, 1965).

Figure 8.1, which is a modification of the conceptual space for dispute processing suggested by Lempert (1978), points to the connections between these styles and the intermediate nature of arbitration. These distinctions are not limited to what are commonly viewed as disputes or legal cases, however. Clinical interventions can also range from mediative to adjudicative. Rueveni characterizes mediative aspects of his clinical work as being

based on a frame of reference that emphasizes the importance of family and friendship systems. When the extended family system is intact but is dysfunctional (as is

STYLE

		Cooperative	Authoritative
STANDARDS APPLIED	Undifferentiated from relational standards	Mediation	Arbitration
	Differentiated from relational standards	Arbitration	Adjudication

FIGURE 8.1. Conceptual space for types of supplemental resolution mechanisms (supplementing the resources of support and control inherent in the disrupted relationship).

> the case in many family problems), the networking efforts are mainly directed toward helping such a system to become less dysfunctional by increasing the communication among its members [1979: 24].

Other clinical strategies, such as psychoanalytic interpretations of childhood events, would be better characterized as arbitrative or adjudicative, involving distinct, authoritatively applied standards. Similarly, medical intervention may range from commonsense remedies to authoritative proclamations. Given these similarities, it is possible to draw conclusions parallel to those regarding dispute processing from a wide range of relational disruptions (see, e.g., Yarrow, Schwartz, Murphy, and Deasy, 1955; Sampson, Messinger, and Towne, 1962; Nall and Speilberg, 1967; Lowenthal and Haven, 1968; Burch, 1972; Myers, Lindenthal, and Pepper, 1975; Cobb, 1976: Rabkin and Struening, 1976; Dean and Lin, 1977: Horwitz, 1977; Langlie, 1977; Andrews, 1978; Gore, 1978; and Lin,Simeone, Ensel, and Kuo, 1979; McCubbin et al., 1980).

The distinctions in Figure 8.1 seem straightforward enough until applied to actual social-control networks. Some control processes do not move in a smooth fashion from one type to another. Rather, they expand and contract and perhaps expand again (e.g., Abel, 1974; Friedman and Percival, 1976; Emerson and Messinger, 1977; Lempert, 1978). At one point the third party mediates, drawing on resources inherent in the ties among actors. At other points a more authoritative imposition of norms or sanctions, distinct from those governing the actors in dispute, may predominate. Thus, a single statement suggesting the trouble was processed by mediation or adjudication is often not enough.

Related to this flexible nature of social-control mechanisms is the simultaneous presence of multiple control networks. When a case is filed in court, the control network clearly moves toward the adjudicative type. As the case becomes enmeshed in legal proceedings, however, another network of relationships comes into play. Attorneys may agree or disagree about the severity of the case, the credibility of the evidence, the propriety of settlement offers, the need to go to trial. In short, secondary disputes may arise. These secondary disputes are likely to be resolved through negotiation, mediation, arbitration, and adjudication according to the same microstructural principles governing the initial decision to transfer the case to court. In such circumstances, it makes sense to characterize the entire control structure as negotiated (or mediated, or arbitrated) adjudication.

The structure of social-control networks may also become difficult to characterize when relational disturbance is chronic and where the third party becomes part of a style of life. As Kidder has suggested in a study of Indian courts, litigation is sometimes pursued "not for its ability to produce conflict resolution, but for its ability to produce advantages (or negate disadvantages) in ongoing antagonistic relationships which are the substance of the community rather than isolated threats to it [1971: 43]." In such situations of chronic disruption, adjudication becomes an integral part of ongoing, sometimes quite tenuous, sets of relations.

These ambiguities in the structure of social-control mechanisms play a central role in disagreements over the long-debated question, What is law? This role can be illustrated by reference to Lempert's (1976) disagreement with Black (1973) over deciding when law has been mobilized. For Black, the mobilization of law is a process by which the legal (governmental) system acquires its cases. In the instance of contract disputes, a contract becomes a relevant case only when a suit has been filed. Otherwise, law has not been mobilized. Lempert finds this definition too restrictive and suggests instead, "If the parties, through their attorneys, settle a contract dispute on the basis of the attorneys' judgment of what a court would do if faced with the case and with the threat of suit constantly in the background, law, in my opinion, has been mobilized [1976: 173]."

The difference between Black's and Lempert's views becomes a matter of degree rather than of kind when we focus on the structural properties of the networks involved in dispute processing. Contracts reduce barriers between disputes and "specific ways in which difficulties can be disengaged from the institutions in which they arose and which they now threaten can then be engaged within the processes of the legal institution [Bohannan, 1965: 34]." With a contract, the law becomes more closely bound to the relationship in question, both through increased access and subjective understanding. In network terms, contracts reduce the *isolation* and *closure* between the disrupted relationship and the legal machinery. In this sense, the contractual relationship is "legalized."

And yet there is a sense in which law is mobilized to a greater extent when a suit is filed than it is when there is no suit. This difference is largely due to structural shifts toward adjudication. The structure inherent in the interpretation of a contract approximates negotiation—negotiation frequently mediated by lawyers. In contrast, the filing of a suit moves closer to the external norms applied in an authoritative manner that characterize the structure of adjudication. The important dimension of variation is the degree of structural differentiation. There is a more distinct, independent actor involved in the processing of a suit than in the writing and interpretation of a contract, but it is not very helpful to suggest that one is law and the other is not. Predicting and understanding the mobilization of law, whether through the writing and interpretation of a contract or through the filing of a suit, is a specific instance of the more general task of exploring factors influencing the probability and degree of structural changes in control efforts.

Seriousness and the Mobilization of Outsiders

In addition to relational resilience, the seriousness of the disruptive event is quite important when predicting structural changes in social control mechanisms.

The more serious the disruptive event, the higher the probability is that the social control network will expand beyond those initially affected.

For example, Gottfredson and Hindelang (1979a) found the single most important influence on victim reports to the police to be the seriousness of the infraction. In addition, it is difficult to imagine anyone disagreeing with the proposition that families confronted with cancer or attempted suicide are more likely to mobilize medical or therapeutic assistance than are families confronted with a cold or minor anxiety. What differentiates the first two events from the latter is the degree of seriousness. Yet, the meaning of seriousness is not always clear. To help clarify its meaning, it is useful to refer to an exchange between Donald Black (1976; 1979) and Michael Gottfredson and Michael Hindelang (1979a; 1979b).

In *The Behavior of Law* (1976), Black presents numerous propositions regarding ways in which law relates to other dimensions of social life. Using data from the National Crime Survey, Gottfredson and Hindelang tested some of Black's propositions in the context of predicting reports of victims' decisions to inform the police. Their general conclusion was that, at best, Black's ideas were only weakly supported. In addition, Gottfredson and Hindelang conclude, on the basis of their data and information from other studies, that Black's framework contains a major omission. It explicitly excludes a proposition stating that the quantity of criminal law varies directly with the seriousness of the infraction.

In reply, Black (1979: 19–20) suggests that Gottfredson's and Hindelang's findings are inadequate for a test of the ideas contained in *The Behavior of Law*. This issue of measurement strategies need not detain us. Rather, the meaning and importance of seriousness is of more interest. Black does not assert that the seriousness of a disruptive event is unimportant. Rather, the disagreement centers on how seriousness should be conceptualized.[3]

For Gottfredson and Hindelang (1979a; 4–5) seriousness is defined by the amount of harm suffered. But harm as judged by whom? By victims, by public opinion, by a set of legal actors? Relying on the work of Sellin and Wolfgang (1964), Gottfredson and Hindelang opt for a scale constructed from responses of judges, police officers, and college students. Black (1976: 9), in contrast, defines seriousness in terms of the situational quantity of social control that the event calls forth. It is for this reason that the seriousness of an event cannot be used to predict the degree of social control within Black's framework. They are one and the same thing.

The position taken in this chapter differs from both perspectives. In contrast to Black, it is assumed that a definitional distinction should be drawn between the seriousness of the disruptive event and the response. The disruptiveness of an event is more than a mere reflection of the level and type of response. Social networks confronted with robbery, rape, martial infidelity, attempted suicide, or a breach of contract may all view the disruption as equally serious and yet, for a number of reasons, respond differently. Some may distrust the police more than others do; some may be more isolated from legal services or alternative therapies than others are. Given this slippage between estimates of seriousness and social-control responses, one should not be defined in terms of the other.

In contrast to the position of Gottfredson and Hindelang, it is assumed here that a theory of social control should explicitly recognize that the same disruptive event, as ranked on a general scale, may have more or less serious implications, depending on the situation, even where there is widespread agreement on rankings. In particular, the

---

[3]This same issue has been addressed in the literature on stress (see, e.g., Holmes and Rahe, 1957; Selye, 1976).

seriousness of any disruptive event is determined by the damage done to network resilience, that is, the ability to absorb environmental stressors. In addition, and equally important, disruptive events should be characterized according to their influence on network isolation and closure. This applies to the "stressfulness" of life events (Holmes and Rahe, 1967) as well as the "seriousness" of crime.

On the social readjustment rating scale developed by Holmes and Rahe (1967), the death of a close family member is rated higher than is being fired at work. It is possible, however, that in some circumstances the death would be less serious. Compare the loss of an elderly grandparent with the mid-career loss of job, calling for a dramatic shift in lifestyle. The important distinction is not between death and job loss but in *the amount of damage done to existing patterns of relationships.* In a similar fashion, when we say that the loss involved in one death is less serious than another, we again imply that the degree of disruption to the pragmatic concerns and affective attachments is greater in one than in the other (Glaser and Strauss, 1964; Bugen, 1977). As Bugen notes: "If the relationship to the deceased is seen as central, the grief reaction will be intense. If the relationship is considered peripheral, the grief reaction will be mild [1977: 197]." This does not deny the possibility of developing general scales for measuring seriousness or stressfulness. Rather, it suggests that the utility of these scales depends on relational disruption remaining constant from one situation to the next. If this does not hold, general scales will be flawed.

The model proposed for the study of relational disruption and structural changes in social-control networks is that in Figure 8.2. Its utility becomes apparent in a number of studies. When identity-defining relationships—that is, those most likely to involve a wide range of emotional attachments, pragmatic dependencies, and shared normative beliefs—are disrupted, we hypothesize, *the more central the disruption, the more likely is the structural elaboration of social control.* This proposition is supported by the data of Gottfredson and Hindelang (1979a) suggesting that within each level of seriousness (as measured by a general ranking

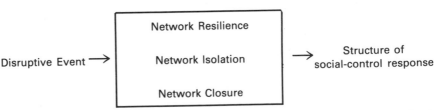

FIGURE 8.2. General model for the study of structural changes in social control networks.

system) victimizations occurring in the home or near home are the most likely to be reported. In a similar fashion, Mayhew and Reiss (1969) found that divorce, alimony, and child support were the only major issues where the incidence of seeing a lawyer showed no relation to income, occupational status, or education, suggesting that the salience of family disruptions is enough to overcome the differential isolation and closure inherent in these other characteristics. Finally, in the area of mental illness, it has been found that "persons who occupy a critical position in the family, generally as indicated by marriage, are more likely to be hospitalized and are hospitalized more quickly than persons not in such a role [Gove and Howell, 1974: 95]."

Without disputing this research, it should also be noted that there is a good deal of evidence suggesting that intimate social ties are more resilient and thus less likely to open up to additional sources of social control (see, e.g., Yarrow et al., 1955; Myers et al., 1975; Black, 1976; Rabkin and Struening, 1976: Langlie, 1977, Dean and Lin, 1977: Gore, 1978: Lin et al., 1979: Horwitz, 1982). It may be that when intimate social ties are disrupted a counterbalancing process is at work. Because these ties define the most central relations, any given disruption has a maximum impact. Because they are also the most resilient relations, any given disruption is more likely to be absorbed by remedies inherent in the exchange, normative and affective resources among actors involved.

Stinchcombe has noted this possibility in his discussion of network permeability and mobilization of the police. Referring to crimes involving coercion in private life, Stinchcombe suggests: "Complaint to the police is something of a betrayal of those to whom we have close personal ties. Once the complaint is made, and the immediate danger and anger past, the personal ties or embarrassment of the complainant quite often reassert themselves, and the main source of evidence refuses to testify further [1963: 154]."

Factors associated with this waxing and waning of network boundaries are not well understood. There is evidence and speculation that individuals tend to "open up," to become less defensive, more amenable to interventive efforts during times of crisis. For example, Weiss found in a study of low-income mothers:

> Desire for support was often expressed by our respondents and, indeed, appeared to be a normal concomitant of trouble. When faced by serious trouble, respondents seemed quite regularly to feel some need for a temporary alliance with an authoritative figure who would symbolically accept their goals as his own and associate his efforts with theirs [1973: 321].

On the other hand, Reiff reports the frustrations experienced by staff of a program designed to help victims of violent crimes stemming from the tendency of victims to make themselves "invisible": "The realistic fear of revictimization accompanied by strong emotional shock often generates high levels of suspicion and distrust. Victims often isolate themselves, virtually hiding in their apartments, refusing to go out after daylight hours and avoiding interaction with strangers [1979: 5]." In addition to the network's tendency to solicit or reject help, the permeability of disrupted networks also depends on intrusive control efforts.[4] These efforts, in turn, may depend in part on the amount of disruption involved. It may take a certain level of disruption before the police are willing to step in, before mental institutions are willing to commit, before courts are willing to hear a case.

Relational disturbances, by their very nature, affect the reservoir of control and support inherent in a given relationship. What was once a strong, resilient, multiplex relationship can become weak, bedraggled, and drained when confronted with certain events. It is because of this structural impact that the "seriousness" of a particular event plays a central role in structural changes in social-control networks.

If we want to study the independent influence of "seriousness," as Gottfredson and Hindelang (1979a) suggest, and at the same time maintain interest in the structural determinants of social control, as Black (1976) has emphasized, it is useful to conceptualize the impact of any given disruptive event according to changes brought in the resilience of interpersonal relationships, as well as shifts in network permeability. It is through its influence on these network properties that any given contract dispute, crime, or illness will be associated with an increased probability of structural changes in social-control efforts.

Structural Changes in Social Control

To this point we have emphasized the probability and degree of structural change in social-control networks. Attention now focuses on the

---

[4]As Black (1973) has pointed out, it is useful to draw a distinction between two types of social control: proactive and reactive. Within a microstructural paradigm, I find it somewhat more useful to substitute "intrusive" and "emergent" for these terms. Emergent structural change in social-control networks is the process of structural change set in motion by those within the disrupted relationship. Intrusive structural changes are initiated by external agents of social control. Any particular structural change might, and frequently does, involve emergent and intrusive dimensions. For example, parties who go to court or call the police may lose control of the process and have a solution imposed. The influence of this on the way police respond to private trouble has been discussed by Goldstein (1960). The loss of control may be one important reason for not going to court, calling the police, or seeking psychiatric assistance (see, e.g., McKinlay, 1972: 130).

pattern of these changes. When faced with disruptions that strain relational resources, in what direction will networks expand? Will persons call the police, hire a lawyer, consult a minister, a psychiatrist, or a faith healer, or join a self-help group? The list is almost endless.

One approach to this question has been to focus on individual resources. Persons turn to lawyers, doctors, or psychiatrists, as opposed to alternatives, according to how much money they have. Also, persons choose between alternative remedies according to their competence (as measured by education) to perceive grievances, illness symptoms, and appropriate remedies. Whether the resource is income, education, or some combination, external sources of social control are utilized according to how rich and discerning are the troubled individuals. As appealing as this argument is (see, e.g., Gove and Howell, 1974), numerous writers (e.g., Kadushin, 1969; Mayhew and Reiss, 1969; Galanter, 1974, 1975: Mayhew, 1975) have argued and offered evidence that things are not quite so simple.

For example, Mayhew and Reiss, in a study of the social organization of contacts with lawyers, concluded: "Citizens are not brought into contact with the legal profession merely by their resources but by their problems, institutionalized definitions, and social organization of problem solution [1969: 317]." This emphasis on "institutionalized definitions" and "the social organization of problem solution" suggests a second general approach to relational disturbances, one that posits a set of overarching macrostructural or cultural influences.Clearly there is merit in this view.Members of many Western cultures are no doubt more likely to call a therapist than an exorcist. Similarly, it is generally the case that most persons in the United States and other modern societies will not call the police for a breach of contract. There are shared institutionalized definitions and beliefs that particular relational disturbances are to be handled in particular ways.

Along these lines, Galanter (1975) has discussed the "litigation mindedness" of different societies. Relational disruptions may be more open to litigated remedies by virtue of shared cultural beliefs and practices. This cultural orientation toward the pragmatic, normative, and symbolic importance of official dispute processing has its obverse in the hypothesized "cultural inpenetrability" of the poor when it comes to the utilization of medical services (see, e.g., Goering and Coe, 1970). The divestment of the criminal law and the emergence of the "therapeutic state" (Kittrie, 1971) suggests a situation in which institutionalized definitions and practices might be shifting. Parallel, too, is the claim that the community health movement, the tendency among clinicians to treat the individual not as an isolated psychological problem but in the context of a broader social milieu, is a rearrangement of cultural beliefs that govern utilization of legal and mental health systems of control (Dinitz and Beran, 1971: Wagenfeld and Robin, 1976: Borus, 1978). Finally, the recent drop in the admission rate of persons 65 and over to mental hospitals can be seen not so much as an improvement in the collective mental health of this group as a structural shift toward increased availability of nursing homes (Dunlop, 1979).

As compelling as the macrostructural approach might seem, there is some rather troublesome evidence. Galanter notes:

> From working with the American material, however, one would not necessarily conclude that belief systems could explain much about dispute processing. Who "believes in" plea bargaining, our overwhelmingly prevalent way of handling criminal cases? A variety of practices of negotiation, compromise, avoidance, and resignation seems to flourish in a population said to be very rights-minded. The converse appears to be the case in India where litigation flourishes alongside an avowed preference for compromise and reconciliation. Comparative exploration of dispute processing certainly cannot ignore the ideology factor; we want to know when and how ideology does have an effect [1975: 365].

This same position is taken by McKinlay in his review of research on clinical service utilization. Referring to such concepts as "values," "social class," and "subcultures," he asserts: "The explanatory power of propositions that incorporate such macro-cosmic concepts appears to be weak because very little attention is given to possibly influenctial intervening mechanisms. As theoretical tools, these concepts can explain too much, and therefore not enough [1972, 131]."

It is at the point of specifying influential intervening mechanisms that a microstructural approach to social control becomes most useful. By focusing on changes in the resilience, closure, and isolation of interpersonal networks—and other analogous variables yet to be discovered— we are better able to understand the ways formal and informal definitions, and macro and micro structures of social control intermesh.

In any response to relational disturbance, an initial definition is fashioned concerning the kind of trouble that occurs: Is this a matter for the police, the courts, the social worker, the minister, the doctor? This jurisdictional decision is an initial determinant of the pattern of structural shifts in social control. One of the major ways the social organization of problem solutions intermeshes with micronetworks of control is through a set of jurisdictional definitions. These definitions are sometimes officially recognized and specified. Prosecutors may refuse to take a case if no "crime" has been committed. Someone was cheated, but the type of cheating involved is a "civil" matter. Likewise, appellate courts may refuse to hear a case for a wide range of reasons. Service bureaucracies may refuse to handle particular matters for policy reasons: "You need to go see ———." In network terms, this becomes a matter of boundary permeability. Official jurisdictional definitions influence the pattern of structural change in control networks by increasing or decreasing the degree of opportunities for interaction (isolation) between the disrupted network and alternative sources of social control.

Decisions about problem types are not based solely on formalized standards, however. The type of problem, and therefore the response, is often a matter of some discussion. As Emerson and Messinger suggest:

> Many troubles, particularly when first noted, appear vague to those concerned. But as steps are taken to remedy or manage that trouble, the trouble itself becomes progressively clarified and specified. In this sense the natural history of a trouble is intimately tied to—and produces—the effort to do something about it. Thus, remedial actions of varying sort—living with, ignoring, isolating, controlling, correcting the trouble—are highly significant events not only in determining the fate of the trouble, but also in shaping how it is first perceived. Conceptually, the definition of a trouble can be seen as the emergent product, as well as the initial precipitant of remedial actions [1977: 123].

Jurisdictional lines are drawn and redrawn as control mechanisms expand, contract, and change direction. Evidence suggests the pattern of this morphogenesis is governed by the principle of structural proximity stated above (see page 212).

In the first stage of expansion close friends or relatives, those in the personal cell of an individual's more extended network (Boissevain 1974: 47), are incorporated. If expansion continues, additional outsiders are drawn in, again, according to their social distance. For example, generalists (ministers, family doctors, police) are more likely to be called, and called at an earlier point, than are specialists, the reason being the reduced social distance between generalist and lay person (Emerson and Messinger, 1977: 127). Similarly, alternative clinics are chosen according to their structural proximity. Kadushin notes, "The circle of friends is thus a key variable in explaining why certain groups are drawn to different types of clinics. In part, people go to different types of clinics because others in their social circles go there [1969: 68]," or, we would add, have knowledge of them.

One important dimension of structural proximity is information flow. It has been found that information is the single best predictor of agency utilization (Katz, Gutek, Kahn, and Barton, 1975). When it comes to the availability of information, "weak ties" are particularly important in that "those to whom we are weakly tied are more likely to move in circles different from our own and will thus have access to information different from that which we receive [Granovetter, 1973: 1371]." The importance of these bridging ties for patterned changes in control networks becomes apparent in decisions to seek psychiatric help (Kadushin, 1969; Horwitz, 1977), medical care (Suchman, 1965), and abortion services (Lee, 1969: Zimmerman, 1977). Their structural location as a "weak tie" also accounts for the importance of lawyers (Lempert, 1976) and the utility of "neighborhood aides" (Mayhew, 1975) in the pursuit of legal remedies. In each case friends, relatives, acquaintances, case finders, and lawyers play an important bridging role between the disrupted network and external sources of social control.

As social-control mechanisms continue to expand, referral networks take on increasing importance in determining patterned changes in the structure of social-control networks. For example, with the emergence of innovative technology, medical care has become more centralized, bureaucratized, and interpersonally complex (Mendelsohn, Swazey, and Traviss, 1971). At the same time, the pattern of information flow has shifted. Networks of relationships, immediately involved in the relational disruption, have become isolated from important sources of information. Given their structural location as a "weak tie," physicians act as important gatekeepers and interpreters of information (Fox and Swazey, 1974). The information available to physicians is in turn influenced by their own referral networks. Personal physicians, removed from large medical centers, are less likely to have access to the latest interpretations of particular diseases and therefore are less likely to suggest these to their patients (Simmons, Klein, and Simmons, 1977).

From beginning to end, the pattern of structural change in social-control networks depends at least as much on microstructural considerations as on cultural beliefs, psychological predispositions, or personal resources. Personal resources and attitudes, as well as macrosystem properties, influence the structural expansion of social-control mechanisms only to the degree that they influence the strength and structure of social links between the disrupted network and alternative sources of control. These links are frequently more flexible than is implied by either the macro or individual resources paradigms. They are governed as much by situational shifts in patterns of exchange, emotional attachments, and normative judgments as by generalized beliefs concerning external sources of social control. This is suggested by research on utilization of medical services by ethnic groups (Nall and Speilberg, 1967), utilization of bureaucratic agencies (Katz et al., 1975), and utilization of the police (Hawkins, 1973).

These findings and conclusions have important methodological implications. For example, the "symptoms-response ratio" suggested by Taylor, Aday, and Anderson (1975) for the measurement of access to medical care may be misleading. This ratio compares the reported number of visits with the number of visits there "should be," as determined by a panel of 40 doctors. "Underutilization" is taken as a measure of lack of access. What "overutilization" means, in terms of access, is unclear. Because the age group 1–5 years is the most likely to "overutilize," does this mean there is too much access for young children? The problem with this indicator is that the comparison of actual usage with normative usage, as determined by a panel of experts, bypasses a number of important stages in the utilization of medical services.

Persons confronted with illness symptoms (and, we might add, potential legal cases) may know of a service, have the opportunity for interaction, and yet not utilize a particular source of support or social control. Medical needs are frequently quite nebulous. Like legal claims, and like trouble in general, decisions as to the "type of case" are made within the context of ongoing interaction and alternative sources of support and control. As in the case with legal services (Mayhew, 1975), indicators of access to medical services should focus on the organized activity of the medical profession or agency and ask how this interlocks via interpersonal relations with more localized networks of social control.

Summary

A general set of propositions has been presented to link properties of interpersonal networks and mechanisms of social control:

The greater the network resilience, the lower is the probability and degree of structural elaboration of social-control mechanisms.

Network, isolation, and closure will influence not only the probability but also the pattern and degree of structural elaboration in social-control mechanisms.

A mark of a useful paradigm is its ability to incorporate a wide range of otherwise diverse findings. The relevance of the preceding propositions to such events as suicide, robbery, physical illness, contract disputes, and marital infidelity has been noted. In addition, it has been suggested that the central characteristic of a disruptive event, as it relates to the structural properties of social control, is its seriousness:

The more serious the disruptive event, the higher the probability is that the social-control network will expand beyond those initially affected.

Seriousness traditionally has been defined either in terms of individual perceptions or generalized public opinion. Within the paradigm presented here, seriousness is defined in terms of the disruptive event's impact on the interpersonal relations among those most directly effected. Among other things, the degree of disruption will vary directly with the centrality of the relationship. At the same time it has been noted that central relationships are, all else being equal, generally more resilient than more peripheral relations. Hence, in many instances there is a counterbalance between the resilience factor and the seriousness factor when it comes to structural changes in social-control mechanisms.

The suggestion that the changes in social-control mechanisms depend largely on the strength and structure of interpersonal relations has important methodological implications for those who would devise indicators of access to various forms of legal, medical, or clinical services. These have been briefly illustrated.

Finally, the discussion has been aimed at bridging the gap between psychological and macrostructural approaches to the study of social control. Whether we are interested in the probability, degree, or pattern of changes in social-control mechanisms, the resilience, isolation, and closure of interpersonal networks offer promising leads for bridging the gap between individualistic perceptions, resources, and tolerance levels, on the one hand, and broader institutionalized values and social structures, on the other.

ACKNOWLEDGMENTS

I thank Donald Black, Larry Cohen, Jack Gibbs, Richard Lempert, and Michael Supancic for useful comments on an earlier draft.

References

Abel, Richard L.
    1974   "A comparative theory of dispute institutions in society." *Law and Society Review* 8: 217–347.
Andrews, Gavin, Christopher Tennant, Daphne Hewson, and George E. Vaillant
    1978   "Life event stress, social support, coping style and risk of psychological impairment." *Journal of Nervous and Mental Disease* 166: 307–316.
Black, Donald
    1973   "The mobilization of law." *Journal of Legal Studies* 2: 125–149.

1976   *The Behavior of Law.* New York: Academic Press.
1979   "Common sense in the sociology of law." *American Sociological Review* 44: 18–27.
Bohannan, Paul
   1965   "The differing realms of the law." Pages 33–42 in *The Ethnography of Law*, edited by Laura Nader. Supplement to *American Anthropologist*, vol. 67.
Boissevain, Jeremy
   1974   *Friends of Friends: Networks, Manipulators and Coalitions.* Oxford: Basil Blackwood.
Borus, Jonathan F.
   1978   "Issues critical to the survival of community mental health." *American Journal of Psychiatry* 135: 1029–1035.
Bugen, Larry
   1977   "Human grief: A model for prediction and intervention." *American Journal of Orthopsychiatry* 47: 196–206.
Burch, J.
   1972   "Recent bereavement in relation to suicide." *Journal of Psychosomatic Research* 16: 361–366.
Burr, W. R.
   1973   *Theory Construction and the Sociology of the Family.* New York: Wiley.
Cahn, Edmond
   1964   *The Sense of Injustice.* Bloomington, Ind.: University of Indiana Press.
Cobb, Sidney
   1976   "Social support as a moderator of life stress." *Psychosomatic Medicine* 38: 300–314.
Danzig, Richard, and Michael J. Lowy
   1975   "Everyday disputes and mediation in the United States: A reply to Professor Felstiner." *Law and Society Review:* 675–706.
Dean, Alfred, and Nan Lin
   1977   "The stress buffering role of social support: Problems and prospects for systematic investigation." *Journal of Nervous and Mental Disease* 165: 403–417.
Dinitz, Simon, and Nancy Beran
   1971   "Community mental health as a boundaryless and boundary-busting system." *Journal of Health and Social Behavior* 12: 99–108.
Dunlop, Burton
   1979   *The Growth of Nursing Home Care.* Lexington, Mass.: Lexington Books.
Emerson, Richard M.
   1962   "Power dependence relations." *American Sociological Review* 27: 31–41.
   1972   "Exchange theory, Part II: Exchange relations and network structures." Pages 58–88 in *Sociological Theories in Progress*, edited by Joseph Berger, Morris Zelditch, and Bo Anderson. New York: Houghton Mifflin.
Emerson, Robert, and Sheldon Messinger
   1977   "The micro-politics of trouble." *Social Problems* 25: 121–132.
Felstiner, William L. F.
   1974   "Influences of social organization on dispute processing." *Law and Society Review* 9: 63–94.
Fox, Renée, and Judith Swazey
   1974   *The Courage to Fail: A Social View of Organ Transplants and Dialysis.* Chicago: University of Chicago Press.

Friedman, Laurence M., and Robert Percival
     1976   "Tale of two courts: Litigation in Alameda and San Benito counties." *Law and
            Society Review* 10: 267–301.
Galanter, Marc
     1974   "Why the haves come out ahead: Speculations on the limits of legal change."
            Law and Society Review 9: 95–106.
     1975   "Afterword: Explaining litigation." *Law and Society Review* 10: 347–368.
     1976   "Delivering legality: Some proposals for the direction of research." *Law and
            Society Review* 11: 245–256.
Gibbs, Jack P.
     1972   "Social Control." New York: Warner Modular Publications, No. 1.
Glaser, Barney, and Anselm Strauss
     1964   "Awareness contexts and social interaction." *American Sociological Review* 29:
            119–121.
Goering, John, and Rodney Coe
     1970   "Cultural versus situational explanations of medical behavior of the poor."
            Social Science Quarterly 51: 309–319.
Goldstein, Joseph
     1960   "Police discretion not to invoke the criminal process: Low visibility decisions in
            the administration of justice." *Yale Law Journal* 69: 543–594.
Gore, Susan
     1978   "The effect of social support in moderating health consequences of unemploy-
            ment." *Journal of Health and Social Behavior* 19: 157–165.
Gottfredson, Michael R., and Michael J. Hindelang
     1979a "A study of *The Behavior of Law.*" *American Sociological Review* 44: 3–18.
     1979b "Theory and research in the sociology of law." *American Sociological Review* 44:
            27–37.
Gove, Walter, and Patrick Howell
     1974   "Individual resources and mental hospitailzation: A comparison and evalua-
            tion of the societal reaction and psychiatric perspectives." *American Sociological
            Review* 39: 86–100.
Granovetter, Mark
     1973   "The strength of weak ties." *American Journal of Sociology* 81: 1287–1303.
Hawkins, Richard O.
     1973   "Who called the cops: Decisions to report criminal victimization." *Law and
            Society Review* 7: 427–444.
Hill, Reuben
     1949   *Families under Stress.* New York: Harper and Brothers.
Holling, C. S.
     1976   "Resilience and stability of ecosystems." Pages 73–92 in *Evolution and Con-
            sciousness: Human Systems,* edited by Erich Jantsch and Conrad Waddington.
            Reading, Mass.: Addison-Wesley.
Holmes, Thomas, and Richard Rahe
     1967   "The social readjustment rating scale." *Journal of Psychosomatic Research* 11:
            213–218.
Horwitz, Allan V.
     1977   "Social networks and pathways to psychiatric treatment." *Social Forces* 56:
            86–104.
     1982   *The Social Control of Mental Illness.* New York: Academic Press.

Kadushin, Charles
   1962   "Social distance between client and professional." *American Journal of Sociology*
           67: 517–531.
   1969   *Why People Go to Psychiatrists*. New York: Atherton Press.
Katz, Daniel, Barbara A. Gutek, Robert L. Kahn, and Eugenia Barton
   1975   *Bureaucratic Encounters: A Pilot Study in the Evaluation of Government Services*. Ann
           Arbor, Mich.: University of Michigan Press.
Kidder, Robert
   1971   The Dynamics of Litigation: A Study of Civil Litigation in South Indian Courts.
           Unpublished doctoral dissertation, Department of Sociology, Northwestern
           University.
Kittrie, Nicholas
   1971   *The Right to Be Different*. Baltimore: Johns Hopkins University Press.
Langlie, Jean K.
   1977   "Social networks, health beliefs, and preventive health behavior." *Journal of
           Health and Social Behavior* 18: 244–260.
Lee, Nancy Howell
   1969   *The Search for an Abortionist*. Chicago: University of Chicago Press.
Lempert, Richard
   1976   "Mobilizing private law: An introductory essay." *Law and Society Review* 11:
           173–189.
   1978   "More tales of two courts: Exploring changes in the dispute settlement function
           of trial courts." *Law and Society Review* 13: 91–138.
Lin, Nan, Ronald S. Simeone, Walter M. Ensel, and Weu Kuo
   1979   "Social support, stressful life events, and illness: A model and an empirical
           test." *Journal of Health and Social Behavior* 20: 108–119.
Lowenthal, Margorie E., and Clayton Haven
   1968   "Interaction and adaptation: Intimacy as a critical variable." *American Sociologi-
           cal Review* 33: 20–30.
McCallister, Lynn and Claude S. Fischer
   1978   "A procedure for surveying personal networks." *Sociological Methods and Re-
           search* 7: (November) 131–148.
McCubbin, Hamilton I., Constance B Joy, A. Elizabeth Cauble, Joan K. Comeau, Joan
M. Patterson, and Richard H. Needle
   1980   "Family stress and coping: A decade of review." *Journal of Marriage and the
           Family* 42: 855–871.
McKinlay, John B.
   1972   "Some approaches and problems in the study of the use of services—an over-
           view." *Journal of Health and Social Behavior* 13: 115–252.
Mayhew, Leon H.
   1975   "Institutions of representation: Civil justice and the public." *Law and Society
           Review* (Spring) 401–429.
Mayhew, Leon, and Albert J. Reiss, Jr.
   1969   "Social organization of legal contacts." *American Sociological Review* 34: 309–318.
Mendelsohn, Everett, Judith Swazey, and Irene Traviss
   1971   *Human Aspects of Biomedical Innovation*. Cambridge, Mass.: Harvard University
           Press.
Miller, F. T., W. K. Bentz, J. F. Aponte, and D. R. Brogan
   1974   "Perception of life crisis events: A comparative study of rural and urban sam-

ples." Pages 259–274 in *Stressful Life Events: Their Nature and Effects*, edited by Barbara S. Dohrenwend and Bruce P. Dohrenwend. New York: Wiley.

Myers, Jerome, Jacob Lindenthal, and Max Pepper
  1975   "Life events, social integration and psychiatric symptomatology." *Journal of Health and Social Behavior* 16: 421–429.

Nader, Laura, and Harry F. Todd, Jr.
  1978   "Introduction: The disputing process." Pages 1–40 in *The Disputing Process— Law in Ten Societies*, edited by Laura Nader and Harry F. Todd, Jr. New York: Columbia University Press.

Nall, Frank, and Joseph Speilberg
  1967   "Social and cultural factors in the responses of Mexican-Americans to medical treatment." *Journal of Health and Social Behavior* 8: 299–308.

Olson, Sheldon
  1975   *Issues in the Sociology of Criminal Justice*. Indianapolis, Ind.: Bobbs-Merrill.

Rabkin, Judith G., and Elmer Struening
  1976   "Life events, stress and illness." *Science* 13: 1013–1020.

Reiff, Robert
  1979   *The Invisible Victim*. New York: Basic Books.

Roberts, Simon
  1979   *Order and Dispute, An Introduction to Legal Anthropology*. New York: St. Martin's Press.

Rossi, Peter, Emily Waite, Christine Bose, and Richard Berk
  1974   "The seriousness of crimes: Normative structure and individual differences." *American Sociological Review* 39: 224–237.

Rueveni, Uri
  1979   *Networking Families in Crisis*. New York: Human Sciences Press.

Sampson, Harold, Sheldon Messinger, and Robert D. Towne
  1962   "Family processes and becoming a mental patient." *American Journal of Sociology* 67: 88–96.

Scott, John F.
  1971   *Internalization of Norms: A Sociological Theory of Moral Commitment*. Englewood Cliffs, N.J.: Prentice-Hall.

Sellin, Thorsten, and Marvin Wolfgang
  1964   *The Measurement of Delinquency*. New York: Wiley.

Selye, Hans
  1976   *The Stress of Life*. Revised edition. New York: McGraw-Hill.

Simmel, Georg
  1908   *The Sociology of Georg Simmel*, edited by Kurt Wolff. Glencoe, Ill.: Free Press, 1960.

Simmons, Robert G., Susan Klein, and Richard Simmons
  1977   *The Social Impact of Transplantation*. New York: Wiley Interscience.

Stinchcombe, Arthur
  1963   "Institutions of privacy in the determination of police administrative practice." *American Journal of Sociology* 69: 150–260.

Suchman, Edward
  1965   "Stages of illness and medical care." *Journal of Health and Social Behavior* 6: 114–228.

Taylor, D. Garth, Lu Ann Aday, Ronald Anderson
  1975   "A social indicator of access to medical care." *Journal of Health and Social Behavior* 16: 38–49.

Turner, Ralph
    1976   "The real self: From institution to impulse." *American Journal of Sociology* 81: 989–1016.
Verbrugge, Lois
    1977   "The structure of adult friendship choices." *Social Forces* 56: 576–597.
Wagenfeld, Morton O., and Stanley S. Robin
    1976   "Boundary busting in the role of the community mental health worker." *Journal of Health and Social Behavior* 17: 111–121.
Weber, Max
    1925   *Max Weber on Law in Economy and Society*, edited by Max Rheinstein. Cambridge, Mass.: Harvard University Press, 1954 (second edition: first edition, 1922).
Weiss, Robert S.
    1973   "Helping relationships: Relationships of clients with physicians, social workers, priests and others." *Social Problems* 20: 319–328.
Yarrow, Marian R., Charlott Green Schwartz, Harriet Murphy, and Leila Calhoun Deasy
    1955   "The psychological meaning of mental illness in the family." *Journal of Social Issues* 11: 12–24.
Yngvesson, Barbara B.
    1978   "The Atlantic fisherman." Pages 59–85 in *The Disputing Process—Law in Ten Societies*, edited by Laura Nader and Harry F. Todd, Jr. New York: Columbia University Press.
Zimmerman, Mary K.
    1977   *Passage through Abortion: The Personal and Social Reality of Women's Experiences.* New York: Praeger.

9

What Is a Dispute About?
The Political Interpretation
of Social Control

BARBARA YNGVESSON

How do we know what a dispute is about? Who decides what the issues are, and how does this shape the outcome? Consider the following case, recorded in a metropolitan setting in the United States: "[A] lower-class black woman called the police . . . to complain that her husband was 'insane,' and that he had threatened to kill her. To this the officer replied that her husband actually was 'only drunk,' and that if they did not go home immediately, both of them would be arrested for 'drunkenness.' Afterward, the observer recorded that, in his opinion, the man was 'insane or at least dangerous' [Black, 1980: 54–55]." Black points out (1980: 114) that typically police define cases such as these as "family trouble," and keep their involvement to a minimum. They may take no action at all, as in this case, or if the situation is more pressing (e.g., a stabbing), they will define the issue as a medical problem rather than as a crime (1980: 113–118).

A case observed by Santos (1977: 70–74) in a Brazilian *favela* (slum settlement) provides another example of the different ways in which a dispute can be defined, although here the dynamic involved in the definition process is quite different. The case was argued before the president of the Residents' Association in the *favela:* Mrs. BW owned a shack that she had rented to Miss AM. Now she wanted Miss AM to leave so she could use the shack for her sister and the latter's three

235

children. Miss AM refused to leave, however. In presenting their case, the disputants defined the issues in moral terms: Mrs. BW argued that she had been compassionate when Miss AM was in need but that the situation of her sister was desperate; Miss AM replied that she and her children must have a place to live and that she could not afford rent elsewhere. Each disputant also, through the use of slander, sought to persuade the president that she was morally superior to the other. Miss AM: "You lived for eleven years with a guy who was crazy and beat you all the time. He committed all kinds of larcenies and finally was caught by the police. Now he is in a mental hospital." Mrs. BW: "The truth of the matter is that she is a prostitute and is full of *cachaca* [alcoholic drink] and of *maconha* [marijuana] all the time. And the shack is always full of *marginais* [criminals] [1977: 71]." Santos argues that the president, after hearing all this, "sensed that the dispute over the shack was secondary and had been triggered by another real dispute between Mrs. BW and Miss AM. They were probably fighting over a man [1977: 74]." The president chose not to become involved in the deeper issues, however, and decided the case on legal grounds (Mrs. BW had a greater right to the shack because she owned it) (1977: 73). Significantly, however, he could not present his decision in those terms "because the fact that *the parties have chosen a moral argumentation* makes such a presentation un-persuasive [1977: 73, italics added]." Thus he induced Miss AM to give in by creating a moral advantage for Mrs. BW: "[She] was very kind to have let you move into the shack and even use her furniture [1977: 71]." On this basis he secured Miss AM's consent to find another place to live.

A final example is drawn from my field notes on a clerk magistrate's hearing at a district court in eastern Massachusetts. The hearings are held in all citizen-initiated cases to determine if a criminal complaint should issue. In this case, A brought her neighbor M to court for threat-ening her with a long-barreled black gun at the door to her (A's) house a few nights earlier. M denied that a gun was at issue in the case. She maintained that the basic issue was an attack by the plaintiff's room-mate's dog on her own dog and that in response she had threatened to use a long black stick to defend her own dog the next time the plaintiff's dog was loose. There was a lengthy exchange between the two dispu-tants, most of it dealing not so much with the threat by the defendant to use the stick or gun, but with the question of whether this was a case "about dogs" or whether it was a case "about a gun." The defendant insisted that her use of the long black stick was simply another stage in the case involving the plaintiff's (roommate's) dog. The plaintiff, on the other hand, insisted that the dog problem had been attended to by the dog officer at an earlier data and that the dog was not restrained; the threat with the gun, she said, was a separate matter, and she had come to court because she was concerned about her safety. She presented detailed and convincing evidence that a gun had in fact been used by the defendant. She described it in detail and said that the police (whom she had called at the time of the incident) had found a gun of that description at the defendant's house. Nevertheless, the clerk who heard this case chose to focus on the issues raised by the defendant, not those raised by the plaintiff; he ruled that this was a case for the dog officer to attend to and did not warrant issuance of a complaint. He did point out to the defendant that she should not "go around threatening people" that way but reprimanded the plaintiff for allowing the dog to run loose. Subsequent to the hearing, the clerk mentioned that the defendant's husband was a local sheriff, who had come in to see him prior to the hearing. The sheriff had stated that his wife did not know how to use a gun and that this was simply a case of threats. The clerk seemed ambivalent about his judgment in the case, but the ruling was not changed.

In this case the decision that the case was "about dogs" was justified by the clerk on the grounds that the alleged gun threat was simply "A's story against M's." Nevertheless, in opting for M's story, he also opted for a particular definition of the issues in the case, as articulated by the structurally more central (rather than the structurally marginal) disputant.

What do the dynamics of these three cases suggest about the relationship of the disputants to one another, and about the relationship between both and the dispute-processing institution? What is the significance of the fact that in the first and third cases the third party (police or clerk magistrate) chose to define the dispute as a family matter and as a neighborhood problem, respectively, rather than as a problem of a criminal nature? What can these decisions tell us about patterns of order in American society? What can the difference in balance of power between the disputants and the third party in the first and third cases, on the one hand, and in the second case, on the other, tell us about the ways power is distributed not only in the disputing forum but also in the broader social context of which the forum is a part?

In this chapter I shall discuss a number of case studies of disputing through which questions such as these can be explored. I shall argue that attention to who defines the categories in which a particular dispute is framed, and consideration of competing efforts to define the same events, can provide us with important, but often neglected, insights into the social control of disputing, as well as into the continuities between this process and fundamental aspects of social order: patterns of integration and marginality, relations of dominance and subordination, and ideas about normal trouble and serious trouble[1] in the relations of individuals and groups in society. Assumptions informing my analysis are the following:

1. A dispute is not simply an "objective fact," but its meaning varies with the circumstances in which it occurs.
2. Any social unit includes individuals and groups with conflicting as well as overlapping interests, and these interests will shape their understanding and interpretation of the events in a dispute. Thus, defining the meaning of a dispute is an act with political implications.
3. Those actors closest to the centers of power in the unit studied typically impose a definition, although meaning may be negotiated. The balance of power in the disputing forum affects this negotiation.
4. The process of negotiating meaning is one of sidestepping certain definitions or transforming them into others. This process is a central feature of disputing and shapes the outcome of disputes in significant ways.

Attention to this perspective on disputing requires a shift not only in the descriptions we provide but also in the theories we employ. Ethnographic descriptions of disputing typically focus on only one layer of meaning, that provided by the dominant actors. The regularities we document assume use of this perspective, and our most basic units of analysis—concepts such as "kin" or "stranger," "family matter" or "crime," "dyad" or "triad"—are shaped by it. By broadening our descriptive base we can develop theories that explore the premises on which regularity is based, and we can suggest the conditions under which a different kind of regularity might operate.

This chapter is divided into two main sections. The first section focuses on ethnographic description, examining case studies from New Guinea, Thailand, and the United States. Special attention will be given to the roles of individuals who seem to be central to the social-control process, with a view to contrasting the perspective of these individuals with that of more marginal actors. Klaus-Friedrich Koch's (1974: 63–66) discussion of the Jalé "big man," an informal leader whose power derives from political skill and ritual knowledge,[2] provided a useful frame-

---

[1]These concepts are used by Emerson (1969: 84) in discussing case management in juvenile court. They are similar to Sudnow's (1965) concept of "normal crime," developed in his study of the operation of a public defender's office.

[2]The concept "big man" is the principal symbol for discussing gradations of power and leadership in Melanesia (see Sahlins, 1963, for an analysis of the role of "big men" and a comparison of this role with other forms of leadership in Melanesia and Polynesia).

work for conceptualizing central figures. Lynn Mather's (1979: 127) discussion of "maverick" attorneys also proved helpful. "Mavericks" are central figures with a deviant perspective: Their visibility makes them useful for highlighting the disparity between official and marginal views. Finally, because I am particularly interested in the ways different actors define acts and persons around which disputes have arisen, I will attend with some care to the language of disputing and to the question of whose language is used in the disputing process. The role of language, official and traditional, is nicely illustrated by David Engel's (1978) study of litigation in Thailand.

The second main part of the chapter will consider the impact of a shift in descriptive focus on our units of analysis and on the kind of theory we develop. In particular, I shall discuss concepts of triadic and dyadic disputing and hypotheses that have been developed about these phenomena. In addition, I shall raise some questions about our understanding of the impact of marginality and rank on the ways disputes are managed.

Description: The Problem of Perspective

> The language of law is to a large extent the language of the officials, and the categories of the law may shortchange the villagers in the distribution of social power [Engel, 1978: 189].[3]

THE JALÉ

Klaus-Friedrich Koch's (1974) ethnography of conflict management[4] among the Jalé of highland New Guinea describes their categories of law and provides numerous materials documenting levels of conflict and responses to conflict. I will argue that these materials primarily represent the ways in which Jalé men—and especially men of ritual knowledge and political skill—conceptualize and deal with conflict, although there are insights into other perspectives as well. Koch does not elaborate on these, however, nor does he pursue the implications of the

---

[3]This and subsequent quotes cited to Engel, 1978 are reprinted from *Code and Custom in a Thai Provincial Court* by David M. Engel by permission of The University of Arizona Press. Copyright © 1978 by The University of Arizona Press.

[4]In accordance with accepted practice, I will reserve the term *dispute* for a conflict that has been asserted publicly. Because many of the cases of conflict reported for the Jalé do not develop into public disputes, I will follow Koch's terminology and use the more general concept *conflict management* in discussing Jalé case processing. I will occasionally use the term *social control* as the most general label for processes used to constrain social behavior.

differences in perspective in his concluding, more theoretical, chapter. His aim is to document regularities in Jalé social control, with a view to developing hypotheses testable elsewhere. My interest is in suggesting an alternate understanding of Jalé social control if the tension points between these regularities (produced by the actions and decisions of the "big men") and the perspective of more marginal people are the focus of attention.

The Jalé raise pigs and cultivate root crops along valleys in the Central Mountains of western New Guinea. Their principal residential units are village subdivisions (wards) in which the main residence is a men's house, known as the "sacred house" (1974: 37). All initiated males of a ward live in the men's house, which is spatially and socially broken down into small groups of agnatically related kinsmen. Koch's analysis of Jalé social structure emphasizes the key role played by these groups (1974: 55–62, 166–172). Their exchanges of women and pigs are a central feature of Jalé political and economic life and provide a basis for the alliances of larger kin-based groups (lineages). Networks created in this way become significant in defining supporters and enemies in times of war; maintenance of the networks and activities related to their expansion are major focuses of action for Jalé males. The largest networks are controlled by the "big men" or "men of knowledge," ritual elders with a large lineage, managerial skill, and verbal eloquence (1974: 54–66).

Another important feature of Jalé society is the spatial separation and ritual differentiation of males and females. Although Koch discusses the psychological effects of male–female dichotomization on male Jalé, he does not pursue its structural and political implications. In fact, the dichotomization of male and female experience is structurally similar to the distinctions drawn between senior (initiated) and junior (uniniti-ated) males. Senior males live in the men's house; their wives, uniniti-ated sons, and unmarried daughters live in separate huts located on the periphery of the men's house. The spatial separation between men and women, on the one hand, and between initiated and uninitiated men, on the other, in which the central position of initiated males is empha-sized, is also reflected in other spheres. Decisions about marriage, trade, and the management of conflict are made by senior males. And in this tribe, as in other culturally similar groups in highland New Guinea, only senior males are permitted to learn the symbols and concepts of ritual knowledge; only they can perform the rituals connected with warfare, life crises, and economic pursuits. The secrecy of this knowledge and that junior men, and women, are considered to operate with simpler levels of knowledge is an important dimension of the power of senior men. It is they who create the categories of knowledge, controlling the distinctions between seniors and juniors and sustaining the male–female dichotomy that "pervades Jalé culture" (1974: 54–55; Barth, 1975). In a sense, as Barth argues, these men "hold all the keys" to reality for others in the tribe (1975: 265).

Jalé strategies of conflict management and their ways of conceptualizing various kinds of conflict are intimately related to the management of trade and the maintenance of extensive networks of debtors by big men. Thus, Koch describes the categorization of Jalé conflict in terms of five modes of antagonistic interaction: altercation (shouting match), scuffle (physical exchange), sorcery, avoidance, and warfare. His data suggest, however, that only certain conflicts, those in which the principal actors are initiated males, are permitted to escalate into altercations, scuffles, or wars. Conflicts between parents and children (which threaten lineage solidarity) or between husbands and wives (threatening the exchange networks of affines) are classified as private matters, of primary concern to the individuals involved. They are termed scoldings or beatings rather than altercations or scuffles, although children and wives may prefer to describe these exchanges in the language of public dispute: A boy "may complain about the altercation with his father; and the latter may speak of having 'scolded' his son. . . . [The] father may even want to emphasize his intention to instruct his son in filial duties and may therefore describe his speech as 'teaching' [1974: 67–68]." Classifying this behavior as teaching or scolding sidesteps structural questions about the relations of parents and children and glosses over potential rifts in the lineage. Similarly, questions about asymmetry in the relations of husbands and wives and problems in the balance of trade of affines are bypassed when the beating of a wife by a husband (for behavior that is permitted in him but sanctioned in her) and her subsequent return home is treated as a marital problem rather than as a political matter. In such cases a wife who returns to her kin "must expect severe reprimands . . . for jeopardizing their exchange relationship with her husband [1974: 108]." Only when senior men on each side choose to become involved—a choice shaped by economic and political considerations— are conflicts such as these permitted to escalate.[5] Thus it is the actions and views of Jalé big men that shape perceptions about the seriousness of conflict in cases such as these, and about its private or public nature.

---

[5]Moore (1972: 67ff.) describes this process as "the principle of expanding disputes." She argues:

> [T]he sociological evaluation of what constitutes a private or a public legal matter depends on the extent of its social effect and its structural importance. . . . The question whether a dispute between individuals will be contained between them or will be allowed to expand into a political confrontation depends not so much on the subject of the dispute as on the desirability of the confrontation from the point of view of the social units potentially involved, and on the question whether the rules apply according to which disputes may be expanded, i.e., whether the relative social positions of the parties lend themselves to opposing alignments [1972: 74–75].

Marginal individuals, and particularly Jalé women, have little to say in defining either the terms in which their conflicts will be conceptualized or the ways in which they will be dealt with by the larger groups of which they are a part.

Similarly, decisions about the escalation of altercations and scuffles into war, and about the nature of the war to be waged, also seem to be influenced by considerations of trade and alliance in which the roles of big men are central. Koch argues that it is structural considerations— whether those involved are affines, whether they are residents of the same ward, or whether they belong to the same men's house group— that determine the escalation of conflict, and particularly the waging of cannibalistic warfare against an enemy. Kin and affines are not edible, because they are "one's own people" or "people whose face is known." Nevertheless, Koch presents several examples of cases where political needs dictate a redefinition of the line between edible and nonedible people, and the evidence suggests that the lines are drawn and altered by men with the broadest base of political support (e.g., case 14, pp. 151–153, and discussion on pp. 80–81). Thus, although structural considerations (distance and proximity of relationship and residence) may influence conflict management in these cases, the question of who is "close" and who is "far" is likely to be a matter of judgment by politically central individuals rather than a social fact agreed on by a broad spectrum of Jalé. The implications of this for hypotheses about conflict management among the Jalé and other similar groups will be discussed in the final section of this chapter.

In sum, then Koch's analysis of Jalé conflict management tells us a great deal about the ways in which conflict is defined and controlled by the most prominent and powerful members of that society. It also provides glimpses of other views of Jalé behavior, reflecting the concerns of more marginal actors. Although Koch does not pursue the implications of these differences in perspective, they suggest a number of questions that might be raised about Jalé social structure and social control. Koch defines the main "blocks" of Jalé society as autonomous groups of coresident male kin (agnates) of approximately equal rank. It is the relations of these groups of kin that are the focus of Jalé economic and political activity. It is the existence of these groups that shapes patterns of escalation and containment of Jalé war. Koch's data suggest, however, that the hierarchical relations of men and women, parents and children, and initiated and uninitiated males are an equally significant dimension of Jalé social structure, and one on which the "official" structure of the big men is dependent for its continued existence. If this is the case, one would expect that the relations of the "official" and "informal" structures would be as important a feature of Jalé politics as the exchanges among autonomous groups of male kin. Case materials presented by Koch suggest that in fact much Jalé conflict is "about" these relations, and specifically about problems in the control of marginal persons or groups rather than what they first appear to be about, such as a pig debt or a raid on someone's garden.[6] Although conflict may be dealt with in the language of pigs or property, disagreement about the object of a conflict and information about how this disagreement is managed can give us clues to the unwritten rules on which the more official order is based and can suggest some of the ways in which this order is maintained.

COURT ATTORNEYS IN LOS ANGELES

Lynn Mather's (1979) study of the ways in which crimes are defined and offenders classified in an urban California court provides a different perspective on issues similar to those raised in Koch's ethnography. Central again is the question of who articulates the rules, who defines the limits of what and who is normal or abnormal, and an analysis of the ways in which "big men" in another system shape the ideology and practice of conflict management. Mather's research is of particular value because of her skill as a fieldworker. Months of observation in the court complement data gathered in formal and unstructured interviews, and a careful use of statistical material documents broader patterns of case disposition. Thus, we have not only an "attorney's perspective" on how cases are managed but also an analysis of implicit rules underlying the behavior of attorneys in the court and a consideration of broader structural features within the court affecting the ways attorneys perceive their cases and the ways in which cases are handled.

Mather argues that the process by which defendants are dealt with in court is governed by clear sets of rules and priorities but that these are for the most part unstated in any formal sense. Rather, to document them it is necessary to discover "what everyone knows" and "what is taken for granted" by those who work in the courts on a regular basis (1979: 139), and this process requires extensive informal interaction with court participants.[7] For the Los Angeles court where Mather carried out

---

[6]See, for example, the cases of The Unruly Wife (pp. 101–104), The Delinquent Husband (pp. 104–107), and The Stubborn Gardener (pp. 125–127).

[7]Mather writes:

I learned a great deal simply by listening to the participants talk to each other about cases. . . . I watched cases being settled by brief phone conversations in attorneys' offices, by meetings by attorneys during court recess, and by discussions in judges' chambers. Then I also observed the official, formal proceedings in court which finalized the guilty-plea settlements. I tried to ask

her research, "what everyone knows" included concepts of "light" and "serious" crimes, of "real" and "legal" crimes, and concepts of the "typical" or "normal" social identity of persons engaging in various types of crime. This shared knowledge shaped decisions about what to do with a case in significant ways. Thus, in distinguishing (or "sorting") first-degree robbery cases, Mather was told:

> On the one hand, you have a small group of really the meanest guys. . . . These mean ones have a background going 'way back to childhood with crimes of vio-lence. Hostile, very aggressive acts. Not usually much dope with these guys. . . . For the rest . . . you get a lot of amateurs. They're not really dangerous guys. Do it more out of feelings of inadequacy. Especially in the black culture, it's a very heroic gesture and a big accomplishment. But most of them aren't dangerous [1979: 102–103].[8]

Only the former, "real" first-degree robbery cases warranted a state prison sentence, according to Los Angeles prosecutors. The others were "legally" first-degree robberies but were more appropriately sanctioned by a term in the county jail. Although "the facts" of a case were invari-ably shaped by perception of moral character, even it was a topic of negotiation. In discussions over a burglary case in which "the guy was caught drilling a hole in the wall next to a safe in a store," assessment of what should be done hinged on a difference of opinion as to the defen-dant's character. The public defender argued that "the guy's just an old drunk," but the district attorney disagreed: "He figured with five priors and drilling a hole in the wall by the safe that the guy's not just an old drunk. That he's a professional burglar [1979: 97]."

Mather raises two important and interrelated questions about the categories shared by court personnel regarding normal crime (Sudnow, 1965) and typical criminals: How were these patterns formed? And whose perspective did they represent? A third question, linked to these, is, Who, if anyone, dominated in the process of categorizing cases? She suggests that the general sentencing pattern—as influenced by judges, probation officers, and district attorney's office policies, as well as by California state law—provides the context within which bargaining takes place (1979: 121). To illustrate this general pattern, Mather pro-

---

participants why certain settlements were chosen and why others were rejected. At the conclusion of a case, I sometimes went with an attorney to his office, asking him about the specific case disposition and about more general patterns in the court. Once in the office, I heard the attorney talk with his colleagues as they came in to report their cases, ask advice, complain about certain judges, and so forth [1979: 8].

[8]This and subsequent quotes cited to Mather, 1979 are reprinted by permission of the publisher from *Plea Bargaining or Trial?* by Lynn M. Mather (Lexington, Mass.: Lexington Books, D. C. Heath and Company, Copyright 1979, D. C. Heath and Company).

vides figures on the distribution of sentences by charged offense and on conviction rates by offense. She argues that it is the outcomes of previous cases that shape the categories in terms of which new cases and new defendants are perceived. Although this analysis was necessarily limited by the goals of her study (i.e., we do not know the basis for judicial sentencing patterns or for district attorney's office policies that shape case outcomes), it suggests nevertheless the limited range of input into definitions of typical crimes and typical criminals in this court. The dominant participants in the process were "attorneys who used legal language to convey social and cultural meanings about cases and court procedures [1979: 9]." Even if one were to go beyond the confines of the particular negotiating team of defense, prosecution, and judge, the process of shaping typical attitudes appears to be largely dominated by attorneys.

In particular, the perspective of indigent defendants, and presumably of others from their sociocultural milieu, and that of other "nonregular" participants in the court is not represented in the court's shared understanding of "typical" crimes and criminals. As Galanter (1974) and Abel (1973) have noted, this insularity is typical of processes dominated by the legal profession, which has a vested interest in "preserving complexity and mystique so that client contact with . . . the law is rendered problematic [Galanter 1974: 118]". Mather notes, in fact, the difficulties caused by "maverick lawyers," who were described by other court regulars as not being "realistic" about how cases should be handled (1979: 127). This lack of realism entailed, in part, sharing all responsibility and decisions with the defendant rather than handling cases in terms of criteria taken for granted (i.e., considered "realistic") by most court regulars.

Although it is clear then who is "left out" of the perspective on normal crimes that Mather's book documents, a related but more subtle question is raised by her analysis: that of who, within the circle of court regulars, plays the more dominant role in determining how cases will be sorted. The district attorney seemed to play a central role in this decision, especially in cases where offense charged and prior record created a "presumption of seriousness [1979: 40]." In the most "serious" cases—for example, homicide, rape, or robbery—bargaining over charge and sentence required that the defense attorney's views converge not only with those of the individual prosecutor but also with those of superiors in the prosecutor's office as well. In addition, in many cases deputy attorneys were expected to conform with "strict office policies [of the district attorney], spelled out in their manuals and periodic directives [1979: 17]." Further, the district attorney played a particularly important role, to the extent that he controlled the charge and alleged prior convictions and thus determined the sentencing alternatives available to the judge. Not unexpectedly, participants considered these cases, in which sentencing stakes were high, to be the important ones and deserving most of the court's attention. In "light" cases, in contrast, the district attorneys were seldom concerned with sentencing, and non-trial dispositions could usually be reached with little conflict between prosecutor and defense attorney. In these cases the role of the judge assumed greater importance, because he possessed ample discretion to impose a lenient sentence and because the defendant's charged offense and lack of prior record indicated a likelihood of probation (1979: 32, 36, 65, 66).

Mather's analysis suggests then that the district attorney (and district attorney's office policy) are particularly important in controlling sentencing alternatives available to the court (i.e., in controlling the limits in terms of which the actions of defendants will be interpreted by the court) in those cases that the court considers most significant. Her study documents the subtlety with which these limits are manipulated by the defense, and the importance to these manipulations of differences in the personality and experience of individual attorneys, but it nevertheless seems clear that the "big men" in this setting are the district attorneys. As was true among the Jalé, individual "big men" become powerful through creating networks of obligations and through "persuasive eloquence": further, their skill in controlling information and access to information are important dimensions of their role. As lawyers, and specifically as employees of the district attorney's office, recruitment to their ranks is controlled to a large extent from within. Their dominance in the disposition process is secured by a number of structural features specific to this court but is influenced as well by a broader set of ideals and organizational features characteristic of the legal profession more generally.

OFFICIALS AND PRIVATE LITIGANTS IN A THAI COURT

The final study I consider is an analysis by David Engel (1978) of litigation in a Thai court. As with the Koch and Mather ethnographies, Engel's research involved field observation and interviews but relied heavily as well on case records contained in court files. This last characteristic of the research means that Engel's book lacks the sense of more immediate involvement in the politics of litigation that is particularly notable in Mather's and Koch's work. Nevertheless, through careful case analyses, carried out in the context of a perceptive discussion of cultural and legal values in Thailand, Engel demonstrates how two different ideologies—one couched in the "language of officials," the other in the more traditional language of custom—are used to define and interpret behavior in Thailand. Unlike the situations described by Mather and Koch, where a relatively uniform (agreed-upon) official ideology (that of "big men" or "district attorneys" and the interests they represent) dominated, the official ideology was a relatively new one in Thailand. Shared agreements had been challenged by a new legal code, and the limits of what was normal were clearly being negotiated as the meaning of behavior was argued by parties and officials in the process of litigation. What we find here is a shift in patterns of dominance in the disputing process and an emergence of new "big persons," accompanying a new language of law.

Engel's analysis focuses on the litigation and negotiation of private wrongs (including private criminal suits and civil "wrongful acts") in the provincial court of the northern Thai province of Chiangmai. Traditionally, private wrongs were mediated in Thailand by *phuyai*, or "big persons," status superiors who could use their influence to bring wrongdoers to terms or to create pressures that would lead disputants to settle their differences (Engel, 1978: 76). The *phuyai* as mediator was a focal dimension of the role patrons were expected to play vis-à-vis their clients in traditional Thai society, and this role continues to be important in modern Thailand despite official efforts to restructure society along other lines.

Mediation, Engel writes, is "of the essence of the hierarchical relations that pervade Thai society [1978: 99]," and he notes that "the concept of hierarchy is generally cited as the primary organizing principle" in Thailand (1978: 69). Even the simplest forms of two-party relationships involve "a delicate probing to determine who is older, who graduated first from what school, what are the respective family backgrounds and social positions [1978: 71]." Larger social hierarchies, developed from links of this kind, involve separate groups formed around a person with rank and resources who acts as a protector and a mediator in a range of circumstances: when clients must deal with government officials or other status superiors, in disputes with equals and others, and so on. At the same time, status superiors can and do make a range of demands on those of lower status (1978: 74, 203), and traditionally little could be done when these demands became excessive.

The transition from this system of justice, which was administered through locally based "big persons," to a system modeled on Western concepts of social order, individual rights, and justice, codified in a national system of laws and administered through a centralized judiciary, was accomplished through a series of reforms at the turn of the century and shortly thereafter. "The new Thai law codes, both explicitly and implicitly, articulated a new and radically different view of the private citizen, the family, the social group, the administrative bureaucracy, and the nation as a whole [1978: 2–3]." Gradually, the impact of this system has been extended throughout Thailand, but it coexists with traditional methods of responding to perceived injury and the concepts of social order in which they are rooted. Increasing numbers of private citizens are using modern Thai courts, but most prefer to avoid handling their disputes in that manner and instead seek out familiar status superiors as mediators. The courts are used far more frequently by authorities "in their historical function of suppressing crime and preserving the peace" than by private individuals or groups who wish to resolve conflicting claims (1978: 45, 46). It is not surprising that this is the case, for *"the language of the law is to a large extent the language of the officials, and the categories of the law may shortchange the villagers in the distribution of social power* [1978: 189, italics added]." Nevertheless, private citizens do choose to resolve some disputes in court and will surely continue to do so in increasing numbers, because "there is an implicit admission that the legal categories created by the central government now occupy the field, that the modern regulations and certification procedures have diminished the authority of the traditional practices that controlled village society over the centuries [1978: 188]."

Engel focuses his research on how traditional expectations modify the ways the disputes of private citizens are handled in the Chiangmai court, and on how interpretation of a dispute is shaped by translation into the language of legal codes. He suggests that the official administrative structure of the court simply serves as a "ready-made hierarchy," filling the gap left by the "missing *phuyai*" when no suitable "big person" linking both parties can be found (1978: 78, 178). This function of the court is demonstrated in the following case, which also shows the ways in which a skillful private citizen who has learned to use the new system and its language is able to wield some degree of control over the acts of status superiors.

A merchant named *Nai* Soem brought a criminal suit against a government official, *Nai* Anan, a "man of status." *Nai* Anan was accused of taking away *Nai* Soem's daughter for indecent purposes and rape. The circumstances surrounding the case suggested, however, that *Nai* Soem's daughter had left her father's home willingly following a quarrel with her father and that *Nai* Soem's goal in the case was simply to obtain the brideprice to which he was entitled as a parent, and which *Nai* Anan refused to pay. Within 2 months following the criminal suit, *Nai* Soem notified the court that *Nai* Anan had paid him "damages," and he withdrew his criminal suit. Engel points out that "what is clearly suggested . . . is that *Nai* Soem obtained the traditional remedy of brideprice by bringing a criminal action against a man who would not otherwise have been obliged to pay him anything at all [1978: 130]." To accomplish this, however, it was necessary to translate a traditional problem into the language of the new codes, thus defining as criminal behavior that would not traditionally have been perceived in that way, and by the same token shifting slightly the limits of what is acceptable in the relations of officials and private citizens. Several other cases cited by Engel illustrate this process and point as well to a peculiar kind of double prism in which "a particular set of events or relationships comes to be ordered and understood according to both of these systems of social order and law [1978: 206]." *Nai* Anan's behavior was defined in traditional terms as "failure to pay brideprice," but it was evidently difficult for *Nai* Soem using traditional means to exact the payment from a government official. *Nai* Anan's behavior was defined as "rape" by *Nai* Soem, simply for purposes of obtaining the payment he sought, yet in doing this he also made a slight dent in traditional expectations that status superiors need not comply with brideprice payments to a status inferior.

Although this example suggests that the new Thai legal codes may be used to alter the traditional structure of power, much of the data Engel presents indicate that the officials remain firmly in control. It is after all "their language," and it is they who most frequently use it, in ways that further their own interests (1978: 51). It appears that although the ideals embodied in the new codes are in conflict with the traditional system of order, many officials and other status superiors have simply translated their old system of dominance into new terms. Thus one finds that several examples are provided by Engel of suits by private citizens against government officials for alleged wrongs but that there is little evidence that these cases were resolved to the advantage of the plaintiff (see cases cited on pp. 191–203). In other lawsuits (tenant versus landlord, female versus male) that brought into question traditional patterns of dominance, cases were decided against the plaintiff on technical grounds (1978: 127), or, as in a case brought by a village woman against a man by whom she was pregnant and who had abandoned her, on the grounds that legally no "wrongful act" had occurred, "even if the facts were found most favorable to plaintiff [1978: 127–128]." Engel argues that it is significant that these cases were taken to the court at all and points to the importance of the courts as forums in which grievances can find new modes of articulation: "The modern legal system in Chaingmai offers remedies for many private wrongs that would go unresolved in the traditional society, if, indeed, they were perceived as wrongful at all [1978: 207]." Although this is surely true, the failure of many of these efforts to define the acts of status superiors as "wrongful" suggests that if the structure of dominance in Thailand is to be altered in any profound way, its central concepts (symbols) will have to be questioned. The *phuyai*, the traditional "big person," is retained in the modern system through the role played by the court and its officials; and it is still "big persons," though in new robes, who control the language of law, setting the limits of what, and who, is to be punished.

SUMMARY

I have argued that the language of law skews case processing in certain predictable ways and that it is important in understanding and explaining the behavior of law to ask "whose language" is being used. Mather describes categories of "serious" and "light" crime used by court officials in Los Angeles, focusing on the role of the district attorney in defining the limits in terms of which cases are perceived and managed. Koch describes forms of conflict engaged in by the Jalé, exploring cirteria they use for distinguishing degrees of violence in the management of conflict and suggesting circumstances that affect choice of a particular form. His data indicate that it is predominantly the criteria used by Jalé men that define gradations of conflict; in particular, it is the "big men," or men of knowledge, who shape the patterning of enmities and alliances, of war and peace. Engel's analysis examines the ways in which the existence of different languages, an official language of law and the traditional language of custom, shapes the disputing process in a Thai provincial court. He provides several cases to illustrate the ways in which private plaintiffs manipulate these two systems of meaning so as to improve their status relative to an opponent. Yet it is the *phuyai*, or "big persons," whether court officials or more traditional status superiors, who remain dominant in the Thai system. Most grievances are still resolved in a manner consonant with traditional concepts of hierarchy advantageous to the *phuyai*; those that do go to court must be argued in language shaped by official and bureaucratic concerns, and these concerns define both who may use the court and the range of possible outcomes.

I have also argued that there is a relationship between the language and concepts of law in a society and broader patterns of social order. Koch's ethnography is particularly illustrative of this, suggesting the ways in which patterns of trade and marital alliance, in which "big men" play a central role, shape the perceptions of Jalé tribesmen as to which injuries should be avenged, and how. These perceptions in turn influence definitions of others as "people whose face is known" or not. In this way the most basic concepts of friend and foe and stranger and kin and ideas of how conflict with an individual or group should be handled are closely tied to the economic and political activities and interests of certain central actors in the society.

Prediction, Explanation, and the Role of the Maverick

> Most of the other P.D.'s [public defenders] could not say "with absolute certainty" what the outcome of a case would be at trial. But they were more willing than the "mavericks" to play the game of predicting the costs and benefits of trial and to impress upon their clients the importance of those predictions [Mather, 1979: 125].

Data presented in the preceding section suggest that in each of the social contexts considered, structural features of each context, deriving from institutionalized relations of dominance, affect the patterning of social control in certain predictable ways. In this section I will consider hypotheses explaining the form of social control, with specific attention to dyadic and triadic forms of managing disputes. In addition, theory explaining variation in the amount and style of social control will be discussed, in the light of the questions of perspective and problems of definition discussed earlier.

DYADS AND TRIADS

The form of conflict management is a topic that has received attention both in field studies as well as in the theoretical literature (Simmel, 1908: Aubert, 1963; Gulliver, 1969, 1973, 1977; Shapiro, 1975). Shapiro, for example, suggests that there is an underlying "social logic" to triads as a means of resolving conflict (1975: 321, 322), and an assumption pervades much of the literature in this area that some form of "stranger" third party is the most desirable way of handling conflict if escalation and violence threatening to the social order is to be avoided (Koch, 1974: 26, 159–175). It has been observed in the field, however, that institutionalized third parties seem to be absent in certain social contexts, and in many of these, conflicts are handled dyadically through a process of negotiation, with each party using various forms of pressure and counterpressure to secure their desired goals (Gulliver, 1969). Although the Ndendeuli studied by Gulliver, and others, such as the Tonga (Colson

1953), seem to be successful in handling conflict in this manner, groups like the Jalé were not.

Koch sought to explain why conflicts tended to escalate among the Jalé, and he suggested that the political segmentation of Jalé local communities into autonomous factions, and the absence of crosscutting group affiliations, combined with certain socialization patterns, were important factors (Koch, 1974: 166). He suggested that institutionalized third parties would not develop in communities with politically autonomous factions but noted that among the Jalé and in other groups, affinal and trading relationships between otherwise autonomous groups served to contain escalation. Thus structural variables (autonomous agnatic power groups, absence or presence of exchange relations between these groups) were important factors contributing to escalation or containment of conflict among the Jalé.

There are several problems with a hypothesis of this type, but a major one concerns how variables (political autonomy, presence or absence of trading relations) are defined. As Koch's analysis of the Jalé suggests, "presence or absence of trading relationships" is not so much a matter of "fact" (whether trade relationships exist) as of the weight given to these relationships, and by whom. Koch's case materials suggest that there are affinal and other exchange relationships between the antagonists in many if not all of the cases in which conflict escalates into war: The conflicts are often about these exchanges. Yet if it is politically convenient, the trade relationships are ignored, opponents are viewed as "people whose faces are not known," and the conflict is escalated. Alternately, blood revenge may be exacted from a lineage or village that is perceived as important economically, by exacting revenge on a village resident with few connections to its dominant kin group, thus minimizing risks of escalation (Koch, 1974: 151–154). Koch's data suggest then that although predictions regarding the likelihood that a conflict will escalate can perhaps be made on the basis of variables such as political autonomy and exchange relations, accurate prediction is contingent on assuming the perspective of the "big men" as to who is kin, affine, or trading partner and as to whose "face is known," for it is these men who control trading patterns and their political consequences (1974: 64).

Another problem with efforts to predict the social-structural correlates of dyads and triads is that the very distinction between these concepts has been questioned. At the very least it can be extremely difficult to define a "pure" dyad in a field situation. Shapiro (1975: 322) points out that although a triad is the most logical form of conflict management, it is unstable and tends to collapse into a dyad as soon as the third party issues a judgment in favor of one side (see also Simmel, 1908: 135–169). Both Shapiro and Gulliver (1977: 35–40) point to the range of interests and biases of the supposedly disinterested third party— whether adjudicator or go-between—and this suggests the potential for a hidden dyad beneath what may on the surface be tripartite. On the other hand, both Barkun and Eisenberg note the "implicit triad" beneath an apparently dyadic confrontation. Barkun (1968: 106) discusses "shared values without a physically present mediator," and Eisenberg suggests that "negotiation conducted jointly by an actor and his allies on an institutionalized basis tends to slide imperceptibly into adjudication by the allies [1976: 662]."

Again, then, we find that defining the presence or absence of some of our most basic analytical concepts—dyads and triads—is difficult, because the boundaries between them are unclear, because a "dyad" may become a "triad" as a conflict proceeds, and because identifying a dyad or triad depends in part on perspective, that is, it is a question of how one looks at things, and not a "fact" easily observed. From whose perspective, and in what sense, is an institution or individual a "disinterested third"? To what extent, in what manner, and in the interests of whom do third parties prevent escalation?

This issue is pertinent to an examination of Engel's suggestion that the modern Thai court can be seen as a crossover point that facilitates negotiations between socially distant disputants (1978: 186). This hypothesis is understandable within the same general theoretical framework as Koch's, which posited the conditions under which such "crossover points" (or third-party institutions) would be lacking and pointed to the social importance of having such institutions. Engel's data suggest, however, that the "crossover points" are not so much *mediating* thirds as a third very much skewed to one side. The modern Thai court is a crossover point if the least powerful party is willing to argue in the other's language and on the other's territory. This fact suggests that what one finds in modern Thailand is not a traid but a somewhat reorganized dyad, with the most socially distant disputants (those farthest from the centers of power) on one side. In conflict between these disputants and others from whom they are separated by differences in age, sex, ethnicity, or rank, the court may serve to facilitate negotiation and to prevent escalation, but because the more powerful of these parties controls the symbols through which communication and negotiation is carried out in court, it is difficult to separate the interests of these parties from those of the "mediating third" (court or judge). Is such a process perceived as tripartite by the socially distant disputants? How are their claims modified by translation into the language of the officials, and what are the implications for them of containment (i.e., preventing escalation) through a shift in the focus of their claims?

The focus on the role of third parties is surely of significance, for the interests they represent seem to play such an important role in shaping the course a conflict takes. But understanding and explaining third parties requires a consideration of political alliances, and of cultural, social, and economic affinities, between third parties and others. Attention to such issues is critical if a general theory of social control is to be developed.

MARGINALITY, RANK, AND LAW

In *The Behavior of Law* (1976), Donald Black proposes an explanation of the quantity and style of law (and other forms of social control) as a function of variance in features of social structure (e.g., rank, marginality, relational distance). Of particular interest for issues raised in this chapter is his suggestion that variation in the amount of law (determined in turn by features of social structure) can explain the application and distribution of concepts such as "criminal behavior," "normal behavior," "deviance," and so on. Thus, for example, Black proposes that the most marginal people in society (and those with the lowest rank) are disproportionately subject to law and have "less law" (less governmental social control) than better integrated people and people of higher rank have. "At every stage of the legal process, a marginal person is more vulnerable to law. Since law varies inversely with the integration of the offender . . . so do criminality and delinquency [1976: 55]." This proposition is another way of stating what Koch's, Mather's, and Engel's data suggest: that those with the highest rank and most central to the seat of government[9]—i.e., the "big men"—will control the application of law and by virtue of this control will set the limits in terms of which behavior is defined as legal or illegal, criminal or normal.

Black's theory provides a highly abstract but clear and logical framework that can serve to focus research and analysis on basic features of the social organization of law: how it is applied, by whom, and with what effect on the ways in which social reality is constructed. Several important issues pertinent to the use of such a theory must be raised, however. These concern the kinds of data necessary if the theory is to be

---

[9] I use the word *government* here in the very general sense of those persons or groups with the greatest degree of control over political and economic affairs in a society.

useful for prediction and the limits of explanation inherent in a theoretical framework of this kind.

Black states that "in a survey about criminal or other legal matters, the questions and answers should pertain to simple matters of fact, since the meaning of legal terminology is by its nature ambiguous and applicable to a variety of facts [1979: 20]"; he suggests further that "direct and unobtrusive observation" is the most reliable way to test the theory of law (1979: 21), for in this way the evaluation implicit in the labels insiders apply to behavior is avoided. Yet as Richard Bernstein notes in an overview of work in phenomenology, "what we take to be an action, and even its proper description, is internally related to the interpretations that are intrinsically constitutive of it. The description and identification of an action are 'shot through with evaluation' [1976: 62]." In identifying and describing acts then, it is important to explain how these are described, *by whom*, and under what circumstances. Understanding crime, or law, or other aspects of social control involves grasping and interpreting the symbolic forms (words, images, institutions, behavior) of social control by considering these forms both as they are viewed from a perspective exterior to the forms and as they are viewed from within. The exterior perspective can be provided by persons or groups who are part of a particular society but are (from the official perspective of those in power) marginal or powerless (Barnett, 1977: 276). Thus we find Mather (1979) noting that the perspective she provides on concepts of crime is that of the court attorneys and is particularly influenced by policies of the district attorney's office and by other court offices (probation, judges). The defendant's perspective is not represented, and she points to the fact that not all defense attorneys (specifically, the "mavericks") share the views of the "court regulars" on severity of crime and typical procedures for managing criminals. Similar differences in perspective can be found in discussions of intrafamily violence. We find, for example, that although battered wives in lower-income neighborhoods in the United States may call the police (suggesting that they perceive battering as "worthy of police attention" and in this sense, "criminal"), "in the view of the police, a typical case of violence between a husband and wife is 'not really a crime' but only a 'family dispute' [Black, 1979: 22; see also earlier]." Black notes further that "there is also evidence that the police are less likely to record as a 'crime' an incident involving people of low status"; it is not clear, however, how people of low status would perceive such behavior. Other examples of this kind are provided in the earlier discussion of Koch's and Engel's material.

These data suggest three levels of interpretation of a particular action, e.g., beating of a wife by a husband: the wife's interpretation of the beating as "worthy of police attention"; the policeman's interpretation of the behavior as "a family dispute" (in which the police should not become involved); and the social scientist's interpretation of the behavior as a failure to apply governmental social control (law) by agents of the government in certain kinds of acts (beating) that occur between certain individuals (husbands and wives) in a specific social context (a lower-income neighborhood in a Western capitalist society). The social scientist's interpretation relates to and helps to explain the interpretation of the police, the official "inside perspective" on the behavior in question. It could validly be argued that this official interpretation is for all intents and purposes the "real one," for reality from the point of view of the "big men" is in fact the dominant reality for most people in society: Even those who question it (maverick attorneys, or a few persistent Thai plaintiffs) must work within its bounds,[10] and the overall pattern of case outcomes is shaped by this reality. The perspectives of battered wives, of indigent defendants, and of maverick attorneys cannot be used to predict case outcomes, and it is this goal that has defined appropriate method in the field and has influenced the development of theory.

Yet a theory in which only the "official" perspective is permitted is surely a limited one, because there is no consideration of the conditions under which the relations posited in the theory might change. What is the "given," what Althusser (1970) terms the "problematic" that explains why the system should work as predicted? If law varies with stratification and with marginality, *why* does it (Michels, 1978: 11)? If sentencing patterns in the Los Angeles court tend to reproduce themselves (along lines, e.g., in which people who are most marginal from the perspective of the court regulars receive the most severe sentences), what fact or facts in the social organization of the court (and of the society of which it is a part) can account for this? What is it about the maverick defense attorneys' approach to case handling that is "unrealistic," and *why* is it unrealistic? In what ways do the premises of maverick attorneys regarding defendants, their role in the criminal process, and the nature of justice differ from those that are shared by other court

---

[10]Bourdieu writes:

Every established order tends to produce . . . the naturalization of its own arbitrariness. Of all the mechanisms tending to produce this effect, the most important and the best concealed is undoubtedly the dialectic of the objective chances and the agents' aspirations, out of which arises the *sense of limits*, commonly called the *sense of reality*, i.e., the correspondence between the objective classes and the internalized classes, social structures and mental structures, which is the basis of the most ineradicable adherence to the established order [1977: 164].

regulars and are reflected in the regular patterning of case outcomes? Mather provides interesting data on these last questions (1979: 124–129); yet it is precisely these questions that are typically left out in the development of theory.

Concluding Comment

Isaiah Berlin suggests that "the first step to understanding of men is the bringing to consciousness of the model or models that dominate their thought and action [quoted in Bernstein, 1976: 233]." Thus we need careful studies both of commonsense constructs (of the "court regulars," of Thai court officials, of Jalé villagers) and studies of regularities of behavior that reveal implicit constraints on action (district attorney's office policies, trading networks of Jalé "big men," the patron–client network of the *phuyai*). The second step to understanding requires an analysis of the model itself (Bernstein, 1976: 233). This requires stepping outside of the model to a sufficient degree that its most fundamental assumptions can be questioned. For example, in Thai case processing as described by Engel we find two ideologies—one based on hierarchy, the other premised on equality—coexisting, and Engel states that the new ideology is gradually becoming dominant (1978: 188ff.). An examination of case outcomes suggests, however, that the "new ideology" has not restructured social relations to any significant extent. Most cases still are managed within a framework in which hierarchy is real and to a large extent unquestioned; on the other hand, some case outcomes reflect a different understanding of the nature of reality, an understanding in which conflict and competition for control of financial resources and political power between villagers and public officials, and between merchants and government officials, is a central factor (1978: 188–189).

An understanding of the behavior of law, in Thailand, in New Guinea, or in a Los Angeles court, requires that the regularities of a particular system be placed in some large context so that the premises underlying regularity are revealed. This is most easily done, in the field, by keeping alert to the mavericks, those individuals situated outside a dominant ideology and whose actions are "unrealistic" in terms of that ideology. This focus brings the question of perspective—of *which* inside point of view is being documented by the observer, and *whose* point of view is dominant in defining the meaning of behavior—to the forefront. The analysis of regularities in social and political life and the paradigms that guide such analysis are critical in approaching this issue. To understand the bases of structural—and ideological—change, however, we must explore perspectives other than the official one. As Berlin acutely points out, "It is in a society that is unanimously agreed upon its goals that a social science would work best that aims at prediction and the reduction of all questions to empirical ones [quoted in Bernstein, 1976: 62]."

ACKNOWLEDGMENTS

I thank Sally Engle Merry, Lynn M. Mather, David M. Engel, and Donald Black for comments on an earlier version of this chapter.

References

Abel, Richard
    1973   "A comparative theory of dispute processing." *Law and Society Review* 8: 217–347.
Althusser, Louis
    1970   *For Marx*, translated by B. Brewster. New York: Vintage.
Aubert, Vilhelm
    1963   "Competition and dissensus: Two types of conflict and of conflict resolution." *Journal of Conflict Resolution* 7: 26–42.
Barkun, Michael
    1968   *Law without Sanctions*. New Haven, Conn.: Yale University Press.
Barnett, Steve
    1977   "Identity choice and caste ideology in contemporary South India." Pages 270–291 in *Symbolic Anthropology*, edited by J. Dolgin, D. Kemnitzer, and D. Schneider. New York: Columbia University Press.
Barth, Frederik
    1975   *Ritual and Knowledge among the Baktaman of New Guinea*. New Haven, Conn.: Yale University Press.
Bernstein, Richard J.
    1976   *The Restructuring of Social and Political Theory*. New York: Harcourt, Brace, Jovanovich.
Black, Donald
    1976   *The Behavior of Law*. New York: Academic Press.
    1979   "Common sense in the sociology of law." *American Sociological Review* 44: 18–27.
    1980   *The Manners and Customs of the Police*. New York: Academic Press.
Bourdieu, Pierre
    1977   *Outline of a Theory of Practice*, translated by Richard Nice. London: Cambridge University Press.
Colson, Elizabeth
    1953   "Social control and vengence in Plateau Tonga society." *Africa* 23: 199–212.
Eisenberg, Melvin A.
    1976   "Private ordering through negotiation: Dispute settlement and rule making." *Harvard Law Review* 89: 637–681.

Emerson, Robert M.
  1969 *Judging Delinquents: Context and Process in Juvenile Court.* Chicago: Aldine Press.
Engel, David M.
  1978 *Code and Custom in a Thai Provincial Court.* Tucson: University of Arizona Press.
Galanter, Marc
  1974 "Why the 'haves' come out ahead: Speculations on the limits of legal change." *Law and Society Review* 9: 95–160.
Gulliver, Philip H.
  1969 "Introduction to Case studies of law in non-Western societies.'" Pages 11–23 in *Law in Culture and Society,* edited by Laura Nader. Chicago: Aldine Press.
  1973 "Negotiations as a mode of dispute settlement: Towards a general model." *Law and Society Review* 7: 667–691.
  1977 "On mediators." Pages 15–52 in *Social Anthropology and Law,* edited by I. Hamnett. New York: Academic Press.
Koch, Klaus-Friedrich
  1974 *War and Peace in Jalémo.* Cambridge, Mass.: Harvard University Press.
Mather, Lynn M.
  1979 *Plea Bargaining or Trial?* Lexington, Mass.: D. C. Heath.
Michaels, Priscilla
  1978 "Review of *The Behavior of Law.*" *Contemporary Sociology* 7: 10–11.
Moore, Sally F.
  1972 "Legal liability and evolutionary interpretation: Some aspects of strict liability, self-help and collective responsibility." Pages 51–107 in *The Allocation of Responsibility,* edited by Max Gluckman. Manchester: Manchester University Press.
Sahlins, Marshall D.
  1963 "Poor man, rich man, big man, chief: Political types in Melanesia and Polynesia." *Comparative Studies in Society and History* 5: 285–303.
Santos, Boaventura de Sousa
  1977 "The law of the oppressed: The construction and reproduction of legality in Pasagarda." *Law and Society Review* 12: 5–126.
Shapiro, Martin
  1975 "Courts." Pages 321–371 in *Handbook of Political Science,* vol. 5, edited by T. Greenstein and N. Polsby. Reading, Mass.: Addison-Wesley.
Simmel, Georg
  1908 *Soziologie, Untersuchungen uber die Formen der Vergesellschaftung.* Leipzig: Verlag von Duncker & Humblot. Portions reprinted in *The Sociology of Georg Simmel,* edited by Kurt H. Wolff. New York: Free Press, 1950: 135–169.
Sudnow, David
  1965 "Normal crimes: Sociological features of the penal code in a public defender's office." *Social Problems* 12: 255–276.

10

Experiments in Social Control

PAT LAUDERDALE

The experimental method probably has had more influence on the conduct of scientific inquiry than has any other methodology (Zelditch, 1961). It has provided a framework of analysis for diverse research problems, including social control. Although experiments in social control have waned since the 1950s, the more general strategy of using randomized experiments has flourished (see Cook and Campbell, 1979: 385). The two major requirements of an experiment, randomization and comparison, cannot always be met, however, the advantages of the approach are not easy to ignore.[1] The experimental strategy is especially useful as a tool for constructing and testing theory.

[1]The advantages and disadvantages of experimentation can be more fully understood by differentiating between types of experiments. For example, the advantages of "laboratory" experiments are the potential for a high degree of control over extraneous factors, the use of different levels of treatment, and the relative ease of utilizing factorial designs (see Zeisel, 1968). The major disadvantage is the problem of generalizing to causal relationships in more complex field settings (see Aronson and Carlsmith, 1968, for a more detailed discussion of these issues). In general, the advantages of "field" experiments are that settings are usually more theoretically or practically relevant and there is a greater possibility to infer cause than there is when we use nonexperimental methods. The major disadvantage is that field experiments cannot readily control extraneous variables, thus making causal inferences more problematic. In both "laboratory" and "field" experiments, the importance of randomization has become apparent in the recent past. The functions of randomization, the types of randomized experiments, the problems with conducting such experiments, and situations conducive to the method have been discussed elsewhere (Campbell and Stanley, 1963; Cook and Campbell, 1976, 1979).

TOWARD A GENERAL THEORY OF SOCIAL CONTROL
Volume 2: Selected Problems

Unfortunately, in the social sciences and, in particular, sociology and criminology, the method has a tarnished reputation. A number of noted field experiments in social reform have led to some of the stigma. These basically attempted to test hypotheses such as those that suggest that community disorganization produces higher crime rates, that economic opportunities are inversely related to juvenile delinquency, and that labeling juveniles as delinquent contributes significantly to their future deviant behavior. The experiments were harshly criticized because they (a) "found effects without making any truly rigorous attempt to exclude competing hypotheses"; (b) permitted extraneous factors "to intrude upon the measurements"; (c) used "recidivism measures which are not all measuring the same thing"; (d) employed "follow-up periods which vary enormously and rarely extend beyond the period of legal supervision"; (e) did not control for "system effects"; (f) ignored replication; and (g) concocted categories "without any theory" (Martinson, 1974: 54).[2] The general conclusion has been that such field experiments in social reform have not been useful and an unintended consequence has been that they have created a disenchantment with the experimental method in general. Although the vast majority of the critiques exist primarily because it is possible to evaluate such research designs relatively easily, most people seemingly have ignored the fact that this accessibility to evaluation is an advantage as well. Hence, there has been a tendency to "throw the baby out with the bath water."[3]

When researchers turn to arenas where the design problems have been resolved fairly well and where more experimental control has been possible, they have tended to focus upon the problems of generalizability of the experimental results. As Zelditch has correctly observed, "No other method makes the contemporary sociologist more suspicious [1961: 529]." Many sociologists feel in particular that laboratory or small-group studies are so contaminated with artificiality that any type of generalization is unwarranted. Consider, for example, a brief description of two classic studies that have been subjected to this criticism.

In a famous study by Sherif (1935; 1936), an experimental situation was created where a person was asked to judge how far a projected spot

---

[2]For a more extensive discussion of the problems with field experiments such as the Chicago Area Projects, the New York Mobilization for Youth Project, the Cambridge–Somerville Youth Study,the Provo Experiment, the Kansas City Experiment, and the Manhattan Bail Project, see Martinson (1974) and Riecken and Boruch (1974).

[3]The tendency to give up on the utility of experimentation has been compounded by the reaction to most comparative work, particularly in regard to prison experiments (see, e.g., Ward, 1979: 155–156).

of light moved in a dark room. The light did not actually move but appeared to do so, due to an optical illusion referred to as the "autokinetic effect." In the process of making a number of judgments, the person typically specified a range of movement. When the person was brought together with two or three other people, the group converged into a group or "normative" judgment; that range was usually somewhat unlike the individual's initial judgment. The group norm persisted when the individuals made their judgments alone at a later point in time.

In a similar study by Asch (1951; 1956), an experimental situation was created where a person was asked to make a judgment regarding which of three lines was closest in length to one other line. Of the three comparison lines, one was obviously closest in length to the comparison line. Before the young man had a chance to announce his judgment, however, he was placed in a group where the experimenter had secretly instructed other people to make incorrect judgments, asking them usually to choose one of the lines that was not closest to the comparison line. The judgments were expressed orally, with the original person making his estimate last. There was a series of 18 separate judgments. In this situation where the group norm contradicted the original person's perceptual judgment, 37% of the original people conformed to the incorrect majority judgment.

Although a more elaborate discussion of the experimental designs and results of these studies should have emphasized their important contributions, the focus has often been on criticizing the unnatural experimental situation. As Cartwright and Zander suggest, however, research such as Sherif's exemplifies the advantages of the method:

> Although Sherif's experimental situation might seem artificial, and even trivial, to the anthropologist or sociologist, this very artificiality gave the findings a generality not ordinarily achieved by naturalistic research. By subjecting a group-level concept, like social norm, to psychological analysis, Sherif helped obliterate what he considered to be the unfortunate categorical separation of individual and group. And his research helped establish among psychologists the view that certain properties of groups have reality, for, as he concluded, "the fact that the norm thus established is peculiar to the group suggests that there is a factual psychological basis in the contentions of social psychologists and sociologists who maintain that new and supra-individual qualities arise in the group situations" [1968: 16].

As is true of most other methodological strategies, the well-done experiment surely has its time and place.[4] Perhaps because much

---

[4]There are two basic concerns regarding the strategy of using experimentation in the study of social control. The first is why such methods should be used at all, and the second

human behavior remains tied to central principles of social control, research testing these principles (largely through the experimental method) has remained relevant to major themes within the social sciences:

> Both formal and informal social pressures are brought to bear on deviant members.
> The informal pressure to conform is illustrated by the experiments of Sherif [1935;
> 1936] and Asch [1951; 1956], which demonstrate that knowledge of the majority
> opinion on some issue is enough to lead some individuals to conform publicly to a
> judgment which differs from the the one they privately hold. . . .
>   The factors which influence the general tendency to conform to group opinion
> are found in the *object* about which the judgment is to be made, in the *subject* who is
> making the judgment, and in the *situation*. The subject will conform more to group
> opinion when the object to be judged is ambiguous, if he must make his opinion
> public, if the majority holding a contrary opinion is large, and if membership in the
> group is highly valued [Hare, 1976: 47–48].

The continuing research also clarified the ambiguous notion of conformity, proposing four major types: (*a*) consistency resulting from the
internalization of values; (*b*) conformance emerging from attraction to an
important reference group; (*c*) compliance resulting from the influence
of authority; and (*d*) convergence based on similar interpretations of
information.

    This chapter concentrates on experiments in social control that exam-
ine the processes that lead to definitions of conformity or deviance and

---

is what questions can be addressed with what possible conclusions once we decide to use
the strategy (see Black, 1979, especially pp. 101–103).
    One basic reason for employing experimentation is to test abstract properties of a
concrete situation. Another related, and more obvious, reason for using the strategy is to
identify important variables that appear theoretically relevant. Nonetheless, these reasons
are typically obscured by researchers' skepticism about the problems of tying these abstract properties to concrete findings.
    Generalizations from experiments typically reflect the idea that "generalization from
any one situation to any other relates, not concrete settings, but abstract properties
[Zelditch, 1961: 536]."

> Concrete similarities are not necessary to generalization: they actually stand in its way. Usually
> complexity makes generalization difficult or impossible: concrete similarities will generally make
> processes complex. For example, the Lippitt-White experiment on democratic leadership was
> exceedingly complex. In this experiment, "leadership" meant not only how directive the leader
> was, but also how socially distant he was, how capricious his rewards were, and how far his
> followers shared his knowledge of the group's future [1969: 31].

Zelditch's point is that researchers in the area of organizations were too zealous in their
generalization; they incorrectly assumed that democratic leadership is a unitary process
while the crucial abstract property was the reward process and its organization.
    Generalizations from experiments are difficult, but so too are most applications of any
theory. This seems to be the case "whether the theory is supported by experiments, or by
field studies, or by surveys, or 'indeed by any evidence whatsoever' [Zelditch, 1961: 538]."

the varied reactions to those processes, definitions, and resultant perceptions of deviant behavior, especially as they occur in group action. The focus is upon primarily two problems that investigators of social control have addressed: first, deviations and deviants in varying social systems, and second, the general dimensions of most social systems as they relate to social control. The intent is not to present a comprehensive description of the literature but, instead, to provide a framework for constructing a manageable research program. A final section suggests some ideas for moving toward a general theory.

Factors in the Reaction to Deviant Behavior

A series of recent studies suggests some factors that lead to variation in the amount of social control that may be imposed on actors or their actions. One set of factors focuses upon the behavioral or attitudinal positions and actions of actors in relation to the norms of a particular group. The most well established include (a) the degree of divergence from particular norms; (b) the direction and distance of movement from an initial judgment on a particular issue; (c) the demeanor of the actors (including the content and rationale associated with their judgments, the type and level of personal contributions to the group, and the overall "presentation of self"); (d) the private or public nature of the action; (e) prior and present levels of commitment and attraction to the group or task; and (f) prior experience and self-confidence (see Larkin and Loman, 1977; Dedrick, 1978; Levine and Ruback, 1980; Nagao and Davis, 1980; Ungar, 1981).

In attempting to reveal the effect of these factors on the amount of social control imposed on group members, Levin argues that the motives of majority group members are centrally important and then presents a useful summary noting that the reaction to deviance is affected by:

> majority members' perceptions of (a) the deviate's current behavior, (b) the social context in which the deviate responds, and (c) the deviate's past behavior.
> . . . One component of the deviate's current behavior is his announced position on the issue under consideration. This issue can vary in importance or relevance to majority members' goals, and the deviate's position can vary in extremity, content, and consistency. . . . The impact of consistency (and probably also extremity and content) can be affected by the size of the minority relative to the majority and by the type of stimulus under consideration (e.g., an "objective" visual item vs. a "subjective" attitudinal issue).
> A second component of the deviate's current behavior is the manner in which he presents his position. One facet of this presentation is the deviate's rationale, or

explanation, for his position. For example, two deviates espousing exactly the same position might elicit very different reactions if one justified his position in terms of values that the majority held sacred whereas the other appealed to values that the majority detested. . . .

Finally, majority members' perceptions of the deviate's past behavior produce "baseline" responses to the deviate . . . , knowledge of the deviate's past opinions, past contributions to the group, typical style of expression, and areas of expertise. Such knowledge often is organized into a set of general and specific role expectations that prescribe, as well as predict, the deviate's behavior in the group. It should be noted that a deviate's role expectations *outside* the group also may influence his treatment within the group, particularly if these expectations confer power that could be used to reward or punish group members. Finally, baseline behavioral responses to the deviate include the amount of time that the deviate is allowed to speak and the care with which the majority members listen to him [1980: 420–421].

Although these factors sensitize us to a range of potentially important variables, it would be premature to suggest how they might fit into a general framework.

Another set of factors focuses upon the status characteristics of group members and the expectation states associated with those characteristics. Although traditionally most of this work has not been directly connected with experimental studies in social control, its core is applicable. The thrust of the work is toward understanding the impact of external status differences on the emergence of power and prestige orders within task-oriented groups. The power and prestige order is reflected in the "distribution of opportunities to perform, in the distribution of performances, in the distribution of evaluations of member contributions, in the overall ratings of group members, and in the relative influence of different members on the final decision of the group [Berger, Cohen, and Zelditch, 1966: 30]." In this context, the emphasis on the resulting allocation of power provides another set of factors that affect the conformity of social actors. They include education, occupation, race, gender, ethnicity, age, and physical characteristics such as size (see Hollander and Willis, 1967; Bonacich and Light, 1978; Lee and Ofshe, 1981). Within the framework developed by Berger and associates (1966), such factors help explain why group members with relatively low-status characteristics yield to the social control of the other members. Their analysis rests largely on the empirical generalization that "when task groups are differentiated with respect to some status characteristic external to the task situation, this differentiation determines the observable power and prestige order within the group, whether or not the external characteristics are related to the group task [1966: 31]."

Although some of the characteristics mentioned here have not been tested adequately (e.g., race and gender), the experimental method is quite amenable to examining such factors. Furthermore, this approach appears to be especially useful for examining some of the more subtle aspects of social control.

Social Control and the Controllers

Unlike the investigations mentioned in the preceding section, another series of studies focuses much less on the actors or actions that can be controlled and more on the context of social control and, to a limited extent, those who exercise social control. The research has a rich tradition linked to the work of investigators such as Sherif and Asch. Unfortunately, two types of criticism have dominated the reaction to this work. One ignores its theoretic utility, belittling it as merely small-group research, whereas another aggrandizes its findings. For example, Sherif did not prove that all groups create norms in the same manner, nor did Asch prove that people typically conform (see Zelditch, 1961). They did contribute to showing why and how under specific conditions actors create norms or typically conform (Sherif, 1935, 1936, 1956; Asch, 1951, 1956). These studies have operated usually from a perspective that includes situational properties, social dynamics, and a structural framework. Each of these elements is discussed in the following subsections.

SITUATIONAL PROPERTIES

Factors that have been identified as important to the operation of social control include: (a) the nature of the group task (e.g., how difficult it is); (b) the group's perception of the relevance of the task; (c) the size of the group; (d) the competency of the group; and (e) the status of the group (see Hare, 1952; Allen, 1956; Mills, 1969; Dion, Baron, and Miller, 1970; Evans and Rozelle, 1973; Arnold and Greenberg, 1980). Existing research suggests that general pressure toward conformity usually increases as the task becomes more difficult and important to the actors. The general pressure toward conformity also appears typically to increase as the group increases in size, competency, and status (Kiesler, 1969).[5]

Although the findings are less conclusive, other research on the phys-

[5]The effect of size is the most ambiguous. Most studies have found that increases in the size of the group beyond three or four persons has only a minimal effect on increasing control. Here is a clear instance, however, where the "laboratory" strategy is inadequate because the setting cannot easily accommodate large collectives.

ical location and reaction of others is significant (see Milgram, 1963: Kiesler, 1969; Latané and Rodin, 1969; Dedrick, 1978). In the renowned Milgram studies, for example, the amount of conformity was often dependent on such factors as well as on the much publicized status of the authority. This controversial series of studies provided an example of overwhelming compliance to authority.[6] Although Milgram was primarily interested in examining the conditions under which obedience to authority existed, the people recruited to participate in the study were told that the purpose was to investigate the effects of punishment on learning. Males were requested to obey an authority's instructions to deliver electric shocks to another person, the learner. In fact, Milgram designed the study so that the shocks would never really be received (the experimenters were the only people who were aware of the deception). The participants were instructed to deliver a shock to the ostensible learner whenever he made an error in the learning task. On subsequent trials, the participants were told to raise the shock-intensity level after each error by the learner. In different conditions of the series of studies, Milgram varied factors such as the status of the authority and the physical distance among the three central actors. Although greater conformity occurred when the *authority* was physically closer to the participant "administering" the shocks, less conformity was demonstrated when the *learner* was closer to the participant "administering" the shocks.

Another major factor is typically referred to as leadership. Investigators usually examine the relationship between the conformity of leaders or high-status actors and their consequent status attainment. The beginning proposition is that there is a positive relationship between initial conformity and status attainment (Hollander and Willis, 1967). The empirical support for the proposition, however, is equivocal (Wahrman, 1970; Wahrman and Pugh, 1972, 1974; Tedeschi, Schlenker, and Bonoma, 1975). The research suggests that in order for actors to increase their status, they must be seen as competent and group oriented rather than

---

[6]The controversy surrounding Milgram's studies centered on the psychological stress of the participants, who thought they were administering severe shocks to the learner. This led to much of the current debate on ethical considerations in social science research. Commenting on Milgram's motivations for conducting the research, Hare cogently notes:

He was motivated by the same concern that was shared by Sherif, Asch, Lewin, and the other social psychologists who had performed experiments on conformity 20 years earlier, at the time of World War II. Given that obedience is a basic element in the structure of social life and that some system of authority is a requirement for all communal living, how is it that the tendency to obey can override training in ethics, sympathy, and moral conduct? In particular, how was it possible for some persons in Germany in 1933–1945 to obey orders to kill millions of people [1976: 40]?

The important debate over the ethics of research such as Milgram's continues.

self-interested. Group members are more likely to accept task contributions that are preceived as group oriented. Members' behaviors are evaluated, however, when they come to the attention of the group, and conforming behavior rarely gets attention. One gets attention by refusing to conform. But, nonconformity is likely to be perceived as indicating self-interest rather than group interest. It seems plausible that *moderate conformity* is usually the optimal condition for status attainment in a group. It will attract attention, and the group can focus upon the positive contributions of the actor without excessive imputation of negative (self-interested) motives (Ridgeway, 1978). The generalization holds only when all else is constant, including the success of the group and similar factors such as the other stages of development of the group.

The study of leadership as a major feature of social control also has one other important implication. The research notes that conformity is not fixed on a single norm, equally applicable to everyone (see Allport's 1934 research on the J-curve for an elaboration of this idea). The thrust of the work has been oriented toward the flexibility allowed to leaders and to their ability to exert disproportionate social control (Sherif, 1956; Hollander, 1960; Sherif, Harvey, White, Hood, and Sherif, 1961; Nagel, 1975; Parker, 1981). Hollander provides clear support for this idea in a series of experimental studies. One of the basic experimental designs consisted of putting individuals (males) into five-person groups and giving them a complex task to be completed in approximately 15 trials. Hollander placed an unusually competent person (the leader) in each group and examined his influence over the series of trials. The influence of the leader grew with subsequent trials, and his suggestions to change major rules of the group (e.g., abandoning majority rule) were more acceptable than were suggestions of the other members, especially when he conformed earlier to group norms.

The conditions under which leaders are able to have such influence have also been examined by Bales (1950) and his critics (Bonacich and Light, 1978). Their research suggests that leaders are able to exercise disproportionate influence either through the need for completion of group tasks or the need for stabilization of socioemotional cohesion. In particular, they have greater ability to introduce novel changes when "the members face new problems or critical situations for which existing guidelines are inadequate [Sherif and Sherif, 1969: 172]."

SOCIAL DYNAMICS

A wide variety of experiments in social control have attempted to use some of the propositions from global explanatory systems that focus on the social dynamics of rewards or imitation (e.g., Bandura and Walters,

1963). These studies have investigated the dynamics of a reward system or imitation process in regard to topics as diverse as education and social intervention (Riecken and Boruch, 1974), behavior modification and juvenile delinquency (Davidson and Seidman, 1974), and social welfare and a guaranteed annual income (Robins, Spiegleman, Weiner, and Bell, 1980). As Cartwright (1979) has pointed out, such studies mirror the World War II concern with the success of the group and the primacy of social control and may therefore involve an overly narrow focus.

On the other hand, there are an expanding number of alternative perspectives that propose important factors in the dynamics or processes of social control. These perspectives reveal much of their emphases by their central concepts, for example, equity, attribution, distributive justice, exchange, social comparison, reactance, dissonance, congruity, and balance. Many of them have common assumptions that basically involve a claim that people try to alter their attitudes to remove inconsistencies between their own discordant attitudes or behaviors. Such similarities are by no means an accident; all share a concern with the inconsistencies created by the impact of conflicting norms on the individual and the group.

The emergence, salience, and transformation of norms are fundamental to the study of social control. For example, the recognition of this range of concerns is notable in experimental studies on procedural justice:

> We suggest that an important key to understanding the effectiveness of the adversary system may be found in two of its properties. The adversary system seems to require (a) the maintenance of a high degree of control over its process by the disputants and, at the same time, (b) a high degree of regulated contentiousness between the disputants themselves. In other words, the disputants have a common interest in limiting the control of the decision maker, while engaging in the competitive pursuit of their opposed self-interests [Thibaut and Walker, 1975: 119].

Thibaut's and Walker's analysis of the adversary system not only exhibits the import of organizational norms (e.g., those regulating the role of judges) and interpersonal norms (e.g., those regulating the disputants) but also reveals the basic advantages of examining the dynamic relationship between such norms within the system. Sherif (1936; 1956) suggests that norms are not only a product of social interaction but also social stimuli that affect individuals and groups (see also Ofshe, 1973). And when equity researchers claim, for example, that judges are personally motivated to see the world as fair and equitable, they note how this personal motivation is largely attributable to group as well as organizational norms concerning justice. Explaining the actions of central agents of social control such as judges (and their associated organizations) requires, at a minimum, the examination of the emergence and impact of norms from a number of theoretical perspectives.

There are two major problems with the use of current social dynamic perspectives for the experimental study of social control. The first is the tendency of social scientists to jump from one new orientation to another. Less than 15 years ago, many researchers were convinced that perspectives such as field theory, systems theory, psychoanalytic theory, the sociometric orientation, or the formal models orientation would provide a stable research focus for an array of studies (see Cartwright and Zander, 1968, for an extensive discussion of these perspectives). Although there has been growth and revision in some of the perspectives, the general reaction has been for researchers to become disenchanted easily and to turn uncritically to new ones.[7] The second problem revolves around the central concepts employed in the social dynamics orientation to social control. Although concepts such as norm, cohesion, locomotion, and stability or instability of the social system provide fertile grounding for experimentation (see, e.g., Schachter, 1951; Emerson, 1954), they are incomplete as a framework for investigating the more abstract properties of social control. These concepts are particularly inadequate when they are employed in analyses that focus upon social processes without a related examination of social structure.

A STRUCTURAL FRAMEWORK

The most crucial aspect of this framework is the manner in which it facilitates the analysis of social structure, those recurrent patterns of social interaction that create the organizational parameters of social action. A structural framework includes dimensions of a social system such as its corporate nature (e.g., whether it is temporary or ongoing), its political structure, its status hierarchies, its goals, its symbolic and physical boundaries, and other organizational factors. The inclusion of only a few of these dimensions into the analysis of social control sheds new light on a variety of experiments. For example, research in the area of group therapy typically ignores the possibility of negative or "casu-

[7]This disenchantment has been heightened by a number of novel problems related to the internal validity of the experiments used to test hypotheses derived from the perspectives. These "sources of contamination" are variously referred to as "demand characteristics," "experimenter bias," "response bias," "evaluation apprehension," "group pressure," "social desirability," "enlightenment effects," and atypical subjects (see Aronson and Carlsmith, 1968; Freese and Rokeach, 1979: 195; Cronkite, 1980).

alty" outcomes from the group experience. Individuals typically join the group in the hope that the therapy will enhance some personal qualities, solve interpersonal problems, or provide a sense of self-worth. Ostensibly, most therapy groups are created to provide uniformly positive effects on the self-concepts of the members; however, a few studies indicate that an unintended consequence of the process of group formation and functioning is negative effects on some of the participants such as drastically lowered self-images or grave confusion regarding future interpersonal relationships (Yalom, 1970; Liberman, Yalom and Miles, 1973; Archer, 1974). Although these studies range from research on group psychotherapy to more member-directed groups such as self-analytic ones, the emergence of the negative consequences appears to stem from the same basic source. The negative experience of a minority of the group members is directly related to their emergent low status within the group. In addition, the degree of their negative experience is directly related to disruptions in the solidarity of the group, its political structure, and its status hierarchies.

Therapy groups are subject to the same basic laws of group dynamics as other small task groups. Although the task for therapy groups is usually identity transformation or maintenance, and although the therapist (or leader) may attempt to produce equality among the members, the surfacing of a status hierarchy with powerful and powerless participants is ubiquitous. The political structure and the status hierarchies of many such groups largely determine the limits of the use of power or control by therapists or other group members. Furthermore, other research suggests that a variety of external threats (e.g., disruptions perceived as outside the group's control) and internal threats (e.g., a leader's disruption of group interaction based on her or his feelings that the group is progressing much too solwly) lead to momentary losses of group solidarity that is typically reestablished by further rejection or stigmatization of the powerless members (Lauderdale, 1976).

In general, therapy group success has depended on the screening of problematic individuals prior to or during the group sessions or the replacement of an inadequate therapist without consideration of the basic structure and dynamics of the proposed type of group therapy. The focus has been disproportionately upon "deviant" patients or therapists. There has been little examination of organizational factors: ones that lead to gross power discrepancies within the groups and contribute to relatively low and discontinuous solidarity.

As with the studies concerning therapy groups, the focus upon a structural framework in most experimental research on social control has been scattered and unconnected to the development of more general theoretic perspectives. There are, however, a number of directions in research that appear worthwhile. Some of the earlier works on political structure (e.g., White and Lippitt, 1960) and their impact on social control have been refined by recent experimental research (Miller and Anderson, 1979; Molm, 1981) and theory (Nagel, 1975). Regardless of whether the social system symbolically defines its political structure by specifying its procedures in terms such as democracy, laissez-faire, autocracy, or actually implements such procedures, these actions produce considerable variation in the amount and kind of social control imposed on members (White and Lippit, 1960). Factors relating to the types of decision making, the distribution of resources, and the allocation of power will be central to future research.

A Theoretical Focus

As was implied earlier, experimental work on the social control of deviants has been quite narrow and typically atheoretical. One alternative is to ground investigation in a structural framework and to attempt to utilize some of its components in a theoretical scheme. For example, two popular sociological theories of deviant behavior, anomie and differential association, view crime and other deviance as the product of the movement of actors across the moral boundaries of a specific social system. Anomie theory explains deviance as resulting from the motivation to achieve success without the legitimate means (Merton, 1938), and differential association presents it as a learning process that occurs during individual involvement with deviant groups (Sutherland and Cressey, 1960). Deviance is simply defined as rule breaking or boundary violation. Deviance, however, can also be viewed as a product of the movement of moral boundaries or rules within the system. Several years ago the present author conducted an experiment designed to explore how the definition and volume of deviance can change in this fashion (Lauderdale, 1976).

In this study people were recruited to join a group that was examining the case history of a male delinquent and were asked to recommend proper correctional treatment for him. One person who was actually an associate of the researcher (the "deviant") consistently adopted an extreme position during the group's evaluation discussions. The other group members were not aware that this experimentally created "deviant" was, in fact, role-playing. In half of the sessions (there were 40 different groups) an additional factor was introduced, an "outside threat." In this threat condition, an observer of the group discussion, a criminal justice expert, commented to the group leader and audibly to the other members that "this group should probably not continue." After the meeting, group members were informed that it might become necessary to reduce the size of the group and were asked to rank each member in terms of their preference for working with them again. Although the "deviant" (the extremist) received dramatically lower preference ratings than did other members, the difference was much greater (i.e., the rejection was much more severe) in the "threat" condition. The results were similar when members were asked separately in an interview if there were any people in their group with whom they did not want to work. The evidence supported the contention that deviants, independent of their actions, will be more severely rejected and stigmatized following an external threat to their corporate social system.

In this type of study, deviance is initially defined when a corporate social system attempts to push actors outside the moral boundary of that system, and deviants are created when actors are ritually stigmatized and placed outside the boundary. Therefore, deviants can be symbolically and/or physically located from within and outside the social system. This suggests that deviance is not necessarily synonymous with nonconformity to the norms of a particular social system.[8] These findings also suggest that the initial effect of an outside threat to a corporate social system is a decrease in the level of solidarity—leading to an increase in the rejection and stigmatization of predefined deviants or to the creation of new deviants, in turn leading to an increase in the level of solidarity. That is, there is not a direct effect from the outside threat to an increase in solidarity of the system, but, instead, the increase is indirect and depends on an intervening process of social control.

In order to maintain its moral boundaries, its corporate structure, and its solidarity, the social system becomes less tolerant of potential or preexisting deviants and increases the level at which it rejects them. The redefinition of those actors as deviants or more deviant, that is, the redefinition of the moral boundaries, creates greater solidarity among the nondeviants of that social system by reaffirming the corporate mem-

---

[8]As was mentioned earlier, the emergence, salience, centrality, and transformation of norms is crucial to future research. The relationship between these aspects of norms and the idea of boundary movement may help us understand and explain why groups reject deviants in some situations independent of their conformity (see Lauderdale, 1980). In these cases, it may be that rejection is based on one or a combination of the following factors: (a) the ease with which low-status actors can be manipulated into deviant roles; (b) the selection of other members whom the high-status members find as posing a threat of disturbance to their position or to the existence of the group; and (c) arbitrary or random selection patterns within systems under stress.

bership. Furthermore, a recent study suggests that social systems under external threat primarily focus on preexisting internal deviants; however, when those internal deviants are not easily identifiable, the social system attempts to create similar sources of solidarity maintenance (Lauderdale, Smith-Cunnien, Parker, and Inverarity, 1983). For example, the group may accomplish this by pulling its members together through blaming another group or other convenient external source.

The idea that groups create internal and external enemies has been influential in research since Durkheim's (1893) explanation of deviance and Simmel's (1908) dissection of social conflict. Explication of this idea, however, remains fragmentary and unintegrated.[9] The research strategy outlined here has the potential to refine these theoretic tenets. It may also redirect the focus of inquiry from one that relies primarily on *ad hoc* accounts of particular historical phenomena (such as a particular witchhunt) to one that emphasizes the construction of a general theory. Further research should specify (*a*) major types of threat and their impact on group cohesion; and (*b*) conditions under which groups respond to various types and degrees of threat by internally scapegoating a member, redefining an existing out-group as an external threat, or forming a coalition with the out-group to cope with the threat.

Much that is learned in an experimental setting can be useful in developing and assessing nonexperimental research data that have been gathered from a wide variety of other settings, for example, observations on the processes of stigmatization in group psychotherapy, extralegal punishment in urban police forces, and the creation of deviance in

---

[9]The thrust of this chapter would be incomplete without some mention of the aspects of social control that are often invisible. Most of the fundamental parts of control are ignored by the steady, persistent workings of most enduring social systems (e.g., groups, organizations, institutions). The subtle dimension of social control can be examined in the power relationships set up by varying decision processes. There are a number of things that a social system does not decide, but controls nonetheless. How do individuals, groups, or organizations decide on their agenda: What will be discussed versus what will not be discussed?

Decisions and nondecisions can be treated as alternative outcomes of a single set of political processes. Studies of decision-making processes usually either test theories about power relationships by predicting decisions or produce generalizations about power relationships from analyses of past decisions. Importantly, however, in some instances a decision is not reached on an issue becase it is not actively contested or because the contest is terminated before it reaches the agenda stage. The function of consensus among the majority of actors is often to prevent certain issues from being considered or to justify the use of extreme tactics against deviants. The methodological problems inherent in research on decision making can be overcome with the aid of experimental research (Meehl, 1974: 374–78). And, experimentation is fundamental to the development of a theory of decision-making.

communal and familial groups. This knowledge can help to identify further social processes such as norm formation, solidarity enhancement, and deviance creation, in terms of other abstract features, which are then analyzed in a variety of specific social contexts varying in scale, complexity, degree of formalization, and historical and cultural setting.

In general, such work will greatly improve future research. The shift from a narrow focus upon the "deviants" to the broader contextual perspective that includes situational properties, dynamics, and a structural perspective is promising for studies of social control.

ACKNOWLEDGMENTS

I wish to thank Rhonda Shapiro and Gray Cavender for their comments on various drafts of this chapter. Donald Black's editorial skill and commitment are especially appreciated. Also, a special acknowledgment is due M. A. Bortner for her detailed contributions to the work: A sensitive yet critical mind is always appreciated. Finally, I am grateful to the University of Minnesota Graduate College for providing funds for part of this research.

References

Allen, V. L.
    1956   "Situational factors in conformity." Pages 133–176 in *Advances in Experimental Social Psychology*, vol. 2, edited by L. Berkowitz. New York: Academic Press.
Allport, F. H.
    1934   "The J-curve hypothesis of conforming behavior." *Journal of Social Psychology* 5: 141–183.
Alvarez, Rodolfo
    1968   "Informal reactions to deviance in simulated work organizations: A laboratory experiment." *American Sociological Review* 33: 895–912.
Archer, Dave
    1974   "Power in groups: Self-concept of powerful and powerless group members." *Journal of Applied Behavioral Sciences* 10: 208–220.
Arnold, David W., and Carl I. Greenberg
    1980   "Deviate rejection within differentially manned groups." *Social Psychology Quarterly* 43: 419–424.
Aronson, Elliot, and J. Merrill Carlsmith
    1968   "Experimentation in social psychology." Pages 1–79 in *Handbook of Social Psychology*, vol. 2, edited by G. Lindzey and E. Aronson. Reading, Mass.: Addison-Wesley.
Aronson, Elliot, and Judson Mills
    1959   "The effects of severity of initiation on liking for a group." *Journal of Abnormal and Social Psychology* 59: 177–181.
Asch, Solomon E.
    1951   "Effects of group pressure upon the modification and distortion of judgments." Pages 177–190 in *Groups, Leadership, and Men*, edited by H. Guetzkow. Pittsburgh: Carnegie Press.

1952 *Social Psychology.* Englewood Cliffs, N.J.: Prentice-Hall.
1956 "Studies of independence and conformity: A minority of one against a unanimous majority." *Psychological Monographs* 70: No. 416.
Bales, Robert F.
 1950 *Interaction Process Analysis: A Method for the Study of Small Groups.* Reading, Mass.: Addison-Wesley.
Bales, Robert F., Fred L. Strodtbeck, Theodore M. Mills, and Mary E. Roseborough
 1951 "Channels of communication in small groups." *American Sociological Review* 16: 461–468.
Bandura, A., and R. H. Walters
 1963 *Social Learning and Personality Development.* New York: Holt, Rinehart and Winston.
Berger, Joseph, Bernard P. Cohen, and Morris Zelditch, Jr.
 1966 "Status characteristics and expectation states." Pages 29–73 in *Sociological Theories in Progress,* edited by J. Berger, M. Zelditch, Jr., and B. P. Cohen. Boston: Houghton Mifflin.
Beutel, Frederick K.
 1957 *Some Potentialities of Experimental Jurisprudence as a New Branch of Social Science.* Lincoln, Nebr.: University of Nebraska Press.
Black, Donald
 1976 *The Behavior of Law.* New York: Academic Press.
 1979 "A note on the measurement of law." *Informationsbrief für Rechtssoziologie,* Sonderheft 2 (April): 92–106.
Bonacich, Phillip, and John Light
 1978 "Laboratory experimentation in sociology." *Annual Review of Sociology* 4: 145–170.
Campbell, Donald T., and Julian C. Stanley
 1963 *Experimental and Quasi-Experimental Designs for Research.* Chicago: Rand McNally.
Caporaso, James A., and Leslie J. Roos, Jr. (editors)
 1973 *Quasi-Experimental Approaches: Testing Theory and Evaluating Policy.* Evanston, Ill.: Northwestern University Press.
Cartwright, Dorwin
 1979 "Contemporary social psychology in historical perspective." *Social Psychology Quarterly* 42: 82–93.
Cartwright, Dorwin, and Alvin Zander
 1968 *Group Dynamics.* New York: Harper & Row.
Chapin, Stuart F.
 1947 *Experimental Designs in Sociological Research.* Revised edition. Westport, Conn.: Greenwood Press.
Cook, Thomas D., and Donald T. Campbell
 1976 "The design and conduct of quasi-experiments and true experiments in field settings." Pages 223–326 in *Handbook of Industrial and Organizational Psychology,* edited by Marvin D. Dunnette. Chicago: Rand McNally.
 1979 *Quasi-Experimentation: Design and Analysis Issues for Field Settings.* Chicago: Rand McNally.
Cronkite, Ruth C.
 1980 "Social psychological simulations: An alternative to experiments?" *Social Psychology Quarterly* 43: 199–216.

Davidson, W., and E. Seidman
  1974 "Studies of behavior modification and juvenile delinquency: A review, methodological critique, and social perspective." *Psychological Bulletin* 81: 998–1011.
Dedrick, Dennis K.
  1978 "Deviance and sanctioning within small groups." *Social Psychology* 41: 94–105.
Dion, K. L., R. S. Baron, and N. Miller
  1970 "Why do groups make riskier decisions than individuals?" Pages 305–377 in *Advances in Experimental Social Psychology*, vol. 5, edited by L. Berkowitz. New York: Academic Press.
Doob, Leonard
  1973 *The Focus on the Individual Deviant*. Stanford, Calif.: Stanford University Press.
Durkheim, Emile
  1893 *The Division of Labor in Society*. New York: Free Press, 1964.
Emerson, Richard M.
  1954 "Deviation and rejection: An experimental replication." *American Sociological Review* 19: 688–693.
Empey, Lamar T., and Maynard L. Erickson
  1972 *The Provo Experiment: Evaluating Community Control of Delinquency*. Lexington, Mass.: D. C. Heath.
Empey, Lamar T., and Steven G. Lubeck
  1971 *The Silverlake Experiment: Testing Delinquency Theory and Community Intervention*. Chicago: Aldine Press.
Evans, Richard, and Richard M. Rozelle
  1973 *Social Psychology in Life*. 2d edition. Boston: Allyn and Bacon.
Fairweather, George W.
  1967 *Methods for Experimental Social Innovation*. New York: Wiley.
  1977 *Experimental Methods for Social Policy Research*. New York: Pergamon Press.
Freedman, Jonathan L., and Anthony N. Doob
  1968 *Deviancy: The Psychology of Being Different*. New York: Academic Press.
Freese, Lee, and Milton Rokeach
  1979 "On the use of alternative interpretations in contemporary social psychology." *Social Psychology Quarterly* 42: 195–201.
Greenwood, Ernest
  1945 *Experimental Sociology: A Study in Method*. New York: King's Crown Press.
Hamblin, Robert L.
  1958 "Leadership and crises." *Sociometry* 21: 322–335.
Haney, Craig, Curtis Banks, and Philip Zimbardo
  1973 "Interpersonal dynamics in a simulated prison." *International Journal of Criminology and Penology* 1: 69–97.
Hare, Alexander P.
  1952 "A study of interaction and consensus in different sized groups." *American Sociological Review* 17: 261–267.
  1976 *Handbook of Small Group Research*. New York: Macmillan.
Harris, Anthony R.
  1977 "Sex and theories of deviance: Toward a functional theory of deviant typescripts." *American Sociological Review* 42: 3–16.
Heider, F.
  1958 *The Psychology of Interpersonal Relations*. New York: Wiley.

Hollander, Edwin P.
   1960   "Competence and conformity in the acceptance of influences." *Journal of Abnormal Social Psychology* 61: 361–365.
Hollander, Edwin P., and Richard H. Willis
   1967   "Procedural rules and the study of deviant behavior." *Social Problems* 21: 159–172.
International Symposium on Alcohol and Drug Addiction.
   1973   *Experimentation in Controlled Environments.* Toronto.
Jones, Edward E., Kenneth J. Gergen, Peter Gumpert, and John W.Thibault
   1965   "Some conditions affecting the use of ingratiation to influence performance evaluation." *Journal of Personality and Social Psychology* 6: 613–625.
Kiesler, Charles A.
   1969   "Group pressure and conformity." Pages 233–306 in *Experimental Social Psychology*, edited by J. Mills. London: Macmillan.
Larkin, William E., and L. Anthony Loman.
   1977   "Labeling in the family context: An experimental study." *Sociology and Social Research* 61: 192–203.
Latané, Bibb, and Judith Rodin
   1969   "A lady in distress: Inhibiting effects of friends and strangers on bystander intervention." *Journal of Experimental Social Psychology* 5: 189–202.
Lauderdale, Pat
   1976   "Deviance and moral boundaries." *American Sociological Review* 41: 660–676.
Lauderdale, Pat (editor)
   1980   *A Political Analysis of Deviance.* Minneapolis: University of Minnesota Press.
Lauderdale, Pat, Phil Smith-Cunnien, Jerry Parker, and James Inverarity
   1983   "External threat and the definition of deviance." *Journal of Personality and Social Psychology* 44: 2211–33.
Lawler, Edward J., and Martha E. Thompson
   1978   "Impact of leader responsibility for inequity on subordinate revolts." *Social Psychology* 41: 264–268.
Lee, Margaret T., and Richard Ofshe
   1981   "The impact of behavioral style and status characteristics on social influence: A test of two competing theories." *Social Psychology Quarterly* 44: 73–82.
Levine, John M.
   1980   "Reaction to opinion deviance in small groups." Pages 375–429 in *Psychology of Group Influence*, edited by P. Paulus. Hillsdale, N.J.: Erlbaum.
Levine, John M., and Barry Ruback
   1980   "Reaction to opinion deviance: Impact on a fence straddler's rationale on majority evaluation." *Social Psychology Quarterly* 43: 73–81.
Liberman, Morton A., Irvin D. Yalom, and Matthew B. Miles
   1973   *Encounter Groups: First Facts.* New York: Basic Books.
Lindzey, Gardner, and Elliott Aronson
   1969   *The Handbook of Social Psychology*, vol. 4. Menlo Park, Calif.: Addison-Wesley.
Martinson, Robert
   1974   "What works? Questions and answers about prison reform." *The Public Interest* 35: 22–54.
Meehl, Paul E.
   1974   "Nuisance variables and the ex post facto design." Pp. 373–390 in *Minnesota Studies in the Philosophy of Science IV*. edited by M. Radner and S. Winohur. Minneapolis: University of Minnesota Press.

Merton, Robert K.
  1938 "Social structure and anomie." *American Sociological Review* 3: 672–682.
Milgram, Stanley
  1963 "Behavioral study of obedience." *Journal of Abnormal and Social Psychology* 67: 371–378.
Miller, Charles E., and Patricia Doede Anderson
  1979 "Group decision rules and the rejections of deviates." *Social Psychology Quarterly* 42: 354–363.
Mills, Judson (editor)
  1969 *Experimental Social Psychology.* London: Macmillan.
Molm, Linda D.
  1981 "The conversion of power imbalance to power use." *Social Psychology Quarterly* 44: 151–163.
Nagao, Dennis H., and James H. Davis
  1980 "The effects of prior experience on mock juror case judgments." *Social Psychology Quarterly* 43: 190–199.
Nagel, Jack
  1975 *The Descriptive Analysis of Power.* New Haven, Conn.: Yale University Press.
Newstetter, Wilber I., Marc J. Feldstein, and Theodore M. Newcomb
  1938 *Group Adjustment: A Study in Experimental Sociology.* Cleveland: Western Reserve University School of Applied Social Sciences.
Ofshe, Richard J. (editor)
  1973 *Interpersonal Behavior in Small Groups.* Englewood Cliffs, N.J.: Prentice-Hall.
Parker, Jerry
  1981 "Durkheim on social organization, law and punishment: Three propositions, two research traditions and some considerations." Unpublished paper, University of Minnesota.
Powers, Edwin, and Helen Witner
  1951 *An Experiment in the Prevention of Delinquency: The Cambridge–Somerville Youth Study.* New York: Columbia University Press.
Reckless, Walter C., and Simon Dinitz
  1972 *The Prevention of Juvenile Delinquency: An Experiment.* Columbus: Ohio State University Press.
Ridgeway, Cecelia
  1978 "Conformity, group-oriented motivation, and status attainment in small groups." *Social Psychology* 41: 175–188.
Riecken, Henry and Robert F. Boruch
  1974 *Social Experimentation: A Method for Planning and Evaluating Social Intervention.* New York: Academic Press.
Robins, Philip K., Robert G. Spiegleman, Samuel Weiner, and Joseph Bell
  1980 *A Guaranteed Annual Income.* New York: Academic Press.
Schachter, Stanley
  1951 "Deviation, rejection and communication." *Journal of Abnormal and Social Psychology* 46: 190–207.
Schur, Edwin M.
  1979 *Interpreting Deviance.* New York: Harper & Row
Schwitzgebel, R.
  1964 *Streetcorner Research: An Experimental Approach to the Delinquent.* Cambridge, Mass.: Harvard University Press.
Sherif, Muzafer
  1935 "A Study of some social factors in perception." *Archives of Psychology* 27: 1–60.

1936   *The Psychology of Social Norms.* New York: Harper.
1956   *An Outline of Social Psychology.* New York: Harper.
Sherif, Muzafer, O. J. Harvey, B. J. White, W. R. Hood, and Carolyn Sherif
    1961   *Intergroup Conflict and Cooperation: The Robber's Cave Experiment.* Norman, Okla.:
            Institute of Group Relations, University of Oklahoma.
Sherif,Muzafer, and Carolyn W. Sherif
    1969   *Social Psychology.* New York: Harper & Row.
Simmel, Georg
    1908   *Conflict and the Web of Group-Affiliations.* New York: Free Press, 1955.
Steffensmeier, Darrell J., and Robert M. Terry (editors)
    1975   *Examining Deviance Experimentally.* Port Washington, N.Y.: Alfred.
Sutherland, Edwin H., and Donald R. Cressey
    1960   *Principles of Criminology.* 6th edition. Philadelphia: J. P. Lippincott (1st edition,
            1924).
Tedeschi, James T., Barry Schlenker, and Thomas Bonoma
    1975   "Compliance to threats as a function of source attractiveness and esteem."
            Sociometry 38: 81–98.
Thibaut, John, and Laurens Walker
    1975   *Procedural Justice: A Psychological Analysis.* New York: Wiley.
Tittle, Charles R., and Alan R. Rowe
    1973   "Moral appeal, sanction threat, and deviance: An experimental test." *Social
            Problems* 20: 488–498.
Ungar, Sheldon
    1981   "The effects of status and excuse on interpersonal reactions to deviant behav-
            ior." *Social Psychology Quarterly* 44: 260–263.
Wahrman, Ralph
    1970   "High status, deviance, and sanctions." *Sociometry* 33: 485–504.
Wahrman, Ralph, and Meredith Pugh
    1972   "Competence and conformity: Another look at Hollander's study." *Sociometry*
            35: 376–386.
    1974   "Sex, nonconformity, and influence." *Sociometry* 37: 137–147.
Ward, David A.
    1979   "Sweden: The middle way to prison reform." Pages 89–167 in *Prisons: Present
            and Possible,* edited by Marvin E. Wolfgang. Lexington, Mass.: D. C. Heath.
White, Ralph K., and Ronald Lippitt
    1960   *Autocracy and Democracy: An Experimental Inquiry.* New York: Harper and
            Brothers.
Yalom, Irvin D.
    1970   *The Theory and Practice of Group Psychotherapy.* New York: Basic Books.
Zeisel, Hans
    1968   "The indirect experiment." *Law and Society Review* 2: 504–508.
Zelditch, Morris Jr.
    1961   "Can you really study an army in a laboratory?" Pages 528–539 in *A Sociological
            Reader on Complex Organizations,* edited by Amitai Etzioni. New York: Holt,
            Rinehart and Winston.
    1969   "Laboratory organizations: A review article." Unpublished paper, Stanford
            University: Laboratory for Social Research.
    1980   "Decisions, nondecisions, and metadecisions." Unpublished paper, Depart-
            ment of Sociology, Stanford University.
Zimbardo, Philip C.
    1972   "Pathology of imprisonment." *Society* 9: 4–8.

11

History and Social Control

WILLIAM E. NELSON

Does history have any distinctive contribution to offer to the development and elaboration of a theory of social control? This is a deceptively simple question that in fact disguises a far more complex one: What can scholars seeking to generate a theory of social control hope to learn from history? The answer depends on social scientists' conceptions of their own intellectual enterprise, their conceptions of the historian's enterprise, and the manner in which the two sets of conceptions overlap.

History as Data

One position is outlined by Peter Winch in *The Idea of a Social Science and Its Relation to Philosophy* (1958). Winch reports that some social scientists see "human history . . . [as] a kind of repository of data." He continues that in the eyes of such theorists the function of "the historian [is to] unearth . . . these data and present . . . them to his more theoretically minded colleagues who then produce scientific generalizations and theories establishing connections between one kind of social situation and another [1958: 182–183]." Social scientists who view history as a mere repository of data, whatever their conception of their own disci-

TOWARD A GENERAL THEORY OF SOCIAL CONTROL
Volume 2: Selected Problems

pline may be, possess a simple inductivist conception of history—a conception related to late nineteenth-century views of social science and to the late nineteenth-century efforts of historians to make their discipline into a science.

The simple inductivist conception of history and the related, simple inductivist conception of science view the historian or scientist as a mere collector and classifier of facts.[1] Although this model today is in some disrepute (see Kuhn, 1970a), it was the predominant view of science when the modern disciplines of social science and history were founded a century ago. As I have written elsewhere (see Nelson, 1982), most American intellectuals in the late 1800s defined the scientific method as the abandonment of abstract principles derived from divine revelation or individual intuition; science, it was thought, should be objective and value free. In place of value judgments, scientists by "classification of facts" substituted "judgments independent of the idiosyncracies of the individual mind [Pearson, 1892: 7]."[2] Late nineteenth-century intellectuals generally believed that scientists simply take "note of all that comes within the range of sensuous experience, and declare whatever may be derived therefrom by a careful induction." "As a philosopher," a late nineteenth-century scientist could "not go farther [Anonymous, 1864: 776]." This simple inductivist model has long exercised a powerful influence on the way in which many practitioners of history and science do their work.[3]

Many historians today still adopt a simple inductivist approach to their research and writing. This is particularly true of the historians whose work will be used for illustrative purposes in this essay—the historians of what has always been a primary form of social control in the United States: the law. Most American legal historians have understood their task to be to recreate the past with objectivity by being "so honest in purpose and so critical of . . . data as to eliminate from [their] conclusions the distorting factors of life and environment [Philbrick,

[1]A leading proponent of the industivist view was the noted American philosopher and educator John Dewey. His principal works in this regard are *Logic: The Theory of Inquiry* (1938) and *Studies in Logical Theory* (1903). Ernest Nagel, a student and supporter of Dewey's pedagogy, has written on the logic of scientific discovery espousing views not too dissimilar from Dewey's (see Cohen and Nagel 1934; Nagel 1956; see also Nagel 1961: 547–606). For earlier inductivist writers, see Note 2.

[2]This concept of science, which Pearson believed to be applicable to the social as well as the physical sciences (1892: 6–7), was picked up by William Graham Sumner, perhaps the leading sociologist of the day (see Sumner, 1940: 127).

[3]For an example of an article that advocates the use of the inductivist method by historians, see Philbrick (1934: 191).

1934: 195]." A leading historian of American law, Julius Goebel, Jr., has written of the need in legal history for "an inquiry into facts" conducted by historians of "patience," "candor," and "industry" in order to complete in a "workmanlike" manner "the delicate task of reconstructing" the history of American law (1944: xxxiv, xxxvi). His colleague, Karl N. Llewellyn, in reviewing a work of legal history, similarly spoke of the need to have the law's past studied by a "patient workman" who is "sensitive to the atmosphere of the facts . . . , trained to caution where caution is called for, instinct with feeling for wholeness, balance, and the limitations of tendencies, joyously willing to sink his own ego in his material [1931: 730]."

Legal historians who have possessed this simple inductivist faith have produced a great deal of valuable scholarship that is as objective and as free of consciously chosen values as any study of the past can be. A significant body of scholarship, for instance, focuses on the creation and operation of the institutions of law (see, e.g., Smith, 1950). Other work traces the history of legal doctrines such as the rules of procedure (see, e.g., Henderson, 1966). Historical analysis of the relationship between legal change and economic growth has also been a common theme (see, e.g., Hurst, 1964; Horwitz, 1977).

Much of this literature in the field of American legal history is probably of little use to scholars striving to generate a theory of social control. But there are some bodies of literature that offer a great deal of useful data to social theorists who are prepared to accept the work of inductivist historians at face value. There is, for example, a vast body of scholarship about the history of criminal law (see, e.g., Preyer, 1982) and of institutions that participate in its enforcement, such as police and prisons (see, e.g., Rothman, 1971; Fogelson, 1977). Another subject that has been studied extensively is the law of slavery and the subsequent law of race relations (see, e.g., Tushnet, 1981). The history of labor law is another topic on which data can be found (see, e.g., Levy, 1957: 166–206). Historians have also given some attention to the role of institutions other than courts, lawyers, and other public officials. George L. Haskins has studied the impact of Puritan ideology on the law of seventeenth-century Massachusetts (see Haskins, 1960); Emil Oberholzer, Jr., has studied how Congregational churches in colonial New England resolved disputes between individuals (see Oberholzer, 1956); and John Phillip Reid has examined how emigrants on the overland trail enforced familiar legal norms in the absence of formal legal institutions (see Reid, 1980). It is possible in an essay of this scope, however, to mention only a few of the many studies that might provide useful data for a theory of social control, and a social scientist interested in such materials should consult appropriate bibliographical sources.[4]

The hard question that a social scientist must face is whether historical studies or even records handed down from past societies can appropriately be treated as mere repositories of data that have been collected in an objective manner free from biases of the historian or record keeper. Most social scientists probably would answer that question negatively. There are two reasons for this answer.

The first reason is that, even among those who most stress the scientific character of history and the objective nature of historical facts, there is an awareness that history is more than merely a descriptive science; it is also a form of art. History has often been said to be both a science and an art and has been thought to lie at the crossroads of science and art. Historians feel a need not only to describe past societies with scientific rigor but also to address fundamental political, social, and human questions that are typically subjects of artistic and philosophical endeavor.[5] These latter questions cannot be addressed, however, wihout the making of fundamental value judgments—a task neither scientific nor objective in character.

A great deal of history has been written in response to questions that demand value judgments. One body of literature, for example, inquires whether American chattel slavery was a benign or brutal institution.[6] But factual information alone—for instance, that many slaves were whipped 39 lashes for particular infractions—will not reveal whether slavery was gentle or harsh. Reaching any conclusion also requires a

[4]Two recent bibliographical sources are Kermit Hall's *A Comprehensive Bibliography of American Constitutional and Legal History* (1984) and William E. Nelson's and John Phillip Reid's *The Literature of American Legal History* (1984).

[5]For writers who have seen history, at least in part, as a form of artistic and philosophical endeavor, see Macaulay (1956: 72); Black (1965: 1–14); White (1965: 7–12); and Fischer (1970: 311–312). Michael Kammen suggests that a concern that history be a form of philosophy—a kind of art—has increased during the past decade (1980: 23–26).

[6]This debate came to a head in 1956 when Kenneth Stampp published his *Peculiar Institution: Slavery in the Ante-bellum South* (1956), in which an attack was leveled against the long-held view of a slavery as a "benign" institution put forth by Ulrich Phillips in *American Negro Slavery* (1918). This same debate, now some 25 years old, is continuing in recent analyses of how the judiciary treated slaves. A. E. Keir Nash, for example, holds to the view that blacks received fair and just treatment in the antebellum courts (1979: 7). In addition, says Nash, any injustice that did occur resulted not from acts of commission but from omission resulting from moral indifference. A similar view has been put forward by Flanigan (1974: 537) and Howington (1975: 249). On the opposing side are scholars who claim that justice was not fairly meted out to slaves and that judicial expressions of compassion were simply meaningless rhetoric (see Cover, 1975; Tushnet, 1975: 119; Hindus, 1976: 575).

theory of just punishment and criteria for comparing penalties meted out to slaves with penalties given to others, and elaborating such a theory and such criteria involves the making of value judgments. A judgment that corporal punishment is more harsh than imprisonment will suggest that slavery was harsh, whereas a contrary judgment that recognizes the brutality of lengthy terms of imprisonment might lead a historian to conclude that slaves were treated more gently than modern American blacks are. By using evaluative words like *benign* and *brutal* in framing questions about the past, historians ensure that their aesthetic and ethical values are deeply interwoven with the facts in the story they tell.

This is not to say that history requiring aesthetic or ethical evaluation of data should be labeled bad history. Indeed, some classical historical works are replete with value judgments (see Beard, 1913; Hofstadter, 1955; Genovese, 1974). Unless critics can do more than point to the value-ladden quality of such history, they cannot fairly call it bad history. But a critic can properly attach the label of unscientific to history that is both descriptive and evaluative. This label is proper because a statement must be value free and objective to qualify as scientific under an inductivist model of science.

The second reason why social scientists should not think of history as a mere repository of objective, value-free data is that the notion of an objective, value-free fact rests on a simple inductivist conception of social science that most social theorists no longer accept. Most social scientists today are more likely to believe in a contrasting model of the scientific method, which might be labeled "Popperian,"[7] after Karl Popper, its earliest and foremost explicator. According to Popper, the scientific method consists of the creative elaboration of hypotheses followed by their rigorous examination in light of all available empirical data. When tested against data, some hypotheses prove false and are then discarded. No hypothesis, Popper maintains, can ever be proven true, although some can be provisionally relied on, as if true, until they are

---

[7]There are many variants to the Popperian approach to science. For example, Thomas S. Kuhn, author of *The Structure of Scientific Revolutions* (1970a) sees himself as a member of the Popperian camp (1970b: 1). Kuhn and others recognize, however, that important differences exist between Kuhn and Popper (see generally Lakatos and Musgrave, 1970; for essays by others who also are essentially philosophers in the Popperian mold, see Lakatos and Musgrave, 1970).

Because a description of these variants is not necessary to understand the contribution that history can make to social theory, I shall merely note that the variants exist and shall say nothing further about them. For the same reason, I shall also make no effort to define the scientific method precisely—a task surely beyond the scope of this essay.

proved false. Because the values of researchers themselves or of the research community to which they belong inevitably enter into the hypotheses they formulate, no empirical findings growing out of those hypotheses can ever be completely objective and totally value free. All science—all empirical research—rests on the methodological, aesthetic, and perhaps ethical assumptions of either scientists themselves or the scientific community to which they belong (see Popper, 1959, 1962; Kuhn, 1970a). Astronomers, for example, who are studying the rings of Saturn make a methodological assumption that the recent *Voyager* probe has provided more accurate and precise observations of Saturn's rings than the best telescope. They also make a further aesthetic or ethical assumption that nature did not alter the rings as the *Voyager* probe approached.[8]

A social scientist who adopts a Popperian view of science and empirical knowledge cannot consistently with that view adopt a simple inductivist view of history. A Popperian social theorist should recognize that all data from the past is inextricably interwined with the perspectives and values of those who assembled the data. Indeed, the Popperian theorist should recognize that a historian's personal perspectives and values are an even more prominent constituent element in historical data than those of a scientist are in scientific data.

The personal perspectives and values of the researcher are so much more important in history than in science because of the greater difficulty that historians have in conclusively proving historical hypotheses to be false. Consider, for example, the scientist's hypotheses that water boils at 100° on the centigrade scale.[9] Scientists can test this hypothesis by structuring precise experiments under varied conditions, and when water fails to boil at 100° centigrade under some conditions—as, for example, at high altitude—they will know that their hypothesis, at least when stated starkly, is false. Compare the hypothesis of the colonial American historian that churches in eighteenth-century New England took cognizance of disputes between individuals. Suppose that church records from a small number of parishes contained no evidence of ecclesiastical cognizance of disputes. Would the existence of such records convince most historians that the hypothesis concerning ecclesiastical resolution of disputes might be false? Unlike scientists, historians would

---

[8]What makes science objective is that once scientists have made assumptions about the questions worthy of study and the methods for studying them, they will not need to make further value judgments as they search for answers. Instead, scientists' questions will direct them to search for specific data, the existence or nonexistence of which will determine their answer.

[9]This example is put forward by Popper's biographer, Bryan Magee (1973: 16).

be unlikely to question this hypothesis because of the substantial possibility that the particular set of records examined was incomplete. Historians, that is, would most likely conclude, on being confronted with sources inconsistent with the hypothesis, that their sources rather than the hypothesis were inaccurate. Of course, scientists might, like historians, conclude that their research had produced a false result rather than that the hypothesis is false when water at a high altitude fails to boil at 100°. But, unlike historians, they can run their experiment again and determine whether the initial result was false. Historians, on the other hand, must usually accept their source material as they find it and can rarely be very confident about how accurately and completely it reveals the past.

The difficulty of falsifying historical hypotheses has two consequences. The first is that historians generally cannot state their hypotheses with the same precision as can scientists. When scientists learn, for example, that water will not boil at 100° at a high altitude, they are not likely to discard their initial hypothesis about the boiling point of water but will more likely state it more precisely—that at sea level water boils at 100° centigrade. Historians, on the other hand, will rarely know whether an initial, imprecise hypothesis is false and hence will generally risk the possibility that narrowing the hypothesis will make it less rather than more accurate. As a result, most historical hypotheses remain broad, general, and imprecise—hence more closely tied to the imaginative act of the historian that gave them birth than to the data against which they have been tested.

My own work (see Nelson, 1978: 902–924) on the power of juries in eighteenth-century America to determine law as well as fact will illustrate how a lack of information prevents precise refinement of historical hypotheses. On completion of my research, I saw that I had no data on the state of the law in eighteenth-century Delaware. Perhaps evidence about the law-finding power of Delaware juries could be obtained by extensive research in manuscript sources, but perhaps it could not. Assuming that evidence is unobtainable, what conclusion should legal historians reach? Because most American jurisdictions, including Delaware's two neighbors, Maryland and Pennsylvania, conferred law-finding power on juries, I would hypothesize that Delaware did as well. In the absence of significant political, economic, or social differences between Delaware and its neighbors, there is little reason to expect that Delaware's law was different. If the facts could be known, perhaps this hypothesis might require refinement, as did my statement of colonial New York law, which had to take into account a 1763 case limiting the jury's law-finding power. In the absence, however, of evidence that probably can never be obtained, the broad statement that eighteenth-century Delaware juries had power to determine law as well as fact is at least as sound as the contrary statement or as the refined statement that the power of Delaware juries was limited.

The second consequence of the difficulty of falsifying historical hypotheses is that historians of a Popperian cast spend more effort than do scientists generating new hypotheses. In a discipline like science, in which falsification and hence refinement of existing hypothesis is often possible, scholars can best establish their reputation by undertaking what has become the paradigmatic scientific task of rigorously testing accepted theories under new factual conditions. In history, on the other hand, rigorous testing of established theories will rarely prove definitively that they are wrong, and accordingly scholars seeking to make their mark will turn to the paradigmatic creative task of imagining a new relationship between historical phenomena. The creative element—that is, the personal perspectives and values of the scholar—therefore play a greater role in historical than in scientific data.

Morton Horwitz's extraordinarily successful book *The Transformation of American Law* (1977) provides an example. In studying the legal history of the period 1780–1860, Horwitz did not attempt to test Willard Hurst's hypothesis that early nineteenth-century courts modified common law rules of tort, contract, and property in order to release creative individual energies and give individuals greater practical control over the environment (see Hurst, 1956: 6). Horwitz instead presented a new Marxist or quasi-Marxist thesis that judges changed the law in order to redistribute wealth from small, landowning farmers to an emerging, entrepreneurial, capitalist class. As a result, legal historians have more than one explanation for early nineteenth-century legal change, but their explanations, unlike those of scientists, have not been and are not likely to be rigorously tested.

Once it is recognized that history is an art as well as a science and that even when history is practiced as a science, a Popperian approach permits individual researchers to intertwine their creative propensities and value preferences with their empirical data, it becomes clear that social scientists cannot look on history as a mere repository of objective, value-free data. Not only historical studies but even records from the past are likely to embody the values and perspectives of those who created them. The records of some colonial New England churches, for instance, no longer contain the names of persons found guilty of fornication because the Victorian custodians of those records, in pursuance of their own value system, obliterated the names. Hence, if scholars seeking to generate a theory of social control naively use historical studies and records as objective sources of data, they will be embedding in their theories other people's values and perspectives that do not belong there.

Contributions of History to a Theory of Social Control

If history cannot contribute objective, value-free data to the elaboration of a theory of social control, then what contributions, if any, can it make? There are at least three.

First, history can provide a source of ideas and hypotheses for social-control theorists. Two studies illustrate the possibilities. One, of which brief mention has already been made, is John Phillip Reid's *Law for the Elephant: Property and Social Behavior on the Overland Trail* (1980). Reid found that, on the overland trail to California in the nineteenth century, a place where there was no legal machinery and individuals told themselves, "there is no law," law continued to flourish. Reid observes, "Definitions of property law were understood by nineteenth-century Americans on the overland trail, [and] personal rights to property remained largely inviolable, even when conditions were trying and people desperate [1980: 335, 359–360]." The significant hypothesis that Reid's book provides for social-control theorists is that an identifiable set of social characteristics—namely, those possessed by emigrants on the overland trail—breeds respect for law to such a great degree that the law will be invoked and obeyed even when law enforcement mechanisms are completely absent.

Another suggestive study is Douglas Greenberg's essay, "Crime, law enforcement, and social control in Colonial America" (1982). Greenberg compares the seventeenth- and eighteenth-century English colonies in America in which the criminal law was successfully enforced with those in which it was contemptuously ignored. He finds that in colonies where the criminal law was successfully administered, a great deal of civil litigation also took place. In colonies in which the criminal law was ignored, on the other hand, few people brought their civil disputes to court. The hypothesis to which Greenberg's essay points is that law penetrates into a community's social life either in its entirety or not at all: that the criminal law can serve as an effective instrument of social control only among people who are accustomed to turning to the institutions of civil law for assistance with the daily problems of their lives.

The studies of Reid, Greenberg, and others, it must always be remembered, do not themselves provide social scientists with objective data in support of a theory of social control; all such studies provide are hypotheses that must be rigorously examined in light of other data in an effort to determine whether the hypotheses are false.Historical studies can, however, also provide data with which to test and perhaps falsify hypotheses. This is, indeed, the second function that history can serve for social-control theorists.

Consider the following example of how historical studies can provide data with which to test hypotheses. Let us suppose that a social scientist has observed that Congregational churches in seventeenth- and eighteenth-century New England adjudicated disputes between individuals and punished other individuals who were guilty of misconduct. The churches thus served as instruments of social control. They were, moreover, nonjudicial instruments of social control; they appear, that is, to have been noncoercive, or what social scientists like to call *informal*, instruments of social control. Social scientists in our own culture who are striving to identify and elaborate informal mechanisms of social control might be tempted to study factors that made ecclesiastical adjudication of disputes and punishment of misconduct possible in colonial New England in an effort to test and elaborate a general theory about the social prerequisites for informal social control. Even so, a sophisticated understanding of history will prove false the hypothesis that churches in colonial New England served as informal instruments of social control. A sound inquiry will reveal that the church in seventeenth- and eighteenth-century New England was not, as it is today, a unofficial entity totally outside the bounds of government. The Congregational churches of colonial New England were, in significant respects, part of government. As I have pointed out in a study entitled *Dispute and Conflict Resolution in Plymouth County, Massachusetts, 1725–1825* (1981), judicial and ecclesiastical institutions for the resolution of disputes were not at all dissimilar. Both had much the same procedures; both had recourse to the same substantive values for law; both ultimately submitted disputes to the collective wisdom of a body of lay people, the jury in the one case and the congregation in the other; both relied heavily on communitarian pressures backed up by coercive sanctions for enforcement of their decisions (1981: 22–44). Although it would be a mistake to conclude that no differences existed between the churches and the courts, it would be equally foolhardy to label churches as informal and courts as official mechanisms of social control and to build a theory of social control on that dichotomy. A careful reading of the historical record will show that a hypothesis that churches acted as informal mechanisms of social control is, if not false, at least in need of some modification.

In addition to testing hypotheses and providing data with which to falsify them, there is a third way in which history can contribute to a theory of social control. The study of history will suggest that there are many, if not an infinite number of, ways in which social control can take place. A social system can, of course, regulate its people with an army and with police and prisons. But these obviously are not the only techniques of social control. In seventeenth-century Massachusetts, an elite magistracy exhorted and intimidated the people with Puritan ideology (see Haskins, 1960). Among Cherokee Indians of the eighteenth century, order was maintained through social pressures imposed by the community as a whole, with ostracism of the recalcitrant as the ultimate weapon (see Reid, 1970: 229–269). In America before the Civil War, where there was little in the way of an army, police force, coherent ideology, or stable and tightly knit community, social control was exercised through the government's distribution of economic largess to those who were willing to uphold and support the existing order (see Nelson, 1975: 206–220)—a method of social control that had also been used in New York City in the eighteenth century (see Hartog, 1979).

The student of history can find in the past apparent examples of all these forms of social control, and undoubtedly many other forms exist as well. The study of history will thus prove that any theory of social control that fails to take into account the large variety of ways in which social control can take place is false. In order to avoid falsification when examined in conjunction with historical materials, a theory of social control must be multifaceted and open-ended. By making this plain, history makes perhaps its most important contribution.

Conclusion

What, then, can history contribute to the development and elaboration of a theory of social control? If social scientists understand that facts exist independently of the perspective with which the world is examined, they can turn to history as a repository of data and construct a theory of social control out of the facts they find there, without concern that the historians whose work is used might have had differing perspectives. If, on the other hand, social scientists adopt an epistemological position that sees all historical writing as a product of historians' imagination as well as of past reality, they can still use history, not as a foundation for a theory of social control, but as a source of ideas and as a check on premature ideas. Whatever their view of their own discipline and of data from the past, social scientists should recognize that history can contribute considerably to a general theory of social control.

References

Anonymous
    1864   Review of *Illustrations of Progress: A Series of Discussions by Herbert Spencer*. *Atlantic Monthly* 13: 775–777.

Beard, Charles A.
    1913   *An Economic Interpretation of the Constitution of the United States*. New York: Macmillan.

Black, John B.
    1965   *The Art of History: A Study of Four Great Historians of the Eighteenth Century*. New York: Russell and Russell.

Cohen, Morris R., and Ernest Nagel
    1934   *An Introduction to Logic and Scientific Method*. New York: Harcourt Brace and Co.

Cover, Robert M.
    1975   *Justice Accused*. New Haven, Conn.: Yale University Press.

Dewey, John
    1903   *Studies in Logical Theory*. Chicago: University of Chicago Press.
    1938   *Logic: The Theory of Inquiry*. New York: Henry Holt.

Fischer, David H.
    1970   *Historian's Fallacies: Toward a Logic of Historical Thought*. New York: Harper & Row.

Flanigan, Daniel J.
    1974   "Criminal procedure in slave trials in the antebellum South." *Journal of Southern History* 40: 537–564.

Fogelson, Robert M.
    1977   *Big-City Police*. Cambridge,Mass.: Harvard University Press.

Genovese, Eugene D.
    1974   *Roll, Jordan, Roll: The World the Slaves Made*. New York: Pantheon Books.

Goebel, Julius
    1944   *Law Enforcement in Colonial New York: A Study in Criminal Procedure (1664–1776)*. New York: The Commonwealth Fund.

Greenberg, Douglas
    1982   "Crime, law enforcement, and social control in Colonial America." *American Journal of Legal History* 26: 293–325.

Hall, Kermit L.
    1984   *A Comprehensive Bibliography of American Legal History*. Milwood, N.Y.: KTO Press.

Hartog, Hendrik
    1979   "Because all the world is not New York City: Governance, property rights, and the state in the changing definition of a corporation, 1730–1860." *Buffalo Law Review* 28: 91–109.

Haskins, George Lee
    1960   *Law and Authority in Early Massachusetts: A Study in Tradition and Design*. New York: Macmillan.

Henderson, Edith Guild
    1966   "The background of the Seventh Amendment." *Harvard Law Review* 80: 289–337.

Hindus, Michael
    1976   "Black justice under white law: Criminal prosecutions of blacks in the antebellum South Carolina." *Journal of American History* 63: 575–599.

Hofstadter, Richard
1955   *The Age of Reform: From Bryan to F.D.R.* New York: Alfred A. Knopf.
Horwitz, Morton J.
1977   *The Transformation of American Law.* Cambridge, Mass.: Harvard University Press.
Howington, Arthur F.
1975   " 'Not in the condition of a horse or an ox': *Ford v. Ford*, the law of testamentary manumission and the Tennessee court's recognition of slave humanity." *Tennessee Historical Quarterly* 34: 249–263.
Hurst, James Willard
1956   *Law and the Conditions of Freedom in the Nineteenth-Century United States.* Madison, Wis.: University of Wisconsin Press.
1964   *Law and Economic Growth: The Legal History of the Lumber Industry in Wisconsin.* Cambridge, Mass.: Harvard University Press.
Kammen, Michael G.
1980   "Introduction: The historian's vocation and the state of the discipline in the United States." Pages 19–46 in *The Past before Us: Contemporary Historical Writing in the United States*, edited by Michael Kammen. Ithaca, N.Y.: Cornell University Press.
Kuhn, Thomas S.
1970a *The Structure of Scientific Revolutions.* Chicago: University of Chicago Press.
1970b "Logic of discovery or psychology of research?" Pages 1–23 in *Criticism and the Growth of Knowledge*, edited by Imre Lakatos and Alan Musgrave. Cambridge: Cambridge University Press.
Lakatos, Imre, and Alan Musgrave (editors)
1970   *Criticism and the Growth of Knowledge.* Cambridge: Cambridge University Press.
Levy, Leonard William
1957   *The Law of the Commonwealth and Chief Justice Shaw.* Cambridge, Mass.: Harvard University Press.
Llewellyn, Karl N.
1931   "Book Review." *Columbia Law Review* 31: 729–732.
Macaulay, Thomas B.
1956   "History." Pages 71–89 in *The Varieties of History from Voltaire to the Present*, edited by Fritz Stern. New York: Meridian Books.
Magee, Bryan
1973   *Karl Popper.* New York: Viking Press.
Nagel, Ernest
1956   *Logic without Metaphysics.* Glencoe, Ill.: Free Press.
1961   *The Structure of Science: Problems in the Logic of Scientific Explanation.* New York: Harcourt, Brace & World.
Nash, A. E. Keir
1979   "Reason of slavery: Understanding the judicial role in the peculiar institution." *Vanderbilt Law Review* 32: 7–218.
Nelson, William E.
1975   *Americanization of the Common Law: The Impact of Legal Change on Massachusetts Society, 1760–1830.* Cambridge, Mass.: Harvard University Press.
1978   "The eighteenth-century background of John Marshall's constitutional jurisprudence." *Michigan Law Review* 76: 893–960.
1981   *Dispute and Conflict Resolution in Plymouth County, Massachusetts, 1725–1825.* Chapel Hill, N.C.: University of North Carolina Press.

1982   *The Roots of American Bureaucracy, 1830–1900.* Cambridge, Mass.: Harvard University Press.
Nelson, William E., and John Phillip Reid
1984   *The Literature of American Legal History.* Dobbs Ferry, N.J.: Oceana Press.
Oberholzer, Emil, Jr.
1956   *Delinquent Saints: Disciplinary Action in the Early Congregational Churches of Massachusetts.* New York: Columbia University Press.
Pearson, Karl
1892   *The Grammar of Science.* London: Adam & Charles Black.
Philbrick, Francis S.
1934   "Possibilities of American legal history." *Law Library Journal* 27: 191–214.
Phillips, Ulrich
1918   *American Negro Slavery.* New York: D. Appleton.
Popper, Karl R.
1945   *The Open Society and Its Enemies.* Princeton, N.J.: Princeton University Press.
1959   *The Logic of Scientific Discovery.* London: Hutchinson.
1962   *Conjectures and Refutations.* New York: Basic Books.
1972   *Objective Knowledge.* Oxford: Oxford University Press.
Preyer, Kathryn
1982   "Penal measures in the American colonies: An overview." *American Journal of Legal History* 26: 326–353.
Reid, John Phillip
1970   *A Law of Blood: The Primitive Law of the Cherokee Nation.* New York: New York University Press.
1980   *Law for the Elephant: Property and Social Behavior on the Overland Trail.* San Marino, Calif.: The Huntington Library.
Rothman, David J.
1971   *The Discovery of the Asylum: Social Order and Disorder in the New Republic.* Boston: Little, Brown.
Smith, Joseph Henry
1950   *Appeals to the Privy Council from the American Plantations.* New York: Columbia University Press.
Stampp, Kenneth M.
1956   *The Peculiar Institution: Slavery in the Antebellum South.* New York: Alfred A. Knopf.
Sumner, William Graham
1940   "The scientific attitude of mind." Pages 127–135 in *Sumner Today: Selected Essays of William Graham Sumner with Comments by American Leaders,* edited by Maurice R. Davie. New Haven, Conn.: Yale University Press.
Tushnet, Mark
1975   "The American law of slavery, 1810–1860: A study in the persistence of legal autonomy." *Law and Society Review* 10: 119–184.
White, Morton G.
1965   *Foundations of Historical Knowledge.* New York: Harper & Row.
Winch, Peter
1958   *The Idea of a Social Science and Its Relation to Philosophy.* New York: Humanities Press.

Author Index

Numbers in italics indicate the pages on which the complete references are listed.

A

Abel, Richard L., 216, *228*, 245, *258*
Aday, Lu Ann, 227, *232*
Allen, John, 7, 8, 9, 11, 15, 17, *21*
Allen, V. L., *267*, *276*
Allport, Floyd H., 269, *276*
Althusser, Louis, 176, *202*, 256, *258*
Alvarez, Rodolfo, *276*
Andenaes, Johannes, 14, *21*
Anderson, Patricia Doede, 273, *280*
Anderson, Ronald, 227, *232*
Andrew, Donna T., 16, *21*
Andrews, Gavin, 216, *228*
Aponte, J. F., 211, *231*
Archer, Dave, 272, *276*
Arendt, Hannah, 17, *21*, 165, *168*
Arensberg, Conrad M., 90, *101*
Arnold, David W., *267*, *276*
Aronson, Elliot, 261, 271, *276*, *279*
Aronson, Harvey, 32, *57*
Asch, Solomon E., 263, 264, *267*, *276*
Aubert, Vilhelm, 79, *101*, 251, *258*

B

Baldick, Robert, 8, 16, *21*, 94, *101*
Bales, Robert F., 269, *277*
Balikci, Asen, 114, *137*
Bandura, A., 269, *277*
Banks, Curtis, *278*
Barker-Benfield, G., 186, *202*
Barkun, Michael, 105, *137*, 253, *258*
Barnett, Steve, 255, *258*
Baron, R. S., *267*, *278*
Barth, Fredrik, 240, 241, *258*
Barthes, Roland, 73, *76*
Barton, Eugenia, 225, 226, *231*
Barton, Roy Franklin, 3, *21*, 115, *137*
Baum, Richard, 144, *168*
Baumgartner, M. P., 7, 9, 11, 18, 19, 20, *21*, 79, 82, 89, 91, 93, 94, 95, *101*
Beard, Charles A., 287, *294*
Beccaria, Cesare, 188, 189, *202*
Becker, Gary, 33, *57*
Becker, Howard S., 9, *21*, 81, *101*
Beidelman, Thomas O., 115, *137*

Bell, Daniel, 144, 145, 146, *168*
Bell, Joseph, 270, *280*
Beloff, Max, 180, *202*
Bendix, Reinhard, 143, 157, *168*
Bennett, Louise B., 144, *168*
Bentz, W. K., 211, *231*
Beran, Nancy, 224, *229*
Berger, Joseph, 266, *277*
Bergesen, Albert, 142, 165, 166, *168*
Berk, Richard, 210, 211, *232*
Berlin, Isaiah, 257, *258*
Berman, Harold J., 90, *101*
Berndt, Ronald M., 114, *137*
Bernstein, Richard J., 255, 257, *258*
Beutel, Frederick K., *277*
Bindoff, S. T., 179, *203*
Black, Donald, 1, 5, 7, 9, 10, 11, 16, 18,
    19, *21*, 79, 89, 91, 94, 97, 98, 99, 100,
    101, 210, 211, 217, 218–219, 221, 222,
    228, 235, 254, 255, 258, 264, 277
Black, John B., 286, *294*
Bloch, Maurice, 95, *101*
Blocker, Jack S., Jr., 187, *203*
Blok, Anton, 17, *21*
Bohannan, Paul, 2, *21*, 30, *57*, 79, 83, 99,
    101, 109, 110, 112, 115, 117, 133, *137*,
    215, 217, *229*
Boissevain, Jeremy, 225, *229*
Bolton, Charlene, 4, 11, *22*
Bolton, Ralph, 4, 5, 11, 17, *22*
Bonacich, Phillip, 266, 269, *277*
Bonoma, Thomas, 268, *281*
Boostrum, Ronald, 189, *203*
Boruch, Robert F., 262, 270, *280*
Borus, Jonathan F., 224, *229*
Bose, Christine, 210, 211, *232*
Bourdieu, Pierre, 107, *137*, 256, *258*
Breslauer, George W., 145, *169*
Bridgham, Philip, 144, *169*
Briggs, Jean, 114, *138*
Brogan, D. R., 211, *231*
Brögger, Jan, 14, *22*
Brown, Claude, 14, 15, *22*
Brown, Paula, 17, *22*
Brzezinski, Zbigniew K., 144, *169*
Buck, Philip, 179, *203*
Buckle, Leonard G., 10, 27, 79, *103*
Bugen, Larry, 220, *229*
Bullough, Vern L., 186, *203*
Burch, J., 216, *229*
Burr, W. R., 210, *229*

C

Cahn, Edmond, 213, *229*
Campbell, Donald T., 261, *277*
Campbell, J. K., 3, *22*
Canderloro, Giorgio, 189, *203*
Caporaso, James A., *277*
Carlsmith, J. Merrill, 261, 271, *276*
Cartwright, Dorwin, 263, 270, 271, *277*
Cassirer, Ernst, 72, 74, *76*
Cauble, A. Elizabeth, 211, 216, *231*
Cavendish, Patrick, 144, *169*
Chagnon, Napoleon A., 4, *22*, 83, *101*, 112,
    114, 124, *138*
Chambliss, William J., 14, *22*
Chance, Norman, 114, *138*
Chapin, Stuart F., *277*
Christie, Nils, 13, *22*, 98, *101*
Chroust, Anton-Hermann, 99, *101*
Clarkson, L. A., 179, *203*
Cleaver, Elridge, 11, *22*
Cloward, Richard A., 20, *22*
Cobb, Sidney, 216, *229*
Coe, Rodney, 223, *230*
Cohen, Albert K., 10, 20, *22*
Cohen, Bernard P., 266, *277*
Cohen, Morris R., 284, *294*
Cohn, Bernard S., 95, *101*
Collier, Jane F., 115, 116, *138*
Colquhoun, Patrick, 191, *203*
Colson, Elizabeth, 98, *101*, 115, *138*, 251,
    258
Comeau, Joan K., 211, 216, *231*
Cominos, Peter, 185, 186, *203*
Conquest, Robert, 144, *169*
Cook, Chris, 179, *206*
Cook, Thomas D., 261, *277*
Cooper, David D., 195, 196, *203*
Cover, Robert M., 286, *294*
Cressey, Donald R., 10, 20, *22*, 26, 273, *281*
Cronkite, Ruth C., 271, *277*
Cunningham, W., 179, *203*

D

Daley, Robert, 56, *57*
Dallin, Alexander, 145, *169*
Danzig, Richard, 211, *229*
Davidson, W., 270, *278*
Davis, David Brion, 196, *203*

Davis, James H., 265, *280*
Dean, Alfred, 216, 221, 229
Deasy, Leila Calhoun, 216, 221, *233*
Dedrick, Dennis K., 265, 268, *278*
De Grazia, Alfred, 157, *169*
De Maris, Ovid, 55, *57*
Dewey, John, 284, *294*
Diamond, Arthur S., 3, 22, 109, *138*
Dillon, Richard G., 18, *22*
DiMaggio, Paul, 107, *138*
Dinitz, Simon, 224, 229, *280*
Dion, K. L., 267, *278*
Donajgrodzki, A. P., 192, 193, *203*
Doob, Anthony N., *278*
Doob, Leonard, *278*
Douglas, Mary, 97, *101*, 142, *169*
Downs, James, 114, *138*
Driver, Edwin D., 6, *22*
Dunlop, Burton, 224, 229
Durkheim, Emile, 109, *138*, 141, 147, 148,
    149, 153, 156, 163, 164, 166, 167, *169*,
    275, *278*

E

Edgerton, Robert B., 4, *22*
Eggan, Fred, 126, *138*
Eggleston, Elizabeth, 8, *22*
Ehrenburg, Ilya, 69, *77*
Eisenberg, Melvin A., 253, *258*
Ekvall, Robert B., 12, 23, 83, *102*
Elias, Norbert, 13, *23*
Embree, Scotty, 176, *203*
Emerson, Richard M., 122, *138*, 210, 229,
    271, *278*
Emerson, Robert M., 213, 216, 225, 229,
    238, *259*
Empey, Lamar T., *278*
Engel, David M., 239, 246–250, 253, 254,
    255, 257, *259*
Engels, Friedrich, 173, 174, 175, 176, 177,
    203, 206
Englehardt, G. Tristam, 186, *204*
Ensel, Walter M., 216, 221, *231*
Erickson, Maynard L., *278*
Erikson, Kai T., 143, 147–148, 149, 150, 151,
    152, 163, 164–165, 168, *169*
Evans, Richard, 267, *278*
Evans-Pritchard, E. E., 8, 15, 20, 23, 83,
    102, 112, 115, 132, *138*

F

Fainsod, Merle, 60, 63, 64, 66, 68, 69, 70, 71,
    77
Fairweather, George W., *278*
Fallers, Lloyd A., 2, 23, 115, *138*
Fallers, M. C., 2, *23*
Farrell, Ronald A., 97, *102*
Fattah, Ezzat A., 13, *23*
Feldstein, Marc J., *280*
Felstiner, William L. F., 79, 84, 97, 100, *102*,
    211, 229
Ferdinand, Theodore N., 193, *204*
Ferracuti, Franco, 7, *27*
Fischer, Claude S., 210, *231*
Fischer, David H., 286, *294*
Flanigan, Daniel J., 286, *294*
Fogelson, Robert M., 285, *294*
Foucault, Michel, 137, *138*, 198, *204*
Fox, Renée, 226, 229
Freedman, Jonathan L., *278*
Freese, Lee, 271, *278*
Fried, Jacob, 4, 11, *23*
Fried, Morton, 121–122, *138*
Friedman, Lawrence M., 216, *230*
Fürer-Haimendorf, Christoph von, 4, *23*,
    97, *102*

G

Galanter, Marc, 84, *102*, 223, 224, *230*, 245,
    259
Gans, Herbert J., 88, 93, *102*
Geer, Blanche, 81, *101*
Geertz, Clifford, *259*
Genovese, Eugene D., *204*, 287, *294*
Gergen, Kenneth J., *279*
Gibbs, Jack P., 210, *230*
Gibbs, James L., Jr., 83, 90, *102*
Glaser, Barney, 81, *102*, 220, *230*
Gluckman, Max, 17, 18, 23, 97, *102*,
    105–106, 109, 110, 115, *138*
Goebel, Julius, Jr., 285, *294*
Goering, John, 223, *230*
Goldschmidt, Walter, 115, *139*
Goldstein, Joseph, 222, *230*
Gore, Susan, 216, 221, *230*
Gottfredson, Michael R., 210, 211, 218–219,
    220, 222, *230*
Gove, Walter, 221, 223, *230*
Graham, Fred, 33, *57*
Granovetter, Mark S., 81, *102*, 226, *230*

Gray, Jack, 144, *169*
Green, Thomas A., 16, *23*
Greenberg, Carl I., 267, *276*
Greenberg, David F., 11, *23*, 171, 188, 200, *204, 205*
Greenberg; Douglas, 291, *294*
Greenwood, Ernest, *278*
Greer, Donald, 144, *169*
Griffin, Clifford S., 196, *204*
Grinnell, George B., *139*
Gross, Jan T., 19
Gulliver, Philip H., 83, 99, *102*, 109, 112, 115, 132, *139*, 251, 253, *259*
Gumpert, Peter, *279*
Gusfield, Joseph R., 145, *169*, 185, 187, *204*
Gutek, Barbara A., 225, 226, *231*
Gutman, Herbert G., 195, *204*

H

Haft-Picker, Cheryl, 7, *23*
Hall, Kermit L., 286, *294*
Haller, Hohn S., Jr., 186, *204*
Haller, Robin M., 186, *204*
Hamblin, Robert L., *278*
Hamilton, Roberta, 181, *204*
Hanawalt, Barbara A., 5, 10, *23*
Haney, Craig, *278*
Hare, Alexander P., 264, 267, 268, *278*
Hare, E. H., 186, *204*
Harner, Michael J., 12, *23*, 83, *102*
Harring, Sidney L., 193, 194, 195, *204*
Harris, Anthony R., *278*
Harrison, Brian, *204*
Hart, C. W. M., 114, *139*
Hartog, Hendrik, 293, *294*
Hartwell, R. M., 198, *204*
Harvey, O. J., 269, *281*
Haskins, George Lee, 285, 293, *294*
Hasluck, Margaret, 5, 12, *23*
Haven, Clayton, 216, *231*
Hawkins, Gordon, 42, *57*
Hawkins, Richard O., 226, *230*
Hay, Douglas, 191, *204*
Heckscher, Eli F., 179, 182, *204*
Heider, F., *278*
Hellerman, Michael, 46, 56, *57*
Henderson, Edith Guild, 285, *294*
Hewson, Daphne, 216, *228*
Hiatt, L. R., 4, *23*
Hill, Christopher, 180, *205*

Hill, Reuben, 211, *230*
Hindelang, Michael J., 210, 211, 218–219, 220, 222, *230*
Hindess, Barry, *205*
Hindus, Michael, 286, *294*
Hirst, Paul, *205*
Hobbes, Thomas, 17, 18, 19, *23*
Hobhouse, L. T., 13, *24*
Hobsbawm, Eric, 12, *24*
Hoebel, E. Adamson, 3, 4, 5, *24*, 31, *57*, 97, *102*, 109, 110, 112, 114, 115, 118, 119, 120, 121, 122, 123, 124, 126, 128, 129, 130, 131, 132, 133, *139, 140*
Hoffman, Stanley, 17, *24*
Hofstadter, Richard, 145, *169*, 187, *205*, 287, *295*
Hogbin, H. Ian, 115, *139*
Hollander, Edwin P., 266, 268, 269, *279*
Holling, C. S., 212, *230*
Holmes, Thomas, 211, 219, 220, *230*
Hood, W. R., 269, *281*
Horowitz, Ruth, 8, *24*
Horwitz, Allan V., 91, *102*, 211, 216, 221, 226, *230*
Horwitz, Morton J., 285, 290, *295*
Howe, Daniel Walker, 184, *205*
Howell, P. P., 3, 8, 15, *24*
Howell, Patrick, 221, 223, *230*
Howington, Arthur F., 286, *295*
Humphries, Drew, 171, 188, *205*
Hurst, James Willard, 285, 290, *295*
Hurstfield, Joel, 179, *205*

I

Ianni, A. J. F., 40, 55, *57*
Ignatieff, Michael, 180, 181, 192, 195, 196, 197, 198, *205*
Inkeles, Alex, 142, 145, 161, *169*
Isaac, Paul E., 187, *205*

J

Jones, Edward E., *279*
Jones, Schuyler, 3, *24*, 95, *102*
Joy, Constance B., 211, 216, *231*

K

Kadushin, Charles, 213, 223, 225, 226, *231*
Kahn, Robert L., 225, 226, *231*

Kammen, Michael G., 286, 295
Kann, Kenneth, 187, 205
Katz, Daniel, 225, 226, 231
Kennan, George F., 75, 77
Kidder, Robert, 217, 231
Kiesler, Charles A., 267, 268, 279
Kimball, Solon T., 90, 101
Kirchheimer, Otto, 157, 169, 181, 196, 207
Kittrie, Nicholas, 223, 231
Klein, Susan, 226, 232
Koch, Klaus-Friedrich, 3, 4, 12, 17, 20, 24, 82, 83, 102, 112, 115, 139, 238, 239–243, 247, 250, 251, 252, 253, 254, 255, 259
Kroeber, Alfred L., 31, 57, 115, 139
Kuhn, Thomas S., 284, 287, 288, 295
Kuo, Weu, 216, 221, 231

L

LaFave, Wayne R., 16, 24
La Fontaine, Jean, 2, 3, 24
Lakatos, Imre, 287, 295
Landes, William, 33, 38, 57
Lane, Roger, 193, 194, 205
Langlie, Jean K., 216, 221, 231
Langness, L. L., 2, 24
LaPalombara, Joseph, 157, 169
Larkin, William E., 265, 279
Latané, Bibb, 268, 279
Lauderdale, Pat, 272, 273, 274, 275, 279
Lawler, Edward J., 279
Lazarsfeld, Paul F., 144, 169
Leach, E. R., 115, 139
Lee, Margaret T., 266, 279
Lee, Nancy Howell, 226, 231
Lee, Rensselaer W., III, 154, 169
Lemert, Edwin M., 14, 24
Lempert, Richard, 117, 215, 216, 217, 226, 231
Lenski, Gerhard, 136–137, 139
Levine, Harry Gene, 185, 186, 187, 205
Levine, John M., 265, 279
Le Vine, Robert A., 15, 24
Levy, Leonard William, 285, 295
Lewis, Arthur W., 158, 169
Lewis, I. M., 3, 24, 83, 103
Lewis, W. David, 196, 198, 205
Liberman, Morton A., 272, 279
Lifton, Robert Jay, 144, 161, 169
Light, John, 266, 269, 277
Lin, Nan, 216, 221, 229, 231

Lindenthal, Jacob, 216, 221, 232
Lindzey, Gardner, 279
Linebaugh, Peter, 195, 198, 205
Linz, Juan J., 66, 77
Lippitt, Ronald, 273, 281
Lipset, S. M., 145, 150, 157, 159, 170
Llewellyn, Karl N., 4, 5, 24, 112, 115, 118, 131, 132, 133, 139, 285, 295
Lockyer, Roger, 179, 205
Loman, L. Anthony, 265, 279
Lowenthal, Margorie E., 216, 231
Lowy, Michael J., 211, 229
Lubeck, Steven G., 278
Lundsgaarde, Henry P., 6, 7, 13, 16, 25

M

Maas, Peter, 46, 56, 58
McCallister, Lynn, 210, 231
Macaulay, Stewart, 35, 58
Macaulay, Thomas B., 286, 295
MacCormack, Geoffrey, 17, 25
McCubbin, Hamilton I., 211, 216, 231
McKinlay, John B., 214, 222, 224, 231
Maddock, Kenneth, 8, 25
Magee, Bryan, 288, 295
Maine, Sir Henry Sumner, 109, 139
Maitland, Frederic William, 13, 26
Malinowski, Bronislaw, 115, 139
Mann, Reinhard, 68, 77
Manning, Peter, 192, 205
Marshall, Lorna, 112, 114, 125, 139
Martinson, Robert, 262, 279
Marx, Karl, 171–177, 183, 184, 199, 205, 206
Mather, Lynn M., 239, 243–246, 247, 250, 251, 254, 255, 257, 259
Matza, David, 13, 25, 26
Maybury-Lewis, David, 4, 25
Mayhew, Leon H., 221, 223, 226, 227, 231
Meehl, Paul E., 275, 279
Mendelsohn, Everett, 226, 231
Merry, Sally Engle, 7, 9, 10, 15, 25, 79, 84, 92, 103
Merton, Robert K., 273, 280
Messinger, Sheldon, 213, 216, 225, 229, 232
Michaels, Priscilla, 256, 259
Middleton, John, 17, 20, 25, 132, 139
Miles, Matthew B., 272, 279
Mileski, Maureen, 79, 101
Milgram, Stanley, 268, 280
Miliband, Ralph, 173, 206

Miller, Charles E., 273, *280*
Miller, F. T., 211, *231*
Miller, N., 267, *278*
Miller, Walter B., 20, *25*
Mills, Judson, 267, 276, *280*
Mills, Theodore M., *277*
Molm, Linda D., 273, *280*
Moore, Sally Falk, 2, 3, *25,* 108, 109, 110, *139,* 241, *259*
Murphy, Harriet, 216, 221, *233*
Murphy, Robert F., 4, *25,* 114, *139*
Murphy, Yolanda, 114, *139*
Musgrave, Alan, 287, *295*
Myers, Jerome K., 216, 221, *232*

N

Nader, Laura, 30, *58,* 79, 94, *103,* 211, 214, *232*
Nagao, Dennis H., 265, *280*
Nagel, Ernest, 284, *294, 295*
Nagel, Jack, 269, 273, *280*
Nall, Frank, 216, 226, *232*
Nash, A. E. Keir, 286, *295*
Nash, June, 2, *25*
Needle, Richard H., 211, 216, *231*
Nelson, William E., 284, 286, 289, 292, 293, *295, 296*
Neuman, R. P., 186, *206*
Newcomb, Theodore M., *280*
Newstetter, Wilber I., *280*
Nozick, Robert, 38–39, *58*

O

Oberholzer, Emil, Jr., 285, *296*
Ofshe, Richard J., 266, 270, *279, 280*
Ohlin, Lloyd E., 20, 22
Olson, Sheldon, *232*
Ostrander, Gilman M., 187, *206*
Otterbein, Charlotte Swanson, 3, *25*
Otterbein, Keith F., 3, *25*

P

Paechter, Heinz, 73, 74, *77*
Parker, Jerry, 269, 275, *279, 280*
Pashukanis, Evgeny B., 196, 197, *206*
Pasqualini, Jean, 74, *77*
Patterson, Joan M., 211, 216, *231*
Pearson, Karl, 284, *296*
Pepper, Max, 216, 221, *232*

Percival, Robert, 216, *230*
Peristiany, J. G., 8, *25*
Perkin, Harold, 184, *206*
Perrin, Constance, 83, *103*
Peters, E. Lloyd, 5, *25*
Petersen, Robert, 52, *58*
Philbrick, Francis S., 284, *296*
Philips, David, 193, 194, *206*
Phillips, Ulrich, 286, *296*
Pike, Luke Owen, 5, 13, *25*
Piliavin, Irvin, 97, *103*
Pilling, A. R., 114, *139*
Pitt-Rivers, Julian A., 8, *26,* 135, *139*
Pollock, Frederick, 13, *26*
Popper, Karl R., 287–288, 290, *296*
Posner, Richard A., 31–32, 33, 35, 38, *57, 58*
Pospisil, Leopold, 83, *103,* 115, *139*
Pound, Roscoe, 13, *26*
Powell, Ken, 179, *206*
Powers, Edwin, *280*
Preyer, Kathryn, 285, *296*
Pugh, Meredith, 268, *281*

R

Rabkin, Judith G., 216, 221, *232*
Radzinowicz, Leon, 180, *206*
Rae, Douglas, 157, *170*
Rahe, Richard, 211, 219, 220, *230*
Raper, Arthur F., 16, *26*
Rattray, R. S., 97, *103,* 115, *139*
Reckless, Walter C., *280*
Redfield, Robert, 30, 31, *58*
Reed, James, 186, *206*
Rees, Alwyn D., 5, *26*
Reid, John Phillip, 3, *26,* 285, 286, 291, 293, *296*
Reiff, Robert, 221, *232*
Reiss, Albert J., Jr., 221, 223, *231*
Renner, Thomas, 46, 56, *57*
Reuter, Peter, 18, 34, 35, 36, 39, 40, 41, 56, *58*
Riasanovsky, Valentin A., 4, *26*
Richardson, James F., 194, *206*
Richardson, Jane, 115, *140*
Ridgeway, Cecelia, 269, *280*
Riecken, Henry, 262, 270, *280*
Rieder, Jonathan, 3
Roberts, Simon, 17, *26,* 113, *140,* 211, 214, *232*
Roberts, W. Lewis, 16, *26*

Robin, Stanley S., 224, 233
Robins, Philip K., 270, 280
Rodin, Judith, 268, 279
Rokeach, Milton, 271, 278
Rokkan, Stein, 157, 158, 170
Roos, Leslie J., Jr., 277
Rosaldo, Michelle Z., 115, 116, 138, 140
Rose, R. B., 190, 206
Roseborough, Mary E., 277
Rossi, Peter, 210, 211, 232
Rothenberger, John E., 5, 26, 90, 95, 103
Rothman, David J., 189, 198, 206, 285, 296
Rowe, Alan R., 281
Rozelle, Richard M., 267, 278
Ruback, Barry, 265, 279
Rueveni, Uri, 215, 232
Rusche, Georg, 181, 196, 207
Rustigan, Michael, 195, 206
Rustow, Dankwart A., 161, 170

S

Sahlins, Marshall D., 106, 111, 127, 128, 140, 238, 259
Sampson, Harold, 216, 232
Santos, Boaventura de Sousa, 235, 236, 259
Schachter, Stanley, 271, 280
Schapera, Isaac, 115, 140
Schlenker, Barry, 268, 281
Schneider, Jane, 12, 26
Schur, Edwin M., 280
Schwartz, Charlott Green, 216, 221, 233
Schwartz, Gary, 8, 24
Schwitzgebel, R., 280
Scott, Austin W., Jr., 16, 24
Scott, James C., 76, 77
Scott, John F., 213, 232
Scull, Andrew T., 191, 195, 202, 207
Seidman, E., 270, 278
Sellin, J. Thorsten, 173, 181, 207, 211, 219, 232
Selye, Hans, 209, 219, 232
Service, Elman, 111, 140
Shapiro, Martin, 251, 252, 253, 259
Sheehan, W. J., 197, 207
Shelton, Walter J., 190, 191, 193, 207
Sherif, Carolyn W., 269, 281
Sherif, Muzafer, 262, 263, 264, 267, 269, 270, 280, 281
Silver, Allan, 190, 191, 207
Simeone, Ronald S., 216, 221, 231

Simmel, Georg, 213, 232, 251, 253, 259, 275, 281
Simmons, Richard, 226, 232
Simmons, Robert G., 226, 232
Siskind, Janet, 114, 120, 140
Smith, Alan G. R., 179, 205
Smith, Joseph Henry, 285, 296
Smith-Cunnien, Phil, 275, 279
Smith-Rosenberg, Carroll, 186, 187, 207
Sodergren, John A., 17, 24
Speilberg, Joseph, 216, 226, 232
Spiegleman, Robert G., 270, 280
Spitzer, Steven, 191, 192, 195, 200, 202, 207
Stammp, Kenneth M., 286, 296
Stanley, Julian C., 261, 277
Stauder, Jack, 12, 26
Steffensmeier, Darrell J., 281
Stevenson, John, 190, 191, 207
Steward, Julian, 114, 140
Stigler, George, 33, 57
Stinchcombe, Arthur, 221, 232
Strauss, Anselm, 220, 230
Strodtbeck Fred L., 277
Struening, Elmer, 216, 221, 232
Suchman, Edward, 226, 232
Sudnow, David, 238, 244, 259
Sumner, William Graham, 284, 296
Sutherland, Edwin H., 20, 26, 273, 281
Suttles, Gerald D., 79, 103
Swanson, Guy E., 150, 155–156, 160, 161, 164, 165, 170
Swazey, Judith, 226, 229, 231
Sweet, Louise E., 12, 26
Swigert, Victoria Lynn, 97, 102
Sykes, Gresham M., 13, 26

T

Tait, David, 17, 25, 132, 139
Tanner, R. E. S., 12, 26
Tarpy, Roger M., 71, 77
Tawney, R. H., 207
Taylor, D. Garth, 227, 232
Tedeschi, James T., 268, 281
Tennant, Christopher, 216, 228
Teresa, Vincent, 56, 58
Terry, Robert M., 281
Theilens, Wagner, Jr., 144, 169
Thibaut, John W., 270, 279, 281
Thoden van Velzen, H. U. E., 3, 27, 99, 103
Thomas, Elizabeth M., 112, 114, 140

Thomas-Buckle, Suzann R., 10, 27, 79, *103*
Thompson, E. P., 10, 27, 180, 190, *207*
Thompson, Martha E., *279*
Timberlake, James H., 187, *207*
Tittle, Charles R., *281*
Todd, Harry F., Jr., 30, *58*, 79, 90, 94, *103*, 211, 214, 232
Torcia, Charles E., 16, *27*
Towne, Robert D., 216, *232*
Traviss, Irene, 226, *231*
Turnbull, Colin M., 5, 27, 114, 125, *140*
Turner, Ralph, 213, *233*
Tushnet, Mark, 285, 286, *296*

U

Ungar, Sheldon, 265, *281*

V

Vaillant, George E., 216, *228*
van den Steenhoven, Geert, 3, 4, 5, *27*
van Velsen, J., 109, *140*
van Wetering, W., 3, 27, 99, *103*
Verbrugge, Lois, 213, *233*
Villano, Anthony, 56, *58*

W

Wagenfeld, Morton O., 224, *233*
Wahrman, Ralph, 268, *281*
Waite, Emily, 210, 211, *232*
Walker, Laurens, 270, *281*
Walker, Samuel, 194, *208*
Wallace, Ernest, 114, 120, 121, *140*
Wallerstein, Immanuel, 136, *140*
Walters, R. H., 269, *277*
Ward, David A., 262, *281*

Ward, J. T., 184, *208*
Warner, W. Lloyd, 4, 27, 114, *140*
Warr, Mark, *168*
Webb, Beatrice, 179, *208*
Webb, Sidney, 179, *208*
Weber, Max, 13, 27, 215, *233*
Weiner, Annette, 115, *140*
Weiner, Myron, 157, *159*
Weiner, Samuel, 270, *280*
Weiss, Robert S., 221, *233*
Werthman, Carl, 8, 27, 97, *103*
White, B. J., 269, *281*
White, Morton G., 286, *296*
White, Ralph K., 273, *281*
Willis, Richard H., 266, 268, *279*
Winch, Peter, 283, *296*
Witner, Helen, *280*
Wolfgang, Marvin E., 6, 7, 27, 211, 219, *232*
Woodburn, James C., 114, *140*

Y

Yablonsky, Lewis, 12, *27*
Yalom, Irvin D., 272, 279, *281*
Yarrow, Marian R., 216, 221, *233*
Yngvesson, Barbara B., 214, 215, *233*

Z

Zander, Alvin, 263, 271, *277*
Zeiger, Henry, 42, 55, 56, *58*
Zeisel, Hans, 261, *281*
Zelditch, Morris, Jr., 261, 262, 264, 266, 267, 277, *281*
Zimbardo, Philip C., 278, *281*
Zimmerman, Mary K., 226, *233*
Zimring, Franklin E., 14, 15, *27*

Subject Index

A

Aborigines of Australia, 4, 8 n. 9
Adjudication, 215–218
Afghanistan, 95
Africa, 2, 83, 97, 116, 158, *see also* individual countries and tribes
Albania, 5
Anomie, and deviant behavior, 273
Arbitration, 34–56, 215–217
  in illegal markets, 34–56
  and problem of enforcement, 37–39
Arbitration services in illegal markets, 34–39, *see also* Arbitration, in illegal markets
  demand for, 34–37
  monopoly of, 38–39
  supply of, 37–39
Arson, as social control, 4, 10
Arusha, 83
Assault, as social control, 7–8, 16
Athens, ancient, 99
Australia, 4, 8 n. 9, 158–159
Avoidance
  and mobility, 96–97, 100
  as strategy of conflict management, 83, 85–86, 96–97, 100, 112–113, 125

B

Belgium, 158
Bena Bena, 2
Bookmaking, 35, 36, 50–51
Boundary crises
  and immanence, 164–166
  in political witch-hunts, 147–155
  sources of, 149–151, 273–275
Brazil, 4
Brideservice, 119–122
Brideservice societies, 111–112, 115–125, 129–131, 134
  claims on women in, 115–117, 123–124
  distinguished from bridewealth societies, 115–118, 129–131, 134
  focus of conflicts in, 121–122, 123–124, 130–131, 134
  organization of inequality in, 117–118, 120
  organization of production in, 119–122
  social control in, 122–125

Bridewealth, 125–128
Bridewealth societies, 111–112, 115–118,
    125–134
  claims on women in, 116–117, 129–130
  distinguished from brideservice so-
      cieties, 115–118, 129–131, 134
  focus of conflicts in, 127–128, 129–131,
      134
  organization of inequality in, 118,
      125–128, 129–130
  organization of production in, 126–128
  social control in, 128–134
Burglary, as social control, 5, 8–9

C

Cameroon, 18 n. 20
Canada, 158–159
Capital punishment, 195–196
Chenchu, 97
Cherokee, 3, 293
Cheyenne, 5, 118, 126, 128–133
China, 73–74, 142–143, 144, 151, 153–154,
    155, 161–162
Church, as agent of social control,
    176–177, 292
Class, see Social class, and social control
Comanche, 31, 118–124, 130–131
Compensation, 3, 6, 112, 114, 132
Conciliatory approaches, as strategy of
        conflict management, 83, 86–88,
        100
Conflict management
  forms of, 251–254
  and morphology, 79–80, 95–100
  and social status, 94–95
Conformity
  and status attainment, 268–269
  types of, 264
Corporateness, 157–167
  of multiparty states, 157–158, 160,
      162–164
  of one-party states, 160–164
  and political witch-hunts, 165–167
  of two-party states, 158–160, 162–164
Corruption, in totalitarian states, 76
Crime, see also Delinquency; Deviance
  political, see Political crime
  as social control, 1–21, 172
  social function of, 147–149, 167–168

Criminology, 188–190, 262
  classical school of, 188–189

D

Death penalty, see Capital punishment
Delinquency, 262, 273, see also Crime;
        Deviance
Denmark, 158
Denunciation, as social control in total-
        itarian states, 67–72
Deviance, see also Crime; Delinquency
  and anomie, 273
  creation of, 147–152, 163–168, 274–276
Disputes
  domestic, 235, 255–256
  expansion of, 241 n. 4
  interpretation of, 237–238, 250, 255–258
Dispute settlement, see also specific types
  in illegal markets, 34–56
  role of mavericks in, 239, 245, 256–257
  in tribal societies, 30–32
Disputing, political context of, 235–258
Domestic violence, 4, 7, 255–256
Dueling, as mode of conflict resolution, 8,
    16, 94

E

East Africa, 4
England, 5, 13 n. 13, 15–16, 158–159, 176,
    178–199
Eskimos, 2–3, 5
Europe, 8, 16, 95, 157, 158, see also indi-
        vidual countries
Execution, see Homicide
Experiments, use in studies of social con-
        trol, 261–276
Expulsion, 97–98

F

Family
  as agent of social control, 176–177
  violence in, see Domestic violence
Feud, 3, 12
Finland, 158
Flight, as social control, 11
France, 94, 142–143, 143–144, 151

G

Germany, 18 n. 21, 68, 94, 158
Gisu, 3
Gossip, as mechanism of social control,
133–134
Greece, 3
Group therapy, 271–272
Gusii, 15

H

Heroin distribution, 36, 37, 40
History
appropriation of, under totalitarianism,
76
contribution to theory of social control,
291–293
evaluation in, 286–287
hypothesis-testing in, 288–290
simple inductivist conception of,
283 291
Homicide, as social control, 2–3, 6–7, 14,
15–16, see also Feud

I

Ideology, of social control, 174–175
Ifugao, 3, 30
Immanence, 155–166
and boundary crises, 164–166
in multiparty states, 157–158, 160,
162–164
in one-party states, 160–164
in two-party states, 158–160, 162–164
India, 4, 6 n. 6, 94–95, 97, 217
Indians
North American, 3, 5, 31, 118–124, 126,
128–133, 293, see also individual
tribes
South American, 83
Industrial capitalism, social control under,
183–199
Information, and social control, 97–98
Intimacy, see Relational distance
Italy, 14 n. 15, 75

J

Jalé, 4, 239–243, 251–252
Judge, 245–246

K

Kalahari Bushmen, 125
Kenya, 15
Kinship ties, and social control, 31–32
Kirghiz, 4
Kpelle, 83

L

Language, and social control, 72–76
Law
anthropology of, 108–110, 111–112
availability of, 18–19
and marginality, 254–257
mobilization of, 88–89, 91, 217–218
and relational distance, 16, 18–19
and self-help, 15–19, see also Self-help,
and the state
and social status, 18–19, 254–257
sociology of, 262–264
Lawyers, 221, 223, 243–246
Lebanon, 95
Liability, collective, 3, 11–12, 31, 131–132
Liberia, 83

M

Mafia, 40–56
dispute settlement by, 40–56
and non-subscribers, 50–51
scope of jurisdiction in, 52–54
organization of, 41–43
origins of, 40–41
Marginality, and law, 254–257
Marijuana distribution, 35, 40, 52–53
Marriage, 111, 119, 120–121, 126–127
in brideservice societies, 119, 120–121
in bridewealth societies, 126–127
Maya Indians, 2
Mbuti Pygmies, 5
McCarthyism, 142–143, 144, 145–146, 151,
155
Mediation, 109–110, 215–217
Melanesia, 83, 127 n. 17, 128
Mental illness, 221, see also Relational
disturbance
Mercantile capitalism, social control un-
der, 177–182
Mercantilism, and regulation of the econ-
omy, 178–179, 181

Meta', 18 n. 20
Mexico, 2, 11, 94
Moravia, 158
Morphology
    and conflict management, 79–80,
        95–100
    and law, 16, 18–19, 254–257

N

Ndendeuli, 251–252
Negotiation, 112, 215–218
New England, 149–150, 185–188, 292, 293
New Guinea, 2, 4, 17, 239–243, 251–252
New Zealand, 158–159
Nigeria, 83, 117 n. 7
Nuer, 8 n. 9, 15 n. 16
Nuristani, 95

O

Organization, and social control, 98–100,
    141–168

P

Penitentiary, creation of, 197–199
Peru, 4, 5, 11
Philippines, 3, 30
Poland, 59–66, 67–68, 69 n. 5
Police, 13, 18–19, 88–89, 190–195,
        218–219, 220–221, 225, 235, 255–256
    establishment of, 190–195
Political crime, 141–155, 164–168
    concept of, 152–154
    institutional setting of, 154–155
Political crime waves, see Political witch-
    hunts
Political witch-hunts, 141–155, 165–168
    boundary crises in, 147–155
    characteristics of, 142–144
    and corporateness, 165–167
    stages of, 149–152
    traditional explanations for, 144–147
Privatization of the state
    and social atomization, 72, 76
    under totalitarianism, 66–72, 76
    and vengeance, 67–72
Prohibition, 40–41, 185, 187–188
Property destruction, see Vandalism

Punishment, proportionality in, 195–197
Purges, see Political witch-hunts

Q

Qolla, 4, 5, 11

R

Rape, as social control, 4, 5
Relational distance, and law, 16, 18–19
Relational disturbance
    and mobilization of nonrelated, third
        parties, 218–222, 228
    and social control, 209–228
Relational networks, 209–228
    closure of, 210, 212, 213–214, 217, 222,
        226, 227–228
    isolation of, 210, 212, 213–214, 217, 222,
        225–226, 227–228
    resilience of, 210, 212–213, 214–218,
        221, 222, 226, 227–228
Reputation, 34–37, 97–98
    and demand for arbitration services,
        34–37
    significance in illegal markets, 34–47
    and social control, 97–98
Revenge, see Self-help; Vengeance
Robbery, as social control, see Theft, as
    social control
Russia, 4, 18 n. 21, 59–66, 69–72, 73–74,
        75, 142–143, 144, 151, 155

S

Sarakatsan shepherds, 3
School, as agent of social control, 176–177
Sedition, see Political crime
Self-discipline, under industrial capital-
    ism, 184–188
Self-help, see also Crime, as social control
    and deterrence, 14–15
    and law, 15–19
    in modern societies, 5–12
    processing of, 15–17
    and the state, 12–14, 17–18
    in tribal societies, 2–5, 19 n. 22
Sexual restraint, under industrial capital-
    ism, 185–187, 200

Sicily, 17, 40
Slaves, 173–174
Social class, and social control, 79–80,
        82–100, 171–199
Social control
    and age, 92–94
    attitudinal factors in, 265–266, 270
    in illegal markets, 17–18, 29–56
    indirect strategies of, 82–96, 100
    under industrial capitalism, 183–199
    and information, 97–98
    and kinship ties, 31–32
    and language, 72–76
    mechanisms of
        under industrial capitalism, 190–199
        under mercantile capitalism, 181
    under mercantile capitalism, 177–182
    and mobility, 96–97
    and morphology, 94–100
    and organization, 98–100, 141–168
    and relational disturbance, 209–228
    situational factors in, 267–269
    and social class, 79–80, 82–100,
        171–199, see also Social control, and
        social status
    and social formation, 171–202
    social psychological theories of, 265–273
    and social status, 105–108, 122–125,
        128–134, 266–267, see also Social
        control, and social class
    in suburbia, 79–100
    under totalitarianism, 18 n. 21, 59–76,
        165
    and weak ties, 94–100
Social formation, and social control,
        171–202
Social status
    and conflict management, 94–95
    and law, 18–19, 254–257
    and social control, 105–108, 122–125,
        128–134, 266–267
Social structure, folk models of, 105–108,
        111, 134–137
Spain, 135–137
State
    privatization of, see Privatization of the
        state
    and self-help, 12–14, 17–18
    and social inequality, 111
Subversion, see Political crime

Sudan, 8 n. 9, 15 n. 16
Switzerland, 158

T

Tanzania, 83, 251–252
Tarahumara Indians, 11
Technology, and social organization,
        106–107
Thailand, 246–250, 253–254, 257
Theft, as social control, 5, 8–10
Therapeutic social control, 91, 215–217,
        223–224
Therapy, group, see Group therapy
Third party, mobilization of, 213, 218–228
Third-party intervention, types of,
        215–217
Tibet, 83
Tiv, 83, 117 n. 7
Tolerance
    and morphology, 96, 100
    as strategy of conflict management,
        83–84, 96, 100, 125, 133
Tonga of Zambia, 251–252
Totalitarian states
    corruption in, 76
    denunciation as social control in, 67–72
    language of, 72–76
    privatization of the state in, 66–72, 76
    social atomization in, 72, 76
Treason, see Political crime

U

Uganda, 3
United States, 6–12, 13, 14, 15, 16–17, 32,
        40–56, 79–100, 110, 135–137,
        142–143, 144, 145–146, 149–151,
        155, 158–159, 173–174, 176, 183,
        185–199, 235, 243–246, 290, 291,
        292, 293

V

Vagrancy, 178, 179, 182
Vandalism, as social control, 4–5, 10–11
Venezuela, 4
Vengeance, 3, 67–72
    through privatization of the state, 67–72

W

Wales, 5
Witchcraft accusations, 96–97, 97–98,
     149–150

Y

Yanomamö, 4
Yurok Indians, 31

Z

Zaire, 5
Zambia, 251–252
Zapotec Indians, 94